Trinity and Truth

Two closely related questions receive distinctively theological
answers in this study: What is truth? and How can we tell whether
what we have said is true? Bruce Marshall proposes that the
Christian community's identification of God as the Trinity serves
as the key to a theologically adequate treatment of these
questions. Professor Marshall argues on trinitarian grounds that
the Christian way of identifying God ought to have unrestricted
primacy when it comes to the justification of belief, and he
proposes a trinitarian way of reshaping the concept of truth.
Direct engagement with the current philosophical debate about
truth, meaning and belief (in Davidson and others) suggests that a
trinitarian account of epistemic justification and truth is also
more philosophically compelling than the approaches generally
favoured in modern theology, as exemplified by Schleiermacher,
Ritschl, Rahner, and others. Marshall offers a contemporary way
of conceiving of the Christian God as "the truth."

BRUCE D. MARSHALL is Professor of Religion at St. Olaf
College, Northfield, Minnesota. He took his doctorate at Yale
University, and has held the Cardin Chair in the Humanities at
Loyola College, Maryland, on a visiting professorship. His
publications include *Christology in Conflict* (1987), and (edited)
Theology and Dialogue: Essays in Conversation with George Lindbeck
(1991).

Cambridge Studies in Christian Doctrine

Edited by
Professor COLIN GUNTON, *King's College London*
Professor DANIEL W. HARDY, *University of Cambridge*

Cambridge Studies in Christian Doctrine is an important new series which aims to engage critically with the traditional doctrines of Christianity, and at the same time to locate and make sense of them within a secular context. Without losing sight of the authority of scripture and the traditions of the church, the books in this series will subject pertinent dogmas and credal statements to careful scrutiny, analyzing them in light of the insights of both church and society, and will thereby practice theology in the fullest sense of the word.

Titles published in the series

1. Self and Salvation: Being Transformed
   DAVID F. FORD

2. Realist Christian Theology in a Postmodern Age
   SUE PATTERSON

3. Trinity and Truth
   BRUCE D. MARSHALL

Titles forthcoming in the series

Theology, Music and Time: The Sound of God
JEREMY BEGBIE

Church, Narrativity and Transcendence
ROBERT JENSON

The Doctrine of Sin
ALASTAIR I. McFADYEN

The Bible, Theology, and Faith: A Study of Abraham and Jesus
R. W. L. MOBERLY

A Political Theology of Nature
PETER SCOTT

Remythologizing Theology: Divine Action and Authorship
KEVIN J. VANHOOZER

Trinity and Truth

Bruce D. Marshall

CAMBRIDGE
UNIVERSITY PRESS

PUBLISHED BY THE PRESS SYNDICATE OF THE UNIVERSITY OF CAMBRIDGE
The Pitt Building, Trumpington Street, Cambridge, United Kingdom

CAMBRIDGE UNIVERSITY PRESS
The Edinburgh Building, Cambridge, CB2 2RU, UK   http://www.cup.cam.ac.uk
40 West 20th Street, New York, NY 10011–4211, USA   http://www.cup.org
10 Stamford Road, Oakleigh, Melbourne 3166, Australia

Printed in the United Kingdom at the University Press, Cambridge

Typeset in 9/13 pt Lexicon (*The Enschedé Font Foundry*), in QuarkXPress™   [SE]

A catalogue record for this book is available from the British Library

Library of Congress cataloguing in publication data
Marshall, Bruce, 1955–
Trinity and truth / Bruce D. Marshall.
        p.   cm. – (Cambridge studies in Christian doctrine)
Includes index.
ISBN 0 521 45335 2 6 (hardback)
ISBN 0 521 77491 8 (paperback)
1. Truth (Christian theology).   2. Trinity.   I. Title.   II. Series
BT50.M29   1999
231′.04–dc21   99–21509 CIP

ISBN 0 521 45335 2 6 hardback
ISBN 0 521 77491 8 paperback

For MY MOTHER AND FATHER, WITH LOVE

Why on earth should we expect to be able to reduce truth to something clearer or more fundamental? After all, the only concept Plato succeeded in defining was mud (dirt and water).

Donald Davidson

Ille homo esset ipsa divina veritas.

Thomas Aquinas

Contents

Preface

The thought of writing this book first took shape years ago when, as a graduate student, I read in manuscript draft chapters of what became George Lindbeck's *Nature of Doctrine*. Lindbeck brought home to me, as did Hans Frei in a different way, the idea that Christians can and should have their own ways of thinking about truth and about deciding what to believe. They need not take their truth claims on loan from some other intellectual or cultural quarter, or regard the only alternative to epistemic servitude as isolation from the broader human conversation about what is true. Little of Lindbeck's own idiom for making these claims remains here, but it will be evident that I think they are correct and important claims to make.

Further reflection suggested that a theological account of truth and the justification of belief which had any hope of success had to engage the analytic philosophical discussion of truth, meaning, and belief in a direct and reasonably detailed way. Save for Wittgenstein, the main figures in this discussion – including some of the century's most important and influential philosophers, like Quine, Davidson, and Dummett – are not much read by theologians. Of course analytic philosophers, including philosophers of religion, usually return the favor. But the modern analytic debate calls into question most of the assumptions which theologians (and not only they) customarily bring to the issues with which this book deals, and offers rigorously argued alternative views. It has therefore seemed indispensable here to try to bridge the gap between theology and analytic philosophy.

At the same time, a genuinely theological account of truth and epistemic justification needs to be robustly trinitarian. It ought to subject whatever ideas it may find useful to the formative discipline of the

Christian community's convictions about the triune God. I have learned this in part from recent trinitarian theology, which, while its historical and systematic claims often seem to me unpersuasive, nonetheless strikes me as basically right in its intuition that a Christian theological account of most matters needs to bear a trinitarian stamp. Most of all, though, I have learned to think about truth and the justification of belief in a trinitarian way by reading Thomas Aquinas, especially his profound and unjustly neglected commentary on the Gospel of John. He is cited often in these pages, both in order to clarify some of the background of the argument, and in the hope of indicating that on the questions at issue here, as on most others, he presents a far different and more compelling figure than is often supposed nowadays by his admirers and detractors alike.

The author of a book which has gestated as long as this one naturally owes much to others.

Jim Buckley, David Cunningham, Louis Dupré, Greg Jones, Bill Placher, Rusty Reno, Mike Root, Robert Wilken, and David Yeago all read drafts of various chapters and took the trouble to comment in detail, often in writing and sometimes on several occasions. My former St. Olaf colleague Fred Stoutland read and helped me improve several drafts of chapter 8; much of my understanding of contemporary philosophy of language I owe to conversations with him. George Lindbeck read the entire original manuscript, nearly twice as long as the present book, and made helpful suggestions about how to shorten it. David Kelsey also offered advice and encouragement on this score.

The Yale/Washington Theology Group read early versions of several chapters. Few of the sentences they saw are in the present book, owing in part to their critical and sympathetic scrutiny. Bits and pieces of chapters 2 and 5 first appeared in "What is Truth?" (*Pro Ecclesia* 4/4 [1995]). I am grateful to the Dogmatics Colloquium of the Center for Catholic and Evangelical Theology for a helpful discussion of that paper. Similarly, parts of chapters 8 and 9 were first published in *Modern Theology* 11/1 (1995), as "'We Shall Bear the Image of the Man of Heaven': Theology and the Concept of Truth." An early version of this paper was given as a lecture at Creighton University, and it was later discussed by the Philosophy Colloquium at St. Olaf College. I learned much from the lively exchanges the paper provoked with both audiences.

Research and writing of initial drafts of chapters 3, 4, and 8 were supported by a College Teacher's Fellowship from the National Endowment for the Humanities. A first version of chapter 6 was written with the help of a Released Time Grant from St. Olaf College, and much of the book's first draft was written during a St. Olaf sabbatical. I am very grateful to both institutions.

My wife Sandy was unfailingly cheerful and encouraging as she heard me say, for years, "I have to go work on my book." In every way, I daily depend on her steadfast love and support. The arrival of our dear daughter Anne Sun Joo in the last months of work on this book held up its completion a bit, but this was the one delay I would not have done without. This book is dedicated with love to my parents, William and Nancy Marshall, in small public token of my gratitude for gifts beyond telling.

A note on translations

With a few exceptions, all the translations are my own, with citations to the original language edition from which the translation was made. In the many cases where citations are most usefully made without page numbers, such as Aquinas's *Summa theologiae* and Schleiermacher's *Christian Faith*, there should be no difficulty, for those who wish to do so, in correlating the cited passages with existing translations. In the case of some works quoted several times and cited by page number, I have also given references to standard translations, indicated by the abbreviation "ET" (with a full reference the first time the translation is cited). In cases where I give a reference to pages but without quotation, the reference is to an existing translation where there is one.

Unless otherwise noted, all biblical extracts are adapted from the *New Revised Standard Version*.

Introduction: theology and truth

Truth as a theological problem

Recall for a moment Jesus' confrontation with Pontius Pilate. As the Gospel of John depicts the scene – in striking contrast to the version shared by Matthew, Mark, and Luke – Jesus engages in an argument with Pilate on kingship and truth. The debate takes a form well known to philosophers ancient and modern; it is an exercise in conceptual clarification. Pilate begins by asking Jesus if he is "the King of the Jews" (18:33). Jesus responds by ascribing to himself a sort of kingship which, while not fully defined by him, is "not from this world" (18:36). Whatever else it involves, this sort of kingship entails that its possessor will not fight to preserve his own life (18:36). Pilate finds this puzzling: "So are you a king?" he asks Jesus (18:37). He appears not to be sure that a plausible concept of kingship can embrace such notions as unworldliness and non-violence. Jesus responds: "You say that I am a king. For this I was born, and for this I have come into the world, to bear witness to the truth. Everyone who is of the truth hears my voice" (18:37). Talk of a sort of kingship which involves not only non-violence but a public commitment to truth only adds to Pilate's confusion. "What is truth?" he asks (18:38). There the debate ends.

Some interpreters of this exchange between Jesus and Pilate (Friedrich Nietzsche, for one) have seen Pilate as the clear winner of the debate, the hero of the story. He cuts short Jesus' talk about bearing witness to the truth by posing what seems to be the most daunting of all philosophical questions – what is truth? – and by knowing better than to venture any answer. Pilate thus speaks for skeptics of every age, not only skeptics about Jesus' claim to bear witness to the truth, but all those who question the usefulness of any human attempt to speak "the truth."

Yet the reader of John's Gospel and Letters, while perhaps daunted by Pilate's question, already knows its answer. The human being Jesus is himself "the way, the truth, and the life" (14:6). Saying that truth is "personal" falls short of capturing John's logic. Truth is not simply personal; for John truth is a person. Even this is too weak: truth is not just any person, but this human being in particular: Jesus of Nazareth, and among human beings only he. Knowing what truth is and deciding about truth, so this Gospel suggests, finally depend on becoming adequately acquainted with this person. In the admirably exact phrase of Thomas Aquinas: *Ille homo esset ipsa divina veritas* – this human being is divine truth itself.[1]

Yet this human being is not "the truth" all by himself. He is "full of truth" (1:14) because and insofar as he comes from another: the Father whose "Word is truth" (17:17), and who has sent that Word to dwell in our flesh and stand trial for his life. Jesus does nothing on his own authority (5:30), but obeys the command of the one who sends him; at the same time Jesus is the truth because he is the eternal Word of the Father in our flesh, to whom the Father gives all that he has (16:15). "Truth comes through Jesus Christ" (1:17) just because, sent by the Father and (in another phrase of Aquinas) "expressing the total being of the Father,"[2] Jesus makes the Father known (1:18). He is "the truth" only in virtue of his unique relation to the Father.

Jesus is "the truth," moreover, not only on account of his bond with the one who sent him, but also on account of his bond with another whom he will send: "the Spirit of truth, who proceeds from the Father" (15:26). In his own way this Spirit is also "the truth" (1 Jn. 5:6), because he leads the world to Jesus himself – and so into "all truth" (Jn. 16:13). As the Father in love gives himself to the world by sending into our flesh and our death the one to whom he has given all that he has, so Jesus gives himself to the world by entrusting himself – all that he has – to the promised Spirit ("he will take what is mine and declare it to you," 16:14). The Spirit leads the world into all truth, into Jesus sent from the Father, by leading the world into the apostolic community: the gathering of those for whose welfare Jesus prays on the eve of his death, together with "those who believe in me through their word" (17:20).

So as John's Gospel and Letters depict it, "truth" is an attribute of the triune God. Indeed, truth is in some deep sense identical with the persons

---

1. *Super Evangelium S. Ioannis Lectura* (hereafter *In Ioannem*), ed. R. Cai, O. P. (Turin: Marietti, 1952) (caput) 1, (lectio) 8 (no. 188).   2. *In Ioannem* 1, 1 (no. 29).

of the Trinity. Apparently both saying what truth is and deciding what is true depend on identifying the triune God, and on being the subject of his community-forming action.[3]

These brief Johannine reflections suggest that the Christian community cannot evade Pilate's question, and should not want to. The church claims to have true beliefs about God. More than that, this community worships and proclaims to the world a God who is himself "the truth," in whom all other truth finds its source and measure. From ancient times the church has thought it needed to give a reflectively explicit account of its belief and practice, and plausible answers to questions which its belief and practice pose. This reflective effort generally goes by the name "theology." By undertaking to speak in the name and on behalf of a God who is "the truth," this community accepts the task of saying in a reflectively explicit way what truth is, and by what right it claims to speak the truth. In this sense truth is a theological problem.

The Christian community's own belief and practice call for an account of the right by which it claims to speak the truth. But one need not be a member of this community, or share its distinctive beliefs, to see that the church is committed to giving a reflectively explicit account of the truth of its talk, or to see what the beliefs are for whose truth it chiefly has to account.

In order to exist as a coherent and identifiable community over time, a human group must, it seems, be united by adherence to certain beliefs and practices – that is, to certain doctrines – which constitute its identity and distinguish it from other communities, and from random and temporary collections of individuals. What these doctrines are can be discerned, empirically, from its practices.

The Christian church is distinguished from other religious and non-religious communities, so this book will argue, primarily by its trinitarian identification of God: God is the Father who has raised the crucified Jew Jesus from the dead and poured out their common Spirit upon all flesh. The one God is identified as the Trinity through the unfolding of a complex narrative which links Israel, Jesus, and the church; this narrative identification of the triune God organizes a comprehensive view of all things, and especially of human nature, history, and destiny. In this sense the Trinity – not in the first place as the focus of a technical debate

---

3. For more on John as a theological entry into the problem of truth, see Hans Urs von Balthasar, *Theologik II: Wahrheit Gottes* (Einsiedeln: Johannes Verlag, 1985), pp. 13–23, and *Theologik III: Der Geist der Wahrheit* (Einsiedeln: Johannes Verlag, 1987), pp. 61–75.

about how to relate one *ousia* and three *hypostases* (though this debate is in its own way crucial), but as specifying the meaning and reference of "God" – may be regarded as the primary Christian doctrine. The Christian community lives by celebrating and serving the deeds, presence, promises, and commands of the God whose identification constitutes this doctrine.

In the modern world the church's claim that its chief doctrines are true has been challenged more vigorously than at any time since the first centuries of Christianity. This challenge has focused to a considerable degree on the right of the Christian community to hold beliefs which seem not to meet the epistemic standards of modernity – broadly speaking, of those views about what we have the right to believe which stem from the Enlightenment. Christian thinkers, both theologians and philosophers, have often attempted to respond to this challenge by taking over distinctively modern notions of truth and epistemic justification. Great intellectual ingenuity has gone into this effort, as we will see. But it has persistently tended to yield unsatisfying results.

Modern theology has repeatedly sought an approximate middle between giving up central Christian beliefs as false and failing to accept the epistemic demands of modernity. The basic strategy has been to offer a reinterpretation of the most central Christian claims (however these are identified) which meets modernity's epistemic standards. The resourcefulness which has gone into these efforts to find a post-Enlightenment epistemic middle for Christian belief has not entirely overcome the criticism, repeatedly voiced, that this is the worst of both worlds: that modern epistemic standards are being applied in at best a half-hearted way, and that what this half-measure succeeds (perhaps) in saving is not finally Christianity after all.

A more satisfying approach to truth as a theological problem, rather than taking the church's central beliefs to be especially in need of epistemic support, will take the church's trinitarian identification of God itself chiefly to confer epistemic right. In order plausibly to maintain that the Trinity and other distinctively Christian doctrines are true, without drastically altering the meaning the Christian community ascribes to them, these doctrines must be regarded as epistemically primary across the board, that is, as themselves the primary criteria of truth. It is not sufficient simply to say that the doctrine is central to Christian identity, and that Christians must therefore hold it true; it must be regarded as the chief test for the truth of the rest of what we want to believe. This means that the very notions of how we decide what is true and of what truth is must be reconfigured in a trinitarian way, transformed by the church's central doctrines from the way we would otherwise expect them to look. This book will be devoted to developing these thoughts, and to addressing objections which they raise.

It might be supposed that according epistemic primacy to the church's trinitarian identification of God can only make the conflict between modernity and Christian belief worse. I will argue that the opposite is the case. Far from being too closely engaged with the modern philosophical debate about meaning, belief, and truth, Christian theology in our century has customarily ignored much of the mainstream argument over these issues, especially that which originates in different ways with Frege and Tarski, and includes Quine, Davidson, and Dummett among its important recent figures. Closer engagement with the main modern debate about truth and the justification of belief tends not to intensify the conflict between plausible epistemic standards and central Christian truth claims, but to make it go away.

That the Trinity is the primary Christian doctrine is contested by much modern theology, and in any case falls short of simply being obvious. The next chapter will therefore try to show that a trinitarian identification of God is central to any recognizably Christian belief system. Chapter 3 considers several of the chief strategies in modern theology for justifying Christian beliefs, while chapter 4 argues that these strategies, whatever the theological desirability of their results, face formidable philosophical problems. An alternative approach, so chapter 5 argues, can satisfy the legitimate aspirations embodied in these strategies without incurring the problems they pose. Coherence with the nexus of central Christian beliefs is decisive when it comes to deciding about truth; consideration of the contents of the central beliefs and of procedures for their plausible interpretation helps to explicate the community's right to make this sweeping epistemic claim. Chapter 6 replies to the objection that this epistemic strategy amounts to the arbitrary and fideistic exaltation of a provincial collection of communal convictions, and takes up a cognate issue: ascribing a decisive epistemic role to particular communal practices may seem to encourage hostility toward other communities – in the first place, but not only, hostility toward their beliefs. Theologically conceived, epistemic justification depends on the mission of the Holy Spirit as well as that of the Son; justified beliefs must not only be christologically coherent, but pneumatologically effective.

Reflection on the epistemic role of the Spirit provides the context for an account of the bearing of communal and individual virtue on deciding about the truth of beliefs (chapter 7).

Chapter 8 shifts the focus from epistemic justification to truth, by distinguishing and evaluating various historical and contemporary accounts of what truth is. In a theological account whatever idea of truth we find most persuasive needs to be subjected to trinitarian discipline. The concept of truth needs to be brought into line with the thought that each of the persons of the triune God is, in his own way, the truth. Chapter 9 suggests a way to do this, and thereby to show how truth and justified belief finally cohere in the *perichoresis*, the mutual indwelling, of the Father, the Son, and the Holy Spirit.

Definitions

Talk about truth, like talk about other large topics, easily flounders for lack of clarity about what is actually being discussed. So we need to be explicit, at least in a preliminary way, about two things: what is being asked, and what it is being asked about.

We are asking what it is for Christian beliefs to be true. The same question might be put by asking what it *means* to say that Christian beliefs are true, or how truth should be *defined* when ascribed to these beliefs (granted that important questions arise about whether and in what sense truth can be defined).

This way of putting the issue – what is it for Christian beliefs to be true? – obviously raises the related question, how should one go about deciding whether Christian beliefs are true? The distinction between these two questions is important, and needs to be marked clearly at the outset. In a word: saying what truth is should not be confused with saying what is true. By itself, an account of what it is for the Christian community's beliefs to be true will not necessarily enable anyone, including Christians, to decide whether those beliefs are actually true. Decisions about the truth of beliefs or utterances require not simply a characterization of truth, but criteria of truth, by appeal to which we can distinguish true beliefs and utterances from false ones, those to which our characterization of truth applies from those to which it does not. To ask what criteria should be applied in deciding whether our beliefs are true, or in testing the truth of our beliefs, is to ask concerning their justification – literally, what gives us the right to hold them.

Deciding that a belief is true is not, however, simply the same as being justified in holding that belief. As I will use the term, to "decide" that a belief is true is to be, or to become, convinced of its truth. Part of being convinced that a belief is true is being clear about what gives one the right to hold it – for example, by establishing that the belief meets relevant criteria of truth. Securing the right to hold beliefs is unavoidable in deciding about their truth; we not only should not, but cannot, simply hold at will whatever beliefs we like. At the same time, as I will argue, an element of willingness cannot always be removed from being or becoming convinced that a belief is true; deciding that a belief is true cannot always be reduced to cognizant possession of the epistemic right to hold the belief. A full account of deciding what is true includes both the notion of epistemic right and that of willingness to believe. Thus deciding about the truth of beliefs is a broader epistemic notion than being justified in holding them, though it always includes the element of justification.

The notion of "justification" is itself ambiguous. At times it gets used in a more normative fashion, at times in a more descriptive one. To call beliefs "justified" can mean that they meet tests which establish or secure their truth, and in that strong and normative sense give their holders the right to hold them. Depending on the type of test involved and the way in which it is (or is not) met, the truth of beliefs might also be regarded as probable, possible, unlikely, and so forth. Communities and individuals ordinarily take beliefs which meet their criteria of truth to be true, and not simply to be beliefs which they are entitled to *hold* true.

But communities and individuals differ about what criteria establish the truth of beliefs, and so about what criteria should be employed to decide about their truth. As a result, a belief which Jack regards as meeting relevant criteria and therefore true, Jill may well regard as false. This does not *require* Jill to regard Jack as "unjustified" in holding his false belief. She may think he is doing the best he can under the circumstances. In that case, to say that Jack's belief is "justified" means he has a right to hold it – that he is living up to his epistemic obligations, so to speak – but not that its truth is secured. This is the weaker, more purely descriptive sense of "justification." But even the descriptive sense of "justified" does not guarantee agreement between speakers about which beliefs each of them has the right to hold. In spite of what she takes to be reasonable epistemic effort on Jack's part, Jill may still regard a belief of Jack's as unjustified, perhaps because he is employing criteria of truth which she (in light, of course, of her own) thinks no one ought to employ.

Thus: a claim to be justified in believing that p may be interpreted as (1) adequately supported or (2) inadequately supported, and a claim the interpreter regards as adequately supported may be taken as (1a) only giving someone the right to hold a belief or (1b) also establishing its truth. The chief difference between (1a) and (1b) is whether the interpreter accepts the justificatory criteria employed in the claim. For present purposes the key point is that a theological account of truth and justification must, for reasons which will emerge in the course of the argument, give an account not only of how the justificatory criteria to which it appeals give Christians the right to hold their beliefs, but of what makes these criteria of truth – criteria which establish or secure the truth of the beliefs which meet them. We are looking, in other words, for a normative, and not only descriptive, account of the justification of beliefs.[4]

This sort of distinction between the question of truth and the question of justification has become commonplace in philosophical discussions of these topics.[5] Even where a distinction between these two issues is made explicitly, however, that distinction is not always observed in practice. Theological debates about truth in particular tend not infrequently to confuse the two matters. A theologian, for example, who argues that belief in Jesus' resurrection need not appeal to types of evidence which non-Christians are likely to find convincing may find herself assailed by other theologians for "ignoring the question of truth." But the question of what sort of evidence, if any, one needs in order to believe reasonably in Jesus' resurrection has to do with the justification of that belief, not its truth. The critic might indeed argue that failure to supply this sort of evidence for such a belief yields an inadequate account of its justification. But on some very standard conceptions of truth – which the critic may well at least covertly share – the belief that Jesus is risen might be true even if one had no evidence or justification for it at all (as realist

4. It is sometimes suggested that the notion of justification be used only descriptively: that the question of what confers the right to hold beliefs has nothing important to do with the question of how we should decide which beliefs are true. Aside from the counterintuitiveness of this stipulation (we regularly suppose that what gives us the right to hold beliefs is that we have employed criteria which settle the matter of their truth), it would be confusing to use the terms this way in an analysis (to be undertaken in chapter 3) of epistemic justification in modern theology. Modern theological proposals about this matter commonly suggest that we only have the right to hold beliefs which have met criteria of a sort which secure their truth.
5. For a classic statement of the distinction see Alfred Tarski, "Truth and Proof," *Alfred Tarski: Collected Papers*, vol. IV, ed. Steven R. Givant and Ralph McKenzie (Basel: Birkhäuser, 1986), pp. 399–423, especially p. 414. For a more recent effort to put the matter, see Jeffrey Stout, *Ethics After Babel* (Boston: Beacon, 1988), especially pp. 24–8, 244–50.

accounts of truth as the "correspondence" of beliefs to reality, or to the "facts," have maintained).

To broaden the point, accounts of truth and accounts of justification can and in practice do vary independently of one another. That is, one might argue that for beliefs to be true is for them (a) to correspond to reality, or (b) to cohere with other beliefs, or (c) to be among those sentences we will find ourselves warranted in asserting at the ideal end of inquiry, or (d) to be what comes out of the barrel of a gun, that is, what we can compel other people to accept, or (e) to be none of the above. All of these ways of saying what "true" means have found defenders, and there are many variants and further possibilities which have as well. But one might also argue that any one of these is the proper or primary criterion for deciding which beliefs are true, and further items may be added to the list, such as (f) to be tied with logical necessity to beliefs which are self-evidently true, which has regularly been invoked as the paradigm of justification, if not as a candidate for an adequate characterization of truth. Moreover, some accounts maintain that truth and justification need to be characterized in the same way. So idealists have often maintained that one or another version of (b) suffices for both, and some pragmatists have said the same for (c). Others seek to combine different items on the list to characterize truth and justification, respectively. Many, for example, argue that truth is a version of (a), while justification is a version of (b), or perhaps (c). Hence the importance of trying to keep the issues straight.

The formative theologians of the last several centuries have not, to be sure, generally written books, or even chapters, on "truth" (Karl Barth and Hans Urs von Balthasar are important exceptions to this generalization).[6] Even less have they devoted thematic attention to "justified belief," or to the relationship between epistemic right and truth. But the difference between the questions I am raising and the preoccupations of modern theologians is more terminological than substantive. As I will try to show, arguments about what it is for Christian beliefs to be true, and how we should give warrant for or decide about their truth, are deeply embedded in modern Christian theology, dispersed across a wide range of rubrics bearing other names: "prolegomena to theology," "theological method," "knowledge of God," "revelation," and so forth.

6. In Barth see especially his treatment of the prophetic office of Jesus Christ under the heading "Jesus Christ, the Truthful Witness," which makes up the whole of *Die kirchliche Dogmatik* IV/3 (Zurich: Evangelischer Verlag, 1932–67 [for the complete work]); ET: *Church Dogmatics* (Edinburgh: T. & T. Clark, 1956–75); in Balthasar see the 3 volumes of his *Theologik*.

What is being asked, then, is what it means to say that Christian beliefs are "true," and by what right the Christian community and its members decide to hold these beliefs. These questions are being asked *about* "Christian beliefs." As I am using the term, a *belief* is an attitude or disposition expressible by holding a sentence true. Thus one cannot have the concept of belief without having the concept of truth (at least as applied to sentences), though for reasons to be explained later our explicit discussion of the concept of truth will be more readily comprehensible if it follows that of justified beliefs. A sentence the meaning of which has been specified by some person or group is, again as I am using the term, a *proposition*; to specify the meaning of a sentence is the same thing as offering an *interpretation* of it. Believing is thus a *propositional attitude*, that is, an attitude (in this case, holding true) toward a sentence the meaning or interpretation of which the believer understands or has specified; there are many other propositional attitudes, such as hoping, doubting, and wishing. The same proposition can be expressed by different sentences (perhaps most obviously when we give the same interpretation for two sentences in different languages), and conversely the same sentence can express different propositions (for example, when two different contexts in which it is held true require two different interpretations of it); I take the relation between concepts and words to work the same way. When a person or group speaks a sentence or proposition they have made an *utterance*; when they speak a sentence or proposition they hold true, they have made an *assertion* or *statement*.

I take these definitions to be non-controversial – not, of course, that the question of what exactly to make of these elemental notions is settled, but simply that the characterizations I have given reflect well-established philosophical usage, and so provide a reasonable place to start. In any case little gain will likely result from arguing about definitions in advance of actual inquiry; it is enough for them to be reasonably clear. Moreover, I take these definitions to entail no ontological commitments beyond the obvious ones: to ask about the truth of beliefs, sentences, and so forth assumes that there are beliefs, sentences, and so forth. In particular, I willingly remain agnostic about whether concepts and propositions are eternal objects, to which our words and sentences are variously attached. Some philosophers devote considerable labor to deciding this matter, especially those who want to ascribe such a status to propositions. But for present purposes, propositions as eternal objects are eliminable in Quine's sense; they add nothing to a consideration of the issue at hand which cannot already be expressed simply by talking about sentences and the interpretation of sentences (and, more specifically, about the equivalence in meaning of one sentence to another).[7]

In raising the questions of truth and of what makes for justified decisions about truth I am thus asking, in the first place, about language. At least at the outset I will mostly consider language – sentences or statements – as the bearer of "true," the subject to which the predicate "true" is applied, and will ask what the Christian community and its members are doing, and by what right they do it, when they apply this predicate to sentences, and also to propositional attitudes (like belief) which include those sentences.[8]

Two other candidates for the bearer or subject of "true" obviously present themselves: the mind, and reality. An ancient tradition maintains that "falsity and truth are not in things . . . but in thought."[9] "True" is a different sort of notion from "good," in that while goodness resides in things, as that which humans and other rational beings desire in them, truth resides in the mind, when it knows things, indeed when things come in a sense to be in the mind.[10] "Truth" thus enters the world with human beings, or more broadly with successful knowers; as Donald Davidson puts the point, "Nothing in the world, no object or event, would be true or false if there were not thinking creatures."[11]

An equally ancient tradition maintains that "the true is that which is,"[12] and ascribes "true" to objects, facts, events, states of affairs, and so forth. Conceiving the bearer of "true" in this way makes "true" more or

7. On the eliminability of propositions taken as ontologically distinct from sentences, see W. V. Quine, *Philosophy of Logic*, 2nd edn (Cambridge, Mass.: Harvard University Press, 1986), p. 10; *Word and Object* (Cambridge, Mass.: MIT Press, 1960), pp. 205ff. Quine also argues a stronger point, viz., that we cannot individuate propositions as objects distinct from sentences, so it is futile to posit their existence; it is about this issue that I remain agnostic for present purposes.

8. Much philosophical debate has been devoted to whether, among linguistic or language-dependent items, sentences, statements, utterances, beliefs, assertions, or propositions should be regarded as the primary (and perhaps sole) bearer of truth. That debate is sometimes regarded as an argument without issue (on which see Susan Haack, *Philosophy of Logics* [Cambridge: Cambridge University Press, 1978], pp. 79–85). It will be peripheral to many of our present concerns, but will play a crucial role when it comes to figuring out what truth is, since a plausible conception of truth depends at least in part on finding a non-question-begging bearer for "true" (see the discussion in chapter 8, pp. 217–23).

9. Aristotle, *Metaphysics* VI, 4 (1027b, 25–7).

10. See Thomas Aquinas, *Summa theologiae* I, 5, 1; 16, 1 (*S. Thomae Aquinatis Summa Theologiae*, 4 vols., ed. P. Caramello [Turin: Marietti, 1948–52]).

11. "The Structure and Content of Truth," *The Journal of Philosophy* 87/6 (1990), pp. 279–328; here: p. 279.

12. Augustine, *Soliloquiorum Libri Duo* II, v, 8. *Patrologiae Cursus Completus, series latina* (=PL), ed. J. P. Migne (Paris: 1844–55), vol. XXXII, 889.

less synonymous with "real"; this usage is not uncommon among theologians, who may also talk about "(the) truth" as roughly equivalent to "the ultimately real."[13]

Any account of truth and deciding about truth will surely have to deal with the connections between language, human beings, and reality. But attending first of all to sentences and beliefs as truth bearers will help avoid begging questions on these complex matters. Conceptions of mind and reality are various and contested, and so as a result are the senses in which "mind" and "reality" may be truth bearers. That sentences and beliefs may be true is by contrast relatively uncontroversial. Whatever else truth may be, it is surely a property or characteristic of some sentences; we regularly regard other people's sentences and our own as true and justified. Figuring out how to construe the truth and justification of sentences – in particular, but not only, of those held true in the Christian community – may then help us get some purchase on the interrelations between language, mind, and reality, and so, eventually, on the senses in which mind and reality as well as language may be truth bearers. This is a common procedure: we may hope to attain a better grasp of vexed and difficult matters by attending to matters less controversial and more accessible, when we have reason to think the matters are linked.

To some theologians, however, taking this linguistic turn irreparably trivializes the issue. A theological account of truth, after all, deals with divine truth itself, with the truth which God himself is, and so with matters of ultimate significance. Why spend a lot of time talking about words – engaged in what Quine calls "semantic ascent" – rather than talking about God?

Because, in a word, our best hope of thinking well about God lies in thinking well about our talk of God. Semantic ascent in theology is not a trivial distraction from the real issue (God), still less a confusion or equation of God with our talk about God. Rather it enables us to see the issue at hand – what God has to do with the truth and justification of our beliefs about God, and about anything else – more clearly than we otherwise could, and to handle the issue in more plausible ways than we would otherwise be able. So, at least, this book will attempt to show. Its argu-

---

13. So for example John Zizioulas poses the theological problem of truth like this: "How can a Christian hold to the idea that truth operates in history and creation when the ultimate character of truth, and its uniqueness, seem irreconcilable with the change and decay to which history and creation are subject?" *Being as Communion: Studies in Personhood and the Church* (London: Darton, Longman & Todd, 1985), p. 70. Zizioulas also talks about truth in other senses.

ment embodies the conviction, which Michael Dummett takes to be the distinguishing mark of analytic philosophy, that "we have no account of thoughts save by reference to language" – whether the thoughts be about God or about anything else.[14]

Of course many theologians do not regard questions about language as trivial. Yet despite their readiness to learn from a wide range of other disciplines, theologians generally continue to keep their distance from analytic philosophy. The reasons for this ongoing reluctance (which, if one takes analytic philosophy to begin basically with Frege, goes back well into the last century) would make an interesting study in its own right. It may have to do with the assumption, common in the humanistic disciplines, that because analytic philosophy's formal apparatus (of quantifiers, variables, sentential operators, and the like) and explanatory concepts form to a certain extent a body of specialist knowledge, the issues it treats and the conclusions it reaches are arcane and lack theological interest. This book proposes that the mainstream analytic debate handles in a rigorous and telling fashion problems about truth and interpretation with which any discipline must deal, and so demands theological attention.

Here a different kind of theological worry comes into view. Theologians no doubt have to draw on philosophical claims and arguments in order to think and talk about God. And it may be that, contrary to the modern theological mainstream, analytic philosophy of language provides the best available conceptual tools for coming to grips with questions about meaning, belief, and truth in theology. But theologians should nonetheless be deliberately eclectic in their philosophical commitments, and correspondingly reserved about making theological claims beholden to any particular philosophical argument or approach. This best assures that theology's truth claims, and even more those of Christian belief itself, will not wind up at the mercy of transient philosophical fashion.

On this score two different issues may usefully be distinguished. When it comes to theology's epistemic priorities, if analytic philosophy (or any other discipline) makes claims which are incompatible with central Christian beliefs, then so much the worse for analytic philosophy. The Christian community and Christian theology are justified, as

---

14. Michael Dummett, *Origins of Analytical Philosophy* (Cambridge, Mass.: Harvard University Press, 1993), p. 11. Not everyone, to be sure, would agree with Dummett's claim about what marks out the analytic tradition in philosophy.

subsequent chapters of this book will argue in detail, in retaining their own epistemic commitments. This is not to say, however, that the Christian community's central beliefs will normally enable theologians to decide which philosophical views have the strongest claim on their attention. Rival philosophical arguments relevant to the issue at hand may alike be compatible with Christian beliefs, and philosophical claims incompatible with Christian beliefs may be supported by better arguments than those which cohere with Christianity. A principled philosophical eclecticism will not likely be of much help in deciding between rival arguments or responding to relevant objections. Theologians, it seems, have to make on their own responsibility the philosophical arguments which bear on the issues they want to treat. I will try to do that here. This book's engagement with analytic philosophy of language aims not to provide a philosophical basis for Christian beliefs, but to make theological use of some of the best available reflection on the topic at hand. It strives to turn an important body of text and argument to specifically theological purposes – to follow, in short, the scriptural injunction to "take every thought captive to obey Christ" (II Cor. 10:5).

We are inquiring, lastly, about the truth of "Christian" beliefs, and about the epistemic right to hold such beliefs. But what counts as "Christian" belief turns out to be a somewhat complicated question. Getting into a position to begin listing Christian beliefs with some reliability requires addressing issues like what identifies the Christian community, what this community's primary criteria of truth are, and how you can tell what these criteria are. It turns out that no one of these questions can be answered without answering them all, an undertaking which begins in the next chapter.

It should at least be clear from the outset, however, that "Christian belief" is not restricted to beliefs which only Christians hold. Any belief might be a "Christian" one, depending on whether and how it fits with the criteria the Christian community employs to assess the truth and falsity of beliefs. A theological account of truth and deciding about truth will not, therefore, apply only to a limited set of beliefs, namely those which are distinctively Christian; in the nature of the case it will turn out to be an account of truth and epistemic right for beliefs in general – for any possible claim which wants to count as true.

One final point needs to be noted explicitly. As the opening paragraphs of this chapter already suggest, I will here follow the New Testament in speaking of Jesus as "the Son" of God, and of this God as "the Father" of Jesus. Since these words take masculine pronouns in English, and the reflexive character of pronouns has no adequate substitute in ordinary language, masculine pronouns will be used for God as well. Whether Christians ought to continue to talk to and about God in this way is of course now much debated. It will be evident that I think the answer to this question is yes, but I will not attempt any systematic defense of this conviction here; that would require a separate book on the Trinity, focused rather differently than this one.

How one handles this difficult problem depends in part, of course, on what one thinks is happening when the Christian community speaks to and about God as "the Father, the Son, and the Holy Spirit." As chapter 2 will argue in more detail, the primal setting of this form of speech is the church's eucharistic liturgy, in which the Holy Spirit invites and enables a human community to join the crucified and risen Jesus in his own eternal love for and knowledge of the Father who sent him, and so to share in the innermost life of God. A straightforward empirical analysis can show, moreover, that this is what the Christian community believes is happening in its liturgy, though it cannot show that this is in fact what is happening. That the persons of the Trinity succeed in inviting us to share their life presumes that they know how to designate and address one another, and in particular that Jesus knows how to address the one who sent him, since our particular place in the life of God is to share, as Jesus' sisters and brothers, in his own loving and knowing address to that one. When Jesus designates that one as "the Father" and invites us to join him, therefore, he issues an invitation which we can of course refuse, but whose terms we cannot define: they are defined by the persons of the Trinity themselves.[15] It is basically for that reason that I think the New Testament designations of the divine persons ought be retained.

The point is a specific one, and suggests nothing about the descriptive (as distinguished from designative or individuating) uses of language about God. One could, to mention only one example, hold that "the Father" is the primary designation of the one who eternally generates the Son and who sends the Son into our flesh, and also hold that a proper

---

15. The idea is an ancient one: "God is to be believed when he speaks of himself, and whatever he grants us to think concerning himself is to be followed" (Hilary of Poitiers, *De Trinitate* IV, 14; *Corpus Christianorum Series Latina* [= CCL], vol. LXII, p. 115, 14–15). Were it otherwise – did speaking truly about the triune God (and especially referring to God) not itself depend on God's own free action, including the gift to us by the divine persons of their own individuating designations for one another – we would perhaps have a much broader choice of words when it came to talking about (and especially referring to) God.

description even of the eternal relationship of "the Father" to the Son, insofar as we are capable of one, necessarily includes maternal as well as paternal aspects – a point of which the trinitarian theological tradition has long been aware.[16]

One could also, as we will see later, hold quite different views of what is going on when Christians speak of God, whether as "the Father" or in other terms. On some alternative accounts, such as those which regard Christian talk of God as chiefly the expression of an inner experience finally too deep for words, it is not at all clear that there would be any justification for retaining the traditional designations. Questions about whether traditional Christian words referring to the persons of the Trinity ought to be retained are thus bound up with much broader questions about the meaning, and the point, of Christian speech.

---

16. As, for example, in the text of the 11th Council of Toledo (675), often cited in contemporary feminist discussions of this point: "One must believe that the Son is begotten and born, not from nothing, nor from some other substance, but from the womb of the Father (*de Patris utero*), that is, from his substance" (DS 526; = Heinrich Denzinger and Adolf Schömetzer, *Enchiridion Symbolorum* [36th edn, Barcelona: Herder, 1976]). Note also Thomas Aquinas's discussion of the *conceptio* of the eternal *Verbum* in *Summa Contra Gentiles* IV, 11 (nos. 3478–9); he concludes: "In the generation of the Word Holy Scripture attributes to the Father all those things which in fleshly generation belong separately to the father and to the mother: thus the Father is said both 'to give life to the Son' and 'to conceive and give birth (*concipere et parturire*)' to the Son" (ed. C. Pera et al. [Turin: Marietti, 1961]).

2

The triune God as the center of Christian belief

The concept of Christian belief

We want to develop, in the first place, a theological account of the justification of beliefs. Such an account will seek to explain in a conceptually precise and maximally plausible way how epistemic justification works for those who hold Christian beliefs. It will obviously try to account for the justification of Christian beliefs themselves. But it will have to say something about the justification of beliefs more generally; there will need at least to be an explanation of how to decide which beliefs belong, or could belong, to a view of the world compatible with holding Christian convictions.

In order to develop such an account, we will naturally have to have a concept of "Christian belief," the sort of concept which will enable us to pick out or identify Christian beliefs. Unless we know how to do this, we obviously will not be able to say how justification works for those who hold such beliefs. What we need, in other words, is the ability to list Christian beliefs; this requires a definition of "Christian belief" which will equip us to form a list in a reliable rather than arbitrary and haphazard way. Once we have the concept of "Christian belief," we should be able to say what individuates a Christian system of beliefs, and thereby say (in principle, not in complete detail) what beliefs may belong to a Christian view of the world.

Arriving at such a concept, and with it acquiring the capacity to identify Christian beliefs, turns out to be a more complex undertaking than one might initially suppose. We might approach the matter by asking particularly adept or knowledgeable Christians what they believe, but here we face a threefold problem. (1) In order for this strategy to work, we would first of all have to know when we were dealing with Christians; this puts us in danger of begging the question, since Christians are (among other things) those who hold certain sorts of beliefs, and it is just those sorts of beliefs that we are not presuming we know how to pick out – including, of course, in our own case, if we identify ourselves as Christians. (2) Even if we assume we know when we are dealing with Christians, we cannot learn to pick out Christian beliefs simply by asking them what they believe, since without a reliable concept of Christian belief already in hand we cannot be sure which of the beliefs they list are Christian ones and which are not. (3) Of course, we might simply ask them to tell us how they pick out Christian beliefs, that is, to tell us what their concept of Christian belief is. But that by itself would give us no way of telling whether a particular individual's concept was a reliable one, rather than an idiosyncratic concept unconnected to the notion of "Christian belief" afoot in the Christian community at large.

This suggests that a more promising approach to a reliable concept of "Christian belief" is to attend to what the Christian community as a whole – the church – holds true, and the practices by which they do so. This obviously avoids the danger of idiosyncrasy, and effectively eliminates the problem of circularity as well: that there is a publicly visible Christian community, made up in our day of a network of more or less closely related groups, will likely be contested by few people within that community, and even fewer outside it. So if by attending to what that community says and does we can discover at work a rule for accepting or rejecting proposals for belief, we will have the concept we seek. That is: in order to discern what the most central, identity-forming beliefs of a community (including the Christian church) are, the first place to look is not in a book, but at what the community *does* – including, of course, the way it talks. What a community's identity-forming beliefs are is essentially an empirical question, to be answered by attending to its practices. A reliable concept of "Christian belief" will therefore be a broadly empirical one; it will be a concept which fits the actual practice of this publicly recognizable community as it decides what counts as its own beliefs.

The boundaries of this community are, to be sure, not entirely clear either to members or non-members. The Quakers, for example, are generally counted as belonging to the Christian community, though they have no sacraments and only minimal public worship; the Mormons generally are not, even though they call upon the name of Jesus in worship, since they have a canonical text not acknowledged by any other community which takes itself to be Christian. But the vagueness of the boundaries does not rule out the possibility of an empirically funded definition of "Christian belief"; it simply counsels us to stick to unambiguous cases when it comes to constructing the needed definition. Even in obvious cases, however, the Christian community presents us with a confusing welter of beliefs and practices from which we hope to discern a rule for what counts as "Christian belief."

We can begin to cut through the confusion by remembering that we are looking for a way to pick out those beliefs which belong to the church as a *community*, and not simply those which happen to belong to the individuals who make up that community. Any human group must, it seems, be united by adherence to particular beliefs and practices if it is to exist as a coherent and publicly discernible community over time. This suggests that we look for beliefs which contribute to the identity of the church, the beliefs which have a role – especially those which have an indispensable role – in its own continuing existence as a coherent community. On every conceivable matter the church's members will naturally have all sorts of opinions which are not essential to the church's own ongoing communal existence. To the extent that these opinions make no contribution to the identity of the church, we can safely exclude them from the domain of "Christian belief." The church as a community has no stake in holding them true (or false), though those who hold the opinions may seek to show that they are compatible with the beliefs to which the church is committed, and so may belong to a Christian view of the world.

Christian beliefs, we can therefore say, are those which contribute to the identity of the Christian community. The concept of "Christian belief" embraces, at its upper limit, beliefs which are permanently essential to the identity of this community, and at its lower limit beliefs which are, at least at some time in its history, beneficial for maintaining communal identity.[1] Those convictions at the upper limit of the range constitute "Christian belief" in the strictest sense, the beliefs the community must hold true in order to maintain its own identity; for present purposes it is these which are our primary concern. The concept of a belief which is essential to ongoing communal identity is nicely captured by William Christian's definition of an "authentic doctrine" of a community: one which that community holds it is "bound to teach."[2]

But we do not yet have an adequate concept of Christian belief, one

1. For a more detailed classification of the Christian community's identity-forming beliefs along these lines, one which usefully takes possible temporal variations into account, see George A. Lindbeck, *The Nature of Doctrine* (Philadelphia: Westminster, 1984), pp. 84–8.
2. William A. Christian, Sr., *Doctrines of Religious Communities: A Philosophical Study* (New Haven: Yale University Press, 1987), p. 74.

which will enable us actually to pick out Christian beliefs. Just knowing that we are looking for those beliefs which actually contribute to Christian communal identity does not by itself enable us to figure out which ones they are. Consider the following complicating factors.

1. We want to identify those beliefs that the church holds as a community, as distinguished from the individual opinions of its members. But we cannot come up with a list of those beliefs by finding out (for example, by taking a poll) which beliefs are held by the greatest majority of the community's members. Even if our poll were sophisticated enough to include a control group of non-members (so that the "The sun rises in the east" did not, on account of its wide acceptance by church members, get counted as a Christian belief), it might be at a given time that most of the community's members hold, perhaps with considerable passion, beliefs which conflict with those convictions which are essential to the church's identity. A community in this sort of condition is, to be sure, one whose continued coherent existence is threatened. But by its own account the church has sometimes found itself in this situation. In much of the fourth century (and in parts of northern Europe until a good deal later) the majority of Christians were probably Arians rather than Nicene trinitarians, famously prompting Jerome to lament (concerning the low point of the Nicene cause in 359) that "the whole world groaned and marveled to find itself Arian."[3]

As this sort of example suggests, the effort to arrive at an empirically significant rather than merely stipulative concept of Christian belief does not, as might be thought, reduce normative questions to purely descriptive ones. For the Christian community itself, the question of what counts as Christian belief is of course a normative one, a question of what the community *ought* to believe. An empirically significant concept of Christian belief therefore cannot be attained just by taking an inventory of beliefs currently held in the community. It requires rather the effort to discover (and not simply assume that one knows) how a particular community in practice decides which beliefs belong to its view of the world and which do not.[4]

2. Nor can we pick out Christian beliefs by finding those that are *distinctive* to the Christian community. That is: supposing that we could find

---

3. *Altercatio Luciferiani et Orthodoxi*, 19 (PL 23, 172C).
4. By the church's (or a Christian) "view of the world" I mean an overall system of belief which is at least compatible with the Christian community's identity-forming convictions – with what I am here calling "Christian beliefs." On the role of "Christian beliefs" in shaping "a Christian view of the world," see chapter 5.

a group of beliefs which were held by all members of the community and only by members of the community, we still could not suppose that we had thereby picked out in an adequate way the beliefs which are essential to this community's identity. The community might very well have beliefs which are utterly essential to its own identity, but which are widely shared by those outside the community. Indeed, there seem to be some communally essential beliefs that the church expects and hopes non-members will share: for example, that Jesus of Nazareth was cru-cified under Pontius Pilate, and that he was born to a Jewish woman named Mary. To be sure, it seems unlikely, and perhaps inconceivable, that a community could have an identity of its own if *all* of its beliefs were shared in this way. But an injunction to look for beliefs distinctive to the church seems an inadequate rule for picking out Christian beliefs.

Moreover, locating those beliefs which are distinctively Christian does not by itself enable us to distinguish those which are permanently essen-tial from those which, while perhaps relevant to the church's identity in a particular place and time, are not. As we have just observed, the concept of Christian belief includes a shading off from the essential to the merely beneficial, and with that from convictions utterly central to its belief structure to those which are more peripheral.[5] Although we will not know until we look, the church is likely not equally committed to all of the beliefs which it holds in common at any given time; only a portion of these beliefs will be really indispensable to the church's identity and central to its system of belief.

3. While the church will likely not regard all of the beliefs to which it is communally committed at a particular time as genuinely essential to its identity, the converse will also be likely to hold: *any* belief might, in the right circumstances, touch on essential matters. Regardless of how remote it may at one time seem from the communally constitutive con-cerns of Christians, any belief might come to be one in the truth or falsity of which the Christian community has a stake, and thus not a matter which belongs only among the individual opinions of its members.

This is perhaps clearest in the area of beliefs about what it is right to do, that is, in ethics. Many Christians in Germany in 1933–34 thought that political support for Adolf Hitler and the National Socialist program was permissible, though not obligatory, for people who belonged to the church; they thought such a political posture was manifestly consistent

---

5. On the overlap between the beliefs "essential" to communal identity and those "central" to its belief system, see the last section of this chapter.

with those convictions which are essential to the church's identity, and had much to recommend it on other grounds for anyone who was concerned about the future flourishing of the German people (there were some – the *Deutsche Christen* – who thought that support for the Hitler regime was positively obligatory for Christians, but they were always in the minority). But as the Confessing Church argued at the time, and virtually all Christians have come to agree, believing what the Nazis believed is not an ecclesially neutral political position, but rather is profoundly inconsistent with those convictions which are most central to the identity of the Christian community.[6] The churches came to take a similar view of South African apartheid. For present purposes the upshot of these considerations is that we cannot exclude any belief *a priori* from the possibility of being a Christian belief. Any belief might not only be included in a Christian view of the world, but might turn out to be beneficial, and perhaps essential, to the church's identity.

We so far lack a usable rule for making judgments about which beliefs are essential to the identity of the Christian community and most central to its belief system. Being widely held in the Christian community, being distinctive to that community, and being apparently remote from the concerns of that community are not reliable guides to those beliefs which do and do not shape the community's identity. Each criterion can indeed be applied to generate a more or less definite class of beliefs. But in each case, it turns out that we cannot judge whether a belief of that class contributes to the community's identity unless we already know what its most central, identity-forming convictions are, and how these convictions shape decisions about what the community ought and ought not to believe.

If this community has a coherent identity at all, however, we ought to be able to discover what that identity is by attending to the community's actual practices. Any community with a coherent and enduring identity must be able to distinguish itself from the mere collection of people who take up a given space at a given time. This will be true even if the membership of the community is virtually coextensive with the inhabitants of a particular geographic area (as has sometimes been the case in Christian history). One way of making this distinction is by public practices which initiate members into the community. It therefore seems reasonable to suppose that one set of practices which will display clearly the church's

---

6. For the best account of these events, see Klaus Scholder, *The Churches in the Third Reich*, 2 vols., trans. John Bowden (Philadelphia: Fortress Press, 1988).

most central beliefs – the ones which are essential to its identity, and therefore help to distinguish it as a community – will be those by which the community receives persons into membership. Here the church is presumably engaged in distinguishing itself as a community from other communities and from its surrounding society or culture at large (though it may do so in many other ways as well).

Virtually all communities which claim the name "Christian" have a distinctive public rite of entry into the community, namely baptism. This rite is public in two senses: (a) it is not simply an action taking place between the person who receives it and the person who gives it, but unites in mutual accountability the recipient to the whole community, and so (b) ordinarily takes place in the midst of the worship of the whole community. This rite – or sacrament, as most Christians call it – does not simply signal that those who receive it are members of the Christian community; it actually makes them members. Regardless of the extent of their previous participation in the life of the community, including its worship, they are not members until they receive this sacrament. The difference between being a member and not being one is neither trivial nor obscure: members are invited to share in the eucharistic rite which is the culmination of ordinary Christian worship (specifically, to eat and drink the consecrated bread and cup), while non-members are not.[7] Conversely, the community has generally regarded exclusion from the eucharist as the strongest sanction it can impose on its members, when in

---

7. For a discussion of baptism as a condition for reception of the eucharist, defended precisely by a theologian inclined to be suspicious of such conditions on account of the eschatological character of the eucharist (in that, as anticipation of and participation in the heavenly banquet prepared by God for all people, the eucharist likewise includes a universal invitation), see Geoffrey Wainwright, *Eucharist and Eschatology*, 2nd edn (London: Epworth, 1978), pp. 130–5. The distinction between members and non-members was even clearer in the ancient church, when those undergoing instruction in the faith but not yet baptized (the catechumens) generally were required to leave the sanctuary after the sermon and before the offertory, viz., before the beginning of the eucharistic liturgy in the narrower sense (the Eastern rite still retains the dismissal of the catechumens, though it is sometimes omitted). Thus they first beheld and first shared in the eucharistic mystery at the same time. Whether the distinction between members and non-members ought to be marked by making the eucharist a quasi-arcane rather than an entirely public "mystery" is of course debatable (see Wainwright's critical remarks, p. 134); the present point is simply that it clearly reflects the church's concern to make the distinction plain.

In the Western churches the relation between baptism and eucharistic participation is complicated by the exclusion from the eucharist of those baptized as infants until they are old enough to be instructed about its meaning (historically, at confirmation). For present purposes these practices can be viewed as a temporal extension of the initiation process, which begins at baptism and is completed at confirmation. The Orthodox clarify the basic relationship between membership and eucharistic reception by communing all baptized members, including infants; in the Western churches the communing of infants and children is now increasingly widespread.

the judgment of the community a member has been unfaithful to the promises he made in his baptism.[8]

Thus the Christian community seems to distinguish itself from others not only by its own rite of membership, but by that particular practice which it reserves only for members. So it seems reasonable to suppose that, among the practices which contribute to the identity of the Christian community, none is more essential than eucharistic worship. And this suggests that one way to get at the most essential and central *beliefs* of this community is to see what sentences the community holds true when it engages in the practice of eucharistic worship. Or, more precisely, we need to see what beliefs are indispensable to eucharistic worship, such that without the public communal holding of these beliefs the practice of eucharistic worship does not take place. Prayer gives the rule for belief, as an ancient Christian adage has it (*lex orandi est lex credendi*), so by looking at the way this community prays, we may hope to discern what its principal beliefs are. This is not, of course, to propose that attention to the beliefs and practices constitutive of eucharistic worship is the only way to get at the most central convictions of the Christian community, rather that it is one readily available way which promises reliable results – surely as reliable as those likely to be obtained in any other fashion.

The liturgical centrality of the Trinity

Here I will not try to provide a detailed analysis of the church's eucharistic liturgy, still less of the rich variety of forms in which it exists. For present purposes there is no need to do so. My aim is to get at those beliefs which are basic to the worship of the Christian community, the beliefs which mark out the rudimentary conceptual structure of this worship. About the beliefs and practices which constitute eucharistic worship there is of course a certain amount of dispute among Christian communities. But there is nonetheless deep agreement of ancient lineage, made more clear by this century's liturgical scholarship and renewal, about what beliefs and practices enable a communal activity to count as eucharistic worship.[9] I will therefore concentrate on the common features of

---

8. In the now vanished days of the *corpus christianum* exclusion from the eucharist could lead to further penalties, including death – but these were imposed by the state, not the church, and so not by the eucharistic community itself.

9. For a widely influential ecumenical proposal which seeks to identify the extensive common ground among Christians in eucharistic practice and belief, see *Baptism –*

eucharistic worship, leaving aside most of its variety. If the foregoing argument is right, these common features will constitute the most central and essential beliefs of the Christian community.

For the sake of clarity I will look primarily at one eucharistic liturgy, an American Lutheran one particularly familiar to me. This liturgy can fairly be taken as a convenient sample of typical Christian worship practice; it has numerous parallels in structure and detail to the eucharistic worship of other Christian communities, to which I will occasionally advert.

Invocation, individuation, and identity

Like almost all eucharistic worship, our sample liturgy of Holy Communion begins with the eucharistic celebrant's invocation: "In the name of the Father, and of the Son, and of the Holy Spirit" (cf. Mt. 28:19) followed by the congregation's assent: "Amen" (195).[10] Or, on those days (especially between Easter and Pentecost) when the eucharist begins without the confession of sins, the celebrant invokes the Father, the Son, and the Holy Spirit by greeting the congregation with a Pauline blessing (II Cor. 13:14) which petitions the presence of these same three among the congregation gathered for worship: "The grace of the Lord Jesus Christ, the love of God, and the communion of the Holy Spirit be with you all" (196). The entire worship to follow takes place in the name invoked at the outset.

The rite of Confession which normally follows the invocation already suggests the basic pattern for worship in this name. Ultimately this community directs its worship toward the Father invoked at the outset. It succeeds in reaching this God, who is at once "almighty" and "most merciful," because it takes place through his Son, whom he "has given to die for us," and in the power of his Holy Spirit, whom he "bestows on" us (195).

The invocation, confession, and greeting thus *name* the God whom the assembly gathered for this liturgy worships; this people's God is the

---

Eucharist – Ministry, Faith and Order Paper 111 (Geneva: World Council of Churches, 1982). For a systematic theological proposal undertaken from a liturgical perspective and well informed about modern liturgical scholarship, see Geoffrey Wainwright, *Doxology: The Praise of God in Worship, Doctrine, and Life* (London: Epworth Press, 1980); on unity and diversity in Christian liturgical practice, see especially pp. 287–323.

10. Parenthetical references are to page numbers in *The Lutheran Book of Worship: Ministers Desk Edition* (Minneapolis: Augsburg, 1978). For a helpful analysis of the common trinitarian structure of Roman Catholic, Orthodox, and Lutheran eucharistic worship, see Matti Kotiranta, "Das Trinitarische Dogma als verbindender Faktor für das liturgische Erbe der Kirchen," *Kerygma und Dogma* 40 (1994), pp. 115–42.

Father, the Son, and the Holy Spirit. Since this God has a name, the community presumably knows how to distinguish him from other real or imagined listeners, whether or not divine, to whom speech might be addressed. So far, however, the liturgy has not shown *how* the worshipping community succeeds in distinguishing its God from everyone (and everything) else to or of whom one might speak. Indeed, the liturgy has not so far made entirely clear whether the bearers of the names "the Father," "the Son," and "the Holy Spirit" are really distinct from one another, or whether these are somehow all names for the same thing. It has not yet *identified* the God upon whom the congregation calls by name.

To *identify* a person or object x is to succeed in distinguishing x from all other persons or objects. At a minimum this requires that we hit on at least one property of x which no other person or object has, one predicate true of x which is not true of any other person or object (in some circumstances, as we will see, more than this minimum is required for identification). When it comes to beings which take up space and time, this can often be done simply by specifying a particular place and time in which the person or object in question is located. "Which one is Jennifer?" I ask, to which my wife responds, "She's the one at the front of the line." Should my wife's sentence be true – should Jennifer be at the front of the line when she utters it – and should she and I believe it to be true, then we will have succeeded in distinguishing Jennifer from all other persons or objects. We will have identified her.

As this example suggests, identifying a person does not require that we have any deep knowledge of her. Identifying a person does not require, in other words, knowledge of that person's *identity*. The identity of a person or object, we can say, consists in whatever makes that person or object the unique individual he, she, or it is. Or, more generally and a bit more precisely, the identity of x is whatever must be true of a person or object in order for that person or object to be x. (I have often spoken of the church's "identity" in just this sense; at present we are looking for communal beliefs which belong to the church's identity as so conceived.) The features which make up x's identity therefore suffice to set x apart from all other persons and objects, actual or possible, while the features by which x is identified need do no more than allow us to distinguish x, at present, from all other actual persons and objects. Thus, as I will use the terms, "identity" is a feature possessed by any individual person or object, whereas "identification" is an activity undertaken by persons who for various purposes want to pick out or distinguish persons and objects (for example, to know more about them). In order to minimize confusion between "identity" and "identify," I will sometimes use "individuate" or "pick out" for the latter – for the action – but never for the feature.

Considerable philosophical debate surrounds the question of what, if anything, constitutes personal identity. At one end of the scale the answer is "everything": all the properties I possess, whatever is true of me, makes me the unique individual I am. This response has the advantage of clarity, including the clarity of making individuation and identity coincide; in order to pick out a person, we would (contrary to the suggestion I have just made) have to know something genuinely identity-constituting about him. It has the disadvantage of implausibility. If this approach is correct, then I am a different person – metaphysically a different individual – for having woken up at 7:17 this morning than I would have been if I had managed to wake up at 7:16, for having had grapefruit rather than orange juice for breakfast, and so forth. This seems counter-intuitive, and suggests the need to find some way of discriminating between the totality of what is true of me and what is genuinely person- or identity-constituting for me.

At the other end of the scale the answer is "nothing": personal identity is elusive beyond our knowing, and perhaps finally illusory. This response has the advantage of frankly facing the epistemic and metaphysical puzzles which surround personal identity, but it also bears the burden of counter-intuitiveness. If this approach were correct I might now be quite another person than I was when I woke up this morning, uneventful as the day has so far been, or at best I would have no way of knowing whether I am the same person as the one who woke up in my bed this morning. This suggests that at least some of what is true of me is genuinely identity-constituting for me, even though it may not always be easy to be sure what this is.

These are challenging philosophical questions – that a conclusion is counter-intuitive does not, after all, mean that it is wrong. For our purposes, however, the problem of what makes for personal identity will arise just in case the liturgy permits us not only to pick out the church's God, but to grasp this God's very identity. As we will see, the liturgy in fact urges us not only to distinguish "the Father," "the Son," and "the Holy Spirit" from one another and from ourselves, but also to lay hold of their own identities, of what ultimately makes each the unique individual he is and the three the unique God they are. For that to happen, however, the liturgy will have to give us a way of telling which of the characteristics we attribute to the divine persons are those which make each person the unique individual he is – if indeed we can find any characteristics which actually accomplish this. It will not be enough to find features which are true of each person, nor even attributes unique to each person; we will need to locate just those features which have to be true of a person in order for that person to be "the Father," "the Son," or "the Holy Spirit." This raises difficult questions, since the liturgy not only directs us to grasp who the divine persons are, but also gives us reasons *not* to equate what constitutes the identity of each person with everything which we may find useful, or even necessary, to identify each. For the moment, however, we can simply attend to the way in which the liturgy individuates the divine persons, and save for later the question whether and how it (or some other Christian practice) actually lets us grasp their identities.

If we are to identify the church's God by way of its worship, the liturgy will at a minimum have to equip us with descriptions of "the Father, the Son, and the Holy Spirit" which attribute to the bearer of this name properties or characteristics which belong to no one else. Similarly the liturgy will enable us to distinguish "the Father," "the Son," and "the Holy Spirit" from one another – to identify them as three persons and not only as one God – should it attribute properties to each, such as distinctive actions, which are not shared by the others. And as the liturgy teaches us to distinguish and relate the bearers of these names, we may expect it to teach us of their distinction from and relation to the gathered community which worships them as God.

Identifying Jesus

The liturgy begins to individuate the God whom the assembly has invoked by indicating that "the Son" upon whom it calls is the same as a particular human being: Jesus of Nazareth, invoked as "Jesus Christ." No practice seems more primitively embedded in the church than that of addressing Jesus, in joy and in want. When the assembly calls upon "the Son," and so upon its God, it calls upon this human being, and when it calls upon this human being, it calls upon the Son who is its God.[11] Thus, singing the Gloria in praise of the triune God, the congregation calls out to Jesus, "Lord Jesus Christ, only Son of the Father, Lord God, Lamb of God: You take away the sins of the world; have mercy on us. You are seated

---

11. On the early identification by the Christian community of the divine "Son" with Jesus of Nazareth (presupposed, for example, in Rom. 1:3), see Martin Hengel, *The Son of God*, trans. John Bowden (Philadelphia: Fortress, 1976), especially pp. 57–84.

at the right hand of the Father; receive our prayer" (198). In its liturgy, the church not only speaks about Jesus, but speaks to him. This community calls upon Jesus in praise and thanksgiving, in petition ("receive our prayer") and intercession, and confidently expects his response to its invocation. We do not yet know how to pick this human being out from the crowd, but we now know explicitly that the congregation regards him as distinct from "the Father," to whom it also speaks, since it attributes to him a condition – being seated at the Father's right hand – which clearly cannot be shared by the Father himself. We know, moreover, that whoever more precisely the church believes Jesus to be, it regards him as someone upon whom it can call.

Calling upon a person presumes a belief about him or her, namely that he or she is not dead. It makes no sense to call upon a person whom you believe to be dead, since the dead cannot hear or respond to your call. So in calling upon Jesus, the church expresses its belief that he is alive, and alive in a distinctive way: exalted to the Father's right hand and sharing completely "in the glory of God the Father" (198).

The liturgy quickly shows, however, that the church not only believes that it can call upon Jesus, but that the one upon whom it calls once was dead – really dead, so that no one could call upon him. This Jesus who "has begun his reign" (200) at the right hand of the Father is "the Lamb who was slain, whose blood set us free to be people of God" (199; cf. Rev. 5:6; 9–10), the one who can say in truth, "I was dead, and behold I am alive for ever and ever, and I hold the keys of death and hell" (Rev. 1:18). In its opening Antiphons the Orthodox Church's Divine Liturgy makes the point even more sharply:

> Only begotten Son and Word of God, although immortal, for our salvation you accepted flesh from the holy Theotokos and ever virgin Mary, and without change became man. Christ our God, you were crucified but trampled down death by death (θανάτῳ θάνατον πατήσας). You are one of the holy Trinity, glorified together with the Father and the Holy Spirit: save us.[12]

Thus by invoking Jesus the church expresses not only its belief that he is alive, but its belief, more precisely, that he is risen from the dead. At the outset of its liturgy the church begins to identify Jesus by calling upon him as the one who is risen from the dead, and who fully shares the Father's glory. If the practice of calling upon Jesus is essential to the

---

12. *The Divine Liturgy of St. John Chrysostom* (Brookline: Holy Cross Orthodox Press), p. 6 (translation altered).

church's identity, then so is the belief that he is risen; the church, it seems, has its communal identity at least in part by making a distinctive – and astonishing – truth claim about Jesus.[13]

While the liturgy displays Jesus' resurrection as indispensable to its identification of him, reference to resurrection does not by itself suffice to individuate Jesus. That Jesus is risen seems to be the chief element in the church's identifying description of him; did the community not believe that Jesus is risen, it could not call upon him, and so could have no liturgy at all. But when the church calls upon Jesus it does not express the belief that just anyone, or someone unknown, has risen from the dead, but specifically that Jesus is risen. Who the church's God is depends on who is risen; did the community suppose that someone else were risen – Lenin, for example, or Genghis Khan – it would back up its invocation of "the (risen) Son" with an utterly different description than it actually does, and so would have a different God. Having begun to identify the three-named God invoked at the outset by saying that the Son is the same as the human being Jesus of Nazareth, the liturgy must now enable the participants – and anyone else who may be on hand – to identify the human being whose resurrection it proclaims.

The church identifies Jesus by telling and hearing a story in which he figures as the central character; the precise sort of identifying description the church has of Jesus is a dramatic narrative, in which acquaintance with the central character comes about through extended attention to what he does and undergoes in a particular sequence of settings – to the cumulative "twists and turns of the deep-laid plot."[14] The name for this

---

13. Christian communities (most of them, at any rate) also call upon the saints, in a way which displays the conviction that they too, like Jesus, live beyond death (and not, like us, before it). A more detailed account would show that the community believes that it can call upon them only because Jesus is risen and seated at the right hand of the Father, and therefore only because the community can call upon him. The church expects from the risen Jesus different and greater things than the saints can give, namely those which can come from God alone (indeed the saints know best of all that they, like we, have no gifts of their own to give, but can only pray for his). On the belief in incarnation which this expectation implies see the first section of chapter 5, in connection with Jesus' universal primacy.

14. To borrow a phrase from Christian, *Doctrines of Religious Communities*, p. 95. It should be noted that the notion of "narrative" is introduced here because the church identifies Jesus, and thereby the triune God, by means of a narrative (one with a textually fixed form, as we shall momentarily observe); in the church's practice, this narrative is not simply a useful way to pick Jesus out from the crowd, but is (this side of the eschaton) permanently necessary for the task. It may further be the case that narratives are necessary uniquely to identify *any* particular person, though I will not argue that more general claim here. The present argument does not depend on its truth, still less on that of the sweeping claims about narrative and "narrativity" sometimes made in theology.

narrative is "the gospel."[15] To the extent that the liturgy as a whole unfolds the narrative which identifies Jesus, the whole liturgy is "gospel," the proclamation of the good news which the church is charged to bring to the world. But that portion of the community's worship which comes between the Gloria (or more precisely the Collect) and the Offertory – the "Liturgy of the Word," as it is often called – is especially devoted to recounting and interpreting the narratives which identify Jesus, and so to the proclamation of the gospel.

The church tells the story of Jesus in its worship specifically by reading and interpreting a limited and invariant set of texts; that only certain texts may be used in this way is part of what it means to say that these texts constitute the church's canon. This community apparently believes that it can succeed in identifying Jesus only by relying on these texts, and by conforming its narration of his story to theirs. The church thus holds its own most essential and central beliefs, whatever they turn out more precisely to be, in a textually controlled and textually dependent way.[16]

The specific sequence of the scriptural readings is informative. They are normally four. Two come from the Old Testament (one is always a Psalm); these tie the present community's worship to the people of Israel, to their election, history, law, and prophets, and so to their God. One comes from the Epistles, and so ties the community's worship to "the *koinonia* of the apostles" (as Acts 2:42 calls the nascent church) by declaring to the present assembly the apostles' teaching, proclamation, and exhortation. The last comes from the Gospels, and ties the community's worship most directly to Jesus Christ by recounting his life, death, and resurrection. Only the last of these readings recounts a narrative in which Jesus actually figures as a character. The readings which link the Gospel narratives identifying Jesus to the people of Israel and to the apostolic community are allowed to stand on their own. Israel and the church speak for

---

15. On the equivalence of "the narratives which identify Jesus" with "the gospel," see, e.g., Luther: "The gospel is and should be nothing other than a chronicle, a story, a narrative (*ein Chronica, historia, legenda*) about Christ, telling who he is, what he did, said, and suffered." D. *Martin Luthers Werke Kritische Gesamtausgabe* (hereafter *WA*) (Weimar: Herman Bohlaus Nachfolger, 1883ff.) 10/1/1, p. 9, 15–17. ET: *Luther's Works* (St. Louis: Concordia and Philadelphia: Fortress, 1955–86), vol. XXXV, pp. 117–18. The gospel not only identifies Jesus, but attributes ultimate and universal significance to him, about which more in a moment; on the logical links between the identification of Jesus and the attribution of significance to him, see Bruce D. Marshall, *Christology in Conflict* (Oxford: Blackwell, 1987).
16. There are, of course, some differences among Christian communities about which texts belong to the scriptural canon – specifically, whether the Old Testament embraces the books included in the Greek Septuagint or only those in the Hebrew Masoretic text. These differences raise important historical and conceptual questions about the Christian canon, but for present purposes they make little practical difference.

themselves in the liturgy, rather than being absorbed into the reading which recounts Jesus' words and deeds; the history of Israel and the church is not simply the implicit prelude and postlude to the action and passion of Jesus. At the same time, the community signals a certain priority of the Gospel among these readings (and over against the sermon as well) by various practices, such as standing for the Gospel reading, acclaiming Christ before and after the reading, making the sign of the cross, or processing with the Gospel text. Here in the Gospel, these practices suggest, beats the inmost heart of the scriptural narrative; the church seems committed to interpreting its canonical text as a whole in a way which is oriented or centered on the Gospels and the story which they, specifically, relate.

As the practices embodied in the Liturgy of the Word show, the church has the narrative that identifies Jesus, the story which tells us precisely who is risen, in the canonical form of four irreducibly distinct but also mutually enriching versions. It begins with the first-born son of the Israelite Mary, renders his words and deeds in the midst of his disciples and the multitudes in Galilee and Jerusalem, turns on the institution of the meal of his broken body and outpoured blood, followed by a voluntary transition from doing to suffering in the garden of Gesthemane, and culminates in his crucifixion and a now involuntary transition from death to resurrection and exaltation. Jesus' resurrection thus forms the climax of a complex dramatic narrative, and does not suffice to pick him out apart from that narrative web. By means of the body of beliefs which constitute this narrative the church remembers Jesus, and by means of this remembrance the church is able to call upon Jesus and enjoy his presence. The practices which make up the Liturgy of the Word thus serve to identify the risen Son whom the entrance rite invokes and praises as the particular historical person, Jesus of Nazareth.

The church's eucharistic practice in the narrower sense – what begins with the Offertory (205) – displays with especial clarity this intimate link between the church's storied memory of Jesus, its invocation of him, and its enjoyment of his presence. In obedience to Jesus' command, the celebrant gives thanks on behalf of the community to God the Father for his goodness and mercy toward human beings, and in particular remembers for the community Jesus' institution of the eucharistic meal, with its explicit reference to his imminent suffering and death: "Take and eat: this is my body, given for you . . . This cup is the new covenant in my blood, shed for you and for all people for the forgiveness of sin" (222). In this way the community remembers anew that Jesus' journey from Bethlehem to Golgotha was undertaken "for the life of the world" (Jn. 6:51) and in order "to give his life as a ransom for many" (Mk. 10:45), and remembers that this particular person and none other is the world's and its own ransom and life, in this very bread and cup which he is about to give to those gathered around the altar. The community responds to the celebrant's remembrance by confessing its faith in Jesus, whom it now knows how to pick out from the crowd: "Christ has died, Christ is risen, Christ will come again" (222). The celebrant then offers to the Father in prayer the people's remembrance of Jesus' death and resurrection, and their anticipation of "his coming in power to share with us the great and promised feast" (222). With its ancient invocation the community then assents to the celebrant's offering, appealing for the presence of the one whom the Liturgy of the Word and the Eucharist has identified: "Amen. Come, Lord Jesus" (222). At the conclusion of the eucharistic prayer, the congregation petitions the Father in the way taught by Jesus ("Our Father . . ."), and in eating and drinking enjoys with unique intimacy the presence of the one upon whom they have called: "The body of Christ, given for you . . . the blood of Christ, shed for you" (227).[17]

In this way the community's identification and recollection of Jesus through the gospel narrative, its invocation of Jesus thus recollected, and Jesus' own gracious self-presentation to the community in his body and blood all belong together. They do so, it is important to note, in a certain order. The community's invocation of Jesus and enjoyment of his presence depend on its grasp of actions or other characteristics unique to him by which it is able to identify him. If the community were unable to identify Jesus, it could not call upon him, nor could it recognize his presence, even if he were to give it.[18] What the community does in the eucharist thus exhibits as utterly central among its beliefs its assent to the identification of Jesus proposed by the church's canonical narrative, and above all to the beliefs embodied in the celebration of the communal meal: that this Jesus who promised to give himself to the community in this meal has died on

---

17. Eucharistic prayers vary considerably in detail, and the differences are sometimes important, but they almost always have the elements which are decisive for the present analysis: remembrance of Jesus, especially of his words over the bread and wine of the supper, and prayer for his presence, both in the context of a thanksgiving to the Father, which includes (as we shall see shortly) a petition for the gift of the Holy Spirit, and usually a personal invocation of the Spirit.

18. This observation is, I will argue later, entirely consistent with the claim that the community's capacity to have true beliefs about Jesus, and so to enjoy his presence, depends entirely upon Jesus himself. See chapter 9, pp. 247–51, also below, note 34.

the cross, is risen from the dead, and will come in glory. If the community did not hold these beliefs it could not have eucharistic worship at all, and a community without eucharistic worship would, it seems, be a gathering of a different kind than the Christian church is and has been.

Identifying the Father

The eucharistic thanksgiving to the Father just mentioned is one of many indications in the liturgy that the church does not invoke Jesus in isolation. The church's canonical narrative individuates Jesus in such a way that the actions and passions by which the community picks him out require reference to the actions of two other persons distinct from him, upon whom the community also calls as God: the Father and the Spirit. In this way calling upon Jesus presumes not only beliefs sufficient to identify Jesus himself, but also beliefs sufficient to identify the Father and the Spirit.

The Gospels depict Jesus' whole journey from Bethlehem to Golgotha as the enactment of a mission enjoined upon him by another. His "food is to do the will of him who sent me, and to accomplish his work" (Jn. 4:34). Jesus calls upon the God who sent him as "the Father," and he invites his followers also to share in the intimacy of this personal address. As the synoptic Gethsemane scene (Mt. 26:36–46; Mk. 14:32–42; Lk. 22:40–46, liturgically recalled particularly during Holy Week) makes especially clear, the chief actions and passions by which the church identifies Jesus depend utterly upon his obedience to the Father. Without his voluntary enactment of the Father's will to send him into the fathomless abyss of abandonment and death there would be no cross and so no resurrection and exaltation. Upon Jesus' mission from the Father, together with his own acceptance of it, depends that sequence of events which makes him the human being upon whom the church calls in worship and prayer.[19]

The eucharistic prayer displays this point in a simple but striking way: it is directed to the Father, not to Jesus.[20] The congregation thanks the

---

19. For two different, though compatible, readings of the Gethsemane scene along these lines, see Karl Barth, *Kirchliche Dogmatik* IV/1, pp. 246–50, 290–300 (ET, pp. 224–8, 264–73); Hans Urs von Balthasar, *Mysterium Paschale*, trans. Aiden Nichols (Grand Rapids: Eerdmans, 1993), pp. 100–7.

20. Though a few eucharistic prayers in the ancient church were addressed to the risen Christ, the pattern of addressing the prayer to the Father is generally established at an early point. In the middle of the second century Justin Martyr already takes it for granted: "Then the bread and vessels of water and of wine are brought to him who presides over the brethren, and he takes them and offers praise and glory to the Father of all in the name of the Son and of the Holy Spirit, and gives thanks at some length that we have been deemed worthy of these things from him." *First Apology*, 65, 3 (Miroslav Marcovich, ed., *Justini Martyris Apologiae pro Christianis* [Berlin: de Gruyter, 1994], p. 126, 8–12; the translation, slightly modified, is that given in Max Thurian and Geoffrey Wainwright, eds., *Baptism*

Father for the totality of Jesus' life, and especially for his death, resurrection, and coming return in glory: "At this end of all the ages, you sent your Son, who in words and deeds proclaimed your kingdom and was obedient to your will, even to giving his life (221) . . . And, believing the witness of his resurrection, we await his coming in power to share with us the great and promised feast" (222). The whole of Jesus' action and passion the community thus receives as a gift from the Father. The church thereby attests liturgically to its belief that all the features unique to Jesus by which it chiefly identifies Jesus belong to him only because he is sent by the Father, and responds in obedience to the mission the Father has for him. Locating these particular features and identifying Jesus by way of them thus requires grasping them as the voluntary enactment of the Father's sending (one would not, for example, have picked out *Jesus'* death by describing an individual dragged kicking and screaming to his cross). In this way picking Jesus out requires reference to the Father, and since we cannot refer to what we cannot in some way identify, we cannot pick Jesus out if we cannot also identify the Father.[21]

As with the Son Jesus, so also with the Father: in order to identify him, we need actions or characteristics unique to him. An obvious place to look for actions of this sort would be the scriptural narrative of Israel's history. Remarkably, eucharistic prayers rarely make reference to God's election of and everlasting covenant with Abraham and his descendants.[22] Even if they did, however, a problem looms at this point.

It seems natural enough to attribute actions like the election of Israel

and Eucharist: Ecumenical Convergence in Celebration, Faith and Order Paper 117 [Geneva: World Council of Churches and Grand Rapids: Eerdmans, 1983], p. 112). On the trinitarian shape of early Christian liturgies, and the role of the liturgy in the formation of the church's explicit trinitarian confession, see Georg Kretschmar, *Studien zur frühchristlichen Trinitätstheologie* (Tübingen: J. C. B. Mohr [Paul Siebeck], 1956), especially pp. 125–223; on Justin, see pp. 184–7.

21. I have taken the community's invocation of Jesus as the entry point for an analysis of its identification of the triune God in whose name it worships, but as the normal structure of the eucharistic prayer clearly suggests, the point of departure could equally well be the church's invocation, through and with Jesus, of the Father. If the temporal actions of the Father, the Son, and the Spirit are related in such a way that identifying any one of them requires identifying the other two, the identification of the three could in principle take place in any sequence, so long as it ended up including all three. As Boris Bobrinskoy observes, "we can discern in the New Testament several 'movements' of trinitarian revelation which complement one another and which all seem to be necessary in their own way." *Le Mystère de la Trinité: Cours de théologie orthodoxe* (Paris: Cerf, 1986), p. 72. In addition to the Christ–Father–Spirit sequence which I am following here, Bobrinskoy finds in the New Testament and the liturgy three (and perhaps four) others, each of which sheds its own distinctive light on the character and aims of the triune God's action in the world; of the six possibilities only the sequence Spirit–Father–Son, he suggests by his silence about it, lacks any attestation in liturgy and scripture (see pp. 70–9; 114).

22. Our sample eucharistic liturgy is an exception: "Through Abraham you promised to bless all nations. You rescued Israel, your chosen people" (221).

and the exodus from Egypt specifically to the Father, not least because the
New Testament often seems to say that the God of Israel is precisely the
Father of Jesus (or perhaps more precisely, it seems to take terms referring
to the God of Israel to be co-extensive with terms referring to the Father).
When the Jew Jesus teaches his Jewish followers to pray to their God "Our
Father . . ." (Mt. 6:9; cf. Lk. 11:2), he presumably does not, from the stand-
point of the church's trinitarian invocation of God, teach them to address
the Trinity as "Father," but apparently teaches them to locate Israel's God
in his inmost personal uniqueness – to individuate this God as "the
Father."[23] When Jesus himself on the cross cries out in the language of
Israel's Psalms "My God, my God, why have you forsaken me" (Mk.
15:34/Mt. 27:46; cf. Ps. 22:1), calling upon the very God whom he had
earlier addressed as "Father" in obedient acceptance of the "cup" he now
has to endure (Mk. 14:36 and parallels), his address to the God of Israel is
presumably not an address to the Trinity – and so in part to himself – but
specifically to the Father who has abandoned him in death.

Such considerations suggest that it should not only be possible but
necessary to identify the God upon whom Jesus and his followers call as
"the Father" by relying on the narratives about Israel, since Jesus'
manner of address to this God seems to assume some prior acquaintance
with him, and so some capacity to pick him out which does not depend
entirely upon Jesus' own words and deeds. "The Father" is apparently
not a heretofore unknown deity, even if he has not previously been
named as "Father."

Yet while these seem like compelling reasons for saying that YHWH,
the God of Israel, is the Father and not the Trinity, there seem to be
equally compelling reasons not to equate the God of Israel with the trinitarian Father. Christians, after all, claim to worship the God of Israel. If
this God is simply identical with the Father, then the Son and the Spirit
are not YHWH and not the God of Israel. Were that the case, then in worshipping them – in giving them glory along with the Father – Christians
would worship that which is not the God of Israel, and thus commit idolatry (cf. Is. 42:8). The seventeenth-century Lutheran theologian Johann
Gerhard puts the point nicely, animated (as were his contemporaries of
every confessional stripe) by a keen interest in showing, against newly

23. There is, to be sure, a substantial exegetical and theological tradition to the contrary;
see Thomas Aquinas, *Summa theologiae* III, 23, 2, c; Bonaventure, *In III Sent.* 10, 2, 3, c (=*S.
Bonaventurae Opera Theologica Selecta*, vol. III [Quaracchi: Collegium S. Bonaventurae, 1941],
p. 229b).

arisen unitarian interpretations of Christianity, that the Trinity is a thoroughly biblical doctrine. The Old Testament as well as the New, he argues, attests the Trinity, as can be inferred "from the divine prohibition in Ps. 81:10 [9]: 'Have among yourselves . . . no new God, and bow down before no foreign God.' If the mystery of the Trinity were entirely unknown in the Old Testament, then a new God would be introduced in the New Testament by the worship of the Son and the Holy Spirit. Is. 43:10: 'No God was formed before me, and none will be after me.' If the Son has become God only in the New Testament, as the Photinians suppose, and begins to be touched by divine worship only in the New Testament, then another God has been formed besides God the Father."[24]

Confronted by what seem like compelling arguments for what seem like incompatible positions (since the Father is not identical with the Trinity, the God of Israel cannot be identical with both), Christian theology from early in its history has oscillated between saying that the God of Israel is the Father and that the God of Israel is the Trinity. A third option further complicates the picture: the God of Israel – the subject of the Old Testament theophanies – is neither the Father nor the Trinity, but Christ. This seems hard to square with the many New Testament passages which seem to require that the God of Israel be the Father (when Christ cries out in agony to Israel's God on the cross, he is surely not talking to himself), but it has to be recognized that this approach too has biblical support (the Israelites in the wilderness, as Paul argues, "drank from the spiritual rock that followed them, and the rock was Christ" [1 Cor. 10:4]), has been elaborately developed in the tradition, and retains vigorous modern advocates (such as the Orthodox theologian Serge Bulgakov).[25]

---

24. *Loci theologici* III (exegesin sive uberiorem explicationem), § 21, ed. Johann Friedrich Cotta (Tübingen: Georg Cotta, 1762–89), vol. III, p. 219.

It may be tempting to dismiss a worry like Gerhard's as anachronistic: clearly the writers of the New Testament, to say nothing of the Old, did not have the later ecclesial doctrine of the Trinity (e.g., the Nicene *homoousion*) in mind when they talked about God, so we should not expect them to take a position on whether the God they talk about is the Trinity. But these writers did have various ways of referring to the God of Israel, and also (at least in the New Testament) to the Father, Jesus, and the Spirit. It is therefore surely in order to ask whether one, two, all, or none of these three are referred to by expressions which refer to the God of Israel. And in any case, as we shall see, what a speaker's words refer to fails to depend in any non-trivial way on what is in his head.

25. "If the Father creates the world by his Word, he makes use of this same Word in his counsel and his revelation in the world. That is why the immediate divine subject of the Old Testament is the same as that of the New: the second hypostasis, the Logos." *Du Verbe Incarné: L'Agneau de Dieu*, trans. Constantin Andronikof, 2nd edn (Lausanne: Age d'Homme, 1982), p. 91; see pp. 117–18, 154.

We cannot here resolve all the perplexities which arise from the Christian claim that in worshipping the Trinity, the church worships the God of Israel. For present purposes we can simply note that the one upon whom Jesus calls as "Father" could not count as *God* unless he were in some sense the same as the one who created the world, rested on the seventh day, elected Abraham and his descendants forever, delivered Israel from Egypt, dwelt in the temple on Mt. Zion, and so forth. Jesus and the apostles are, after all, Jews. The story of Jesus' slaying and raising could be recognized by the apostles themselves as "the gospel of God" (Rom. 1:1) – the one true God – only if it included reference to the actions by which this God initially proves himself divine, and so distinguishes himself from all other candidates for worship: the election and deliverance of Israel. In at least this sense the story of Israel seems indispensable for identifying the God whom Christians worship.

At the same time, if the God whom Christians worship is the God of Israel, then Jesus and the Spirit must also in some sense be the same as the one who elects and delivers Israel, though of course they cannot be the same as each other. Since the God of Israel apparently cannot simply be the same as any one person of the Trinity, the actions by which YHWH initially displays himself to the world as God will have to be shared in some way by all the persons of the Trinity. Since in order adequately to individuate the persons of the Trinity we need actions unique to each, it seems as though the narratives about Israel will not by themselves be sufficient to enable us to distinguish the persons of the Trinity from one another.[26]

The eucharistic liturgy does, nonetheless, enable us to identify the Father. The actions typically attributed to the Father in eucharistic prayers are three: creating the world, sending Jesus into the world for the world's redemption, and perfecting or consummating the world in a promised future. Of these creation and consummation fail to individuate the Father, the latter in part because it has not yet happened, and both for the reason we have just indicated: they are shared by all three divine persons. Even though these actions are shared by each in a different way, as we will see later on, the fact that they are shared requires that we already be able to pick out the divine persons in order to ascribe the common actions to each in a distinctive way.

This leaves the sending of Jesus as the most promising candidate for

26. For more on these issues see my essays, "Does the Church Worship the God of Israel?", *Knowing the Triune God*, ed. James J. Buckley and David Yeago (Grand Rapids: Eerdmans, forthcoming), and "The Jewish People and Christian Theology," *The Cambridge Companion to Christian Doctrine*, ed. Colin Gunton (Cambridge: Cambridge University Press, 1997), especially pp. 95–8.

an action unique to the Father by which we can identify him. The community thanks the Father, as we have observed, for sending Jesus to undertake the action, passion, and resurrection by which we are redeemed from sin and death, the very features which enable us to pick out Jesus from the crowd. Sending is not a reflexive act; I cannot be the direct object of my own sending, though of course I can be its indirect object (that is, I can send a package to myself, but I cannot send myself). Jesus does not send himself to the upper room and the cross. He is sent by the Father, and that action of his which corresponds to this sending is his obedience. More than that: the Father's mission seems to issue not only in the features by which the church chiefly identifies Jesus, but in his entire life and destiny. As the Anglican liturgy has it, "You, in your mercy, sent Jesus Christ, your only and eternal Son, to share our human nature, to live and die as one of us, to reconcile us to you, the God and Father of all."[27]

Jesus is thus the direct object of the Father's sending, and we are its indirect object. And this is sufficient to distinguish Jesus both from the Father and ourselves. The sending of Jesus into our flesh and death is an action unique to the Father, and seems to be the clearest way in which the eucharistic liturgy identifies him: the Father is the one who sent Jesus. Sending Jesus to us at once distinguishes the Father from him and from us, and inextricably links our identification of the Father to our identification of Jesus. We can identify the persons of the Trinity in several different sequences, but we can identify them at all – adequately distinguish them from one another – only because Jesus has appeared on the scene.[28]

Eucharistic prayers regularly suggest a further set of features by which

27. *Book of Common Prayer* 1979, p. 362. See Gal. 4:6: "God sent his Son, born of a woman . . ."
28. Trinitarian theology has lately put particular stress on this point. Thus Bobrinskoy: "It is the person and the mystery of Christ, Word incarnate and Son of Mary exalted to the right hand of the Father in the power of the Holy Spirit, who permits the discernment and specification of what is particular to Christian worship," and with that of "the mystery of God . . . of his 'tri-unity'" (*Le Mystère de la Trinité*, pp. 159, 71). Similarly Hans Urs von Balthasar, *Theodramatik* II/2 (Einsiedeln: Johannes Verlag, 1978): "In Christianity such a distinction of a plurality in God is only possible on the basis of the action of Jesus Christ. In him alone is the Trinity opened up and accessible. Thus is verified . . . the principle that theological persons cannot be defined apart from their dramatic action" (pp. 465–6; ET: *Theo-Drama*, vol. III, trans. Graham Harrison [San Francisco: Ignatius Press, 1992], p. 508). Also Wolfhart Pannenberg, *Systematische Theologie*, vol. I (Göttingen: Vandenhoeck and Ruprecht, 1988): "The heavenly Father whom [Jesus] proclaims is so closely bound up with Jesus' own appearance and action that only *thereby* is he identified as Father" (p. 288; ET: *Systematic Theology*, vol. I, trans. Geoffrey W. Bromiley [Grand Rapids: Eerdmans, 1991], p. 264); thus "a systematic grounding and elaboration of the doctrine of the Trinity must set out from the revelation of God in Jesus Christ" (p. 326; ET, p. 300).
    As Bobrinskoy rightly suggests, the present claim – (a) We can identify the persons of the Trinity only if we can identify Jesus – does not imply (b) We can identify the persons of the Trinity only if we have already identified Jesus; (a) fails to imply, in other words, that we have to identify Jesus first in the trinitarian sequence.

Jesus and the Father may each be identified. For example the Anglican liturgy just cited calls the human being Jesus Christ the Father's "eternal Son," and suggests a reason why the whole human life of Jesus, from its first origin in Mary's womb, may be characterized as the outcome of a mission from the Father: because Jesus' human life as a whole is what happens when the "eternal Son" willingly accepts the Father's command that he "share our human nature." The Nicene Creed will already have made clear that the "Lord Jesus Christ," who as the Gospels narrate "was crucified for us under Pontius Pilate," is in the strictest sense (namely numerical identity: ἕνα) the same as "the only-begotten Son of God, who was begotten of the Father eternally."[29] Jesus thus has a feature unique to him – being (the only one) "begotten" by the Father – which, like being sent, is correlated with a feature apparently unique to the Father, namely being the "begetter" of Jesus, of the eternal Son now in our flesh. Unlike sending and being sent, however, which are temporal, begetting and being begotten are eternal.[30] Sending and being sent also have an inherently voluntary element which begetting and being begotten seem to lack. Sending thus seems contingent in a way that begetting is not; however the two fit together, they cannot simply be equated with one another. The introduction of this pair of apparently non-contingent features into the identification of Jesus and the Father is one indication that the liturgy wants to let us in on their very identities, and not simply allow us to pick them out. The liturgy thus begins pressing us to isolate those features of Jesus and the Father which are genuinely identity-constituting for them.[31]

Identifying the Spirit

Distinguishing Jesus from all other persons or objects seems to depend not only on being able to identify the Father, but on being able to identify the Spirit. On the one hand, Jesus' human existence depends *ab initio* upon the Spirit (cf. Lk. 1:35, and the creedal "conceived by the power of the Holy Spirit" [204], which regularly finds its way into eucharistic prayers).[32] The mission for which he was born and came into the world

---

29. I follow here the Greek text of the Creed of 381 in DS 150.
30. More precisely: begetting is eternal with respect both to the act and the term of the act, while sending may be eternal with respect to the act, but is temporal with respect to its term.
31. For more on this see the discussion in chapter 9, pp. 259–65.
32. As these prayers and the New Testament (especially Lk. 1) make plain, Jesus' human existence depends on the Israelite Mary as well as on the Spirit; the Spirit brings about

(cf. Jn. 18:37), namely to undertake the journey from Bethlehem to Golgotha for us, can take place only because of the Father's gift of the Spirit to him at (or at least manifested in) his baptism (cf. Mt. 3:16–17 and parallels). The main features by which the church identifies Jesus are the outcome, as we have argued, of his utter acceptance and enactment of his mission from the Father. But this unique relationship to the Father, and with it the identification of Jesus, itself depends on his being "filled with the Spirit" from the Father (Lk. 4:1), or as Luke elsewhere puts it, his "rejoicing in the Holy Spirit" (10:21).[33]

On the other hand Jesus promises that upon his exaltation to and by the Father he will send the Spirit he has received irrevocably into the world, in order to draw the world into the intimacy of his own unique relationship to the Father (cf. Jn. 14:16, 15:26; Acts 2:33). By making this promise Jesus entrusts the completion and fulfillment of his own mission – that is entrusts his own self, his own total reality – to the future mission of another who is irreducibly distinct from himself. He does so precisely in death, offering back to the silent Father the Spirit he has received from the Father (Lk. 23:46; Jn. 19:30), trusting that the Father who has abandoned him in death (Mt. 27:46; Mk. 15:34) will not forever exclude him from the bond of love in their common Spirit – trusting, in other words, that the absent Father will raise him from the dead, in the power of that Spirit. Here too, at the decisive point of resurrection, the features by which the church identifies Jesus depend upon the action of the Father's Spirit; he is "made alive in the Spirit" (1 Pet. 3:18; cf. Rom. 1:4, 8:11; 1 Tim. 3:16).

How then shall the Spirit himself be identified? Eucharistic liturgies typically call upon the Father to send the Spirit, just as they thank him for having sent the Son. "Send now, we pray, your Holy Spirit, the spirit of our Lord and of his resurrection, that we who receive the Lord's body and blood may live to the praise of your glory and receive our inheritance with all your saints in light" (223). As prayers of this sort make plain, the church picks out the Holy Spirit as "the spirit of our Lord and of his resurrection,"

Jesus' human existence precisely by eliciting Mary's willing acceptance of her own unique place in the history of salvation.

33. Bobrinskoy comments: "This verse constitutes the hidden key of the whole mystery of the communion of the Father and the Son. The Son prays to, names, and reveals the Father 'in the Spirit.' At the same time the Father is well pleased with his incarnate Son, and 'the Holy Spirit, under the form of a dove, confirms the Word of the Father' (Troparion of the Theophany of the Lord)" (*Le Mystère de la Trinité*, p. 86). Or as Pannenberg puts the point: "The Gospels trace back Jesus' bond with the God whom he proclaims to the presence and action of the Spirit of God in him" (*Systematische Theologie*, vol. I, p. 290; ET, p. 266).

and so only in relation to the Father and the Son. Thereby they suggest the need, once again, to locate actions or features unique to this divine person by which the assembly can distinguish him from the others, in this case from the Father and the Son.

The various actions of the Spirit for which the congregation prays seem rooted in a particular feature which it confidently expects that he will possess, namely the very sending which it asks of the Father. Given the logic of sending and being sent, calling upon the Spirit as sendable by the Father to undertake certain actions seems adequate to distinguish the Spirit from the Father. This works whether the Spirit's action be understood as directed toward the congregation alone, or also toward the gifts of bread and wine (a point which remains disputed among Christian communities). Of course the Son is also sent by the Father. Being sent from the Father therefore does not by itself distinguish the Spirit from the Son, and so fails to enable us to identify him.

The quick way to deal with this problem is to characterize the Spirit as sent by the Son as well as by the Father; the logic of sending and being sent would thereby distinguish the Spirit from the Son as well as from the Father. Eucharistic prayers sometimes do this (following the New Testament), but more usually they do not. The actions for which the Spirit is eucharistically invoked do normally include, however, those by which the Spirit brings about a relationship of the assembly to the Son. We call upon the Spirit to unite us to Christ by way of Christ's presence in the elements of the communal meal, and thereby to unite us to one another. In this way the eucharistic mission of the Spirit presupposes the sending of the Son into our flesh and the availability of the Son's flesh for the communal meal. More than that, the eucharistic epiclesis hopes for an action of the Spirit which the Son does not himself undertake. The Son, it seems, receives the eucharistic assembly's unity with him as a gift from the Spirit, and might even, indeed, be understood to receive his own unity with the eucharistic elements as a gift from the Spirit. If the action of uniting the assembly or the elements with the Son is the result of a mission from the Father, it must therefore be a different mission from any which belongs to the Son, and so has to characterize a different agent. The Spirit can, it seems, be picked out as the one to whom this mission uniquely belongs. In this way we may distinguish the Spirit liturgically from the Son and ourselves as well as from the Father.

Thus the church's worship, its "narrative about Christ" in liturgy and canonical text, exhibits the features by which it picks Jesus out, and to that extent his personal uniqueness, as inextricable from, though irreducible to, those features by which it picks out the Father and the Spirit. As it turns out, in other words, by invoking Jesus the church invokes the Trinity. More precisely: if, as we have already suggested, calling upon Jesus is essential and central for this community, then so is the identification of this person upon whom the community calls. Jesus cannot be identified in the church's canonical narrative except in relation to and distinction from the Father and the Spirit; therefore the identification of the Father and the Spirit is equally essential and central for this community.[34] *What* the church identifies when it calls upon the Father, Jesus, and the Spirit is of course God, so we can sum up these reflections on the church's central beliefs like this: the church's liturgical practice exhibits the body of beliefs which identify the triune God as most central for it.

Of course, there is much more to it than this. The God identified in the church's invocation – the triune God – the church holds to be the creator, redeemer, and perfecter (or consummator) of the world, and in particular of human life and history. To put the point at the highest level of generality, the church holds the triune God and the actions of that God to be of ultimate and universal significance, and has an open-ended variety of ways to characterize this significance. The church also believes that the creative, redemptive, and perfecting actions of the triune God elicit certain ways of life in the world, and exclude others. These judgments of significance (for example, that God was in Christ "reconciling the world to himself") and prescriptions for action (for example, "you shall love your neighbor as yourself") naturally occupy an essential place in the church's body of belief. But the church believes not simply in creation, redemption, and consummation. The church believes that the triune God – the Father, the Son, and the Holy Spirit – creates, redeems, and perfects the world; these actions and their significance may be attributed to the triune God and to no one else. Consequently the church's beliefs about what is ultimately significant and morally right presuppose the beliefs which constitute its trinitarian identification of God; we must have identified the subject of these judgments of significance in order to be able to make the judgments (or make them rightly) in the first place.

34. To say that the church's existence as a coherent community depends upon its identification of the Father, the Son, and the Holy Spirit is not to deny that this identification is itself the work of the Trinity. As the petitions for the presence of Christ and the Spirit indicate, the community understands its liturgy as a whole to depend utterly upon the action of the Father at whom the assembly's worship aims, through the Son whom he has given and the Spirit whom he bestows. The gospel and the sacraments are thus the means by which the Father, the Son, and the Holy Spirit identify *themselves* in and for the world, and invite the world to share in their life, which is the very life of the one God.

Thus among the beliefs which are most central for the Christian community the trinitarian identification of God has a certain priority over all the rest, since the others depend on that identification.

Communal centrality and epistemic primacy

We are trying to understand how epistemic justification works for those who hold Christian beliefs. Given our proposal about what the most central Christian beliefs actually are, the question now has a more definite shape: how does the Christian community decide that its trinitarian identification of God is true? By what epistemic right does the church believe in the Trinity? We can get a handle on the question by reflecting a bit more on the kindred notions of "essential" and "central" beliefs.

Essential beliefs are those which are necessary to a community's identity, those upon which its survival depends. If most of the members of a community cease to hold its essential beliefs, then the community will cease to exist; all of those persons who were its members may live on, but they will no longer constitute a community, or at least not the same community they did before. Decisions about which beliefs are "essential" to the identity of a given community are not merely arbitrary, nor do we have to make them simply by taking the word of this or that member of the community. Ongoing communal practice displays essential beliefs. The empirical criterion for communally essential beliefs is, we could say, persistent adherence, especially adherence in the face of adversity. A community's most essential beliefs will be those which it is least willing to give up, and least willing to modify or reinterpret. Essential beliefs are highlighted by the community's insistence on maintaining them, even at considerable cost (such as loss of membership, or persecution), when there are plausible and attractive alternatives available which would require dropping or modifying the beliefs in question.

Understood in this way, a community's essential beliefs will naturally be co-extensive with its central beliefs. In a particular system of belief or worldview, "central" beliefs are those which are the least dispensable among the convictions which belong to that system or outlook, and so can be regarded as the most characteristic among that particular collection of beliefs. Calling a belief "central" thus relates it primarily to other beliefs, rather than to a community of believers. But the beliefs which a community is least willing to give up, those which are most deeply constitutive of its identity, will *eo ipso* be those which are most characteristic of its worldview or outlook. The beliefs which are least dispensable when compared with the rest of the convictions the community actually has or might possibly have will be precisely those which the community, by the practices which display its persistent adherence, is least willing to let go of or modify. They are thus the convictions which are most central to the community's overall collection of beliefs.

Now the concept of belief depends on the concept of truth, in that to have a belief just is to be disposed to hold a sentence true which expresses the contents of that belief. Beliefs, therefore, are truth claims. Thus our empirical criterion for which beliefs are most central to a community's identity tells us something important about how that community decides which beliefs are true. According to this empirical criterion, a community regards belief A as central with respect to belief B if and only if, should conflict arise between A and B, the community persists in holding A true, and rejects or modifies B. But this is simply to say that the community regards A as a criterion for deciding about the truth of B. Faced with the incompatibility of the two beliefs – that is, the inconsistency which belongs to logical contradictions – it holds A true, and finds that it must therefore hold B false. The community, we can say, regards A as *epistemically primary* with respect to B. The larger the range of beliefs across which this relationship applies, the more central A is within the community's belief system, and, correlatively, the broader the scope of A's epistemic primacy. At limit, as we shall see, that primacy might be unrestricted; it might apply across the full range of possible beliefs.[35]

---

35. Unlike the relationship of incompatibility or inconsistency, it will be noted, the relationship of epistemic primacy is not reversible. The community holds B false because it holds A true; it does not hold A true because it holds B false. If beliefs A and B are incompatible, holding A true requires holding B false, but holding B false does not require holding A true; the two beliefs might be contraries rather than contradictories. That is: $[-(A \cdot B); A, \therefore -B]$ is valid (A, $\therefore -B$ is the logical "because" of two sentences back); $[-(A \cdot B); -B, \therefore A)]$ is invalid.

This discussion, it should also be noted, assumes that the community recognizes the incompatibility of A and B, and that it is committed to avoid holding incompatible beliefs. In a complex belief system like Christianity it is easy to miss contraries and contradictories, and the church at any given time no doubt holds some beliefs the incompatibility of which has so far gone unrecognized, or is the subject of ongoing communal debate. On the commitment to hold a consistent set of beliefs, by contrast, seems to depend the very possibility of having a communal identity, and so of being publicly recognizable as a community. Suppose a community holds true a certain . statement, P, and so regards the belief that P as belonging to its belief system. But the community also wants to hold true −P (or wants to suppose that holding P true does not require holding −P false). Holding true P admits to the community's belief system all statements consistent with P; holding true −P admits all statements consistent with −P. All possible statements are consistent with either P or −P, so the community's belief system admits all possible beliefs. Having a communal identity seems to depend on holding in common some beliefs and not others, so the communal admission of contradictory beliefs would seem to exclude having a communal identity at all (and, as a condition for communal identity, having a belief system at all).

This may sound arcane, but we are entirely familiar with the relationship of epistemic primacy, and make judgments all the time which display our conviction that one belief is epistemically primary with respect to another. Suppose, for example, that I believe (A) that Bill Clinton is a good president, and (B) that good presidents don't raise taxes. Since these two beliefs are in conflict (they cannot both be true, since Clinton has raised taxes), I will have to make a decision about which one is true, and drop or revise the other. If I want to go on thinking that Clinton is a good president, I will have to change my beliefs about the revenue policies of good presidents (thus taking A as epistemically primary with respect to B), and if I want to go on thinking that good presidents don't raise taxes, then I will have to change my beliefs about Clinton's capacities as a chief executive (thus taking B as epistemically primary with respect to A).

We can call the opposite relationship *epistemic subordination*. If belief A is epistemically primary with respect to belief B, then B is epistemically subordinate with respect to A, in that should conflict (inconsistency) arise between the two beliefs, B will be rejected or modified, and A will be held true. To regard one belief as epistemically subordinate with respect to another is not at all to regard the subordinate belief as unimportant or peripheral with respect to the other, but to stipulate a logical relationship between the two: B must fail to conflict with A in order for me to hold B true. The relationship of epistemic subordination implies a kind of *epistemic dependence*. Where belief B is held to be subordinate to belief A, holding B true depends upon its being consistent with A. The converse of course does not obtain; holding A true does not depend upon its consistency with B.

In the case of the Christian community, I have suggested, our empirical criterion for centrality of belief points to the church's trinitarian identification of God. It seems that no practice is more primitively embedded and persistently maintained in the Christian community than that of calling upon Jesus, or, we could equally well say, of calling upon the Father through and with Jesus in the Spirit. Therefore the beliefs upon which this practice chiefly depends are the ones which are most central for this community: those which identify the crucified Israelite Jesus as raised by the Father, in the Spirit whom Jesus and the Father have poured out on all flesh; by constituting the narrative of these actions the same body of beliefs identifies the Father and the Spirit as well.

If this way of locating the church's central body of beliefs is correct, then these beliefs will be epistemically primary for the church. That is, the church will decide about the truth of other beliefs by seeing how well they fit, or cohere, with the beliefs which constitute its identification of the triune God; beliefs which conflict with the church's identification of God will have to be dropped or modified. So we have a preliminary answer to the question of how the church decides that its most central beliefs, namely its trinitarian identification of God, are true. The church determines that its trinitarian identification of God is true by taking that body of beliefs as the standard by coherence with which the truth of other beliefs is to be decided; in so doing the church obviously takes the beliefs by which it identifies God to be true, since beliefs which are standards of truth must themselves be regarded as true. The precise range of beliefs over which the epistemic primacy of the narratives which identify the Trinity extends is an important and more complex question, to which we will attend in chapter 5. That any belief might touch on essential matters indicates that the range might be unrestricted, but whether this is actually the case awaits a closer examination of the central beliefs themselves.[36]

The epistemic primacy of the church's central beliefs also gives us the concept of "Christian belief" which we sought at the outset. If the trinitarian identification of God is epistemically primary in the Christian community, then the chief rule for picking out "Christian beliefs" is that they be at least compatible with the nest of convictions which make up this identification. As a way of saying what can count as Christian belief this rule has the advantage of empirical cash value; it avoids both circularity and stipulation. There is, as we shall see, a good deal more to it. No doubt many matters of concern to the community will not be decidable by recourse to that set of beliefs alone, and compatibility alone will not be enough to distinguish beliefs which actually make a contribution to the church's identity from those which do not. But we can take the first and most basic step towards individuating a Christian view of the world by adverting to the epistemic status of the narratives which identify Jesus, and with him the Trinity.

36. This argument does not, it should be noted, involve the claim that the convictions which make up its trinitarian identification of God are the only essential (and therefore central) beliefs of the community, but simply that they clearly belong among those which are essential; no doubt others are as well. But if the trinitarian identification of God is in fact essential, then any further essential beliefs (e.g., what I have called "judgments of significance" about the actions of the Trinity) will have to be consistent with it, since essential beliefs are just those the contradictories of which the community has to reject.

It is arresting to observe, therefore, that modern theology has usually followed the opposite epistemic procedure. Since around the end of the seventeenth century, it has seemed obvious to theologians of otherwise quite different outlook that the Christian community must decide about the truth of its own most central convictions by seeing how well these comport with other beliefs – in particular, though not exclusively, with those currently dominant in one or another stretch of high culture. Now given an empirically plausible way of locating Christian beliefs, this seems incoherent. If a community holds true the identification of God as Father, Son, and Holy Spirit only insofar as that identification fails to conflict with some other beliefs, then those other beliefs, not the trinitarian identification, will be the ones this community is least willing to give up. Therefore that community will not, supposing our location of the most centrally Christian beliefs is correct, be the Christian community. On the contrary: instead of seeing how well they fit with other beliefs, the Christian community will have to decide that its own most central beliefs are true by recognizing that their centrality presumes their epistemic primacy; it presumes of them the distinctive status of those beliefs with which others must fit in order to be true.

Surely, though, this will not do. The question we want to answer is, "How do we decide which of our beliefs are true?" And the Christian community's answer, according to the argument I have just proposed, is, "In the final analysis, by seeing whether they agree with our own most central convictions." But the same argument works equally well for any other community, at least any community with a worldview of reasonably broad scope. On pain of forfeiting its identity and dissolving the ties which bind it together, *any* such community must, according to this argument, regard its own most central beliefs as true, and revise or reject other beliefs which conflict with those central convictions. This goes for other existing communities whose central beliefs conflict with those of the church, and for communities which are now defunct just because nobody any longer thinks their beliefs are true, like the community of Ptolemaic astronomers, who numbered among their central convictions the belief that the sun and planets revolved around the earth. The argument so far may indicate why the Christian community naturally regards its own most central beliefs as true and epistemically primary, but it does little to explain what *right* the community has to do so.

Considerations like these have fueled the conviction of many modern theologians that they must look elsewhere than the church's own most central beliefs for the conferral of epistemic right. Before pursuing any further the thought that the church's trinitarian identification of God itself enjoys epistemic primacy, it will be quite useful to look at some of the chief modern strategies for the justification of Christian belief.

3

Epistemic justification in modern theology

50   Though extended explicit discussions of the topic are uncommon in modern Christian theology, we can identify five assumptions or implicit theses about epistemic justification and truth which have proven deeply persistent since the late seventeenth century. This chapter will concentrate on three theses about justification:

(1) An *interiority* thesis, according to which Christian beliefs are justified to the extent that they adequately express certain inner experiences.

(2) A *foundationalist* thesis, according to which justified beliefs (including Christian ones) must either be tied in virtue of their meaning to self-evident or incorrigible data, or logically grounded in beliefs which are.

(3) An *epistemic dependence* thesis, according to which the primary criteria for deciding about the truth of Christian beliefs, at least in part and perhaps as a whole, must not themselves be distinctively Christian.

While none of these three epistemic claims logically requires either of the others, they have tended to go together in modern theology (especially the first two). Two further theses, one having to do with justification, the other with truth, will come up for discussion in later chapters.

(4) A *pragmatic* thesis, according to which Christian beliefs are justified by the communal and individual practices bound up with holding them true (chapter 7).

(5) A *correspondence* thesis, according to which the truth of beliefs, including Christian ones, consists in their agreement or correspondence with reality (chapters 8–9).

As the examples which follow will suggest, part of the staying power of the assumptions about justification with which this chapter will be concerned has lain in their susceptibility to ongoing reformulation and improvement. This has enabled them to attract people of otherwise different conviction, drawn by the promise that these theses could, if properly worked out, secure the epistemic right to have Christian beliefs. But compelling as interiority, foundationalism, and epistemic dependence have each seemed, all three are beset by difficulties so serious that Christian theology can best try to account for its epistemic rights by giving them up, and pursuing an alternative course.

Three theses on justification: a case study

Friedrich Schleiermacher's theology and philosophy evince a strong commitment – and one formative of much subsequent theological reflection – to all three of the characteristically modern theses about justification with which we are concerned here. He thus makes an especially illuminating case study, against which we will be able to contrast alternative versions of each thesis. With Schleiermacher, as with the other test cases, our present interest is limited to matters of epistemic principle (we will have to set aside, for example, the important differences in content between his basic list of central Christian beliefs and the one suggested in the previous chapter).

Interiority

For Schleiermacher Christian beliefs, or what he calls "propositions of Christian faith" (*christliche Glaubenssätze*) are "apprehensions of Christian religious states of feeling set forth in speech" (§ 15, *Leitsatz*).[1] These distinctive states of feeling or religious affections (*Gemütszustände*) are not universal, but quite specific to Christians. They do include a universal aspect, namely "God-consciousness" or "the feeling of absolute dependence"; "God is given to us in feeling in a primordial (*ursprüngliche*) way" (§ 4,4). This religious feeling common to all humans is, however, never experienced by itself, but only in inextricable connection with the totality of our cognitive, volitional, and affective interaction with the world (see § 5). As a result there is not one religious emotion but a rich array of them; the distinctiveness of Christian religious emotions lies at once in the central feeling around which they are all ordered and shaped, namely the experience of redemption (conceived as a transition from the painful suppression of the God-consciousness in the totality of our active

---

1. Friedrich Schleiermacher, *Der christliche Glaube*, 2nd edn (ed. Martin Redeker, Berlin: de Gruyter, 1960). All references to this work will be by paragraph (§) and section number in the text ("*Leitsatz*" = the proposition at the head of the paragraph) (ET: *The Christian Faith*, trans. H. R. Mackintosh and J. S. Stewart [Philadelphia: Fortress, 1976]).

and receptive life to the pleasure of its domination; see § 62), and the "historical constant" (§ 10, *Leitsatz*) which is the sole and sufficient source or cause of that experience, namely the particular historical person Jesus of Nazareth (§ 11).

The constellation of Christian religious affections is related to explicit Christian beliefs as "inner" to "outer," and therefore, on Schleiermacher's view, as that which is truly basic and primitive in the human being to that which is, however indispensable, secondary and dependent. "The propositions are only derivative; it is the inner state of feeling which is original."[2] To be sure, the inner religious emotions share with the whole of our interior life an urge to express themselves and so to make themselves outwardly known. This movement from the inside out begins with overt physical gestures and culminates in explicit speech, which is alone the adequate outward expression (*Ausdruck*) of those inner affections (see § 15,1).

Schleiermacher does not try to locate precisely the point in this expressive process at which language emerges ("even inwardly, thought does not proceed without the use of language"; § 15,1). But the discourse of the Christian community, the "propositions of faith" distinctive to it, depend for their very existence upon the Christian religious emotions which they express. "Propositions of faith of all forms have their ultimate basis so exclusively in the stirrings of the religious self-consciousness that where the latter do not exist, the former cannot come into being" (§ 15,2). This in turn suggests that Christian discourse derives its meaning or sense, and therefore its communicative power, primarily from the Christian religious emotions which it expresses; one therefore grasps the meaning of the discourse chiefly by relating it to the inward source from which it springs.[3] Even dogmatic propositions, though they are the most

---

2. Friedrich Schleiermacher, "Zweites Sendschreiben an Dr. Lücke," *F. D. E. Schleiermacher Kritische Gesamtausgabe* (hereafter KG), division I, vol. X, ed. Hans-Joachim Birkner et al. (Berlin: de Gruyter, 1990), p. 343 (ET: *On the Glaubenslehre*, trans. James Duke and Francis Fiorenza [Chico: Scholars Press, 1981], p. 59). This goes for all verbal (indeed, all outward) products of the Christian religious consciousness, including the technical formulations of Christian theology; in relation to "the state of piety (*der Zustand der Frömmigkeit*)," the propositions of both dogmatics and ethics "are not original, rather they are secondary (*nicht ein ursprüngliches, sondern ein zweites*)" (Friedrich Schleiermacher, *Die christliche Sitte nach den Grundsätzen der evangelischen Kirche im Zusammenhange dargestellt*, ed. Ludwig Jonas, *Friedrich Schleiermacher's sämmtliche Werke*, division I, vol. XII [Berlin: G. Reimer, 1843], p. 20).

3. As his lectures on hermeneutics show, Schleiermacher's conception of meaning and interpretation is more complex than this (see *Hermeneutics: The Handwritten Manuscripts*, trans. James Duke and Jack Forstman [Missoula: Scholars Press, 1977]). For Schleiermacher understanding involves grasping the various linguistic relations of a given discourse as

technical and remote from the inward Christian affections, can be formed and adequately interpreted only by a direct apprehension of and comparison with the interior religious consciousness itself (see § 17,2).[4]

It is precisely by repairing to their own inner states that Christians *decide* which sentences are true (at least among those purporting to express or describe the content of the states). The believer's recourse to her own religious affections is apparently direct: she discerns which sentences she is justified in holding true by immediate access to her own inner *Gemützustände*, which enables her to compare their content with that of the language in question and thereby decide whether this language constitutes an adequate expression of those inner states. If a sentence does this, it is true. Access to their own interior condition provides Christians with a criterion sufficient for deciding about the truth of putative *Glaubenssätze*; Christian faith is "a holding-true which rests on feeling."[5] For Schleiermacher, as for interiorists generally, this holds good whatever the manifest subject matter of the propositions in question. They need not actually be about religious feelings, but can equally well be about the attributes of God, Christ's redemptive work, and so forth (see § 30). Inner states of feeling justify beliefs in a strong sense: the truth of propositions which adequately express Christian religious affections is guaranteed. "Everyone who shares the faith verifies (*bewährt*) [propositions belonging to Christian faith] at once by the certainty of his or her own immediate religious self-consciousness."[6]

It will be seen that on an account like Schleiermacher's, theological decisions about which sentences are true depend on decisions about which ones are genuinely Christian, in such a way that to establish the properly Christian character of a sentence is *eo ipso* to establish its truth.

well as apprehending the inner experiences from which it arises. In theology, however, this latter "technical" and "divinatory" aspect takes on special prominence and decisiveness. See Bruce D. Marshall, "Hermeneutics and Dogmatics in Schleiermacher's Theology," *The Journal of Religion* 67/1 (1987), pp. 14–32.

4. To be sure Schleiermacher, like most interiorists after him, also wants to insist that the inward religious consciousness of Christians must be "awakened" (§ 6,2) and "mediated" by language. For him this is not only a matter of hermeneutical principle, but of Christian dogmatic necessity: "The entire effectiveness of the redeemer himself was conditioned by the communicability of his self-consciousness by means of speech" (§ 15,2). On the extent to which this coheres with his apparent conviction that generating and recognizing "propositions of faith" depends on already having the inward Christian religious consciousness, see the discussion below, p. 77.

5. As Schleiermacher observes in a handwritten marginal note to his own copy of *The Christian Faith*, endorsing August Twesten's notion of faith. See Redeker, ed., *Der christliche Glaube*, vol. I, p. 94, note c.

6. Friedrich Schleiermacher, *Kurze Darstellung des theologischen Studiums*, ed. Heinrich Scholz (Leipzig, 1910), § 209.

To dogmatic theology falls the task of individuating the body of properly Christian belief, of identifying from among the welter of sentences held true in a given social and historical location those which "can only be derived from the domain of inner [Christian] experience" (§ 30,2), and so are at once genuine *Glaubenssätze* and true propositions. That a proposition fails to be a *Glaubenssatz* does not, of course, imply its falsity. Its truth may be ascertained in other ways, as Schleiermacher realizes (see the discussion below of epistemic dependence).

Schleiermacher's theology thus nicely embodies one characteristically modern epistemic claim, which we have called the interiority thesis: Christian beliefs may be justified by appeal to inner experiences, upon which depend the contents of the beliefs and the meaning of the sentences which express them. Direct access to these experiences is available at least for Christians, and in virtually all modern versions of the thesis, Christian experience includes (although it is not reducible to) aspects or structures which are common to all people, and introspectively available to everyone. In a word: "self-consciousness is the place of truth" (§ 34,1).

Foundationalism

In much modern theology this first thesis is closely intertwined with a second, foundationalist thesis. By "foundationalism" I mean a set of three claims tightly connected by adherents of the thesis:

(F 1) that with regard to at least some of the sentences we hold true, we have direct or immediate access to states of affairs, events, or experiences in virtue of which those sentences are true;

(F 2) that this direct access guarantees the truth of these sentences, and so justifies us in, or serves as the ultimate evidence for, holding them true;

(F 3) that the rest of our beliefs must be justified by establishing some suitable kind of warranting link with those which are directly tied to the world (and thereby serve as the justificatory "foundation" for the rest).

In this century most philosophical foundationalisms have been vigorously empiricist in character (with the exception of a few doughty Cartesians, like Husserl); the search has been for sensory data, experiences, or events which could serve as the ground for legitimate truth claims. In modern theology, by contrast, the foundationalist thesis has almost always complemented the interiority thesis.

On the one hand interiority appears tailor-made for foundationalist epistemological ends: foundationalism depends on immediate access to states of affairs which justify us in holding some sentences true, and the interiority thesis promises just that. We all have direct access to our own inner religious experiences, and these include for all human beings an experience of God as the "whence" of our feeling of absolute dependence, and for Christians an experience of the redemptive release of that consciousness by Christ. Thus Christians are justified in holding true sentences about God, Christ, and so forth, so long as they express the content of these emotions. On the other hand, though, our feelings sometimes deceive us. Why then take our religious affections as securing the right to hold true the beliefs which express them – still less as *guaranteeing* the truth of those beliefs?

Here Schleiermacher extends the interiority thesis into a foundationalist account of the justification of Christian belief. The inner religious experiences of Christians are not only directly accessible, they are incorrigible. Christians are certain of them: not merely certain that they have them, but certain of the content they deliver.[7] To feel oneself absolutely dependent involves being certain of one's absolute dependence, and to be certain of one's dependence involves being certain that this dependence has an adequate cause outside oneself, namely God, who is ineluctably co-present in the experience itself; the same applies to certainty of the experience of redemption and to Christ as its cause (see § 14,1).[8]

Seen in this foundationalist light, Christian beliefs as a whole "rest on a given" (§ 13, *Zusatz*), namely inward Christian experience. The Christian religious affections are "givens," Schleiermacher seems to suppose, in that they authenticate themselves; to have Christian faith is to have experiences which are at once incorrigible and veridical (that is, reliable bearers of truth). Such experiences may therefore not be regarded as derived from or dependent upon a source about which we would have to know in order to be sure of their reliability, and so be sure that what they lead us to believe is true. The experiences of absolute dependence and redemption of course point to sources outside the subject, but these are not experiences which require for their certainty and reliability, or even for their existence, that we have independent knowledge of their sources. Rather we apprehend God as absolute, creative causality and Jesus as redeemer precisely through our experiences of

---

7. Thus faith is "the certainty accompanying a state of the higher self-consciousness, which is therefore different from, but definitely not less than, the certainty which accompanies the objective consciousness" (in natural science, for example) (§ 14,1).
8. For just this reason Schleiermacher is not concerned that anything will be lost by interpreting all Christian beliefs as "descriptions of human states" (§ 30).

dependence and redemption.[9] The Christian religious consciousness and its sources are "given" in a unique inward way necessarily different from that of an empirical object (cf. § 4,3). This precludes any action upon or alteration of either the consciousness or its sources by us, which would interfere with their epistemic reliability.

This suggests, moreover, that these experiences are "given" in that having them does not depend on having any beliefs about them, or on having any particular beliefs at all. Rather, as the interiority thesis already suggests, having beliefs which express these experiences depends upon having the experiences; the outward linguistic formulation of the experiences is revisable and correctable, but not the experiences themselves. Thus it is not possible to inquire behind the Christian religious consciousness or to call its content (as distinguished from the explicit formulation of that content) into question. Christian faith is at bottom "a purely factual [rather than theoretical] certainty, but that of a completely interior fact" (§ 14,1). Christian beliefs neither have nor need any foundation besides the "factual certainty" of the Christian religious affections themselves. "For the Christian doctrine of faith the presentation (*Darstellung*) is at the same time the foundation (*Begründung*), since everything in it can only be grounded by being shown to be the correct expression of the Christian self-consciousness. For the person who cannot find this in his own self-consciousness, no foundation is possible."[10]

Epistemic dependence

Schleiermacher's interiorist and foundationalist account of justification leaves open two allied questions of great importance: what difference do

---

9. With regard to the general God-consciousness, it must strictly be denied that "this feeling of dependence is conditioned by any previous knowledge of God" (§ 4,4). With regard to the Christian experience of redemption the matter is, as Schleiermacher well knows, more complicated, since the presumed source of that experience is a particular historical person who, it seems plausible to suppose, can only be located as the source of inwardly experienced redemption by appeal to some "previous," or at least independently available, knowledge. Nonetheless, everything which needs to be said about Christ in Christian dogmatics is made up of "immediate expressions of our Christian self-consciousness," in which "it is explained how, on the basis of this consciousness, the redeemer is posited" (*wie vermöge dieses Bewußtseins der Erlöser gesetzt ist*) (§ 91,2). No appeal to independent historical knowledge of Jesus, Schleiermacher here supposes, is necessary.
10. "Zweites Sendschreiben," *KG* I/10, p. 373 (ET, p. 78). This means that there can be no proof of Christian beliefs on Schleiermacher's view. For the believer no such proof is needed, since she already apprehends the inward fact upon which all of her explicit beliefs are adequately based. For the non-believer no such proof is possible, since no amount of argument from "generally recognized and communicable propositions" (§ 13, *Zusatz*) could engender that "given" in inner experience from which alone Christian beliefs genuinely originate, and which guarantees their truth.

the rest of our beliefs make for whether or not we hold Christian claims true, and conversely, what difference does holding Christian beliefs make for decisions regarding the rest of the claims we are going to hold true? Schleiermacher is well aware of these twin questions, and he deals with them mainly by charting the relationship between Christianity, especially Christian theology, and *Wissenschaft* – the burgeoning results and philosophically articulated methods of the modern sciences of nature and history, freed by the Enlightenment to pursue their inquiries wherever they lead without external compulsion or restraint. For Schleiermacher this relationship always has two sides.

1. There must be no identification or confusion of Christian beliefs with other types of belief. Since beliefs and types of belief are picked out or identified for Schleiermacher by reference to their sources, the imperative to avoid confusion means that Christian theology must always clearly distinguish those beliefs whose primary origin is the inward Christian self-consciousness from those whose origin is our interaction with the world of objects, events, and persons – from those which stem from what Schleiermacher calls "the objective consciousness" (see § 18,3). In particular, dogmatics must guard against illicit entry into the realm of Christian belief by propositions which look like *Glaubenssätze*, but are in fact "speculative," that is, which properly belong in the realm of metaphysics or transcendental philosophy.[11] Dogmatics on the one hand, and natural science, history, and "speculation" on the other, each have their own "territory" (*Gebiet*); the latter are all "produced on the soil of *Wissenschaft*, and thus belong to the objective consciousness and its fundamental conditions, independently of the inner [Christian] experience and the facts of the higher self-consciousness" (§ 30,2).

Correlatively, each has its own distinctive procedures for establishing the truth of beliefs. A proposition which someone "wanted to ground objectively [that is, 'scientifically'], without going back to the higher self-consciousness, would no longer be a *Glaubenssatz* and would not at all belong on our territory" (§ 17,2; cf. § 33, *Zusatz*). The imperative to limit diverse epistemic procedures to the appropriate "territory" implies, as Schleiermacher is well aware (see § 13, *Zusatz*; 28,2), that Christian beliefs cannot claim the same sort of epistemic rights as natural and historical science, and even "speculation," in particular the right to expect universal

---

11. "A proposition which originated from the speculative activity [viz., "the purely *wissenschaftlich* striving which has the intuition of being as its task"], no matter how closely related in content to our own, would no longer be a dogmatic one" (§ 16, *Zusatz*).

assent based on generally recognized rational principles and empirical judgments. It excludes, moreover, any synthesis of Christian belief and *wissenschaftlich* results; there can be no attempt to combine the two "into *one* whole" (§ 16, *Zusatz*). This is not to say, of course, that the truth of Christian beliefs is in question, only that it is grasped and guaranteed in a different way.

2. There must be no conflict or competition between Christian beliefs and the methods and results of modern *Wissenschaft*. Although it follows its own epistemic procedures, dogmatics must always strive to formulate Christian beliefs in a way which is consistent with the results of natural and historical science. It must seek to show that "every teaching which really represents an element of our Christian consciousness can be conceived in such a way that it leaves us free from entanglement with *Wissenschaft*," that is, free from making claims about territory which is not our own, and so risking conflict with the highest intellectual achievements of our culture.[12] Otherwise, Schleiermacher warns in a famous rhetorical flourish, "the knot of history" may come undone, and "Christianity be allied with barbarism, science with unbelief."[13]

Consistency with the results of natural science requires revision in beliefs long held to be of the essence of Christianity, particularly those surrounding the doctrine of creation and of God as creator and preserver.[14] Likewise, dogmatics always aims for consistency with critical historical investigation, with similarly revisionary consequences.[15] The crucial test case is the doctrine, upon which for Schleiermacher the whole Christian enterprise turns, that Jesus is the unique historical redeemer. Upholding this belief requires showing how it can be coherent to say that Jesus is the unique and irreplaceable ideal or archetype of human religious perfection (concretely, that he constantly has an absolutely unimpeded God-consciousness), and at the same time is a genuinely historical (and so genuinely human) person, fully subject to the ordinary laws of human historical development and as such accessible to critical historical research in the same way as any other human being (cf. § 93).

Schleiermacher deploys all of his considerable ingenuity to show that

---

12. "Zweites Sendschreiben," *KG* I/10, p. 351 (ET, p. 64).

13. "Zweites Sendschreiben," *KG* I/10, p. 347 (ET, p. 61).

14. See § 39,2 and "Zweites Sendschreiben," *KG* I/10, pp. 346–7, 356, for general statements of the point (ET, pp. 60–2, 67). Whether the world has a temporal beginning is among the traditional claims which must be left to science (see §§ 41,2; 52,1).

15. "We must be scrupulous that we bring nothing in [to dogmatics] which conflicts with generally recognized results of historical research" ("Zweites Sendschreiben," *KG* I/10, p. 355; ET, p. 67).

this strikingly revised version of the traditional doctrine of incarnation can coherently satisfy both faith's commitment to Jesus' unique redemptive significance and the commitment of historical *Wissenschaft* to free critical investigation regulated by its own laws (unsuccessfully, so Ferdinand Christian Baur and David Friedrich Strauss in their own day, and others since, have argued – but we can leave that aside for present purposes). At the same time he regards the traditional doctrine itself – that the whole life of Jesus is the life of the eternal Logos of God in the full reality of our flesh – as incapable of meeting the demands of historical science, and at the same time (though not *because* of its scientific implausibility) incapable of being regarded as a proper expression of the Christian religious consciousness (see §§ 95–8).

Schleiermacher thus proposes a relationship of non-competing autonomy between Christian belief and the rest of what modern *wissenschaftlich* people (whether Christians or not) have good reason to believe. What he says about "speculative knowledge of God" applies to the relationship between Christian belief and *Wissenschaft* generally: "For me these two always remain outside one another, because, so I am convinced, although they must agree with one another, they do not belong together, and are not determined by one another."[16]

This way of thinking about Christian faith and modern *Wissenschaft* exhibits a thesis. Christian beliefs are epistemically dependent on the results of natural and historical science, in the sense outlined at the end of the last chapter: we have the right to hold Christian beliefs only if they are consistent with certain beliefs not distinctively Christian, in this case the recognized results of modern science. Christian beliefs are therefore also epistemically subordinate to established *wissenschaftlich* outcomes. Should conflict arise between the two, it is the Christian beliefs which will have to be dropped or revised. Or more precisely: if a given belief conflicts with scientifically justified claims, and so must be rejected, it cannot be recognized as a genuine expression of Christian piety.

This may seem like an odd way to put the epistemic point Schleiermacher wants to make. He insists on the autonomy – the *independence* – of both Christian faith and modern science, and apparently holds that their agreement with one another must be mutual. Christian

---

16. "Erstes Sendschreiben an Lücke," *KG* I/10, p. 333 (ET, p. 52). Similarly, theology must seek "to establish an eternal covenant between living Christian faith and scientific research – which works for itself, independently, and is emancipated on all sides – such that faith does not hinder science, and science does not exclude faith" ("Zweites Sendschreiben," *KG* I/10, p. 351; ET, p. 64).

faith and theology, however, are never in a position to impose this agreement on natural and historical science. Theology must accept the "generally recognized results" of *Wissenschaft* as they come, and cannot attempt to bring science into line with those beliefs which meet the distinctively Christian criteria of truth. Rather, it must always attempt to show that beliefs which meet this standard can be articulated in such a way that they are compatible with scientifically justified beliefs. The *epistemic* relation between faith and *Wissenschaft* is thus not mutual, but one in which holding Christian beliefs true depends on finding them consistent with certain other claims.[17]

The concept of different "territories" or regions of belief is Schleiermacher's device for securing the autonomy of both faith and science while minimizing (though not eliminating) the epistemic dependence of Christian belief. Given a distinction between different types of belief, different epistemic procedures appropriate to the various territories can be assigned to each, and each procedure confined to its own territory. Whether a belief belongs on Christian territory depends, however, not on its epistemic role but on its contents, and thereby on the meanings of the sentences which state its contents. In order to distinguish between different regions of belief, therefore, we need to be able to fix the meanings of particular sentences. This allows us to grasp the contents of a speaker's beliefs and so to discern whether or not those beliefs belong on Christian territory (in Schleiermacher's version of the thesis, by locating their point of origin within the subject – the "religious consciousness" or the "objective consciousness").

On this view it seems that the meaning of sentences must be determined, and regions of belief thereby distinguished, independently of decisions about the truth of sentences and beliefs. The investment of dependence theorists in this important assumption about meaning is not hard to understand. Advocates of the thesis want to display the credibility of Christianity to a modern culture grown skeptical of its truth. While this requires that Christian beliefs be at minimum consistent with the established claims of modern thought, it cannot be up to science, or any other cultural accomplishment, to tell Christians what beliefs they are committed to holding. Although Christian beliefs about history or the human subject have to meet the same standards of truth

---

17. No epistemically informative relationship *could* be mutual (as Schleiermacher realizes), since simply observing that two sets of beliefs are supposed to be consistent with one another gives us no clue about what to do should conflict arise between them.

as those of, say, Marxists or Freudians, Christians rightly resist, so dependence theorists invariably maintain, any reductive explanation of what their beliefs mean, or are "really about" – such as those regularly offered by Marxists and Freudians. Sharing criteria of truth for Christian belief with Marxists or Freudians must not, in other words, require that one share a Marxist or Freudian interpretation of those beliefs.

The dependence project seems to stand or fall with the assumption that the process of deciding about the meaning of the sentences Christians hold true must employ different standards, and proceed in a different way, from the process of deciding about whether those sentences are true. Theologians committed to the project have thus sought various ways of identifying the beliefs which are central to Christianity without relying on the wider set of claims, at least in part not distinctively Christian, by which they have sought to secure the epistemic right to maintain central Christian convictions. Figuring out what genuinely Christian claims mean yields a list of beliefs "internal" to Christianity (as it is often put), by contrast with which the rest of what people believe is naturally "external." Establishing the epistemic right to hold Christian beliefs requires some kind of appeal to external standards, but this process presupposes that the meaning or content of the beliefs internal to Christianity has been fixed.[18]

Of course Schleiermacher, like many dependence theorists, thinks Christian beliefs also have internal criteria of truth. He thus proposes what could be called a *harmonist* version of the dependence thesis. Theology and modern *Wissenschaft* each enjoy a genuine autonomy of epistemic *procedure*; theology must not only refrain from making incursions into external territory, but must also resist attempts to impose external procedures (even *wissenschaftlich* ones) directly on its own territory. At the same time, Christian beliefs remain epistemically dependent on scientific *results*, even though they cannot at all be derived from any adequately justified external beliefs.

---

[18]. Dependence theorists are not, however, alone in supposing an epistemic need to distinguish between beliefs internal and external to Christianity, and correlatively in assuming that decisions about the meaning of sentences can float free of decisions about their truth. Theologians vigorously opposed to any epistemic dependence of Christian claims on "external" beliefs sometimes insist on both assumptions. Not least by some of his advocates Karl Barth is often read this way, though I think mistakenly. See Bruce D. Marshall, "Rhetoric and Realism in Barth," *Toronto Journal of Theology* 10/1 (1994), pp. 9–16, and my review of Richard H. Roberts, *A Theology on Its Way? Essays on Karl Barth*, *The Journal of Theological Studies* 44/1 (1993), pp. 453–8.

Variations

By combining the interiority, foundationalist, and dependence theses, Schleiermacher constructs a manifestly attractive position: if the theses can be sustained, he will have developed an account of the Christian claim to truth which honors the seeming requirements of both theology and modernity. He will have shown how Christians may regard their own most central beliefs as true – indeed be infallibly certain of their truth – without any prior appeal to external epistemic authority (whether that of scripture or church) of the sort the Enlightenment rules out. He will have shown that Christians may secure the truth of their beliefs in a way that modernity regularly suggests truth be found – by looking to the interior – while upholding the Christian conviction that our reality and our redemption are wholly dependent upon a source outside ourselves. He will have shown that accepting Christian beliefs is an intelligible possibility for everyone, since everyone is religious, without reducing the content of those beliefs to convictions held by (or even available to) all reasonable people, and without denying that actually to hold these beliefs requires participation in the practices of a particular historical community. Finally he will have shown that everything truly essential and central in Christianity may be accepted without rejecting anything which the wider culture of modernity gives people good reason to believe – and, conversely, that Christian beliefs spring from a distinctive and irreducible epistemic source which renders them unassailable (when properly formulated) from any other cultural quarter.

Modern Christian theologians have been widely convinced (whether or not they followed, or even read, Schleiermacher) that a successful presentation of the Christian claim to truth in their distinctive cultural situation must meet these demands, and have also generally supposed that one or more of the theses here outlined is an indispensable means to realizing this aim. They have not, to be sure, agreed on just how these theses should be developed. Here I can only indicate briefly, by attention to some more recent theologians, a few of the more striking possibilities for developing alternative versions of the three theses.

Interior foundations

While less than universal, interiorist and foundationalist strategies have been so common in Protestant theology since Schleiermacher that it has come to seem unnecessary to justify, or even to explain in detail, theological appeals to "experience." Most of the arguments on the Protestant side have not been about whether theology could or should appeal to experience in order to secure Christian claims to truth, but about what sorts of experiences – or more recently whose experiences – may be taken as epistemically authoritative. These debates are important, because decisions about which experiences are epistemically authoritative shape decisions about which beliefs or formulations may be regarded as justified. But they do not alter the basic structure of, or the linkage between, the interiorist and foundationalist theses.

By contrast the Roman Catholic theologian Karl Rahner offers a genuinely alternative version of the two theses: for him a robust appeal to interior epistemic foundations does not circumvent, but rather establishes, the claim that Christian beliefs are true because God says so, and indeed because God says so through the scripturally normed teaching authority which he has established in the church. Rahner's aim is to develop a theological epistemology which both honors the modern demand that beliefs about matters of ultimate significance have an adequate epistemic grounding in the inner depths of the human subject, and at the same time upholds the traditional Catholic teaching that saving faith is an assent to what the church teaches – one "more firm than any other [assent], on account of the authority of the revealing God himself."[19]

Human experience for Rahner always includes a certain depth dimension, a "wordless" (*satzlos*) interior aspect which constitutes our "original ... knowing (*wissendes*) possession of a reality," and so serves as the basis or foundation for explicit belief.[20] This interior contact of the self-present human subject with what it knows seems for Rahner to be self-authenticating and incorrigible, and as such founds whatever certainty may belong to ordinary empirical knowledge.[21] At its very heart this "transcendental" and "unthematic" dimension of experience includes

19. Karl Rahner, *Grundkurs des Glaubens* (Freiburg: Herder, 1976), p. 20; ET: *Foundations of Christian Faith*, trans. William V. Dych (New York: Seabury, 1978), p. 8. Rahner's language here echoes that of the Dogmatic Constitution "Dei Filius" of Vatican I (1870); see DS 3008.
20. Karl Rahner, "Zur Frage der Dogmenentwicklung," *Schriften zur Theologie* (Einsiedeln: Benziger Verlag, 1954–84), vol. I, p. 77; ET: *Theological Investigations* (New York: Seabury and Crossroads, 1961–), vol. I, pp. 64–5.
21. See "Ideologie und Christentum" (*Schriften zur Theologie*, vol. VI, p. 66): "Transcendental implications are necessarily co-posited in every spiritual and free act of existence, and carry their light and their certainty in themselves"; as such "transcendental experience" serves as "the unthematic ground of every empirical experience and knowledge of the truth" (ET, vol. VI, p. 49).

an awareness of God, not simply as the infinitely distant holy mystery upon which all things depend, but as the one who graciously offers himself to each person in love, in a free but complete self-communication. At the same time, we necessarily strive to explicate or mediate this interior knowledge with increasing fullness and clarity. The criterion for the success of this reflective effort is the interior knowledge itself, to which direct access must therefore be available.[22]

So far Rahner sounds a lot like Schleiermacher, although he describes in a somewhat different way the inner experiences which serve as the incorrigible epistemic foundation for measuring the truth of explicit Christian beliefs. The argument takes a characteristic twist when Rahner presses the question about what can count as an adequate verbal mediation of the transcendental experience of God and of grace. Why take the teaching of scripture and church, as Rahner assumes the Christian believer and Christian theology must do, to be the uniquely adequate and permanently normative linguistic mediation of the primordial experience of God's saving self-offer?

At just this point Rahner insists upon the insufficiency of appealing *only* to the believer's recognition that explicit Christian beliefs constitute a correct verbal expression of the pre-linguistic depths of her experience. Expressive adequacy is a necessary but not sufficient criterion by which to test for the truth of Christian beliefs. Rahner's argument here combines two trains of thought.

1. If Jesus is the absolute objective or "categorial" mediator of the inward experience of saving grace, then this experience can only be mediated in a fully adequate and definitive way if people have knowledge of him in a strong sense; we need a grasp of the truth about him which is in some way guaranteed and unrevisable. Since Jesus of Nazareth is a particular historical person, those who live after him can only know about him categorially, that is, only by means of explicit beliefs about him, and so of sentences held true which rightly identify him (as the crucified and risen

---

22. "Such an explication ... measures a sentence which is offered as a conceptual expression (*Aussprache*) of experience by the original experience, and finds it correct by that standard" ("Dogmenentwicklung," *Schriften zur Theologie*, vol. I, p. 78; ET, vol. I, p. 66). For a later version of the same sort of argument, see *Grundkurs*, p. 28 (ET, p. 17). First the interiority thesis: "we should always be coming to know better in a conceptual way what we have already experienced and lived through prior to such conceptualization, even if not absolutely without it." Then the foundationalist complement: "conversely, we should show again and again that this whole ... conceptuality does not bring about the givenness of reality to the human being from the outside, but is rather the expression of what has already been experienced and lived through in the depths of existence in a more original way."

Jew of Nazareth) and describe him (as God's eschatological offer of himself to the world, or as God's incarnation). Transcendental experience alone cannot guarantee the truth of such sentences. It can guarantee that they are its own veridical linguistic objectification, but not that there is a categorial or objective state of affairs to which they correspond.

2. This definitive categorial mediation of God's interior offer of saving grace must fully involve the historical and social character of human existence, and in particular the fact that our historical and communal location is for the most part given to us: we do not create the most basic and formative human communities to which we belong, but without them distinctively human existence would be impossible. This means that each person can expect to receive God's final self-offer, namely Jesus Christ, precisely in her distinctive historical present, and only by being invited to join in a community which confronts her with this self-offer. That confrontation will in the nature of the case be authoritative; each person will run up against the church as a communal reality not created by him, a communal reality which is not simply the objectification of his own transcendental experience, but makes a claim that addresses his most profound need for an adequate mediation of his experience of grace.[23]

Taken together, these two lines of argument suggest that Jesus Christ can only be grasped from out of the depths of human subjectivity as God's eschatological self-offer to the world if there is a concrete human community which is the bearer of authoritative teaching about him. Only if the truth of the church's talk of Christ – its living communal voice, normed by scripture but not itself a text – is guaranteed can Christ be received as the absolute mediator of the inward experience of God and grace. The church is not, of course, the guarantor of the truth of its own teaching; for this there can be no inner-worldly guarantee. Rather the church as authoritative teacher about Jesus Christ must be included in God's eschatological gift of himself to the world in Christ if that gift is to be received with the unreserved embrace it intrinsically demands. The church's proclamation of and teaching about Christ must, in other words, be true because God guarantees it – because God says so. Thus "regardless of how it is worked out in concrete detail, the Christian has to anticipate an authoritative church," and the Roman Catholic *magisterium* falls within the horizon of this anticipation.[24]

23. On the last two paragraphs see *Grundkurs*, pp. 332–5 (ET, pp. 342–6).
24. *Grundkurs*, pp. 336–7; see pp. 366–75 (ET, p. 347; pp. 378–88).

This is not, of course, a deductive proof of church authority, still less of the specifically Roman teaching office. It can neither replace nor bring about acceptance in faith of the church's teaching, including its claims to authority. Rather the argument explicitly presupposes belief in Jesus Christ as the absolute mediator of salvation, and tries to show the need for an "authoritative church" only on the basis of this assumption. As with Rahner's transcendental arguments generally, the point is not so much to convince non-Christians to accept Christian beliefs as to show that these beliefs are adequately grounded in, though they cannot be wholly derived from, the depths of human subjectivity. Starting from standard modern assumptions about interior foundations for the justification and truth of Christian belief, Rahner strives to show that something like the Roman Catholic *magisterium* must be in place if these very foundations are to hold.

Epistemic dependence

Harmonist versions of the dependence thesis (like Schleiermacher's) have proven quite durable as an epistemic strategy in modern theology. As Schleiermacher himself clearly senses, however, this approach is inherently unstable. The Christian religious consciousness functions as an indispensable criterion, internal to Christian "territory," by which the truth of Christian beliefs is supposedly guaranteed, yet at the same time those beliefs have to agree with the independently established results of natural and historical science. Of this proposal for an epistemic "covenant" between faith and *Wissenschaft* there can be, Schleiermacher seems willing to grant, no theoretical demonstration. It functions more like a working ideal, rooted in the conviction that since the religious self-consciousness and the striving for objective knowledge are alike ineradicable elements of the human spirit, there can be no ultimate conflict between them (cf. § 28,3).

Modern theologians have not always shared Schleiermacher's confidence. How should theology proceed when persistent efforts at reconciliation leave Christian beliefs in conflict with claims modern culture widely regards as warranted? This seems to signal a breakdown of epistemic harmony which is best acknowledged and dealt with, lest decisions about which beliefs are true and which should be revised or discarded end up happening at random. So theologians have regularly argued that the credibility of Christianity depends on ascribing consistent primacy to beliefs shared with (or at least sharable by) Christians and non-Christians alike. Only this will provide an adequate basis for the hope (shared with harmonist views) that Christians will not find their own distinctive claims at odds with what they otherwise have good reasons to hold true. Accepting the epistemic dependence of Christian beliefs, they have sought to develop *universalist* versions of it.

On accounts of this kind the primary criteria of truth for Christian belief must be shared by all rational people – they must be, at least implicitly, universal. Schubert Ogden, for example, repudiates any appeal to "special criteria of truth" for Christian beliefs, and argues that these beliefs can be regarded as true only if they meet universally acknowledged criteria of credibility.[25] To be sure, agreement on just how to state these universal criteria of truth is elusive, but without "situation-invariant" criteria the Christian claim to truth itself cannot be sustained. It belongs to the very meaning of Christian beliefs about God, human existence, and salvation through Christ that they purport to be true for everybody, and this requires that their truth be established (or not) on grounds everybody accepts.[26]

Like harmonist versions of the dependence thesis, this strong universalism assumes the need to distinguish clearly between procedures for identifying and fixing the meaning of central Christian beliefs, and procedures for deciding about their truth. A proposal for belief can count as Christian (as theologically "appropriate," in Ogden's phrase) only if its meaning is congruent with that of the Christian " 'datum' discourse," namely the historically reconstructed witness of the apostles found in, but not identical with, the New Testament.[27] In order to figure out whether an utterance has more or less the same sense as that of the Christian "datum discourse," we have to know how to fix the meaning of the apostolic witness itself; both are presumably part of a single process of locating and interpreting those beliefs which are centrally Christian. Since, however, these beliefs naturally lack the universal acceptance which criteria of truth require, they can play no role in the process of deciding about the truth of beliefs. In particular they can have no role when it comes to deciding about the truth of Christian claims themselves. The credibility of

25. A "credible" theological statement is one which "meets the relevant conditions of truth universally established with human existence" (Schubert M. Ogden, *On Theology* [San Francisco: Harper, 1986], p. 5). On "special criteria," see p. 103.

26. That Christianity presents at least some claims as "universally valid means that there have to be at least some reasons correspondingly general or universal for accepting them, if their acceptance is to be at all rationally motivated" (*On Theology*, p. 84).

27. *Ibid.*, p. 4.

genuinely Christian beliefs requires, it seems, that determining the meaning and deciding about the truth of sentences and beliefs be two different undertakings.

Procedures for fixing meaning allow for distinctions between various regions of belief. Once a belief has been placed in the appropriate region (most basically, whether its meaning or content locates it as "internal" or "external" to Christianity), its truth can be decided. Here too a similarity with harmonist approaches may be discerned, but to the opposite end: though there is a distinctively Christian region of belief, it has no epistemic criteria of its own. For a strict universalist like Ogden, the epistemic right to hold Christian beliefs depends entirely on finding them adequately supported by universally acknowledged criteria of truth. Should there be conflict between these criteria and distinctively Christian claims, it is the Christian beliefs which will have to be dropped or revised.

Not all universalists are so strict. David Tracy agrees with Ogden on the need to distinguish criteria of truth for Christian beliefs from criteria of appropriateness; showing that a belief has a content appropriate to Christianity is not, as a rule, sufficient to show that the belief is true. In order responsibly to claim truth for Christian beliefs, and *a fortiori* to establish their truth, theologians must always have recourse to "public" criteria of truth.[28] While "public" criteria are in general those which tend toward universal acceptance, it turns out that theology's criteria of truth aim at an internally differentiated, and perhaps elusive, sort of universality. Theology must address three different though interrelated "publics": the academy, the church, and the wider society, each of which advances its own truth claims and epistemic criteria. For each "public" there is a specific theological discipline whose chief business is to engage that public (fundamental, systematic, and practical theology, respectively). Between theological disciplines the criteria of truth will differ not only in content but in logical status; they will be "universal" in analogical, rather than identical, ways.

Though in principle a "disclosive" interpretation of distinctively Christian events and texts is available to any reasonable person, systematic theology (which addresses specifically Christian truth claims) will find success in its public enterprise more elusive than will fundamental theology (which mainly concerns religious experience shared by all people). Systematic theology's criteria of truth are less universally compelling and less tied to cognitive factors than are those of fundamental

---

28. See David Tracy, *The Analogical Imagination: Christian Theology and the Culture of Pluralism* (New York: Crossroad, 1981), pp. 49–54, 80–1, 131–2.

theology, and so reasonable people will find it easier not to be persuaded by its claims. Tracy grants that this leaves open the possibility of tension between the truth claims and criteria of fundamental theology (oriented more to the universal) and those of systematic theology (oriented more to the particular).[29] Since there are on his view no super-criteria to adjudicate these disputes, Tracy's universalist version of the dependence thesis leans a bit toward a harmonist version. But for a genuine harmonist like Schleiermacher, two disparate sets of criteria for truth must each be kept within their own limits, while Tracy aims at synthesis: the criteria of truth for Christian theology are finally one, universal, and public, even if in an internally differentiated, analogous, and elusive sense.

Especially in universalist versions, the dependence thesis usually goes hand in hand with revisionist interpretations of Christian beliefs. Ogden and Tracy both exemplify this pattern, but some universalists much more extensively advocate traditional theological claims. Wolfhart Pannenberg, for example, distinguishes in the usual fashion of the dependence thesis between questions about the content or meaning of Christian beliefs and questions about their truth. Again characteristically, he argues that because Christian beliefs inherently claim universal truth (claim to be "truth for all" and not simply "my truth"), they require a justification which displays their epistemic dependence on the totality of "knowledge external to theology."[30] Providing such justification is the chief task of theology, which must treat the truth of Christian belief as its goal, not its presupposition.[31] For Pannenberg, more than Ogden or Tracy, the criteria for universal epistemic justification are mainly those beliefs for which good reasons can be given, which ought to lead any reasonable person to accept them, and not necessarily those which are universally, or even widely, held. (Correlatively, he differs from many universalists in rejecting the interiority thesis, often regarded as the best way to make plausible claims about beliefs at once universally held and existentially important, and thereby epistemically decisive.)[32] The truth Christianity claims about God is ineluctably historical, which for

29. On these tensions and Tracy's confidence that they may be overcome, see *ibid.*, pp. 54–62.

30. Agreement with the full range of "knowledge external to theology (*außertheologischen Wissens*)" is "a matter of the universal coherence and consequently of the truth of Christian doctrine." Wolfhart Pannenberg, *Systematische Theologie*, vol. 1 (Göttingen: Vandenhoeck and Ruprecht, 1988), p. 59 (ET, p. 49). On "my truth" see p. 60 (ET, p. 51).

31. See *Systematische Theologie*, vol. 1, p. 60 (ET, p. 50).

32. Pannenberg thus rejects "consensus" as a sufficient criterion of truth; see *ibid.*, pp. 22–3, 34 (ET, pp. 12–13, 24); the main opponent here is Jürgen Habermas. Justificatory appeals to experience in theology are finally unable to escape subjectivism and even "irrational fanaticism" (p. 57; see pp. 76–7; ET, pp. 47, 66–7).

Pannenberg entails that whether the claim really is true can only be fully settled at the eschaton.[33] In the meantime, theology has to show that and how these claims agree with everything else we have good reason to believe. And, Pannenberg maintains, it can. In contrast with Ogden and Tracy, he covers the full range of traditional theological *loci* in detail, including robust accounts of the doctrines of the Trinity, the incarnation, and Jesus' resurrection. These complexes of belief are absolutely central, Pannenberg argues, to Christian faith and theology, and all are capable of reasoned articulation which renders them as credible as any beliefs can be short of the eschaton.[34]

Universalist versions of the dependence thesis now often meet vigorous resistance from what could be called *localist* versions of it. Liberation theologies perhaps most clearly represent the type. The experiences of suffering and the struggles for liberation of particular oppressed communities generate criteria of truth which all beliefs, including Christian ones, must meet, but it is neither likely nor necessary (for the justification of beliefs) that people outside a particular oppressed community will share those criteria. James Cone, to cite an early example, identifies two "sources" for Christian theology, scripture and the experience of oppressed black Americans ("experience" here has the sense of "the social and political location of a community and its members"; Cone makes no interiorist appeal).[35] Only those beliefs can count as Christian which have scriptural support, but only those interpretations of scripture (and so of Christian beliefs about God and Christ) can be true which cohere with the black community's experience of oppression and liberation. Consistency alone, however, is not enough to warrant the truth of proposals for Christian belief. In order to be true, such proposals must not simply be compatible with black experience, but positively serve the struggle for liberation and, he sometimes suggests, arise directly out of it.[36] Whether Christian beliefs held by the black community meet criteria

---

33. See *ibid.*, p. 26 (ET, p. 16). All Christian beliefs should therefore be treated as hypotheses awaiting eschatological confirmation (see *ibid.*, pp. 66–9; ET, pp. 56–8), though in this they do not differ from any other sort of belief (see "Wahrheit, Gewißheit und Glaube," *Grundfragen systematischer Theologie: Gesammelte Aufsätze*, vol. ii [Göttingen: Vandenhoeck and Ruprecht, 1980], especially pp. 246–8).

34. Over against Ogden and Tracy Pannenberg is basically right, I think, to suggest that justification (and truth) is a genuinely dogmatic issue, and not simply a prolegomenal or foundational one; this book will do the same. The problem is not where he locates the issue but the way he treats it.

35. See James H. Cone, *God of the Oppressed* (New York: Seabury, 1975), pp. 8, 30–6.

36. See *ibid.*, pp. 34, 124. When he speaks of two discrete sources (which are also norms or epistemic criteria) of Christian theology which need to be dialectically (or even

of truth other than those generated by its own experience, let alone universally held ones (if there are any), is irrelevant to whether they are true. Their coherence with black experience – or, more precisely, with scripture as interpreted in the black community – is sufficient to establish their truth.[37]

paradoxically) related, Cone sounds like a harmonist, if perhaps an uneasy one (see p. 113). But on the whole he seems to regard the primary criteria of truth for Christian belief as an ordered unity; scripture is a source and criterion because black experience requires it (see pp. 31, 113), so that the primary epistemic criterion is scripture as interpreted by the black community's distinctive experience.

37. Social practices structured by radical inequalities of power and freedom inevitably give rise to criteria of truth which not only differ, but conflict; black theologians should expect disagreements with white theologians over what is true to be utterly basic. "White people use such terms as 'rationality' and 'law' as they suit their interests" (ibid., p. 204; see pp. 7–8).

4

Problems about justification

Theological attempts to justify Christian beliefs by appealing to inner experience, foundations, or epistemic dependence all face daunting problems. The arguments which suggest these difficulties are in part philosophical, both in the obvious sense that they have been proposed mainly by philosophers, and in the more important sense that they trade on assumptions which one does not have to hold distinctively Christian beliefs to accept.

The logical links between these three theses are loose enough that it would be possible to accept any one of them without accepting the other two. I group them together not only because modern theology has tended to do so, but also for my own purposes: these three theses seem to me alike unsalvageable. That a theological claim faces philosophical problems does not, to be sure, necessarily require abandoning it. If central Christian beliefs require the thesis, then ways will have to be found to defend it. Later chapters will argue that this is not the case with any of the present theses, mainly by trying to show that a plausible theological account of epistemic justification may be developed which forgoes any appeal to them, and which makes constructive use of the philosophical arguments which suggest that they are beyond rescue.

The belief-dependence of inner experience

Emotion and intention

In theology, justificatory appeals to inner experience tend to turn on a claim about the relation between these experiences and the beliefs which express or describe them. For the interiorist the relevant experiences, while in some sense pre-linguistic or "wordless," give rise to beliefs and sentences which publicly express and communicate the experiences. Having a certain kind of belief depends upon having a certain kind of experience, and the dependence is unidirectional; having such an experience does not depend upon having the belief which properly expresses it. This dependence of beliefs upon experiences seems to be both causal and interpretive. So Schleiermacher argues that Christian beliefs can come about only if the person who holds them has the experiences they are supposed to express, and also suggests that making sense of the sentences the believer holds true requires that the interpreter have the experiences from which they are held to spring. At bottom we interpret the discourse by way of the experiences, not the experiences by way of the discourse.

This interiorist picture of the relation between "inner" experiences or affections and "outer" beliefs and utterances appears implausible. The generally religious and more distinctively Christian experiences or emotions to which interiorists appeal are each supposed to have a specific content, by which they may be identified and distinguished from other religious and non-religious experiences people may have. Interiorists claim not simply that we experience, but that we experience "absolute dependence" or "holy mystery" or "unrestricted love." An inner religious experience is, in Schleiermacher's phrase, a "determinate consciousness"; without determinate content, it could do no epistemic work, since there would be nothing specific with which to compare explicit beliefs and see if they matched up, and so were sure to be true. The implausibility lies in supposing that inner experiences or emotions can have determinate content without depending upon having specific beliefs.

The specific content of an emotion (and so the emotion itself) seems to depend on the object of the emotion. Correlatively, identifying and attributing emotions depends on specifying their objects for the one to whom they are attributed. Emotions, and more broadly the sorts of experiences to which theological interiorists appeal, are "intentional": they cannot be identified and distinguished from one another save by reference to an object. Being in an intentional state thus presupposes the ability to refer to objects.[1]

The link of intentional states (including emotions) to their objects is

---

1. As Hilary Putnam argues: "Intentions are not mental events that *cause* words to refer: intentions . . . have reference as an integral *component*" (*Reason, Truth and History* [Cambridge: Cambridge University Press, 1981], p. 43). On the intentionality of emotions, see Wayne Proudfoot, *Religious Experience* (Berkeley: University of California Press, 1985). Proudfoot there develops an extended argument against what I am calling the interiority thesis, with reference to Schleiermacher in particular (see especially pp. 31–40).

most simply expressed prepositionally: "fear of heights," "craving for Indian food," and so forth. The intentional object which specifies an emotion need not be all that definite (there are many kinds of heights), but having an intentional object is a necessary condition for having an emotion. Noticing someone on the observation deck of the Empire State Building whose palms and face were sweaty, who was trembling slightly and tugging at his collar, I might suppose that he was afraid of heights, but it could be that he was coming down with the flu. Discovering whether the surface symptoms result from an emotion or a virus depends on being able to specify the emotion (fear of . . .), and that depends on identifying an object which caused it (heights).

The situation is the same in the first person; identifying an intentional object is not simply a condition for attributing an emotion to another, but for having one myself. I am somewhat afraid of heights, so I would likely not take these surface symptoms in this situation to indicate the flu (I might be wrong, of course, but I would have to return to street level before I could begin to tell the difference); if I had no fear of heights, I would immediately begin to think I had a virus. The difference between trembling from fear and trembling from the flu is that one requires an intentional object and the other does not. Not only distinctions between emotions and other states, but also the fine discriminations we make between emotions, require reference to their objects. Fear of flying differs from fear of heights; even though airplanes go high, some people reluctant to ascend tall buildings can fly without qualms. The two differ in that one is directed toward airplanes and the other toward high places; the sweaty palms, dizziness, and nausea attendant upon each may be indistinguishable, and the dread or foreboding perhaps bound up with each is itself distinguished from kindred emotions by reference to its intentional object.

Emotions, or what Schleiermacher calls modifications of feeling, require objects to which they are intentionally related; an emotion has to be *about* something. But having intentional objects requires having both concepts and beliefs. To be afraid of heights I have to intend high objects, and this requires me to have the concept "high," which (if I am to have it at all) I must be able to distinguish from the concept "low"; it also requires me to have the concept of falling, which requires me to have the concepts of up and down, of a material body, of time, and so forth. Only armed with a large battery of concepts can I intend high places in such a way as to fear them. And I must also have an unspecifiably wide range of beliefs: I must believe that I am a material body, that material bodies tend to fall from high places, and so forth. This open range of interconnected beliefs outlines what Donald Davidson calls the "logical and epistemic space" within which emotions, like all other propositional attitudes, may be identified and their content specified.[2]

Having an emotion therefore depends on having many beliefs.[3] It depends, more precisely, on having beliefs one is convinced are true. Suppose that I feel a modest joy over having constructed this argument. This joy depends on my beliefs that it is a good argument, and that theological interiorism much needs refuting. I do not, of course, *infer* my joy from these beliefs; the joy just wells up, but its upwelling depends on my holding the beliefs.[4] Should an interiorist objection now occur to me which the argument does not address, my joy would vanish with my belief that I have constructed a good argument. The emotion clearly does not depend on the truth of all the beliefs which help to constitute it, but it does depend on my holding them true. My emotions or affections cannot remain fixed if my beliefs change in relevant or sufficiently extensive ways, though since there is no one-to-one correspondence between beliefs and emotions (one emotion requires many beliefs), there is no general rule for what counts as "relevant" and "extensive" change.

Religious experience and Christian belief

The inner experiences, feelings, or emotions to which theological interiorists appeal are, like emotions generally, intentional states: specifying their content depends upon identification of and reference to their objects. So Rahner speaks of a "pre-thematic" experience "of holy mystery" or "of self-communicating love." Schleiermacher's "feeling of absolute dependence" appears at first glance to be different, since "absolute dependence" specifies the content of the experience but makes no explicit reference to an object ("dependence" is obviously not the *object* of the feeling; rather, so to speak, its genus). However, the difference is only

---

2. Donald Davidson, "Thought and Talk," *Inquiries into Truth and Interpretation* (Oxford: Clarendon Press, 1985), pp. 156–7, 162; see also "Rational Animals," *Actions and Events,* ed. Ernest LePore and Brian McLaughlin (Oxford: Blackwell, 1985), p. 475. Davidson here speaks of "thoughts," a term he uses to include all propositional attitudes ("Rational Animals," p. 478).

3. A person's interior life depends, of course, on much more than her beliefs: her biological makeup, the specific and contingent events which have taken place in her own history, and so forth. None of this detracts from the dependence of emotions, and intentional experiences generally, on beliefs.

4. A point Proudfoot stresses; see *Religious Experience*, pp. 19, 62, 163f.

apparent. Schleiermacher realizes, indeed insists, that an experience of dependence has to be an experience of dependence *on* something; we undergo the experience of absolute dependence only insofar as that on which we are dependent is "co-posited" as integral to the experience itself. Thus the experience of oneself and all finite being as absolutely dependent necessarily involves reference to an adequate source of this felt universal dependence, an omnicausal "whence" to which dependence on this scale may rightly be attributed.

Since the feeling of absolute dependence involves an intentional object, in order to have that experience one must be able to identify or locate its object, what Schleiermacher calls its "whence." Schleiermacher in fact devotes much of the first part of *The Christian Faith* (the discussions of God as creator and preserver, and of God's attributes) to a detailed analysis of the concepts and beliefs necessary in order adequately to locate and describe the object of the feeling of absolute dependence, insofar as that feeling is presupposed and contained in the specifically Christian religious consciousness. He proposes, of course, that these beliefs (and perhaps the concepts as well) depend unilaterally on the inner feeling, but this picture seems to have the relationship backwards. Without these beliefs a person would not be able to have a feeling of absolute dependence, because he could not specify the object upon which he was dependent. A feeling of dependence with no specifiable object would not be dependence on anything, and so not dependence at all, while a feeling with a different object, specified by different beliefs (say, without beliefs about absolute causality), would be a different feeling (of less than absolute dependence).

Interiorists will quickly point out that "God" or "holy mystery" is not an "object" of the deep experience in which each is present the way airplanes are the "object" of the fear of flying. Part of the point about these experiences is that they transcend (or precede) the split between "subject" and "object."

As an objection to the argument that inward experiences are belief-dependent, this observation turns on an equivocation regarding the notion of an "object." The object of an intentional state may be capable of only vague description; it need not have a spatio-temporal location, indeed it need not exist at all. For an intentional state to have an object in the relevant sense, it must simply be possible to describe the state by using a prepositional phrase: the experience, emotion, or thought needs to be "of" something, "about" something, or similarly linked to a term. Interiorists like Schleiermacher and Rahner clearly think the epistemically decisive experiences to which they appeal are susceptible of such description, and so they clearly hold that these experiences have "objects" in the relevant sense.

Interiorists will also point out that on their view, these inward experiences necessarily give rise to explicit beliefs. Although the experiences are prior to and do not depend for their existence upon the beliefs which express or mediate them, one nevertheless cannot have the experiences without having appropriate beliefs, and having contact with a linguistic community which shares those beliefs. Experiences are inward and original while beliefs are outward and derivative, but interiorists argue vigorously that the two are inseparable.[5] There seem to be two possible construals of this reply.

1. The appeal to mediation might mean that in order to have a particular religious experience, one must have a specifiable range of beliefs. If so, it seems that having the experience depends on having the beliefs. Understood in this way, the reply does not counter the anti-interiorist argument we have been developing, but confirms it.

2. The appeal might mean that in order to have a particular religious experience, a person must have some beliefs, but it does not matter what the beliefs are; any and all beliefs are equally capable of mediating the experience. This is a genuine reply to the anti-interiorist argument, but an unconvincing one. If all beliefs may succeed in mediating the feeling of absolute dependence (for example), then the belief that $-p$ (that the "whence" of this feeling has no causal power) does the job as well as the belief that p (that the "whence" of this feeling has causal power). But this means that an intentional object of the feeling cannot be specified, since it seems impossible that contradictory beliefs could identify the same object (thus, for example, a "whence" without causal power must be a different intentional object from one with causal power; the same intentional object presumably cannot both not have and have any given property). And without specifiable intentional objects, one feeling seems not to differ or be distinguishable (even for the person who has it) from another. Interiorists sometimes try to avoid this problem by suggesting that while all beliefs may mediate the experiences in question, some do it much better than others. But this seems not to help: the belief that $-p$ does not locate poorly the same object the belief that p locates well; contradictory beliefs identify different intentional objects.

---

5. See chapter 3, note 4.

As a claim about the relation between emotions, including religious ones, and beliefs the interiority thesis seems to have the basic lines of dependence reversed. The same goes, it could be argued, for the interiorist suggestion that the meaning and interpretation of a person's utterances depend on interior experiences they express. Nothing interior – no intention, purpose, mental act, or experience on the part of the speaker (including yourself) – enables you to fix the sense of the sentences a speaker utters. Perhaps the most familiar way of supporting this claim is Wittgenstein's argument against the possibility of a private language.[6] This claim is also, as we will argue in connection with the truth-dependence of meaning, one of the requirements for a theory of interpretation which is genuinely radical and non-question-begging. For the moment, however, we need to consider the epistemic implications of the dependence of inner experience upon belief. Here two problems arise.

(a) According to the justificatory picture favored by interiorists, Christians test the truth of their beliefs by introspection; they locate an inward experience and try to determine whether the belief in question originates from that experience and expresses its content in a relatively adequate way. In this way they may rightly decide whether sentences describing beliefs or other inward states should be regarded as true. For present purposes we can grant the plausibility of the interiorist picture in the case of sentences like

(1) I, Jill, feel that I am absolutely dependent on God.

The plausibility of this picture rests chiefly on two assumptions which, while disputed, are certainly defensible: (i) such sentences, at least when spoken in the first person and the present tense (and prescinding from the intention to deceive a listener – or oneself), are usually true, and (ii) the speaker's apprehension of their truth may be introspective; it need not come about by attention to her own overt speech and action.[7] Still, having an experience such that (1) is true depends on having a great many beliefs, and so on holding true many other sentences. Among such sentences is presumably

(2) I, Jill, am absolutely dependent on God.

---

6. Fergus Kerr gives a sustained reading of Wittgenstein aimed at supporting anti-interiorist theological purposes in *Theology After Wittgenstein* (Oxford: Blackwell, 1986); on private language, see especially pp. 84–90.

7. Putnam among others thinks (ii) must be wrong, since " 'meanings' just ain't in the *head*." See "The Meaning of 'Meaning,'" *Mind, Language and Reality: Philosophical Papers*, vol. II (Cambridge: Cambridge University Press, 1975), pp. 215–71; the quoted phrase is from p. 227. Cf. "Knowing One's Own Mind," *Proceedings of the American Philosophical Association* 60 (1986–7), pp. 441–58.

This, and numerous other sentences which Jill must be disposed to hold true in order to have a feeling of absolute dependence, do not at all express or describe that experience. They are not about that particular feeling or about any other inner experience. The truth of the beliefs whose content they state cannot depend, therefore, on whether the believer has or does not have any inner experience. So talk of justifying *these* beliefs by introspection makes no sense. Nothing which could be apprehended introspectively will be likely to have any bearing on whether or not they should be taken as true. Their truth is much more readily assailable than that of beliefs expressed by sentences like (1), and while introspection might be a person's way of finding out that she holds the beliefs which having the experience of dependence requires, it will not begin to help her decide whether she ought to hold them.

(b) The truth of sentences describing and attributing propositional attitudes (like 1) neither requires nor implies the truth of sentences which state the contents of the attitudes (like 2). Either can be true while the other is false; this happens all the time.

(3) Junior Ortiz feels that he is a better catcher than Johnny Bench

is, Junior tells us, true, while

(4) He (Junior) is a better catcher than Johnny Bench

is surely false. More generally, while a person must *hold* many beliefs true in order to have an emotion or other intentional experience, having the experience does not require that the beliefs actually *be* true.

This applies particularly to the beliefs which locate the object of the experience. I may be frightened because I believe there is a snake in the grass underfoot, while my hiking companion realizes that the rustling we both hear is actually caused by a mouse. In that case "I'm frightened that there is a snake underfoot" would be true, while my belief, "There is a snake underfoot," would be false, although other beliefs upon which the experience depends ("Snakes are sometimes dangerous") might still be true. This means that being justified (whether introspectively or otherwise) in the attribution of an inner experience, emotion, or attitude contributes nothing toward the justification of the beliefs upon which the experience depends. To whatever test of truth sentences about inner experiences may be held, they can meet that test and beliefs upon which the experience depends can still be false.

So while I have to believe that I am absolutely dependent upon God in order to have the feeling or experience of absolute dependence upon God, I will have to justify that belief in some other way than by appeal to the experience or to the fact that I have it. Of course a feeling may lead or incline a person to hold a certain belief which is not itself an attribution or description of the feeling; the feeling of absolute dependence may (as Schleiermacher argues) lead someone to believe that God is omnipotent. Since there is no one-to-one relationship between emotions and beliefs, a person may surely come to hold beliefs at least in part in order to satisfy an emotion they already have.[8] But invoking the feeling makes no contribution to *justifying* the belief it inclines one to hold. The feeling, more precisely, has no justificatory force of its own. When it comes to epistemic right, appeal to the feeling simply refers one to the justificatory force of the beliefs on which the feeling itself depends. Justificatory appeals to inner experience will achieve no more than appeals to these beliefs.

In sum: theological interiorists argue that our inner experiences put us in touch with the way things ultimately are, and that our beliefs about the ultimate nature of things are justified by these experiences. To the contrary, however, there are good reasons to suppose that having experiences which put us in touch with the ultimate (or anything else) depends on having true beliefs about it, and that deciding which experiences lead us on the right epistemic track depends on deciding which beliefs are true.

Only beliefs justify beliefs

Two types of anti-foundationalism

Few theologians any longer will admit to being foundationalists. None, in fact, ever did; theological interest in "foundationalism" followed upon various philosophical criticisms of foundationalist views, so that theologians generally discuss it mainly in order to reject it as an epistemic option.[9] Philosophical arguments against foundationalism tend to be of two different sorts, which need not go together: one attacks the claim that we only have the right to hold beliefs which meet foundationalist standards, while the other goes further, and attacks the notion that the world – states of affairs or events – either can or needs to justify beliefs in the

---

8. Chapter 7 will explore this possibility in more detail.
9. George A. Lindbeck, *The Nature of Doctrine* (Philadelphia: Westminster, 1984), Ronald F. Thiemann, *Revelation and Theology* (Notre Dame: University of Notre Dame Press, 1985), Francis Schüssler Fiorenza, *Foundational Theology* (New York: Crossroad, 1986), William C. Placher, *Unapologetic Theology* (Philadelphia: Westminster, 1989), and John E. Thiel, *Imagination and Authority* (Philadelphia: Fortress, 1991) adduce somewhat different anti-foundationalist philosophical arguments for various theological purposes. Lindbeck, Thiemann, and Placher think foundationalist assumptions detract from the plausibility of various strains of modern theology (e.g., those stemming from Schleiermacher), while Thiel doubts that these traditions are foundationalist in any problematic sense.

first place. The first strategy targets (F 3) among the foundationalist claims we have identified, while the second and more radical strategy targets (F 1) and (F 2).[10] In order to be clear about what is supposed to be wrong with foundationalism, and what does (and does not) follow from rejecting it, we need to look at these two different types of argument.

The foundationalist strategy has been to identify one or more types of belief whose truth is sufficiently secure to serve as the basis for all other beliefs, and then to propose instances of the type. The candidates are several.

(A) *Self-evident* or *self-authenticating* beliefs, which impress themselves on us with such clarity that we cannot doubt their truth, and require no recourse to other beliefs in order for us to see that they are true. Proposed instances include basic logical laws, and so-called "analytic truths," like "All bachelors are unmarried men."

(B) *Empirically evident* beliefs, which can be construed in two ways.
(i) They have their truth directly guaranteed, though perhaps only for the moment, by certain percepts, sensations, sense data, or the like, whose content they state. An instance might be "I am appeared to treely (or greenly)," which might itself be taken as empirically evident to the one who holds it, or might be taken as directly based on an experience regarded as a bit more primitive (like "Green here now!"). These veridical beliefs about sensations then justify further beliefs about an objective world, that is, about matters other than beliefs and sensations ("There is a tree").
(ii) They are themselves about an objective world, and so state more than the content of sensations (again, "There is a tree"), but are directly justified by sensations.

(C) *Incorrigible beliefs*, which cannot be false, or, in one current idiom, are true in every possible world, and so must be true in the actual one. The examples given for (A) and (B) might also be incorrigible, but a belief might belong to neither category and still be incorrigible, though perhaps not foundational – complex truths of arithmetic (such as $89 \times 125 = 11,125$) are standard examples, since it seems impossible for them to be false, but they are not self-evident, at least to most of us.

(D) Beliefs which are certain, in that the holder is fully convinced that they are true, and indeed, at limit, cannot coherently conceive the possibility of doubting them. The Cartesian *cogito* is a classic proposal of this type.

Not least among theologians, anti-foundationalism is often equated with rejection of the claim that there can be beliefs of any of these types.

10. See above, p. 54.

The first sort of argument against foundationalism, however, grants that there are beliefs of all these types. Alvin Plantinga, for example, thinks that all four classes are well populated, and so endorses claims (F 1) and (F 2) of the foundationalist thesis. Yet the foundationalist strategy – at least in what Plantinga calls its "classical" version, marked by a commitment to (F 3) – remains unpersuasive.

Self-reference is the problem. According to the foundationalist proposition, a rationally justified system of belief will consist of sentences held true which are either (1) self-evident, empirically evident, or incorrigible, or (2) evidentially supported by beliefs of the types gathered in (1). But by these criteria the foundationalist proposition is not itself a rationally justified belief, since it is not self-evident, empirically evident, or incorrigible, and seems not to be supported by any evidential relationships to beliefs which are of these types (at least no foundationalist has provided, or even tried to provide, an argument which displays such relationships). So the rationally justified course for foundationalists (and *a fortiori*, everybody else), by their own criteria of justification, is to reject the foundationalist proposition.[11] This clears the way for taking various Christian beliefs as "properly basic," even though they do not fall into the classes of belief gathered in (1). They may be believed with full epistemic right, but without recourse to evidential support, in particular support from other beliefs.

It might seem as though a more radical sort of anti-foundationalist argument would proceed by trying to sweep away the various types of belief to which foundationalists appeal. Yet even then the broader epistemic outlook which underwrites foundationalism can remain in place. As Davidson in particular has argued, getting rid of foundationalist claims (F 1) and (F 2) finally requires getting rid of the epistemic dualism of scheme and content.[12]

A "scheme" in this sense is a system of beliefs and concepts, while the

11. For Plantinga's argument, see "Reason and Belief in God," *Faith and Rationality*, ed. Alvin Plantinga and Nicholas Wolterstorff (Notre Dame: University of Notre Dame Press, 1983), especially pp. 59–63, and more recently *Warrant: The Current Debate* (Oxford: Oxford University Press, 1993), pp. 66–96, and *Warrant and Proper Function* (Oxford: Oxford University Press, 1993), pp. 176–85.

12. On this see Donald Davidson, "On the Very Idea of a Conceptual Scheme," *Inquiries*, pp. 183–98; "A Coherence Theory of Truth and Knowledge," *Truth and Interpretation: Perspectives on the Philosophy of Donald Davidson*, ed. E. LePore (Oxford: Blackwell, 1986), pp. 307–19; "The Myth of the Subjective," *Relativism: Interpretation and Confrontation*, ed. Michael Krausz (Notre Dame: University of Notre Dame Press, 1989), pp. 159–72; "Meaning, Truth and Evidence," *Perspectives on Quine*, ed. R. Barrett and R. Gibson (Oxford: Blackwell, 1990), pp. 68–79.

"content" is some type of experience or sensation (or, less plausibly, "reality" or "the world" as a whole). The scheme (as Kant was perhaps the first clearly to suggest) interprets, organizes, fits, or copes with the content (perhaps in manifold, even incompatible, ways), while the content is simply given, susceptible of interpretation by the scheme but not itself an interpretation of anything else. This sort of distinction between scheme and content underwrites foundationalism by making it seem plausible that the uninterpreted data of experience, the givens of sensation, can serve as *evidence* for a system of beliefs, indeed conclusive evidence: at least some of our beliefs may come to be justified in an absolute and incorrigible way, so this outlook suggests, since the evidence for them is a non-verbal, sensuous given which is beyond epistemic manipulation. Given this picture foundations become an urgent epistemic need. Since concepts are subject to our manipulation while the evidential given is not, it becomes imperative to anchor scheme in content. Without the sort of justification which arises when scheme is confronted by content, our whole system of belief will end up losing its tie to the world, and we will no longer be able to tell the difference between true belief and mere invention.

By dispensing with the standard types of foundational belief, a view like Quine's revises the scheme-content distinction, and attenuates its foundationalist force. Now the whole of our sense experience confronts our whole conceptual scheme, rather than individual sentences facing isolated bits of sensuous data.[13] This rules out (B) empirically evident and (A) self-evident beliefs at a stroke, since it eliminates both the possibility of specifying uniquely the experiences which would confirm or disconfirm any one belief, and the possibility of confirming or disconfirming any one belief without doing the same to an unspecifiably diverse number of others at the same time (thus blocking the notion of a *self-evident belief*, and with that the distinction of "analytically" from "synthetically" true beliefs). Consequently appeals to (C) incorrigible beliefs and (D) certain beliefs (at least in the limit sense of those not rationally dubitable) must also be given up.

Quine thus drops the notion of direct access ingredient in standard versions of foundationalist claims (F 1) and (F 2). But his talk of statements about the external world "facing" the tribunal of sense experience

13. "Our statements about the external world," Quine famously proposes, "face the tribunal of sense experience not individually but only as a corporate body." Willard Van Orman Quine, "Two Dogmas of Empiricism," *From a Logical Point of View*, 2nd edn (Cambridge, Mass.: Harvard University Press, 1980), p. 41.

continues to enshrine an epistemic outlook which turns on a confrontation between linguistic or conceptual scheme and given empirical or
experiential content. So also does his later distinction between "report
and invention, substance and style, cues and conceptualization," which
holds out the promise that we can investigate the world and ourselves in
such a way that, "subtracting his cues from his world view, we get man's
net contribution as the difference. This difference marks the extent of
man's conceptual sovereignty – the domain within which he can revise
theory while saving the data."[14] What remains of the scheme–content
dualism here, and so of foundationalism, is the notion of a type of evidence or justification for beliefs which is not itself a belief, and which reliably informs us, in the crucial basic cases, about the truth of beliefs.

One can attack a dualism from either side, and Davidson mounts arguments against both the notion of "scheme" and that of "content" which
versions of the dualism employ. His arguments against the scheme side of
the dualism are perhaps the more familiar of the two.[15] Their upshot is
that the notion of alternative conceptual schemes organizing or fitting
the world or experience in different (and perhaps contradictory) ways is
finally unintelligible. As a result serious conceptual relativism cannot
even be formulated; we must all largely share a largely true picture of the
world. For present purposes, however, Davidson's attack on the content
side of the dualism has more telling implications. He approaches the
issue by observing how foundationalist notions of content prop open the
door to skepticism.

About the world we regularly if unsystematically find that our beliefs
are mistaken, which may prompt the (foundationalist) thought that for
at least some of our beliefs about the world we need a type of evidence
about which we cannot be mistaken. The content of sense experience is
supposed to be able to serve as evidence for the beliefs which make up a
conceptual scheme because this content – when properly distinguished
from both the world (about which we can be mistaken) and the scheme
(which is what needs to be justified) – is incorrigible, at least for the
person who has it. In this sense the ultimate epistemic evidence is subjective, and just for that reason secured from the uncertainty which to some
degree the world always has for us. However more precisely conceived,

---

14. W. V. Quine, *Word and Object* (Cambridge, Mass.: MIT Press, 1960), p. 5.
15. As developed especially in "On the Very Idea of a Conceptual Scheme." For a presentation
of Davidson's anti-scheme arguments oriented toward the epistemological assumptions
and problems of modern western religious thought, see Jeffrey L. Stout, *The Flight from
Authority* (Notre Dame: University of Notre Dame Press, 1981), especially pp. 165–71.

empirical content fills its evidentiary role by taking up an intermediate position between the world and the scheme. My belief, "There is a tree," is presumably true if and only if a tree is there, but the evidence for that belief is neither a tree nor other beliefs – neither the world nor the scheme – but something in between, namely what goes on at or beneath my skin, the content (on Quine's view) of my surface irritations or sensations.

How, though, can we be sure the evidence so conceived is reliable? In whatever way we think of our beliefs, our sense experience, and the objects we normally take our beliefs to be about, we are apparently unable to take up a position independent of our beliefs and our sense experience so as to compare them with the objects and thereby tell which beliefs are true and which experiences reliable. This being the case, taking the contents of sense experience as the ultimate evidence for our beliefs about the world fails to overcome skeptical worries. Indeed interposing any sort of entity, sensuous content or otherwise, as an epistemic intermediary between our beliefs and the objects the beliefs are about sets up an epistemic situation in which these worries become unavoidable. Granting for present purposes that we cannot be mistaken about the contents of our sense experience, we nonetheless have no way to tell whether it is reliably informing us about the world. Even on a highly refined version of the scheme–content dualism like Quine's, it remains quite conceivable that the sensuous contents which serve as the evidence for our beliefs might massively mislead us, prompting us to hold beliefs which are mostly false.[16]

One might, of course, try to solve this problem by finding a reliable intermediary, but this seems highly unpromising – indeed, since we have no way of checking on the reliability of epistemic intermediaries, incoherent. It seems more plausible to drop the epistemic role of empirical content altogether, that is, to drop the notion of an epistemic intermediary which is supposed to serve as evidence or justification for beliefs about the world. As Davidson proposes: "Since we can't swear intermediaries to truthfulness, we should allow no intermediaries between our beliefs and their objects in the world. Of course there are causal intermediaries. What we must guard against are epistemic intermediaries."[17]

16. Quine himself, to be sure, has no expressed interest in the search for epistemic foundations or the problem of skepticism, in part because he is quite willing to grant that humans beings might, within the range of their "conceptual sovereignty," organize the "cues" their experience provides by means of schemes utterly different from any now in use.   17. "A Coherence Theory of Truth and Knowledge," p. 312.

Distinguishing in this way between causal and epistemic intermediaries, and declining to ascribe any epistemic role to whatever causal intermediaries there are between the objects our beliefs are about and our beliefs about those objects, makes it impossible even to formulate *either* global skepticism about the deliverances of the senses *or* the sort of foundationalism which seeks to overcome it, whether in the forms proposed by traditional empiricism or those for which the untraditional, Quinean variety continues to leave room. Since on this picture sense experience plays no epistemic role – no role in our decisions about what sentences mean and which ones are true – both worries over whether the senses are reliably informing us about the world and attempts to identify reliable sensuous informers will be irrelevant to these decisions. And since it is only in connection with these epistemic decisions that it occurs to anyone either to worry globally about the reliability of sense experience or to seek foundationalist relief, both the worry and the quest seem to be pointless.[18]

Davidson's argument here is not, it should be noted, that we can get rid of scheme–content dualisms simply by doing away with the notion of "uninterpreted experience." Quine, for example, argues vigorously against the possibility of uninterpreted experience (experience "free of theory"), yet seems to assume the scheme–content distinction, and so views our actual experience of the world as a kind of insoluble compound of scheme and content, theory and data.[19] As Davidson sees it, the problem lies not in the notion of uninterpreted contents of experience, but in the epistemic role such contents are supposed to play; he gets rid of an epistemic reliance on uninterpreted experience by dropping the notion of epistemic intermediaries altogether, interpreted or otherwise. This is genuinely radical surgery. With no epistemic role for the contents of sense experience, there is nothing left for schemes to organize or fit; "scheme and content ... came as a pair; we can let them go together."[20]

Theological consequences of anti-foundationalism

What then follows from rejecting foundationalism, whether in Plantinga's manner or Davidson's?

It does *not* follow that we have to deny the existence or possibility of the various types of belief to which foundationalists usually appeal as

---

18. See "The Myth of the Subjective," pp. 165–6. Davidson's argument here depends not only on his rejection of epistemic intermediaries, but also on his own positive account of the relations between meaning, truth, belief, and evidence, about which we will have more to say in connection with the dependence thesis.   19. See *Word and Object*, p. 39.
20. "The Myth of the Subjective," p. 165.

evidence, namely types (A) through (D). Like Quine, one can be a foundationalist without them, and, like Plantinga, one can be an anti-foundationalist with them. One could, moreover, accept Davidson's anti-foundationalist argument (at least on its content-oriented side) and still suppose that most of these types of belief can be maintained; while Davidson himself dispenses with all four on various (mostly Quinean) grounds, his argument against foundationalism only *requires* him, so far as I can tell, to reject (B). Philosophical announcements of the collapse of foundationalism have been celebrated in some quarters, and denounced in others, for bringing an end to presumed or inherited certainties and putting all beliefs up for grabs – casting us into the open sea, as it were, without even a plank from Neurath's boat for support. But such claims, whether a case can be made for them, or even sense made of them, go far beyond what the rejection of foundationalism, taken by itself, can plausibly be invoked to support.

If Davidson's way of rejecting foundationalism is correct, however, an important epistemic consequence comes to light. His argument aims to eliminate all objects, events, or states of affairs which might intervene epistemically between beliefs and what the beliefs are about. All that remains to justify beliefs, therefore, is other beliefs. Supposing that anything which is not a belief might justify beliefs needlessly creates skeptical quandaries. But more than that, it proves difficult to explain without circularity how anything but a belief could justify – that is, how things like objects, events, or experiences could function as a reason or evidence for holding a belief without recourse to the concept of belief.

Suppose, for example, a question arises about what justifies my belief that there is a tree in front of me. It seems natural to say that I am justified in believing that there is a tree in front of me because I see the tree with my own eyes. Can this be taken to mean that the seeing itself – the sensory event, my being appeared to treely – is doing the justifying, rather than any belief? Suppose I believe that I do not see a tree, or I believe that the relevant sensory event, the seeing of a treely kind, is *not* taking place. Would the seeing (the event) still justify my belief that there is a tree in front of me? Surely if I believe that I am not seeing a tree, I cannot be justified in believing that there is a tree in front of me. I might in fact be justified in believing that there is not a tree in front of me, though my belief could well be false. It is thus my belief about the seeing, not the seeing itself, which does epistemic work. A similar sort of argument can be made against attempts to attribute justificatory significance to any object or event in the causal chain which links the tree and my belief about it (obviously including the tree itself); the causes themselves do not justify, though of course beliefs about them may. One outcome of the collapse of foundationalism – at least where claims (F 1) and (F 2) are implicated in its downfall – is thus that justification can only be a matter of coherence among beliefs. The world – objects, events (including experiences), and states of affairs – does not justify beliefs; justification is a relation not between beliefs and the world, but between beliefs and beliefs.[21]

To be sure, accepting a coherentist view of justification throws into sharp relief a quite basic choice which must be made when it comes to saying what *truth* is. Having characterized justification as a matter of coherence among beliefs, one might go on to characterize truth in the same way, as, say, what we are presently, or perhaps ideally, justified in asserting (whoever "we" are). But the coherentist view of justification which seems to follow from rejecting foundationalist accounts of what can count as evidence does not entail a coherence theory of truth. A coherentist about justification need not characterize truth itself as coherence, and may instead offer a different account of what truth is (whether in traditional realist fashion, or by taking the alternative course Davidson, among others, follows). This is to propose an irreducible distinction, at least in this life, between what it is for a belief to be justified and what it is for the same belief to be true; if one follows this course, justification is a matter of coherence among beliefs, while truth cannot be. I will later advocate a mixed view of this kind. As we shall see such a view obligates its holder to answer a question which does not arise for a pure coherentist: why should we suppose that beliefs related to one another in a suitably coherent way are true?[22]

---

21. As Davidson puts the point, "what distinguishes a coherence theory is simply the claim that nothing can count as a reason for holding a belief except another belief. Its partisan rejects as unintelligible the request for a ground or source of justification of another ilk" ("A Coherence Theory of Truth and Knowledge," p. 310; on the argument of the foregoing paragraph cf. pp. 310–12).

Plantinga argues that this view is implausible: "In the typical case I will not believe that I see a tree on the basis of a proposition about my experience," and so this sort of belief should typically be regarded as itself basic ("Reason and Belief in God," p. 49). It is no doubt true that I usually need not advert to any beliefs about my experience in order to be justified in holding beliefs about what I see or otherwise perceive. But the question is whether perceptions themselves *can* play any justificatory role, or whether, should it become necessary to invoke perceptions for justificatory purposes, that role rather belongs to beliefs about them. Moreover, I can presumably hold innumerable beliefs to which I do not explicitly advert at any given time, but some of which may nonetheless play an important role in the justification of a particular belief (think, once again, of how the epistemic picture changes if we withdraw one or another such background belief).

22. On these questions, see chapters 8–9.

Truth as "disclosure"

Before we leave foundationalism behind, it may be useful to look briefly at the notion of truth as "disclosure," which some recent theologians and philosophers of religion see as a complement or alternative to the "models" of truth as correspondence and as coherence.[23] The language of "disclosure" (*Entbergung* or *Unverborgenheit* – "unhiddenness") stems mainly from Heidegger, in particular from his essay "On the Essence of Truth" and the remarks on truth in *Being and Time*, § 44. On Heidegger's account, we ordinarily understand truth as an "agreement" (*Übereinstimmung*) between a sentence or utterance and a thing. In order to become comprehensible to us, truth so understood needs to find root in a more "primordial" (*ursprünglich*) relationship between human beings and the world they inhabit. This relationship consists, roughly, in a human way of acting or a "comportment" (*Verhältnis*) which "lets beings be" – which opens us to the openness which every being has for us. Freely to be open to beings, to let them dispose of us and measure our speech rather than trying to force them to fit our preconceived ideas, is to have beings disclose themselves to us, and in this the primordial essence of truth consists. This open comportment finds its completion in the utterance of sentences which speak of things as they are, and alone makes possible such utterances.[24]

Exactly what to make of these passages from Heidegger is a bit difficult to say. This might be taken for foundationalism of an exceptionally bold sort. Instead of painstakingly trying to build on bits of sensuous data to the point where they can justify beliefs about the grass, the trees, and the stars, Heidegger sometimes seems to say that the grass, the trees, and the stars will simply tell us what sentences to hold true, if only we will let them. This thought readily lends itself to theological application. God discloses himself in a unique way to those who are open to his free and personal revelation; this disclosure constitutes incorrigible evidence for the truth of Christian beliefs. What remains puzzling is how beings or God disclose themselves to us in such a way that they enable us to decide what to say – what sentences to hold true. In Heidegger's idiom: how does the

---

23. For a helpful brief account of this line of thought, see Louis Dupré, "Reflections on the Truth of Religion," *Faith and Philosophy* 6 (1989), pp. 260–74; see also the remarks on "manifestation" in David Tracy, *Plurality and Ambiguity* (San Francisco: Harper and Row, 1987), pp. 28–30.

24. See Martin Heidegger, "Vom Wesen der Wahrheit," *Wegmarken* (*Martin Heidegger Gesamtausgabe*, division I, vol. IX [Frankfurt: Klostermann, 1976]), especially pp. 182–91 (ET: "On the Essence of Truth," *Martin Heidegger: Basic Writings*, ed. David Farrell Krell [New York: Harper and Row, 1977]).

comportment which "lets beings be" find its completion or fulfillment (*Vollzug*) in true utterances?[25] Apparently we cannot link our beliefs to the beings our beliefs are about in an epistemically useful way by invoking "disclosure" as a middle term which securely joins the two. If we do not believe that a being has disclosed itself to us, it is hard to see how the occurrence of the disclosure (however more precisely understood) could justify us in holding any sentences true; if we do believe it, then the believing, not the disclosure, is doing the justificatory work.

But one might just as readily read the Heidegger of these passages not as a foundationalist at all, but as a pathbreaking anti-foundationalist – and, as several interpreters have lately suggested, an unusual sort of pragmatist.[26] On this reading "disclosure" is not a foundation for beliefs, an epistemic intermediary between human beings and the world they seek to know, but names what happens when human beings wrapped up in social practices use language for the myriad purposes which constitute those practices (including practices of deciding which beliefs are true).

We need not decide here whether talk of truth as disclosure is best read in foundationalist or non-foundationalist terms. To the extent that "disclosure" invites us to think in foundationalist terms, it faces the sort of objections to foundationalism just considered; to the extent that it does not, it invites the development of non-foundationalist accounts of justification.

The truth-dependence of meaning and interpretation

In all of its versions (harmonist, universalist, and localist), the epistemic dependence thesis hangs on the assumption that the meaning of Christian beliefs is unaffected by the way in which their truth is assessed. Theological dependence theorists are of course not alone in supposing that the meaning of sentences and the contents of beliefs can be fixed without trying to decide whether they are true. It seems obvious enough that whether a sentence is true depends at least in part on what it means ("Schnee ist weiß" is true if it means "Snow is white," but not if it means "Pigs do fly"). From this philosophers have often

25. See "Vom Wesen der Wahrheit," p. 184 (ET, p. 124).
26. E.g., Richard Rorty, *Essays on Heidegger and Others* (Cambridge: Cambridge University Press, 1991), in particular "Heidegger, Contingency, and Pragmatism," pp. 27–49. Rorty draws heavily on the pragmatist interpretations of Heidegger by Robert Brandom and Mark Okrent.

inferred that in general we have to grasp what sentences mean before we can try to establish their truth value: we can and should hold for meaning while testing for truth.

Much modern philosophy has, nonetheless, argued that this traditional picture essentially has the matter backwards, and for this reason can offer no plausible or informative account of how we actually succeed in figuring out what sentences mean. In order to develop such an account, we have to view meaning as truth-dependent: we cannot, on the whole, decide what sentences mean except by deciding whether they are true. If the common modern philosophical view is right, as I will argue here, then the dependence thesis, which assumes the contrary, cannot be sustained – although a full account of the deficiencies of the thesis will await the introduction of specifically theological considerations in the next chapter.

One way to state the common modern view is in terms first explicitly proposed by Frege: the meaning of a sentence is, or is given by, its truth conditions. Correlatively, to understand the meaning of a sentence is to grasp its truth conditions.[27] Related to this is the context principle: "Only in the context of a sentence do words mean anything."[28] Taken together these principles imply that the meaning of words or phrases consists in the role they play in establishing the truth conditions of the sentences in which they may appear. But philosophers since Frege have argued for the truth- (or more precisely, truth-conditional-) dependence of sentence meaning and the correlative context dependence of word meaning in different ways, tied to quite different philosophical projects. It will be useful here to consider two divergent ways of making this case: that of Donald Davidson, to which we will recur at several points in subsequent chapters, and, more briefly, that of Michael Dummett.

Davidson on truth, belief, and meaning

A theory of meaning, Davidson observes, aims to explain what it is for words to have the meaning they do. Interpretation theory, a cognate enterprise, will have to show how we are consistently able to figure out what the utterances (or inscriptions) of speakers (or writers) of a language

---

27. See Gottlob Frege, *Grundgesetze der Arithmetik*, 2nd edn (Hildesheim: Georg Olms Verlagsbuchhandlung, 1962), I, § 32 (ET of part I by Montgomery Furth, *The Basic Laws of Arithmetic* [Berkeley: University of California Press, 1964]). See the discussion in Michael Dummett, *Frege: Philosophy of Language*, 2nd edn (Cambridge, Mass.: Harvard University Press, 1981), pp. 358–9.

28. Gottlob Frege, *Die Grundlagen der Arithmetik* (Breslau: Verlag von Wilhelm Koebner, 1884), § 62; see p. x (ET by J. L. Austin, *The Foundations of Arithmetic*, 2nd edn [Oxford: Blackwell, 1953]). See Dummett, *Frege: Philosophy of Language*, pp. 192–6.

mean. A successful theory will, moreover, have to avoid begging its own question. In explaining how we are able to understand what words mean, a non-question-begging theory of interpretation must forgo any appeal to information or evidence which itself depends on knowing the meaning of the words under interpretation. In particular, a plausible theory of how we figure out what language means cannot presume knowledge on the part of the interpreter of the propositional attitudes – the beliefs, desires, intentions, and so forth – of the speakers of the language he is trying to interpret. Or, in a different philosophical idiom, a plausible interpretation theory cannot assume that the interpreter knows the speaker's way of being in the world, or final horizon, or inner experience.

The reason for this is not far to seek, though regularly overlooked in theories of interpretation: knowing what a speaker's propositional attitudes are depends on knowing what her words mean. All the propositional attitudes are tied to belief (what a person wants, hopes for, and so forth depends on what she believes), and knowing what a person believes depends on knowing the meaning of the sentences she holds true. A noncircular theory of interpretation will thus systematically discourage efforts to justify claims about what a speaker means by her words which depend on appeals to her beliefs and intentions. Correlatively, such a theory will view meaning, belief, and intention as bound up with one another in such a way that they can only be attributed to speakers, and explicated conceptually, as a package; none can be the basis for the attribution and explication of the others.[29]

These considerations may be summed up by saying that a successful theory of interpretation (or a theory of meaning, though for Davidson these are not exactly the same thing) must be able to account for the possibility of radical interpretation. The problematic of radical interpretation is most obvious if we imagine ourselves in the position of the field linguist, who comes upon a group of people making sounds which seem to be words or sentences in a language, but one with which the linguist is wholly unfamiliar. How will the linguist, innocent of the meaning of native utterances and so of the contents of native beliefs, manage to assign correct interpretations to the natives' words and sentences?

This, Davidson suggests, is the problem of interpretation at its most

29. On requirements of a non-question-begging theory of interpretation, see *Inquiries*, pp. xiii, 127, 134, 215; "The Structure and Content of Truth," *The Journal of Philosophy* 87/6 (1990), pp. 315–16.

basic, where questions are least likely to be begged. It is thus an especially useful test for an informative, non-circular theory of interpretation. Upon solving this problem turns not only the possibility of interpreting native discourse, but of recognizing the natives as speakers of a language; noises or inscriptions which we can make no headway in interpreting – which is to say, in practice, of translating into our own tongue – we will eventually have to categorize as something other than utterances in a language, and the noisemakers as something other than speakers of a language. While the task of translating a previously unknown language poses most sharply the problem a theory of interpretation has to solve, all interpretation involves a radical element. We may suppose that expressions in our own language tend to have the same meaning each time they are used by us and our fellow speakers, but it remains to account for this assumption – as, indeed, for the assumption that another person is speaking the same language as we.[30]

Confronted with this radical problem, Davidson argues, the interpreter's only recourse is to get at meaning, and with it belief, by way of truth. Interpretation will have to hold for truth while testing for meaning. The interpreter, that is, will have to proceed by assigning meanings to native utterances which allow him to maximize the ascription of truth to those same utterances. If we find ourselves interpreting native speakers in such a way that we have to regard them as in the main mistaken – if, that is, we have to take the beliefs our interpretation of their speech leads us to attribute to them as massively false – then the only plausible course is to locate the problem in the meanings we assign to their utterances, rather than in the truth of their beliefs. Talk of "maximizing" agreement among language users somewhat oversimplifies the matter, since quantity is not the only factor which affects agreement in belief. The firmness or intensity of conviction with which beliefs are held is another, as is the relative centrality or primacy of a belief within the total belief system of a speaker. It might be better, Davidson suggests, to talk of "optimizing" agreement, of interpreting in such a way as to find the "best fit" between the meanings and beliefs we attribute to speakers and the beliefs we ourselves hold true.[31]

---

30. On this see "Radical Interpretation," *Inquiries*, p. 125. The problem of radical interpretation, Davidson observes, has considerable affinity with that addressed by Bayesian decision theory; he exploits the connections in his proposed solution of the problem. See *Inquiries*, pp. 144–8, 160–6, and "The Structure and Content of Truth," pp. 316–18, 322–4.

31. "Thought and Talk," *Inquiries*, p. 169; "Radical Interpretation," *Inquiries*, p. 136.

Successful interpretation depends, in a word, on applying the "principle of charity" across the board, that is, to all the actual and possible utterances of a group of speakers, and thus to their language as a whole. The "principle of charity" applies a holistic constraint to interpretation. Its force is to optimize agreement between speakers and interpreters about which sentences are true. The principle requires us to interpret the discourse of others in such a way that, to the fullest extent possible, the sentences we hold true, they hold true as well. The interpreter thus reads her own standards of truth into the discourse of the speaker in the effort to understand him – the only standards, of course, which she has to go on.

The unit across which the principle of charity requires interpreters to maximize agreement is thus the whole natural language of the speakers; a successful theory of interpretation for a particular language must in principle be able to assign a meaning to any sentence uttered in that language, and this means that all sentences possible in the language must fall within the field throughout which agreement needs to be maximized. The assumption that native discourse is for the most part true gives us something germane to go on as we try to figure out what it means, since we know that truth and meaning must be linked (such that, as we have already observed, whether a sentence is true depends at least in part on what it means). "What makes interpretation possible," as Davidson puts the point, "is the fact that we can dismiss a priori the chance of massive error."[32]

What entitles us to rely on the principle of charity is that any disagreement in belief is only possible against the background of extensive agreement in belief.[33] You and I may disagree about whether the Uspensky Sobor is the most beautiful church in Moscow, but in order to do so we have to share innumerable beliefs which locate Moscow, describe its geography, identify the Uspensky Sobor, characterize the features of the church, and so forth. If in our effort to convince one another regarding the aesthetic merits of the Sobor we found ourselves disagreeing about where the church was located, what it looked like, and so forth, we would not come to the conclusion that we disagreed

---

32. "Thought and Talk," *Inquiries*, pp. 168–9. On the "principle of charity," see also *Inquiries*, pp. xvii, 136–7, 152–3, 199–201, and "The Structure and Content of Truth," pp. 318–20; the basic idea is owed to Quine, though Davidson deliberately uses it "in ways that deviate, sometimes substantially, from his" ("Structure and Content," p. 319). On the principle of charity as a "holistic constraint," see, e.g., *Inquiries*, p. 139.
33. See "Radical Interpretation," *Inquiries*, p. 137.

about its beauty, but that we were talking about different things. Eventually, disagreement in belief simply changes the subject under discussion, and thereby ceases to be disagreement; disagreement inevitably becomes mere difference well before it threatens to overwhelm the background of agreement. Applied to the problem of radical interpretation, this means that when interpreters attribute extensive error to speakers, the speakers must simply be talking about something else than the interpreters suppose – in other words, that the interpretation must be incorrect.

Knowing that we have to maximize the ascription of truth to speakers in order to interpret them correctly does not, by itself, enable us to make any headway in understanding their actual utterances. In order to begin assigning meanings to particular native utterances, we will (so the principle of charity suggests) have to have a good grip on two things: when the native thinks she is making a true utterance, and what the truth conditions of the utterance are. For this the publicly observable speech behavior of the natives provides the necessary evidence. Even when we do not understand a speaker's language, we can regularly tell when her utterances are made with assent, and we can also regularly tell what it is about the speaker's environment that, in the specific situations where a particular utterance is made, prompts or causes the assent. The evidence is of course cumulative, and the principle of charity is our guide; if in the experimental process of assigning meanings to native utterances on the basis of the prompted assent of native speakers we find ourselves ascribing extensive falsity to the speakers, we will need to reconsider what we take to signal assent, or (more likely) what we take to prompt or cause it. But in either case the possibilities are limited and the evidence plentiful, so the task cannot be impossible to accomplish.[34]

The thought, then, is that the pattern of a speaker's prompted assents to similar or identical sentences in similar circumstances enables the interpreter, tutored by the principle of charity, to locate the truth conditions of those sentences (or utterances; the problem of what parts of utterances to count as sentences need not detain us here). Coupled with the thought that the meaning of a sentence is, or is adequately given by, its truth conditions, we have a non-circular way of assigning meanings to

---

34. On the evidential role of prompted assent in a non-circular theory of interpretation, see, besides the passages cited in notes 30 and 31 above, "A Coherence Theory of Truth and Knowledge," pp. 315f.

native sentences, and thus contents to native beliefs – we have, in other words, a plausible theory of radical interpretation.[35]

Though it inevitably oversimplifies the matter to a considerable degree, one of Davidson's examples will help here. Suppose we encounter an unfamiliar speech community, one of whose members, Erich (though it takes a while for us to figure out that this is his *name*, and not, say, his favorite food) appears untroubled by our habit of following him around and listening in on his conversations. It is winter, and one of his utterances upon which we quickly fasten is "Es schneit." We observe that he and the rest of those who seem to speak his language make this utterance only when it is snowing on or about them. A pattern appears: although Erich often says "Ist kalt" under the same circumstances that prompt "Es schneit," he sometimes says "Ist kalt" when we leave the cottage on sunny, though frigid, days, and usually says "Es schneit" when he looks out the window when snow is falling, even though he is sweating in front of a roaring fire. We conclude (though the conclusion is open to revision as we attend to more of Erich's talk) that what prompts "Es schneit" is snow, falling.

This enables us to construct a formula of the following type, which states the truth conditions for that sentence: "'Es schneit' is true if and only if it is snowing." This formula gives necessary and sufficient conditions for "Es schneit" to be true, and thus truth conditions unique, in Erich's language, to "Es schneit." It thereby gives us the meaning of "Es schneit," since grasping the conditions under which this sentence, and it alone (in the language under interpretation), is true amounts to understanding what the sentence means. The formula also gives us a translation. As English speakers we are entirely confident of the formula, "'It is snowing' is true if and only if it is snowing," and so we know that any sentence which can rightly be substituted for the English sentence named on the left side of this biconditional formula must mean "It is snowing." Our observation of Erich's prompted assents is what warrants our substitution of "Es schneit" in that position, and so warrants our decision to translate his sentence as "It is snowing," and not, for example, as "It is

---

35. By trading freely on both the idea of maximizing the ascription of *truth* to native utterances and that of maximizing *agreement* with native beliefs, Davidson's deployment of the principle of charity raises, we should note, an obvious problem. Agreement is not truth; speaker and interpreter can clearly agree on false beliefs. One can grant, it might therefore be argued, that interpretation has to maximize agreement between speaker and interpreter, without supposing that what speaker and interpreter agree on is true; the principle of charity may require that meaning be agreement-dependent, but not that it be truth-dependent. For Davidson's reply, see chapter 8, pp. 237–8.

cold." And since we now know not only that Erich thinks this utterance is true, but what his words mean, we know what he believes when he utters them, namely that it is snowing.[36]

As Davidson often observes, the matter is a good deal more complicated than this. The procedure just sketched obviously works well only for occasion sentences (those whose truth conditions are overt but variable features of a world common to speakers and interpreters, such that the assent or dissent of speakers changes with the presence or absence of the features). The less occasional the sentence, the more heavily the interpreter will have to rely on the principle of charity, and the less on prompted assent, in fixing the meaning of the speaker's utterances; this process will also depend on finding native equivalents for the logical constants, identity, and the rest of the apparatus of first-order predicate logic.[37]

We need not pursue these complications further here.[38] For present purposes, it suffices to observe that the truth-dependence of meaning stands out clearly in a non-circular account of how we understand the discourse of others. We can interpret native utterances in a non-circular way if we can correctly locate their truth conditions. The chief test for whether we have done so is whether we can count as true most of the sentences the native holds true. Of course there is also a meaning-dependence of truth: whether a sentence is true depends, in part, on what it

36. For Davidson's deployment of this sort of example, see "Radical Interpretation" and (also in *Inquiries*) "Belief and the Basis of Meaning." The theory of interpretation which recommends the procedure just sketched turns on adapting Tarski's theory of truth as a theory of meaning. Davidson's original argument for this is in "Truth and Meaning" (*Inquiries*, especially pp. 22–4); the strategy recurs in all of his articles on truth and interpretation.

For more on Tarski's theory of truth, especially his formula for perspicuously stating truth conditions (the so-called T-sentences, exemplified here by " 'It is snowing' is true if and only if it is snowing"), see chapter 8.

37. For a summary of these complicating factors, see *Inquiries*, p. 136.

38. One of the criticisms of Davidson's theory of interpretation, made especially by philosophers of language sympathetic to Wittgenstein, turns on the notion that meaning is not truth-dependent, but use-dependent (for one version of this argument, see Charles Taylor, "Theories of Meaning," *Human Agency and Language: Philosophical Papers*, vol. 1 [Cambridge: Cambridge University Press, 1985], pp. 248–92). To the extent that appeals to "use" invoke the purposes, desires, interests, and so forth of speakers in order to interpret their utterances (rather than relying on their publicly observable practices of holding sentences true in specific circumstances), the requirements of radical interpretation, Davidson argues in reply, cannot be met; this sort of appeal to use guarantees that the question will be begged. See chapter 7 for more on this; for a brief but illuminating analysis of the differences between Davidsonian and Wittgensteinian approaches to interpretation, from a philosopher who finds neither convincing, see Michael Dummett, *Origins of Analytical Philosophy* (Cambridge, Mass.: Harvard University Press, 1993), pp. 15–21.

means. This does not contradict, but highlights, the sense in which meaning hangs on truth. What a sentence means depends on its truth conditions, so that whether a sentence is true depends on only two factors: what its truth conditions are (that is, what it means), and whether those conditions are met. Interpretation exploits these connections between meaning and truth by assuming that truth conditions are generally met when speakers take them to be.

If Davidson's view of the way meaning and interpretation hang on truth is roughly right, then a basic assumption about meaning and truth which informs the epistemic dependence thesis in theology must be wrong. It will be impossible, as the different versions of the thesis attempt in their various ways, to hold for meaning while testing for truth. On the contrary: the very effort to construe Christian beliefs as epistemically dependent will largely determine the meaning one assigns to the sentences which express those beliefs.

Our truth commitments determine, on the whole, the meanings we assign to words. The more relevant we think a particular set of beliefs (that is, truth commitments) is to interpreting some discourse – the closer we suppose those beliefs are to this discourse within the total epistemic field – the more clearly and forcefully the beliefs determine the assignment of meaning. The dependence thesis in theology is the view that a certain set beliefs ("universal," "public," "*wissenschaftlich*," or whatever) is not only uniquely relevant to deciding about the truth of Christian beliefs, but has a fixed truth value, at least with respect to Christian beliefs: they can never be rejected for failure of consistency with Christian claims. Far from being unaffected by the dependence theorist's truth commitments, therefore, the interpretation of the Christian "datum discourse" or the contents ascribed to the Christian religious consciousness (insofar as these may be ascertained by interpreting the sentences Christians utter) will be determined by those beliefs most of all.

This may seem overstated. While we cannot hold for meaning while testing for truth on the whole, we can certainly do so in particular cases; otherwise we could understand only those sentences whose truth value we had already decided, which is absurd. One of the benefits of knowing a language is the capacity to grasp the meaning of novel sentences even if we do not know whether they are true, since we can grasp the meanings of the words even though they have not appeared in that particular sentence before. We can then perform various operations (like scientific experiments) to try to figure out whether they are true. It therefore seems quite plausible to view Christian beliefs as among those (a distinct minority, to be sure) whose truth value has not been decided, and to try to decide it by reference to other beliefs. Recognizing the truth-dependence of meaning thus seems entirely consistent with the dependence thesis.

The problem, however, is that theological dependence theorists aim to justify Christian beliefs, not to falsify them. The dependence thesis is a commitment not only to deciding about the truth of Christian beliefs by appeal to standards which lie outside the border it draws around those beliefs, but also to holding Christian beliefs true by those standards (albeit, in some cases, tentatively and provisionally). This combination of commitments creates enormous pressure for revisionist interpretations of Christian beliefs; it is in the nature of the case, and not by accident, that epistemic dependence as a view of justification in theology tends to go together with revisionism about the meaning of Christian claims. But the dependence thesis not only prompts revisionist interpretations, it systematically increases the likelihood that these interpretations will be implausible.

While we surely can test the truth of sentences of whose meaning we are already confident, our right to be confident in the meaning we have assigned to those sentences depends on our willingness to find them false. This is not simply a gesture toward open-mindedness, but a systemic requirement imposed by a non-circular theory of meaning. Such an account bids us to maximize agreement with speakers of the discourse we are interpreting about which of their sentences are true. But sometimes we will have to count others mistaken – regard as false sentences they hold true – precisely in order to increase agreement with them on the whole, and so best understand them.[39] That is: we will sometimes find ourselves confronted with a choice between ascribing implausible or unlikely meanings to sentences people hold true, and regarding those sentences and beliefs as false. If meaning is truth-dependent, unlikely interpretations of particular sentences will be just those which tend to increase falsity on the whole. This happens if, in order to hold a particular sentence true, we attribute to its words meanings which, when those same words are used in a number of further sentences held true in other contexts, require us to hold the further sentences false.

39. In Davidson's formulation: "The best we can do is cope with error holistically, that is, we interpret so as to make an agent as intelligible as possible, given his actions, his utterances and his place in the world. About some things we will find him wrong, as the necessary cost of finding him elsewhere right" ("A Coherence Theory of Truth and Knowledge," p. 318).

We may try sometimes to avoid this problem by assigning to a particular word or phrase a sense quite different from, or more nearly opposed to, that which it has in the other sentences we hold true, but this only brings out the unlikelihood of the interpretation of the troublesome term. Rather than resorting to strained and unlikely assignments of meaning, a viable interpretive procedure will take the more efficient course, and count false those sentences which could only be saved by such resort.

The dependence thesis, however, is structured in such a way as to preclude this interpretive efficiency. The truth commitments by which dependence theorists test Christian beliefs naturally have a considerable effect on the interpretation of those beliefs. Add their determination not simply to assess, but to hold true, Christian beliefs by the standard of these commitments, and the interpretive effect of the commitments becomes overwhelming. Normally the natural language in which beliefs are stated serves on the whole as a check against implausible interpretation. But here the check cannot do its work, since its force is precisely to allow that the most plausible interpretation may be one which, by the dependence theorist's standards of truth, makes the beliefs in question come out false. (The assumption that the meaning of sentences and beliefs can be fixed on the whole without deciding about their truth helps keep this from being noticed.) The regular result is the assignment of meanings to Christian claims which are so extended that interpretive plausibility and efficiency would be better served simply by taking the claims as false. We will pursue some theological applications of this important point in chapter 5.

Hermeneutics

Recent theological discussions of the meaning, interpretation, and truth of Christian discourse regularly draw upon figures in the hermeneutical tradition, especially Paul Ricoeur and, to a lesser extent, Hans-Georg Gadamer.[40] There is no room here to look at the views of these two writers in detail. I ought at least briefly to indicate, though, why their approaches to meaning and interpretation seem to me less compelling, and to that extent less theologically pertinent, than those analyzed in this chapter.[41]

40. For sustained theological engagements with Ricoeur, see Kevin Vanhoozer, *Biblical Narrative in the Philosophy of Paul Ricoeur* (Cambridge: Cambridge University Press, 1990) and James Fodor, *Christian Hermeneutics: Paul Ricoeur and the Refiguring of Theology* (Oxford: Oxford University Press, 1995).
41. For detailed criticisms, both philosophical and theological, of Ricoeur in particular, see Nicholas Wolterstorff, *Divine Discourse: Philosophical Reflections on the Claim that God Speaks*

Philosophers of language like Quine, Davidson, and Dummett suppose that questions about meaning and interpretation are philosophically central and have wide purchase. In this they agree with the hermeneutical tradition, against those analytic philosophers who regard meaning as trivial and assume that philosophical questions (especially metaphysical ones) can safely be addressed without attending to matters of meaning.[42] These meaning-oriented philosophers of language seek a theory which will explain what it is for words to have the meaning they do, and, closely connected to that, a theory which will explain what we have to know in order to interpret or understand words, and their speakers, correctly. Whatever else it might try to do, a hermeneutical theory of the sort sought by philosophers like Gadamer and Ricoeur will presumably offer answers on both counts.

At just this point, though, the recommendations of hermeneutical theorists tend to be a bit elusive. For Gadamer interpretation takes place through a fusion of the interpreter's "horizon" – his beliefs, attitudes, prejudices, and so forth – with that of the author or speaker; for Ricoeur through a grasp of the "world" or "way of being in the world" disclosed or referred to by a text.[43] Each philosopher offers a complex description of the process or event of interpretation so conceived, tied to extensive discussions of sense, reference, truth, and kindred notions. How, though, does either of these views of interpretation actually account for our ability to figure out what a speaker's words mean (or, if this formulation seems to prejudice the issue in favor of authorial intention, to figure out the meaning of whatever words we may come across)? Engaged with a wide range of issues and often suggestive, these discussions nonetheless leave one unsure how to cope with the situation of radical interpretation. They tell us little about what it is that English speakers would have to know in order to grasp that "Es schneit" means "It is snowing," if they did not already know German and had to write their own grammar and lexicon.

What tends to be missing is any clear connection between the large-scale descriptions of the interpretive process offered by hermeneutical

(Cambridge: Cambridge University Press, 1995) especially pp. 130–52, 171–3. Wolterstorff's chief worries are a bit different from my own.

42. For an appreciation of Gadamer from an analytic point of view, see John McDowell, *Mind and World* (Cambridge, Mass.: Harvard University Press, 1994), pp. 115–19, 184–6.

43. In Ricoeur's formulation: "What has to be understood is . . . a possible world . . . the world-propositions opened up by the reference of the text. To understand a text is to follow its movement from sense to reference: from what it says to what it talks about." *Interpretation Theory: Discourse and the Surplus of Meaning* (Fort Worth: Texas Christian University Press, 1976), pp. 87–8.

theorists and the meaning of actual utterances (or inscriptions). Suppose that we could know, in advance of interpreting his utterances, that Erich's mode of being in the world is that of infinite resignation in the face of solitude and death, and that "Es schneit" is among the utterances which most passionately embody this mode of being. The possession of such knowledge would still be of little help when it came to figuring out that this utterance means "It's snowing" and not "It's raining" or "It's white." Such a scenario is, moreover, counterfactual. We can acquire this sort of knowledge of other persons only by becoming competent radical interpreters of their utterances and inscriptions. Presumably we cannot grasp a speaker's horizon or way of being without knowing the meaning of his words, any more than we can grasp his intentions and other propositional attitudes in advance of interpreting what he says. A theory of interpretation which has trouble giving an informative and non-question-begging account of an utterance like "Es schneit" is perhaps not the most promising point of departure for a consideration of more complex linguistic phenomena (like metaphor).

At times, particularly when discussing the problem of interpreting a speaker whose beliefs are greatly different from our own, hermeneutical theorists suggest that grasping the horizon or mode of being displayed by a speaker or text and figuring out what the words of each mean are not in fact so closely tied as their general picture of interpretation would lead one to suppose. It sometimes seems as though knowing what a speaker's words mean is one thing, a manageable technical project, but "understanding" the speaker requires a different and more difficult undertaking, namely grasping the speaker's horizon or the possible world disclosed by the text. The hard part, though, is figuring out what the words mean. If we know that, we know what it would be for the sentences in which they appear to be true, and this just is, presumably, to grasp the possible (and perhaps actual) world the sentences are about.

To be sure, the proposals of hermeneutical theorists could be developed in ways which made them more informative. Gadamer's idea of an interpretive fusion of horizons might be taken as a gesture at the principle of charity; Ricoeur's idea that understanding a text involves grasping the world to which it refers might be taken as a suggestion to interpret sentences by trying to locate their publicly available truth conditions. In either case, an explicit tie to a clear concept of truth would offer hope of a useful explanation of meaning and interpretation. Whether overtures of this kind would be entirely acceptable to these writers is perhaps open to doubt. If they were, it would indicate that they do not so much desire an alternative to analytic views of the kind we have been considering, as suggest implicitly a truth-dependent account of meaning such as the analytic tradition has sought to make explicit.[44]

Dummett's anti-realism

Michael Dummett's theory of meaning conceives meaning, truth, belief and their interrelations in ways quite different from the Davidsonian account just outlined. Like Davidson, Dummett basically agrees with Frege that the meaning of a sentence is given by its truth conditions, and that to understand a sentence is to grasp its truth conditions. Again like Davidson, he agrees with Wittgenstein that meaning is use, in at least one important sense which can be assigned to that multivalent dictum: meaning is public, in that "the knowledge in which a speaker's understanding of a sentence consists must be capable of being fully manifested by his linguistic practice."[45] In order to uphold both Frege's point and Wittgenstein's, however, we must on Dummett's account come up with a quite different notion of truth than we are likely used to, and with that we must reconceive the way the truth conditions for a sentence give its meaning.

Dummett's argument to this point is quite complex, and there is no room here to give more than a very rough sketch of it.[46] For many sentences in our language, Dummett points out, we lack any way of deciding whether or not they are true. Sometimes this lack is a want of insight or skill on our part (a procedure for justifying the assertion or denial of a sentence is available to us, but we are ignorant of it or inept at carrying it

---

44. By suggesting that Gadamer and Ricoeur miss the salience of truth for meaning, I must, it might be assumed, disagree *a fortiori* with the interpretive outlook of Hans Frei, since Frei criticizes them (and others) for not distinguishing questions of meaning sharply enough from those of truth. Unlike some analytic philosophers of language or the hermeneutical theorists, though, Frei offers no general theory of interpretation, and so no general claims about the connections between truth and meaning. Sometimes Frei does suggest (mistakenly, it seems to me) that probably no such claims can be made plausible, and that in any case Christian theology should have no stake in them. But his chief concern, especially in *The Eclipse of Biblical Narrative* (New Haven: Yale University Press, 1974), is with biblical interpretation, and with the way in which some historically and conceptually particular notions of what it would be for (key parts of) the bible to be true yield implausible interpretations of it. To *that* concern a truth-dependent theory of meaning, as the last section of chapter 5 will argue in detail, offers considerable support.
45. Michael Dummett, "What does the Appeal to Use Do for the Theory of Meaning?" *The Seas of Language* (Oxford: Clarendon Press, 1993), p. 116.
46. For clarification of Dummett's views I am indebted to my colleague Frederick Stoutland, especially the chapter on Dummett in his *Recent Theories of Meaning* (forthcoming).

out), but in many cases there apparently is no procedure available to us by which we could fix the truth value of a sentence. Statements about the remote future are obvious cases ("A city will some day be built here") as are statements about the past where we have no way to obtain evidence which would decide their truth or falsity ("Socrates talked at one," as opposed, say, to "Socrates drank hemlock"). An adequate theory of meaning must account for a speaker's ability to understand just such problematic sentences. It must do so (here Dummett and Davidson agree) without appealing to any occult knowledge on the speaker's part. A speaker's linguistic and non-linguistic practice together must fully display the speaker's ability to grasp the truth conditions, and thereby the meaning, of the sentences he speaks; otherwise we violate the (suitably interpreted) principle that meaning is use.[47]

Whatever we make of truth, we are likely to assume that all declarative sentences are either true or false. We tend to assume, in other words, that the law of excluded middle applies to all such sentences, and so that they all have a truth value (Dummett calls this application of the law of excluded middle "bivalence").[48] This assumption about truth, however, makes it impossible to give an account of meaning in terms of truth conditions for the sort of sentences we have been considering – those whose truth value we cannot decide – without invoking occult knowledge.

To grasp the meaning of a sentence is to grasp its truth conditions. If bivalence holds, then undecidable sentences will be determinately true or false. But in that case we would have to attribute to speakers who understood such sentences a grasp of the truth conditions for the sentences, even though the speakers could never recognize whether those conditions were actually met. This is an ability which it is not clear that any speaker could have, since it requires him to grasp definite truth conditions for a sentence even though there is nothing he can actually recognize as establishing its truth or falsity. It is, moreover, an ability which the public practices of speakers cannot give us any warrant to attribute to

---

47. See "Use for the Theory of Meaning," p. 113.
48. Dummett distinguishes four interpretations of the law of excluded middle, of which bivalence is only one. In particular, he discriminates between bivalence, which he rejects, and *tertium non datur* – the principle that there are no truth values for an indicative sentence to have other than "true" and "false" (or, if one admits many-valued logics, that the others are not on a semantic par with these), so that if a sentence has one, its negation must have the other. The latter he accepts. See Dummett's "Preface" to his *Truth and Other Enigmas* (Cambridge, Mass.: Harvard University Press, 1978), pp. xviii–xix, xxiii, and *The Logical Basis of Metaphysics* (Cambridge, Mass.: Harvard University Press, 1991), pp. 9–10, 74–81.

them, since it would be an ability which bore no relation to their publicly manifest capacity to assent to or dissent from sentences precisely when they can recognize that conditions obtain which entitle them to do so.

What we *can* attribute to speakers on the basis of their public practices is the ability to recognize when conditions obtain which justify them in asserting and in denying particular sentences, and the ability to recognize when no conditions obtain which justify them in either asserting or denying particular sentences. So: if we want to maintain that meaning is public and account for it in terms of truth conditions, we have to give up the notion that sentences can have truth conditions unrecognizable by us, and thereby incapable of being grasped in a way which our public practices of assertion, denial, and indecision could display. With that we have to give up the notion that sentences can be determinately true or false independently of our capacity to recognize them as such, that is, independently of our justified assertion or denial of them. We have to give up, in other words, on realism about truth.[49]

For a sentence to be true, therefore, just is for us to be justified in asserting it, in the strongest sense: to have "conclusively established" it as true. For a sentence to be false just is for us to be justified in this strong sense in denying it. Many sentences we can neither verify nor falsify, so these must be regarded as having no truth value. Undecidables are not, Dummett proposes, thereby meaningless (indeed what launches his theory is the effort to comprehend how we could grasp their meaning); we can conceive a justification or verification procedure for them, even if it is not one we could ever actually carry out, and this conception constitutes that grasp of their truth conditions in which our understanding of them consists.[50]

Dummett calls this view of meaning and truth "anti-realism," in order to highlight its abandonment of the principle which he takes to be the

---

49. Realism has to go, that is, insofar as "we may ... characterize realism concerning a given class of statements as the assumption that each statement of that class is determinately either true or false." "What is a Theory of Meaning? (II)," *The Seas of Language*, p. 56.

50. "On this account, an understanding of a statement consists in a capacity to recognize whatever is counted as verifying it, i.e., as conclusively establishing it as true. It is not necessary that we should have any means of deciding the truth or falsity of the statement, only that we be capable of recognizing when its truth has been established. The advantage of this conception is that the condition for a statement's being verified, unlike the condition for its truth under the assumption of bivalence, is one which we must be credited with the capacity for effectively recognizing when it obtains; hence there is no difficulty in stating what an implicit knowledge of such a condition consists in – once again, it is directly displayed by our linguistic practice." "What is a Theory of Meaning? (II)," pp. 70–1.

chief mark of any realist account of these issues, namely bivalence about truth.[51] In equating truth for sentences with recognizable conditions which would justify us in asserting them, Dummett takes sides in one important way with coherentist and pragmatist conceptions of truth, though his basic concern is rather different than theirs: they reject realism because they worry that realists make truth inaccessible to us; Dummett worries that a realist conception of truth makes *meaning* inaccessible to us. As Dummett is well aware, anti-realism has deep and perhaps troubling consequences; it implies that reality itself is indeterminate beyond the limits of our capacity to decide which sentences are true.[52] To these issues we will return in more detail in chapter 8.

For the moment the chief point is that one need not agree with Davidson about the relations between meaning, truth, and belief in order to find the assumptions of the theological dependence theory about these issues unpersuasive. Dummett's account is fundamentally different from Davidson's, in particular on the matter of anti-realism, which Davidson consistently rejects (on this, as the ensuing argument will show, I agree with Davidson). But for Dummett, perhaps even more clearly than for Davidson, we cannot figure out what sentences mean except in the process of deciding about their truth value (or, as the case may be, their lack of it) – except, that is, by grasping the conditions under which we could recognize that we were justified in asserting them.

Introducing the notion of anti-realism also helps point up a different sort of difficulty regularly faced by the dependence thesis. Especially when the thesis goes universalist, its advocates sometimes appear unsure whether they want to be realists or anti-realists. Ogden and Pannenberg, for example, both sometimes seem to equate "credible" and "true"; only those statements may be regarded as "universally true" which are universally credible, that is, which meet justificatory standards which everybody holds (or perhaps ought to hold). This suggests commitment to an

51. Dummett praises the "middle" Wittgenstein for clearly grasping this point about what notion of truth can do duty in the theory of meaning: "It is what is regarded as the justification of an assertion that constitutes the sense of the assertion" (Wittgenstein, *Philosophical Grammar*, I § 40, cited in "Use for the Theory of Meaning," p. 111; see *The Logical Basis of Metaphysics*, p. 314). The "later" Wittgenstein, by contrast, draws fire for giving up on this earlier insight.

52. "It is hard to swallow such a conclusion," Dummett observes of his own anti-realism, "because it has profound metaphysical repercussions: it means that we cannot operate, in general, with a picture of our language as bearing a sense that enables us to talk about a determinate, objective reality which renders what we say determinately true or false independently of whether we have the means to recognize its truth or falsity" ("Use for the Theory of Meaning," p. 116).

anti-realist account of truth in the sense just defined: for beliefs to be true just is for us to be able to recognize that their truth conditions obtain, and so be fully justified in believing them. But dependence theorists also tend to juxtapose such suggestions with the observation that Christian faith and theology involve commitment to an "understanding of the way things ultimately are" for which truth is claimed.[53] This suggests a realist notion of truth according to which "the way things are" makes every indicative sentence determinately true or false.

Now, if one wants to be a realist, then the need for Christian beliefs to be justified by appeal to universally shared criteria cannot be derived from the observation that they are supposed to be true for everybody, since on realist accounts (a) every indicative sentence, and so every belief, is determinately true or false regardless of whether anyone is justified in believing it, and (b) a true belief is therefore true for everybody, even those who do not hold it (or even entertain it). A realist might argue, of course, that only those beliefs should be *held* true which meet the sort of criteria Ogden and Pannenberg propose, but on realist grounds the question would remain why only those beliefs could *be* true which were held true on universal grounds. If by contrast one wants to be an anti-realist, then one needs to explain why beliefs whose truth consists in meeting our current justificatory standards, even granted that those standards are universally accepted, should be taken to bear on "the way things ultimately are."

The argument of this chapter suggests a certain progression in the difficulties faced by modern theological accounts of epistemic justification. Beliefs, distinctively Christian or otherwise, cannot be justified by appeal to inner experiences; beliefs cannot, indeed, be justified except by appeal to other beliefs; and we cannot even figure out what sentences mean, and therefore what the contents of beliefs are, without relying on the concept of truth and the processes by which we decide whether sentences are true (though dispute arises concerning the form this reliance should take). Pointing up the problems faced by modern theological accounts of epistemic justification does not, of course, accomplish anything positive, but only raises anew the question: how, without recourse to the interiority, foundationalist, or dependence thesis, *are* we going to account for the justification of Christian beliefs?

---

53. The phrase is Ogden's, from *On Theology* (San Francisco: Harper, 1986), p. 11.

5

The epistemic primacy of belief in the Trinity

An investigation of its practices has suggested that the church can endure as a coherent community only if it continually tests other beliefs for truth or falsity by seeing whether they are consistent with its trinitarian identification of God. Should this distinctive epistemic procedure be incoherent or otherwise unreasonable, then what follows is presumably not the continuing embrace of irrational practices, but their abandonment, and so a basic change in communal identity. We therefore need to determine whether the church has the epistemic right to regard its own most central beliefs as the primary criteria of truth, and if so, what confers this right. This requires a closer look at the contents of the church's trinitarian nexus of belief.

Jesus' universal primacy

Jesus undertakes his journey from Bethlehem to Golgotha, so the church believes, for the life of the world (cf. Jn. 6:51). The gift of life which Jesus undertakes to give the world is not, it seems, an event or state of affairs which comes to pass apart from or in addition to his acceptance and enactment of the mission from the Father which leads to the cross. Rather the world's deliverance from death, its redemption and reconciliation to God, coincide with the particular and unrepeatable sequence of actions and events by which the church identifies Jesus. Jesus' death does not simply symbolize or promise the world's deliverance, but actually puts death to death; Jesus' resurrection, ascension, and his gift of the Spirit do not simply symbolize or promise new life from the dead, they bring it about and impart it.[1] This means that what happens on the way

---

1. The language here is in part that of the Orthodox Divine Liturgy, but the thought is not a uniquely Eastern one. Thus Augustine: "The immortal one took on mortality in order that

from Bethlehem to Golgotha and the Emmaus road has universal scope. If Jesus' action and passion are genuinely for the life of *the world*, then their power and significance extends to all creation. And the difference Jesus makes to the rest of reality is not superficial or transitory, but utterly basic; it is the difference between death and life, between non-being and being, for every particular thing.

It thus seems that a garden-variety belief in redemption through Jesus entails belief in Jesus' unrestricted primacy with respect to all created reality. If in virtue of his life, death, and resurrection Jesus is "for the life of the world," he must have what the New Testament calls "primacy in everything" (Col. 1:18). *That* creatures are and *what* they are must depend on Jesus himself – and so on what comes to pass between Bethlehem and the Emmaus road – if he is to be their redeemer. Only one upon whom creatures depend for their existence, qualities, and relations can give them forgiveness and new life – can make them be what they were not and not be what they were. And all creatures must be dependent upon Jesus if any creature is to be redeemed by him. Any creature outside the scope of this dependence might be capable not only of resisting Jesus' bestowal of life in his own case, but of counteracting it in others. Jesus can be the redeemer of the world, it seems, only if he is the one in whom "all things hold together" (Col. 1:17), and through whom "all things came into being" (Jn. 1:3; cf. 1 Cor. 8:6).[2]

All this may seem more than a little paradoxical, since the one on whom this argument supposes that all creation depends is himself a creature, who as such came to be at a particular moment, before which he was not, and who lived in a particular and therefore limited stretch of space and time. This appears to generate wildly incoherent claims. If all creation depends on Jesus in the manner I have described, then what came to be before Jesus was born depended for its existence on Jesus. But Jesus did not yet exist. So what existed before him depended on what did not exist. But surely nothing can depend for its existence on what does not exist, so what existed before Jesus cannot have depended on him. The New Testament claim that in the human being Jesus "all things hold together"

---

he might die for us, and by his death put to death our death." Sermo 23A, 3, *CCL*, vol. XLI, p. 322.

2. All this, it should be stressed, is said in the New Testament of the particular human being Jesus. The one through whom "all things came into being" in Jn. 1:3 is the Logos, but precisely the Logos who became flesh (Jn. 1:14); the one in whom "all things hold together" in Col. 1:17 is the same as "the firstborn from the dead" (1:18), who "has made peace through the blood of his cross" (1:20); the one Lord "through whom are all things" in 1 Cor. 8:6 is the same as the human being who died for those who now eat in the temples of Corinthian idols (see 8:11). See also note 8 below.

and through him "all things came into being" seems thoroughly self-contradictory.

Col. 1, which has helped to organize these last reflections, handles this problem by recourse to the Christian community's trinitarian identification of God, and in particular by characterizing Jesus as "the icon (εἰκών) of the unseen God" (1:15). In this context the Father is clearly the "unseen God" of whom Jesus is the "icon" or image. To characterize Jesus as the Father's image suggests that his human visibility depicts the Father in the world, in virtue of a resemblance or likeness to the one whose image he is. While unseen in himself, the Father enables the world to see him in another, or to see him by seeing this other. As Paul puts the point, the face of Jesus Christ is the very image of God (cf. II Cor. 4:6,4). And Jesus' human face is not a partial or transitory, and therefore perfectible or replaceable, image of the Father; rather, in the expressive phrase of Heb., Jesus "bears the exact imprint of God's very being" (1:3). Without prejudice to his full humanity, so these texts propose, this human being completely shares the attributes of the God whom he calls "the Father"; if he is the Father's perfect image, then "in him all the fullness of God was pleased to dwell" (Col. 1:19; cf. 2:9 for Θεότητος).[3]

The New Testament's characterization of Jesus as the image of the unseen God conceptualizes, we could say, the incarnational logical structure of the narratives which identify him. These narratives attribute the actions and passions of this human being to God (such as dying on the cross), and the actions of God to this human being (such as forgiving sins). Statements which conform to this logical pattern imply that the one who dies on the cross and the one who forgives the paralytic's sins – and in whom all things hold together – are the same, in the strict sense: they must, if such statements are true, be numerically identical. By having this implication, these statements give rise to the traditional Christian doctrine of incarnation, insofar as this doctrine is concerned (perhaps chiefly concerned) to assert explicitly that "our Lord Jesus Christ" is "one and the same (ἕνα καὶ τον αὐτὸν) . . . the same one perfect in divinity and the same one perfect in humanity."[4]

3. For an analysis of the extensive modern exegetical debate on this passage from Col., see Pierre Benoit, "L'hymne christologique de Col. 1, 15–20," Exégèse et théologie, vol. IV (Paris: Cerf, 1982), pp. 159–203. Alois Grillmeier charts the role of the passage in the christological debates of the ancient church in Jesus Christus im Glauben der Kirche, vol. I, 2nd edn (Freiburg: Herder, 1982), pp. 102–21. For a theological reflection see Hans Urs von Balthasar, Theodramatik II/2 (Einsiedeln: Johannes Verlag, 1978), pp. 229–38 (ET, pp. 250–9).

4. DS 301 (the definition of Chalcedon). Chalcedon's repeated insistence on the logical point that the one who is perfect (that is, complete) ἐν ἀνθρωπότητι is numerically the

In the prologue to John's Gospel the church has generally found the chief paradigm for this teaching. Jesus is there described as the Word of God become our flesh. That is: the Word "expresses the total reality of the Father" (to recall a phrase of Thomas Aquinas), and the human being Jesus is himself this Word, incarnate; therefore Jesus himself expresses the total reality of – is the perfect image of – the Father.[5] Col. 1, we can see, reverses the subject–predicate relation of the Johannine paradigm. Whereas John takes the Logos as subject and ascribes "flesh" to him, Col. takes the crucified human being Jesus as subject and ascribes "the fullness of God" to him. These two paradigms jointly display the logical pattern which governs the developed doctrine of incarnation, and is clearly at work in the claim that in the creature Jesus, all things hold together: whatever is true of the human being Jesus of Nazareth is true of God (John) and whatever is true of God is true of the human being Jesus of Nazareth (Col.).[6]

For present purposes, the crucial outcome of these reflections on Jesus as the icon of the Father is that he shares fully in the Father's creative power. Only if this human being fully possesses the Father's divine capacity to give being in every respect is it true to say that in him, "all things hold together." But because the capacity to create is shared by the Father and Jesus (and also of course by the Spirit, about whom more in a moment), the actual work of creation, of making all things and making everything hold together, will also be shared by them. The work, like the capacity, will however be shared in a certain order. It will originate with the Father, who is the source, himself unoriginate, of the Son and the

same – τὸν αὐτὸν – as the one who is complete ἐν Θεότητι, gives the rule, as it were, for its subsequent use of the notions of person, hypostasis, and nature (see DS 302). A detailed discussion of Chalcedon's doctrine is beyond the scope of this book, but we may observe that the definition's main concern is not to make an arcane metaphysical point, but to make explicit a pattern for uttering true sentences about Jesus Christ. It thereby addresses a matter of basic Christian concern: worship of Jesus presumes that sentences uttered according to this pattern are true, otherwise such worship would be idolatry.

5. See chapter 1, note 2. This suggests that in describing Jesus as the perfect image of the Father we have located for at least one of the divine persons a feature of the sort for which the liturgy suggests we look: a characteristic not only unique to him, but non-contingent, and therefore constitutive (at least in part) of his identity. On this see chapter 9, pp. 269–71.

6. The medievals developed in considerable detail the use of logical devices to articulate Chalcedon's doctrine (see Marshall, *Christology in Conflict*, chapter 5), but this procedure stems from the sometimes self-conscious preoccupation of ancient Christian theology with what can and cannot be *said* christologically. See, for example, Cyril of Alexandria's 4th anathema against Nestorius: "Whoever allocates the terms contained in the gospels and apostolic writings and applied to Christ . . . to two persons or hypostases and attaches some to the man considered separately from the Word of God, some as divine to the Word of God the Father alone, shall be anathema." Lionel R. Wickham, ed. and trans., *Cyril of Alexandria: Select Letters* (Oxford: Clarendon Press, 1983), p. 30; for applications of this rule see Cyril's *Quod unus sit Christus, Patrologiae Cursus Completus, series graeca* (=PG), ed. J. P. Migne (Paris: 1857–66), vol. LXXV, 1289B–1293A; 1327B–1329D.

Spirit, and it will be received and accepted by the Son and by the Spirit. The Father and the Son will each therefore have their own distinct role in the one work of creation, as of redemption, though the roles will be inseparable.[7]

The work of the Trinity in making all things hold together in the one who is the Father's image has two aspects with particular epistemic significance. Col. 1 expresses these by saying "all things have been created (a) through him (δι' αὐτοῦ) and (b) for him (εἰς αὐτὸν)" (1:16).

Saying (a) that the Father creates through Jesus suggests that as the Father eternally wills to create a temporal world, his own Word in the flesh accepts this intention and shares in its enactment – or, if it helps put down the specter of incoherence which led us to go incarnational as well as trinitarian in thinking about creation, his own Word who is to become flesh (the traditional *Verbum incarnandum*).[8] He is himself, with the Father, the agent of creation, upon whom all creation entirely depends. More than that: to say that the Father creates through Jesus suggests that when the Father wills to create the world, he sees and knows it – indeed sees and knows all possible worlds – in and through his Word in the flesh. The Word in the flesh is, to use the traditional term, the "exemplar" for the Father of all things, real and possible. That the Father sees all things in the enfleshed Word does not mean that Jesus himself is all things, but rather that all things have their reality and particular character in virtue of their relation and ordering to him.

The complementary phrase from Col. 1 brings this out: (b) "all things have been created *for* him." As he wills to create the world, the Father

---

7. On this see the discussion in chapter 9, pp. 251–8.

8. It seems, however, to make no substantive difference whether one speaks of the Word incarnate (*Verbum incarnatum*) or the Word "to be incarnate" (*Verbum incarnandum*), since from God's point of view – which is the one that counts in the present case – the Word is *always* incarnate. Like divine acts generally, the Father's sending of the Son into human flesh, the Son's acceptance of this mission, and the Spirit's creation of the humanity of Mary's first child by uniting that humanity to the eternal Son – everything which makes up the incarnation from God's side – is always actual in and for God. The created terms of this act of incarnation – the humanity of Jesus and its union with the Word – are temporal; they come to be at a particular time. One therefore need not resort to talk of the *Verbum incarnandum* for fear of paradoxical or incoherent consequences which might follow from speaking of creation through the *Verbum incarnatum*; for the creating God the two come to the same thing. On this see, e.g., Thomas Aquinas on the missions of the divine persons: "Divine action (*operatio*) can be considered in two ways: either from the side of the agent, with respect to whom it is eternal, or from the side of the effect of the action, with respect to which it can be temporal. But God's action is not a medium between himself and his effect, rather his action is in him and is his entire substance; therefore his action is by its very essence eternal, but the effect is temporal." *Scriptum super Sententiis* I, 14, 1, 1, ad 3 (ed. R. P. Mandonnet and M. F. Moos, 4 vols. [Paris: Lethielleux, 1929–47]) (hereafter *In Sent.*).

orders each thing, and all things together, around his own Word in the flesh; the Father wills a world which fits, in its totality, with Jesus Christ. The fitness is twofold; it embraces both the origin and the destiny, the beginning and the end, of all things. That is: the Father wills a world in which all particular things and their various properties and relations "hold together" in Jesus, and all particular things reach the goal the Father wills only on account of Jesus' cross and resurrection – in the event, despite their own refusal of the goal and consequent captivity to evil, so that their attainment of the final goal is not only creation, but reconciliation and redemption. And the Son in turn glorifies the Father by accepting and enacting the particular role the Father appoints in the creation and redemption of the world the Father wills.[9]

Only by the outpouring of the Spirit, however, will all things actually reach the goal that the Father and the Son, each in his own particular way, establishes for them. That goal, briefly put, is for all things to share as fully as each is capable in the infinite beauty, goodness, and truth of the divine being and life, which the Father rejoices eternally to share in its totality with his Son and his Spirit, and which they together rejoice to receive from him. The Father creates a world which expresses, and thereby resembles, him by conforming all things to his incarnate Word – to the one who alone fully expresses his own total reality. The Father creates a world which not only resembles him, but radically desires him and succeeds in attaining him, because he makes that world by his Spirit.

The Spirit's distinctive role in the triune God's act of making "all things hold together" is perhaps clearest with regard to the destiny of creatures. It belongs chiefly to the Spirit to give all things their proper share in the divine life. Let loose on "all flesh" (Acts 2:17) at Pentecost by the risen and exalted Christ (cf. Acts 2:33), the Spirit enlivens and moves

---

9. On this see, e.g., Barth's treatment of creation as a work of the triune God in *Kirchliche Dogmatik* III/1 (Zurich: Evangelischer Verlag, 1932–67 [for the complete work]): "In view of this one, his Son, who would become a human being and the bearer of human sin, God loved humanity from eternity, before he created it, and with humanity the whole world – in and in spite of its complete lowliness, non-divinity, and indeed anti-divinity. And he created it precisely because he loved it in his own Son, who stood eternally before his eyes as the one rejected and slain on account of its sin" (pp. 53–4; [ET, pp. 50–1]). The suggestion that the Father envisions the world (indeed any world) through and for the particular human being Jesus of Nazareth raises, to be sure, a host of difficult questions about the relation between creation, sin, and redemption which cannot be treated in detail here. Col., at any rate, is quite clear about the basic claim which raises the problems: the one through whom and for whom "all things have been created," and in whom "all things hold together" (1:16, 17), is the crucified Jesus, viz., the very same one (αὐτός) "through whom [God] was pleased to reconcile all things to himself, making peace through the blood of his cross" (1:20).

every creature in the way suitable to it so that, joined to the Father's crucified and risen εἰκών, all may enjoy the good which the Father intends for
them. The Spirit is thus the agent who immediately brings it about that
all things receive the life of God by holding together in Christ, and is in
that sense the principal agent who moves them to their final goal.[10] So
while willing that there be a world at all which holds together through
union with his Word in the flesh belongs chiefly to the Father, and willing
to be the flesh to which all things are ordered belongs chiefly to the Word,
the realization of this will in creatures belongs chiefly to the Spirit.[11]

But the Spirit's distinctive role in creation, like that of the Son, per-
tains to the origin as well as the destiny of all things. Pentecost is the
definitive enactment of the Spirit's mission to join all things to the incarnate Son, but that mission is already anticipated and prepared, so the
church's trinitarian exegesis has regularly proposed, from the beginning
of creation: it is the same Holy Spirit who moves over, and then gives form
to, the formless chaos of Gen. 1:2, who is breathed into the first human
beings to give them life (Gen. 2:7) – and who is then withdrawn from
them on account of sin (cf. Gen. 3:19).[12]

The Spirit, this suggests, is a secondary exemplar, as well as the chief
agent, of the movement of creatures into the life of God. The love of the
Father and the Son for one another seems bound up with the person of
the Spirit in a distinctive way (though precisely how this is so remains a
matter of theological dispute).[13] The Father loves the Son Jesus, in eternity and in time, precisely by giving him the gift of the Spirit – the one
gift equal to and so worthy of both the giver and the receiver – to repose in
and on him; the Son loves the Father precisely by gratefully receiving and
rejoicing in this gift, and (in time) by sharing the gift with the world.
Father and Son are thus eternally united or joined with one another in

---

10. As Aquinas argues: "In [created] things, the motion which is from God seems to be
attributed properly to the Holy Spirit." *Summa Contra Gentiles* IV, 20 (no. 3571).

11. The Word's willing to be flesh is shared with the Father and the Spirit, not, of course,
the being flesh itself. The former can therefore be appropriated to him, while the latter, as
unique or proper to him, cannot.

12. For a sketch of the classic exegesis, see Boris Bobrinskoy, *Le Mystère de la Trinité: Cours de
théologie orthodoxe* (Paris: Cerf, 1986), pp. 21–70.

13. Viz., as to whether the mutual love of the Father and the Son in the Spirit requires, or
even permits, the affirmation that the Spirit eternally proceeds *ex Patre Filioque*. For some
reflection on how traditional East–West disputes about the eternal procession of the Holy
Spirit might embody a disagreement which makes no difference there is any need to
resolve, see Bruce D. Marshall, "Action and Person: Do Palamas and Aquinas Agree about
the Spirit?" *St. Vladimir's Theological Quarterly* 39/4 (1995), pp. 379–408. For a different
argument to a similar conclusion from the Orthodox side, see Serge Bulgakov, *Le Paraclet*,
trans. Constantin Andronikof (Paris: Cerf, 1946), pp. 87–143.

and through the Holy Spirit as a person distinct from both, though the love which unites them, as it springs only from fullness and not from lack, does not have the distinctive note of desire. That creatures succeed in attaining the God who perfectly expresses himself in Jesus Christ results from the gift of this Spirit; that they, made from nothing and so lacking all, cannot help desiring union with this God, whether or not he ever wills to pour out his Spirit so that they may attain him, results from their creation in the image of this same Spirit. Anything which is, however remotely, *like* the Spirit to whom it eternally belongs to unite the Father and the Son in love, will naturally seek its own share in that love.[14]

Epistemic right as christological coherence

What then of deciding about truth? We undertook this exploration of the church's trinitarian identification of God in the hope of answering the question by what right the church takes the beliefs which make up that identification as primary when it decides about truth. What does the content of these beliefs suggest about their epistemic status?

Identification of Jesus as epistemic trump

As he is identified by the church's canonical narrative, the particular person Jesus of Nazareth holds all things together, with regard to both

14. These last remarks are suggested by medieval Western views of the Spirit as not only agent but exemplar of the love of creatures for the Father in the Son. Thus, e.g., Bonaventure, commenting on John 17:22: "In prayer the Lord asks that his disciples be united, not by nature, but by love (*dilectionis*), in conformity to the highest unity. Now the members of Christ are united by mutual love (*amorem*). Therefore in the divine there is an exemplar of this," namely "the third person, who proceeds in the manner of mutual love (*caritatis*)." *In* 1 *Sent.* 10, 1, 3, a (*Opera Selecta* I, p. 160a). With regard to all creation, and linked to the exemplarity of the Son: "All creatures come forth from God by thought and will. But in the divine we have to suppose, prior to the production of creatures, the eternal emanation of the Word, in whom the Father laid out all things that were to be done. For the same reason, therefore, it was necessary that a person emanate in whom he willed and gave all things" (*In* 1 *Sent.* 10, 1, 1, d; *Opera Selecta* I, p. 156a). While not always thought of as having Bonaventure's interest in exemplarism, Aquinas makes a similar argument (though without the suggestion that knowledge and will in God not only explicate, but demonstrate, the trinitarian processions). "Assuming, according to our faith, the procession of the divine persons in a unity of essence (which no argument can be found to prove), the coming forth of the persons, which is perfect, will be the pattern (*rationem*) and cause of the coming forth of creatures ... Thus the coming forth of the creature, insofar as it stems from the generosity of the divine will, may be traced back to one principle, which is as it were the pattern (*quasi ratio*) of this entire generous conferral ... and this is the Holy Spirit," that is, "a person ... in the divine who comes forth in the mode of love" (*In* 1 *Sent.* 10, 1, c; see *In* 1 *Sent.*, prologus: "Just as a waterway is diverted from a river, so is the temporal procession of creatures from the eternal procession of persons."). On these texts see Gilles Emery, *La Trinité créatrice* (Paris: J. Vrin, 1995).

their creation and their redemption. Only that can be whose existence and attributes fit with his; even that in creation which comes to oppose him must be wholly capable of being redeemed by him. This fitness between Jesus and other creatures is an asymmetrical rather than a mutual relationship. The being of other creatures is not simply compatible with his own, but as a whole causally dependent upon him; he is not simply the exemplar but the agent of creation – together, of course, with the Father and the Spirit, each in his own way.

This suggests that when it comes to the epistemic relation between beliefs – when it comes to deciding what is true – the identification of Jesus which relies on the church's canonical narrative must have primacy. When we ascend from the content of the church's central beliefs to the question of their epistemic status, these beliefs seem to require that we accept the following conditional: if identifying descriptions of Jesus in the church's canonical narrative are held true, then the sentences by which we identify and describe other things must, if we are to hold *them* true, at least be compatible with (that is, not contradict) the sentences by which we identify and describe Jesus. This consistency relationship too is asymmetrical; holding true the beliefs by which the church identifies Jesus requires deciding about the truth of other beliefs by seeing whether they are at least consistent with the narrative identification of Jesus, and not deciding about the truth of that narrative identification by seeing whether the beliefs which make it up are consistent with others. The narratives which identify Jesus are epistemic trump; if it comes to conflict between these narratives and any other sentences proposed for belief, the narratives win.

That the meaning of the narratives which identify Jesus implies their epistemic primacy may perhaps most clearly be seen by considering the obvious alternative.[15] It might be held that when conflict with other beliefs arises, then beliefs expressed by holding these narratives true lose the epistemic confrontation.[16] This epistemic decentralization of the narratives which identify Jesus might be maintained as a general principle, or it might be proposed *ad hoc*; the range of sentences with respect to

15. The implication is, more precisely, that if the narratives are held true, they must be held to be epistemically primary, and if they are true, they must be epistemically primary.
16. There might of course be cases where the consistency of this or that belief with the canonical narrative was undecidable by us, at least in our present state of ability to work out the logical relations among our beliefs. This would have no bearing on the epistemic primacy of central Christian beliefs, since the rule which defines this primacy is that conflicts must always be decided in favor of the Christian beliefs, not that we can always tell when there are conflicts.

which the narratives were epistemically subordinate might be wide or narrow. Either way, when beliefs constitutive of the narrative identification of Jesus are held false, it becomes impossible to believe that in Jesus so identified, all things hold together. To regard as false chief elements in the New Testament's identification of Jesus is to hold that there is no one who meets or satisfies that description.[17] And if there is no one who answers to the New Testament's identifying description of Jesus, then all things cannot hold together in him, since nothing can hold together in that which is not. More precisely: to hold false sentences indispensable to the New Testament's identification of Jesus because holding them true would create conflict with some other beliefs is to suppose that states of affairs obtain which are incompatible in some way with Jesus' existence and the attributes unique to him. The status of "that which holds all things together" might or might not be ascribed to such states of affairs; in either case, the canonically identified person Jesus would not be the one who holds all things together. If he is, then the nexus of belief by which the church identifies him cannot lose epistemic conflicts with other beliefs.[18]

So if all things hold together in Jesus, crucified and risen, then at the epistemic level it seems that all true beliefs must hold together in – be logically consistent with – the narratives which identify him, and the triune God with him. He must have "primacy in everything," including decisions about truth.

Unrestricted epistemic primacy

As this line of argument already suggests, the epistemic primacy of the church's narrative identification of Jesus, and with him of the triune God, must be unrestricted; it must range across all possible beliefs. There can be no type or area of belief which is exempt from the requirement that it be at least consistent with the body of beliefs which identify the crucified and risen Jesus. That is: no matter what the contents of our various

---

17. This holds good regardless of how one specifies what these chief elements are. The present claim is *not*, therefore, that everything in the New Testament, or in the Gospels, is equally important to the identification of Jesus. That the narratives of the passion and resurrection are among the principal elements, as here supposed, is relatively non-controversial.

18. The same point can be put in terms of Tarski–Davidson definitions of truth for sentences. If all things in fact hold together in Jesus Christ, then the right branch of any T-sentence whose *left* branch could possibly be true must state truth conditions for the sentence on its left which are compatible with the truth conditions (also as stated by T-sentences) of the narratives which identify Jesus and the triune God.

beliefs, no matter how remote the meaning of many sentences we hold true may be from that of the church's canonical narrative, those sentences must still be tested for truth against the church's most central beliefs. If we hold true the canonical identification of Jesus, then we cannot decide about the truth of our philosophy, our politics, or even our science without seeing whether those beliefs are consistent with, and to that extent subject to correction by, the beliefs which identify Jesus.

This is, once again, required by the content of the beliefs themselves. Suppose we hold beliefs, or at least accept the possibility of beliefs, which do not have to be tested for their consistency with the narrative identification of Jesus. We then build into our epistemic structure the possibility that there are objects, events, or states of affairs, whether past, present, or future, which in one way or another do not fit with Jesus Christ crucified and risen, which are incompatible with his existence and attributes, and so with creation and redemption through him. He will therefore not "have the primacy" with respect to those things; they will not "hold together" in him; rather, on account of them, he will lack the features ascribed to him in the canonical narrative. Thus if *all* things, not just some things, hold together in Jesus, then it seems that all beliefs, not just some beliefs, must fall within the epistemic range of the beliefs which identify him.

Believing the gospel (that is, the narratives which identify Jesus and the triune God), therefore, necessarily commits believers to a comprehensive view of the world centered epistemically on the gospel narrative itself. On such a view there will be no regions of belief and practice which can isolate themselves from the epistemic reach of the gospel. But conversely having such a comprehensive view also means that Christians will not be able to isolate the gospel from the rest of their beliefs, to be held true for whatever restricted purposes, pious or otherwise, Christians may want to use it. On the contrary, believing the gospel at all means that Christians must always venture forth, prepared to engage as best they can all life and reality – to interpret and assess whatever alien or novel beliefs they may encounter – in light of the narratives which identify Jesus.[19]

Taking the narrative identification of Jesus and the Trinity as *primary* in decisions about truth, and that without restriction, is not at all the same thing as taking the beliefs which make up that identification as the *sole* criteria of truth. Nor does the unrestricted epistemic primacy of this

19. On this see chapter 6.

nexus of belief require this sort of implausible epistemic exclusivity. Many, indeed the great majority, of our decisions about what is true cannot be made by appeal to the church's central beliefs alone, but require that we advert to other relevant beliefs. Consistency with the narratives which identify Jesus is the condition *sine qua non* which all other beliefs must meet in order to be true, but this condition will rarely be sufficient to decide about the truth of philosophical, political, natural scientific, or other beliefs, or to settle disputes between competing claims in those areas. Thus the unrestricted epistemic primacy of the church's central beliefs can be stated only negatively: no sentences which are *in*consistent with these beliefs can be true (including any other beliefs – such as logical laws – to which we may advert epistemically), but consistency with the church's central beliefs does not normally guarantee, all by itself, that other beliefs are true.[20]

It is important to observe that one can, at least in principle, fail to maintain the unrestricted epistemic primacy of the gospel narrative without regarding any elements of the narrative as false. Holding aspects of the narrative false is, of course, the clearest way of denying its epistemic primacy. But the fact that one holds the narrative true need not indicate anything more than that one has a consistent system of belief. In any consistent belief structure even those members which have the lowest epistemic status will win conflicts with beliefs which are inconsistent with them. By itself, a consistent belief system says nothing about the epistemic priorities of those who hold the beliefs.

Epistemic primacy is by contrast a normative relationship, such that for any beliefs A and B, A is epistemically primary with respect to B if and only if, should inconsistency arise between A and B, A is held true, and B rejected or modified. When taken as A, the narratives which identify Jesus and the triune God will be epistemically primary without restriction just in case B could be any other possible belief. To ascribe unrestricted epistemic primacy to the gospel narrative is thus not simply to hold, as a matter of fact, no beliefs which are inconsistent with it, but to be prepared to reject any possible belief which is inconsistent with it.

Of course questions about one's epistemic priorities normally come up only when conflict arises among beliefs one is pretty deeply committed to

---

20. This formulation guarantees that unrestricted epistemic primacy belongs *exclusively* to the narrative identification of Jesus; saying that *all* other beliefs must be consistent with these ensures at a stroke both that these are unrestrictedly primary and that the rest are not.

holding true. Faced with conflict, one might attempt to maintain a consistent system of belief which included the chief elements in the church's narrative identification of Jesus, but at the same time reversed the epistemic priorities implied by the narrative. Resolving epistemic conflict in this fashion is the aim of the dependence thesis in theology. Some reflection later in this chapter on the belief that Jesus is risen will suggest how difficult this turns out to be in practice.

Epistemic primacy and highest truth

If we hold true the narratives which identify Jesus and the Trinity, we are committed by the content of those narratives to regarding them as epistemically primary across the board. This implies that a community which has the beliefs expressed by holding these narratives true must regard that body of beliefs as what could be called the *highest* truth – not only the highest available truth, but the highest truth there can be. To say that central Christian beliefs have unrestricted epistemic primacy means that any possible belief which contradicts them must be false. Ascribing genuinely *unrestricted* primacy to these particular beliefs, moreover, preempts the application of the category; no other beliefs will be able to enjoy this logical status. From this it follows that no true belief can contradict the narratives which identify Jesus and the Trinity. If these narratives are believed, therefore, those who hold them true cannot consistently suppose that they could possibly turn out to be false. And this is just what it means to say, at least when it comes to deciding about truth, that a set of beliefs is the highest truth.

That the narratives which identify Jesus and the Trinity have to function, if held true at all, as the highest truth helps give a clearer picture of the idea that epistemic justification is finally christological and (thereby) trinitarian coherence. On this view, the totality of beliefs which human beings might hold can be seen as forming an open field, ordered around a christological and trinitarian center. This center is also, as it were, a peak or summit from which the whole field can be surveyed, though of course its distant parts will be seen less clearly from the center than those close by. Every part of the field is contiguous with every other part, since nothing can belong to the field – can count as a sentence or belief – unless we can assign to it a meaning or content, which links it in manifold ways to the rest of the field. There are thus no regions inaccessible from the rest of the field, no boundaries which the intrepid and interested explorer cannot cross. The distance between sentences and beliefs in this logical space follows upon their difference or similarity of meaning and content; those sentences are closer to one another whose meanings are more alike, more intimately connected.

In this open field of possible sentences or beliefs, no belief which fails of consistency with the christological center can be counted as true. Consistency is of course the most minimal kind of coherence among beliefs, but for just that reason it enables us to define the unlimited epistemic reach of the narratives which identify Jesus in a precise and informative way. Since no two inconsistent sentences can both be true, regardless of what the sentences mean, consistency with these narratives can be required of all sentences as a test of truth, and we have readily available interpretive and inferential procedures for figuring out whether the test has been met in most cases. Ascertaining whether this minimal sort of coherence with the canonical narrative obtains will leave the truth of a great many beliefs undecided, but it will already configure the field of belief in quite definite ways, by eliminating lots of beliefs which lack consistency with those which are centrally Christian.

Coherence of course comes in many varieties. If the minimal kind of coherence among beliefs is consistency, the maximum is identity. A set of sentences are consistent when its members are all possibly true; the sentences in the set are identical, for present purposes, when they all mean the same thing. So we normally assume that "Grass is green" and "Schnee ist weiß," while they mean quite different things, are consistent with one another (they can both be true), and yield compatible beliefs; we normally assume that "Grass is green" and "Gras ist grün" mean the same thing, and that those who hold these sentences true have the same belief. A sentence proposed for belief which meant the same thing as one of the sentences which make up the church's narrative about Jesus and the Trinity would thus have the maximal sort of coherence with those beliefs to which unrestricted epistemic primacy belongs.

If consistency with the beliefs which are epistemically primary is necessary for any other belief to be regarded as true, it would seem that identity (of meaning) with the primary beliefs would have to be regarded as guaranteeing truth. Almost as strong a form of coherence as identity of meaning is necessary implication; logically necessary inference from those beliefs which are epistemically primary would likewise seem to guarantee truth to whatever sentences were inferred. A weaker form of coherence, but still stronger than consistency, is what the medievals called *convenientia*. One belief coheres with another *ex convenientia* when the one makes it particularly fitting or appropriate, but not necessary, to believe the other. So belief in the incarnation, for example, fits in an especially beautiful way with belief in the infinite and selfless goodness of God, but (insofar as the incarnation is also believed to be a contingent act of divine freedom) it is not a necessary implication of God's goodness; the truth of belief in God's goodness does not by itself, therefore, guarantee the truth of belief in God's incarnation.[21]

Instead of continuing this general taxonomy of christological coherence, this and subsequent chapters will attend to particular cases. These general remarks indicate, however, that when it comes to the varieties of christological coherence, scope and decisiveness vary inversely. The more narrow the range of beliefs across which a particular type of coherence with the church's central narrative can function as a relevant test of truth, the more coherence tends to guarantee truth. Conversely, the wider the range across which the test applies, the more it tends simply to permit truth rather than support or guarantee it. Taken by itself, consistency with the christological and trinitarian center does not guarantee truth, but it does, crucially, guarantee falsity to those beliefs which lack it, and that on the widest possible scale. It alone applies as a relevant test to all possible beliefs; its scope is unlimited, and so it alone can serve to define the epistemic primacy of the church's central narrative.

The Father's epistemic role

By what right, then, does the Christian community finally take its narrative identification of Jesus as epistemically primary across the board, and so as the highest truth? The answer proposed by the content of the narratives, read in their full trinitarian depth, is that Jesus is the icon of the Father. This human being perfectly expresses the Father in the world – not all by himself, in isolation from everything else, but by being the one in whom all other things hold together.

When the Father envisions this and any world which he might actually will to create, and when he wills that this world in fact be and be redeemed, he orders it in its totality around his Word in the flesh.[22] It is

---

21. For the scholastics themselves, it was normally states of affairs which were *conveniens*, rather than beliefs about them (the incarnation of God, rather than the belief that God is incarnate). For examples regarding the case at hand, see Aquinas, *Summa theologiae* III, 1, 1; Bonaventure, *In III Sent.* 1, 2, 1 (who speaks of *congruitas* rather than *convenientia*).
22. As Eph. 1 also suggests: the mystery of the Father's will now made known in Christ (v. 9) is his resolve (v. 9b) "before the foundation of the world" (v. 4) to gather up all things in heaven and on earth under Christ as their one head (v. 10). See the comments of Heinrich Schlier, *Der Brief an die Epheser*, 6th edn (Düsseldorf: Patmos Verlag, 1968), pp. 63–6.

entirely natural for the Father to order the world in this way. As the Father's own Word become our flesh, who alone makes the human journey from Bethlehem to Golgotha and the Emmaus road, Jesus is the Father's very image, the one who perfectly expresses the total reality of the Father. What the crucified and risen Jesus expresses naturally includes the Father's mind and will, which he shares not simply by qualitative but by numerical identity.[23] Indeed, as the Father's Word and image incarnate, Jesus Christ is the Father's way of uttering or expressing the very Trinity of divine persons, as well as every creature the Trinity creates.[24] As a result the whole ordering of creation will have to fit with – hold together in relation to – what happens in the crib at Bethlehem, on the cross of Golgotha, and with the disciples on the Emmaus road. Any ordering of creation as a whole which did not fit with the features by which the church identifies this particular person would on that account fail to fit with the Father's own mind and will (since it would be incompatible with what perfectly expresses that mind and will); on any such ordering the Father would, *per impossibile*, be at war with himself.

The upshot of these trinitarian considerations is that we have reached the end of the epistemic road. The Father's knowledge is definitive. This means more than that his knowledge cannot be mistaken. The Father is, together with his Word and Spirit who come forth from him, the source of all things in their entirety, and so of their order and relation. As such the Father (and therefore the triune God) cannot be thought of as waiting, the way we must, for things to exist in order to know them. His very knowledge of them must be productive of their existence and attributes (presuming, of course, that he knows that they exist; their existence itself must, on the same assumption that the triune God is the source of all things, be wholly dependent on his will). The Father is the final measure of all things; nothing can be other than as he orders it, other than it is in his mind and will.[25]

---

23. The enfleshed Word expresses the will of the Father in two different senses: (i) he fully shares that capacity to act which belongs to the Father's divinity, and is communicated to him by eternal generation, and (ii) he freely accepts the Father's eternal but contingent decision that he in fact be enfleshed, viz., that he be Jesus of Nazareth.

24. As Thomas Aquinas suggests: "The whole Trinity is spoken in the Word, and every creature as well" (*Summa theologiae* I, 34, 1, ad 3). See Anselm, *De Processione Spiritus Sancti* 11: "One who sees the Son sees the Holy Spirit, just as he sees the Father." F. S. Schmitt, ed., *S. Anselmi Opera Omnia* (Edinburgh: Thomas Nelson, 1946–61), vol. II, p. 208, 23–4.

25. Or: nothing can be incompatible with the Father's mind and will, since all things are just because he (and with him the Son and Spirit) knows and wills them. This obviously brings to mind conceptual problems about evil which I cannot pursue in detail here. It may simply be observed that the argument here about epistemic primacy coheres with two

Thus if we believe things to be other than they are, and are ordered, in the Father's mind and will (other than the Father believes them to be, we would say, if the Father had beliefs), our belief cannot be true. In the Father's mind and will, all things are ordered to Jesus, crucified and risen. Consequently to hold any belief inconsistent with the narrative identification of Jesus is to believe things to be other than they are in the Father's mind and will. And any such belief must be false. In sum: if the Father expresses his own total reality by ordering all things around the crucified and risen Jesus – if Jesus is the Father's icon – then we will have the epistemic right to hold only those beliefs which are ordered around (at minimum, are consistent with) the beliefs which identify Jesus. Beyond the Father's knowledge no further or more basic justification for the unrestricted primacy of the church's central beliefs could reasonably be sought, or given, since none can be conceived.

That all things hold together in Jesus Christ, crucified and risen, is the work not only of Jesus and the Father, but of the Spirit in whom they are united in love, and whom they pour out upon all flesh. As exemplar the Spirit orients all things to the Father's icon as their chief desire, and as agent the Spirit chiefly brings about the realization of this desire. This suggests that the epistemic habits which define Christian identity are skills only the Spirit can teach us. Ordering all of our beliefs around the gospel of Christ requires a massive reversal of our settled epistemic habits and inclinations, of our usual ways of deciding what is true. Only the Holy Spirit is up to the epistemic effort involved. The Spirit alone can teach us to recognize in the narratively identified Jesus the Father's own icon, and to interpret and assess all of our beliefs accordingly. To the way the Spirit carries out his distinctive epistemic role we will return in detail in a later chapter.

But we already have the outline of an answer to our question about epistemic justification. The Christian community decides what is true by learning from the Spirit to read the narratives which identify Jesus in

traditional solutions to these conceptual problems. (1) To say that nothing can be inconsistent with the Father's knowledge and will is not to say that the Father wills evil, nor that he fails to know it (since in knowing it he would produce it) but that evil is not, strictly speaking, part of creation; it is the privation of goodness and therefore being, and so not what the Father wills, which *eo ipso* comes to *be*. (2) There is a sense in which, given this privative metaphysical status, evil "fits" with creation in that nothing which suffers it will fail to be redeemed; the ordering here claimed of the origin and destiny of all things around Jesus would only prove incoherent if there was evil inherently beyond the scope of redemption, evil not destined, however mysteriously, to be made good, and in that way to disappear.

their full trinitarian depth, and so to recognize the crucified and risen Jesus as the perfect icon of the Father; the church finds in the New Testament depiction of this distinctive relationship between Jesus and the Father the ultimate warrant for taking the trinitarian narratives as epistemically primary across the board. When it comes to epistemic right, this is the force of saying, "Jesus Christ is the truth."

Precedents

Here there is no room to explore some of the deep precedents in the tradition for this epistemic outlook. We may simply indicate that theologians agree on it who are often thought to have utterly divergent epistemic commitments. Along lines we have sought to make explicit Thomas Aquinas, for example, argues that "The chief matter in the teaching of the Christian faith is the salvation accomplished by the cross of Christ," which is foolishness to the world "since it includes something which seems impossible according to human wisdom, namely that God dies (*Deus moriatur*), and that the omnipotent becomes subject to the power of the violent."[26] This requires that Christians and Christian theology keep their epistemic priorities straight – as Aquinas concretely and colorfully puts it, "Whatever is not in agreement with Christ is to be spewed out ... because he is God."[27] But Luther's approach to matters epistemic, while motivated by concerns quite unlike Thomas's and expressed in a very different way, is, as I have argued elsewhere, basically the same in substance.[28]

The epistemic picture developed here is also drawn with remarkable clarity and economy by Anselm, in a text from the *De concordia*. Anselm here speaks simply of consistency with scripture rather than specifically with the narratives identifying Jesus, and the concepts I have used are not entirely Anselm's own. But little of the foregoing argument is not stated or implied in his remark; indeed one key feature of Anselm's picture – the epistemic relation between the church's central beliefs and what seems supported by "evident reason" – we have yet to treat in detail. His words can stand as an apt summary of the argument so far.

---

26. *In I Cor.* 1, 3 (nos. 45, 47). *S. Thomae Aquinatis super Epistolas S. Pauli Lectura*, vol. I, 8th edn, ed. R. Cai, O. P. (Turin: Marietti, 1953).
27. *In Col.* 2, 2 (nos. 95–6). *S. Thomae Aquinatis super Epistolas S. Pauli Lectura*, vol. II. In a more familiar idiom: "It does not belong to sacred doctrine to prove the principles of the other sciences, but only to judge them: for whatever is found in other sciences which contradicts the truth of this science is totally to be rejected as false, according to II Cor. 10:[5]" (*Summa theologiae* I, 1, 6, ad 2).
28. See my "Faith and Reason Reconsidered: Aquinas and Luther on Deciding What is True," *The Thomist* 63/1 (1999), pp. 1–48.

We proclaim nothing of use to spiritual salvation which holy scripture, made fruitful by a miracle of the Holy Spirit, does not either put forward directly or contain within itself. For if at times we say something by reason which we cannot either point out explicitly in what scripture says or prove on that basis, we can know by scripture whether it is to be accepted or rejected, in the following way. If it is gathered by evident reason, and scripture at no point contradicts it (since scripture, just as it is opposed to no truth, also supports no falsity), then what is said by reason is taken under the authority of scripture, by the very fact that scripture does not negate it. But if scripture opposes our view beyond any doubt, then although our reasoning may seem unavoidable to us, we cannot suppose that it is supported by any truth. Thus holy scripture contains within it authority over every truth which reason gathers, since scripture either openly affirms it or at least does not negate it.[29]

Epistemic priorities, truth commitments, and plausible interpretation

The unrestricted epistemic primacy of those beliefs which are most central for the Christian community has so far come to light as a necessary implication of their content. To hold these beliefs true at all, so an analysis of their content suggests, requires treating them as epistemic trump. Recalling the philosophical considerations about the truth-dependence of meaning introduced earlier reinforces this conclusion. The key issue is how we may plausibly connect the truth value, the meaning, and the epistemic status we assign to sentences.

The last chapter argued that we cannot on the whole interpret sentences plausibly (assign meanings to them) except by maximizing the ascription of truth to sentences which speakers hold true, and so by optimizing agreement between speakers. This is one way (mainly Davidson's) of working out in a full-scale, non-question-begging theory of interpretation Frege's contention that the meaning of a sentence is given by its truth conditions, and the meaning of the constituents of a sentence (in a

29. *De concordia* III, 6, F. S. Schmitt, ed., *S. Anselmi Opera Omnia* vol. II, pp. 271, 26–272, 7. See *Cur Deus homo* I, 18: "It is certain that if I say anything which without doubt contradicts holy scripture, it is false, and I would not want to hold it if I knew" (*Opera*, vol. II, p. 82, 8–10). Commenting on these passages, Michel Corbin asks rhetorically, "Can we say that . . . [Anselm] has taken so seriously the christological titles *Logos* (Jn. 1:1) and *sophia* (I Cor. 1:22) that only that to which faith gives its assent is rational?" (cf. "justified"). "Louange et grâce, nuit et jour," Michel Corbin and Henri Rochais, eds., *L'œuvre de S. Anselm de Cantorbery*, vol. V (Paris: Cerf, 1988), p. 25.

natural language, the words) is the contribution they make to the meaning of sentences in which they might be used.[30] We need now to develop this thought so as to factor in the issue of epistemic primacy. How is the epistemic status of a sentence related to belief and meaning – to the truth value we assign the sentence and the interpretation we give it?

The argument – to state its conclusion at the outset – will display the great strength of the links between the epistemic status of a sentence, its plausible interpretation, and the truth value we set on it. A change in any one of these variables affects the others in quite specific ways. These connections have the look of logical bonds rather than merely psychological ones; attempts to break them (whether or not deliberate) lead in predictable ways to incoherence or implausibility. Since we want to test the claim that when central Christian beliefs are held true they must function with unrestricted epistemic primacy, our chief concern for the moment is the link between truth value (that is, the assignment of positive truth value, or belief) and epistemic status.

At first glance, the link between truth value and epistemic status looks obvious: roughly put, the more persistently we try to uphold the truth of a belief, the wider the range of beliefs over which it has epistemic primacy, and thus the higher (or more deeply rooted) the epistemic status it has for us. We can grasp the significance of this bond by looking at what happens to interpretation when theologians committed to the dependence thesis try to break it.

Interpreting Jesus' resurrection

The dependence thesis is the claim that we may hold central Christian beliefs true without regarding them as epistemically primary; on this, so the argument goes, rests the possibility of being an intellectually responsible Christian in the modern world. Some reflection on belief in Jesus' resurrection will provide a useful demonstration of the difficulties inherent in this epistemic procedure.[31] Though dependence theorists differ on which beliefs are essential to Christianity, many would agree with the

---

30. Davidson's holistic formulation takes the matter a step further: "Frege said that only in the context of a sentence does a word have meaning; in the same vein he might have added that only in the context of the language does a sentence (and therefore a word) have meaning" ("Truth and Meaning," *Inquiries into Truth and Interpretation* [Oxford: Clarendon Press 1985], p. 22).

31. For a cognate argument, suggested by both Luther and Aquinas, regarding belief in the incarnation, see Marshall, "Faith and Reason Reconsidered," pp. 33–46.

claim made in chapter 2 that belief in Jesus' resurrection is central to communal and individual Christian identity (though perhaps for reasons different from the ones there offered). For present purposes the decisive question is whether it is possible to give a plausible interpretation of "Jesus is risen" when, in dependence-theoretical fashion, one *both* (a) wants to hold it true, even in the face of epistemic conflict, and (b) treats it as epistemically subordinate to and dependent upon other beliefs, with which conflict may arise.

The New Testament's talk of Jesus' resurrection is of course complex. But the meaning of "Jesus is risen," whatever else it may involve, seems at least to include the predicates placed on the lips of the glorified Jesus himself in Revelation: "I was dead, and behold I am alive forever and ever" (Rev. 1:18). This seems to capture the basic action of the Gospel stories of Jesus' resurrection, which narrate (a) that Jesus once was dead, and (b) that now he lives forever, such that people can now encounter him in person. "Is risen" appears, in other words, to be basically a two part predicate, composed of "was dead" and "lives forever." "Dead" and "lives" have their usual meanings; the astonishment lies in conjoining them in this sequence – in saying that there is a temporal point at which "lives" may rightly be applied to this person which follows the point at which "is dead" may rightly be applied to him. This, to be sure, gives rise to some novel connotations of "lives," such that it can, for example, now be joined to "forever." Using the standard logical form of attribution, the New Testament applies this two part predicate to "Jesus." "Was dead" and "lives forever" are (in that sequence) both said to be true of the person Jesus, and this same person is the subject of both of these predicates (a point on which the Gospel narratives, with their references to the risen Jesus bearing the wounds of his crucifixion, lay particular stress). To believe that Jesus is risen, therefore, means at least to believe that

(1) Jesus was dead,

(2) Jesus now lives,

and that

(3) "Jesus" has the same referent in both (1) and (2).

Theologians committed to the dependence thesis, striving to make "Jesus is risen" come out true while avoiding conflict with what they regard as the primary standards of truth for that sentence, have tended to come up with two different interpretations of it. Schleiermacher can represent the first proposal, and Rudolf Bultmann the second (and much more common) one.

In his lengthy discussion of the resurrection and ascension narratives at the end of *Das Leben Jesu*, Schleiermacher insists that Jesus must have appeared to and conversed with his disciples after his crucifixion and burial. Otherwise the historical reliability of all the Gospel reports of the appearance of the redeemer and of the redemptive impression he made upon his followers would be void.[32] This means that he is committed to the truth of the resurrection (or more precisely, the appearance) narratives, but also to (3) – that is, to accepting the logical form which attributes "is risen" as a genuine predicate to Jesus, and not to anyone or anything else. The question is what to make of the predicate itself, that is, of (1) and (2).

Schleiermacher insists with particular clarity on the interpretation of (2). Jesus' "second life" with his disciples after his cross and burial is a wholly natural one, a return to the same sort of human life he enjoyed before the cross.[33] This follows naturally from his epistemic priorities. In order to harmonize Christian claims with the best deliverances of scientific and historical reason, we should not hold any beliefs which invoke the supernatural or miraculous.[34] The resurrection narratives are true; therefore they must be interpreted in a way which attributes to Jesus a life after the cross entirely continuous with his life before it. What then of (1)?

In a remarkable passage, Schleiermacher proposes that it makes no difference to our interpretation of the New Testament's talk of Jesus' resurrection whether or not we take the text to mean that Jesus actually died. The one sure sign of death, he argues, is the onset of bodily decomposition, and we do not know whether Jesus' body began to decompose; he might simply have been catatonic, and thus only have appeared to be dead. Our ignorance need not concern us, since what matters about Jesus'

32. See Friedrich Schleiermacher, *Das Leben Jesu*, ed. K. A. Rütenik, *Friedrich Schleiermacher's sämmtliche Werke*, pt. I, vol. VI (Berlin: G. Reimer, 1864), p. 471. ET: *The Life of Jesus*, trans. S. MacLean Gilmour (Philadelphia: Fortress Press, 1975), p. 442.

33. "Through the resurrection Christ returned to a genuinely human life"; the risen Jesus "says explicitly that he is not a being existing outside the ordinary course of nature, but a fully human body." Therefore "one should think of his condition as the restoration of his life entirely in the former manner," and interpret any contrary indications in the texts (such as the risen Jesus passing through closed doors) accordingly (*Das Leben Jesu*, pp. 498; 473, ET, pp. 469, 444).

34. Except insofar as the very existence of the redeemer is a miracle, in that it could not have been caused by any antecedent natural or historical states of affairs. See *Das Leben Jesu*, p. 474 (ET, p. 445); *Der christliche Glaube*, 2nd edn (ed. Martin Redeker, Berlin: de Gruyter, 1960), § 93,3.

death is not whether it actually occurred, but his attitude toward it, the continuance of his fully unimpeded God-consciousness even in his suffering.[35]

For Schleiermacher this is not simply an historical hypothesis to the effect that Jesus might not actually have died on the cross, but also a proposal about what the Gospels actually mean when they say that Jesus "died." He does not hold, as one might expect, that the Gospels clearly affirm Jesus' death on the cross, but we cannot be sure whether what they say is true. He seems, rather, to be sure that what they say is true, but not to be sure what they mean. He finds the problem acute because he has already fixed on an interpretation of the resurrection narratives which requires the elimination of miraculous or supernatural elements from Jesus' life after the tomb. The task is now to find a plausible interpretation of the accounts of the crucifixion which fits with this reading of the resurrection narratives. He hits on the solution of saying that when ascribed to Jesus in the New Testament, "dead" can be taken to mean "no longer alive," but it can equally well be taken to mean "asleep," that is, "not no longer alive."

Of course this proposal does not interpret the troublesome term, but rather fails to interpret it. To propose that a stretch of discourse really supports contradictory interpretations ascribes to the discourse a level of vagueness or confusion which puts it at the margins of intelligibility, where we are not sure we are dealing with language at all. As an interpretive recourse this suggestion can be employed only sparingly, and as a last resort. Failure to arrive at a consistent interpretation signals with far greater likelihood that one's interpretive effort has somewhere gone astray.

In fact Schleiermacher never suggests that the problem is unusual vagueness or incomprehensibility in the texts. Having said that both interpretations are permissible he instead struggles to strike some sort of balance between the two, oscillating between a plausible interpretation

---

35. See *Das Leben Jesu*, pp. 443–5 (ET, pp. 415–17). Schleiermacher sometimes seems to lean toward denying that Jesus died on the cross: one "has to grant that in Christ's situation there was not yet the least beginning of decomposition, and thus not death." But there is finally no need to decide the issue: "In this matter we can take a position of complete equanimity, and give an unbiased account of the details without any particular interest in whether it comes out one way or the other" (p. 444; ET, pp. 416–17). Though he probably strives to find more consistency than the texts actually have to offer (they are, after all, student lecture notes), Emanuel Hirsch's reading may do better justice than the texts themselves to Schleiermacher's aims. See his *Geschichte der neuern evangelischen Theologie*, vol. v (Gütersloh: Bertelsman, 1954), pp. 37–8.

which does not fit with his epistemic priorities and an implausible one which does.

To take "dead" here to mean "no longer alive" is to take it in the usual sense, and so to take the New Testament's affirmation that Jesus is risen along the lines suggested in (1)–(3) above. But it is hard to see how this interpretation could square with Schleiermacher's epistemic commitments. In that case to hold true "Jesus is risen" allows for an event in time which at best fits very poorly with the expectations of natural and historical science as Schleiermacher understands them. So this interpretation is quite plausible, but given his epistemic commitments should lead Schleiermacher to hold "Jesus is risen" false. To take "dead" to mean "asleep" or "catatonic" is, by contrast, much more congenial to Schleiermacher's epistemic commitments, since it allows him to understand Jesus' life after this "death" to be entirely natural and continuous with that before it, lacking any undesirable miraculous or supernatural element. But this is a wholly unsatisfactory interpretation of "dead": were we to take speakers this way when we find them holding true "x is dead" we would have to find them massively false; we should therefore not interpret the troublesome term this way.[36]

When it comes to "Jesus is risen," therefore, Schleiermacher seems unable to link up his epistemic commitments, the truth value he assigns to the sentence, and a plausible interpretation of it. If he holds to his epistemic priorities and remains committed to regarding the sentence as true, the result, while it cleaves to the manifest logical form of the sentence, is an astonishingly forced interpretation of the predicate. A workable theory of interpretation requires us to adjust the meanings we assign to a speaker's utterances in order to find her right most of the time. This sometimes requires us to assign meanings to the speaker's words which make particular sentences the speaker holds true come out false, as the price of assigning meanings to those same words which allow us to find her right most of the time. If this Davidsonian suggestion is basically correct, then given Schleiermacher's epistemic priorities, the interpretively efficient adjustment would simply be to find "Jesus is risen" false,

---

36. Schleiermacher's willingness to forgo interpretive plausibility here for the sake of his epistemic commitments is, as Hans Frei observes, startling. "Far more remarkable [than Schleiermacher's skepticism about physical miracles] is the fact that, no matter what he may have chosen to believe about the facts of the case, it never occurred to him that there is something unfitting, indeed ludicrous, about rendering the story of Jesus in a way that makes such a thundering anticlimax possible." *The Eclipse of Biblical Narrative* (New Haven: Yale University Press, 1974), p. 313.

rather than hold it true at the cost of systematic interpretive implausibility. The apparent alternative would be to adjust one's epistemic priorities – to seek a way of construing one's relevant beliefs about nature and history, and the inferences which must, may, and may not be made from them, which is at least consistent with "Jesus is risen," plausibly interpreted.

Together with almost all modern readers of the resurrection narratives who are committed to the dependence thesis, Bultmann disagrees with Schleiermacher about where the main interpretive difficulty lies. While Schleiermacher never quite proposes any definite interpretation of (1), Bultmann takes it for granted that the New Testament asserts that Jesus died on the cross, and he interprets "died" in the usual sense. The problem becomes what to make of (2) – of the sense in which Jesus "lives" after his genuine death.

Were we to interpret the resurrection stories according to their mythological surface meaning, Bultmann assumes, we would surely have to regard them as false.[37] But this does not mean they actually are false; Bultmann is utterly committed to the truth of the New Testament proclamation of Jesus' cross and resurrection. Instead it means that we have to interpret the narratives differently, so that they are consistent with, and thus can come out true by, the same standards which would otherwise make them come out false – we have to "demythologize" them. Like Schleiermacher, therefore, he proposes his account of "Jesus is risen" as an interpretation of what the New Testament actually says, of the sentences to be found there, and not as an alternative to sentences which he thinks he has to hold false.

In some famous passages, Bultmann argues that to believe in the resurrection of Jesus just is to believe in the saving significance of his death, to grasp the cross as God's definitive promise of salvation or authentic existence.[38] Jesus' resurrection is not, by contrast, to be thought of as a spatio-temporal event which happens to a dead person.[39] As Bultmann

37. In the well-known throw-away line: "One cannot use the electric light and the radio … and at the same time believe in the New Testament world of spirits and miracles." "Neues Testament und Mythologie," *Kerygma und Mythos*, vol. I, ed. Hans Werner Bartsch (Hamburg: Evangelischer Verlag, 1948), p. 18; on the resurrection specifically, see p. 21 (ET: "New Testament and Mythology," *Kerygma and Myth: A Theological Debate* [New York: Harper, 1961], pp. 5, 8).
38. "*Faith in the resurrection is nothing other than faith in the cross as the saving event*, in the cross as the cross of Christ" ("Neues Testament und Mythologie," p. 50; the emphasis is Bultmann's [ET, p. 41]).
39. In the New Testament, "next to the historical event of the cross stands the resurrection, which is no historical event." So "it is not as though the cross could be seen as simply the

sees it, the problem with believing in the occurrence of such an event is not simply that it runs counter to our most basic assumptions about what can happen in nature and history. We should not think of locating the resurrection in the realm of "objective" happenings to begin with; unlike the cross it is not datable, even in principle.[40] To take Jesus' resurrection as a spatio-temporal event would require numbering "Jesus is risen" among our historical and natural-scientific beliefs, where we are entitled to hold only those sentences true for which proof can be offered. In the case of the belief that Jesus is risen no such proof is available. If we want to maintain these epistemic priorities and still hold "Jesus is risen" true, we will have to find an interpretation according to which "Jesus is risen" does not assert that "rises" – that is, "lives" – is a spatio-temporal event which happens to the dead Jesus.[41]

Bultmann develops this interpretation by elaborating the suggestion that believing in Jesus' resurrection is the same thing as believing in the saving significance of his cross. To the historical event of the cross is "added" the present proclamation of the significance of that event as

death and disappearance of Jesus, upon which the resurrection followed, reversing the death" ("Neues Testament und Mythologie," pp. 44, 48; ET, pp. 34, 38).

40. See Rudolf Bultmann, "Zum Problem der Entmythologisierung," *Kerygma und Mythos*, vol. II, ed. Hans Werner Bartsch (Hamburg: Evangelischer Verlag, 1952), p. 206 (partial ET: "Bultmann Replies to his Critics," *Kerygma and Myth*; here, p. 209).

41. "Certainly," Bultmann emphasizes, "*faith's relation to its object cannot be proven*. That faith cannot be proven is, however, precisely its strength, as Wilhelm Herrmann taught. To assert that faith could be proven would be to assert that God can be known and ascertained outside of faith, and consequently to put God at the level of the world, which is always at hand and subject to objectification. Here the demand for proof is indeed appropriate" ("Zum Problem der Entmythologisierung," pp. 199–200; see p. 207 [ET, p. 201]).

Here Bultmann evidently follows the strategy, widespread among dependence theorists, of treating "history" and "faith" as wholly discrete (though, so the argument usually goes, not conflicting) epistemic realms, correlated with quite different sorts of things ("the objective world," "God"). How, though, do we decide which sentences to put into which box? If sentences having to do with "history" must be susceptible of proof, we will have to assign countless sentences about the past, and not simply those having to do with God or divine action, to that realm, outside "the world subject to objectification," which is for Bultmann the homeland of faith. "Napoleon had a red handkerchief in his pocket at Waterloo" is no more susceptible of historical *proof* than "Jesus is risen"; short of the eschaton we will very likely lack evidence which would conclusively establish either one as true. If states of affairs with regard to which the only beliefs we can have are unprovable must be moved outside the objective world, then what Napoleon had in his pocket when Marshal Ney charged Wellington's line is no less outside the sphere of objective reality than Jesus' resurrection – and so, presumably, is no less the object of saving faith. One might reply that "Jesus is risen" belongs to "faith," while "Napoleon had a red handkerchief in his pocket at Waterloo" belongs to "history," because the former has to do with God and salvation, while the latter does not. But this seems wholly arbitrary; why we need to assign sentences about God and sentences about the past to two discrete epistemic realms in the first place is just the question at issue. If not being subject to proof fails to move the contents of Napoleon's pockets outside the objective world, then there is apparently no cause to suppose that it moves Jesus' resurrection there either.

God's ever new offer of salvation. To proclaim Jesus' resurrection, it seems, just is to proclaim his cross as saving, even as to believe in the resurrection just is to believe in the cross, preached. Jesus' resurrection thus appears to be identical with the event of its proclamation, and faith in the resurrection with faith in that proclamation.[42] There is life after the cross, to be sure, but what lives seems not to be the crucified Jesus. What "lives" are the words which proclaim his cross as the event of salvation, and the faith of those who find their lives transformed by this proclamation. Jesus dies a human being, but what rises are words and faith; while the cross is clearly an event which happens to Jesus, the resurrection is an event which happens not to him, but to us.

Or so it often seems. Like Schleiermacher, though, Bultmann wavers between an implausible interpretation of "Jesus is risen" which squares with his epistemic priorities and a more plausible and standard one which appears inconsistent with those priorities, and with what he says about the resurrection when he adverts to them.[43] Here too interpretive irresolution results from an effort to hold the gospel proclamation of the resurrection true in the face of apparently conflicting beliefs, without regarding it as epistemically primary over against those beliefs (that is, without having to give up beliefs with which the gospel proclamation apparently conflicts). This allows him either his epistemic priorities or a plausible interpretation of the resurrection texts, but not both. As with Schleiermacher, we need not settle which interpretation he finally decides on; indeed there may be no way to settle it.[44]

42. "It is the word [of reconciliation] which is 'added' to the cross and, by demanding faith, makes the cross comprehensible as the saving event" ("Neues Testament und Mythologie," p. 51; ET, p. 42).

43. Side by side with the remarks just cited, Bultmann insists that it is "Christ the crucified *and risen* [who] encounters us in the word of proclamation"; this suggests that Jesus' resurrection is the content (and not simply the event) of the proclamation, and indeed that in hearing the proclamation which has this content we encounter the risen – living – Jesus himself, the very one who died on the cross ("Neues Testament und Mythologie," p. 50, my emphasis; ET, p. 41).

44. Not unreasonably taking his cues from Bultmann's explicit epistemic priorities (though he does not call them that), Karl Barth reads Bultmann as settling for a thoroughly forced reading of the New Testament resurrection texts, and poses some trenchant questions about the possibility, necessity, and desirability of such an interpretation (see *Kirchliche Dogmatik* III/2, pp. 531–7; 541–5 [ET, pp. 442–7, 451–4], also *Rudolf Bultmann: ein Versuch, ihn zu verstehen* [Theologische Studien 34, 2nd edn, Zurich: Evangelischer Verlag, 1953]). Arguing *inter alia* against readings of Bultmann influenced by Barth, James F. Kay plays up the passages (like those cited in the previous note) which suggest Bultmann's commitment to a more plausible interpretation (see *Christus Praesens: A Reconsideration of Rudolf Bultmann's Christology* [Grand Rapids: Wm. B. Eerdmans, 1994]). Both ways of reading Bultmann probably seek more consistency than the texts actually exhibit (which is not to say they are both equally persuasive); the reason each side can

The problem with an approach like Bultmann's lies not in the interpretation of (1) "was dead," nor even primarily of (2) "now lives," but in the way he handles (3) – the logical form by which the New Testament attributes both (1) and (2) to "Jesus." Whereas Schleiermacher took the logical form of "Jesus is risen" in a plausible way but leaned toward a highly unlikely interpretation of the predicate, Bultmann makes somewhat better sense of the predicate at the cost of losing track of the logical form of the sentence. One way to get at the difficulty which arises here is to ask whether Bultmann's interpretation of "Jesus is risen" succeeds in fixing the referent of "Jesus" in a consistent way.

He clearly has no trouble agreeing to "Jesus died on the cross," which implies that "Jesus" refers to "the person who died on the cross" (this slightly vague formulation could easily be indexed in order to guarantee uniqueness of reference). He also wants to hold true "Jesus is risen"; let us say this means that he in fact wants to hold true "Jesus now lives." Since "Jesus" refers to "the person who died on the cross," assent to these last two sentences requires assent to "The person who died on the cross is risen" and "The person who died on the cross now lives"; save in oblique contexts, singular terms refer to the same thing just in case we can substitute one for the other *salva veritate*.

But now, it seems, Bultmann clearly wants to demur. To hold true "The person who died on the cross is risen" and "The person who died on the cross now lives" is to say that resurrection is an event which happens to a dead person. This our epistemic priorities require us to deny. But Bultmann, committed to avoiding any interpretive outcome on which "Jesus is risen" ends up false, seems to opt for saying that "Jesus is risen" and (let us suppose) "Jesus now lives" are indeed true, but "Jesus" in these sentences does *not* refer to the person who died on the cross; it refers rather to the proclamation of his cross as saving, or to faith in that proclamation. So (1) "Jesus was dead" and (2) "Jesus now lives" both come out true, but at the cost of denying (3) outright: "Jesus" does not refer to the same thing in both sentences. This in turn calls for an extended or metaphorical interpretation of the predicate in (2), one which captures the sense in which "lives" may rightly be applied to the experience of faith in the proclamation of Jesus' death or (still more extended) to the words of the proclamation themselves, as distinguished from the sense in which it

always find ammunition against the other is that the conflict between Bultmann's epistemic priorities and his truth commitments bars him from coming up with a consistent interpretation in the first place.

applies to persons. Thus by varying the referent of "Jesus" (by denying [3]), Bultmann ends up taking "Jesus is risen" to mean something like "Because Jesus died on the cross, we can now experience authentic existence."

Fixing the reference of singular terms plays a basic role in the interpretation of any language, since without it we will have scarcely any idea of what the speakers of the language are talking about. The complexities of reference need not concern us here, save to observe that here the Davidsonian (and Quinian) principle of charity has important work to do: if we fix the reference of a singular term in such a way that we have to count as false most of what our speakers assert about it, the great likelihood is that we have the reference wrong. Bultmann wants to count the "speakers" of the New Testament right when they assert "is risen" of "Jesus," but at the dimly acknowledged cost – given his epistemic priorities – of counting them wrong in the rest of the assertions they make about him. Obviously words and faith did not die on the cross, but a person did; if "Jesus" refers to words and faith, as it often seems to do in Bultmann's interpretation of "Jesus is risen," then "Jesus died on the cross" will be false, as will "Jesus was born around 4 BC," "Jesus was a Jew," and so forth (or perhaps these and similar sentences will have to be counted not so much as false but as nonsensical – an equally good sign that interpretation has taken a wrong turn, since the point of interpretation is presumably to make *sense* of speakers' utterances). Better to avoid such implausible interpretive desperation, take "Jesus" to refer consistently to "the person who died on the cross" (as Bultmann himself obviously wants to do, most of the time), and if our epistemic priorities forbid us to assert "now lives" of "the one who died on the cross," regard the New Testament speakers as simply mistaken in their belief that Jesus is risen. The alternative, once again, is to adjust our epistemic priorities – to reassess our assumption that tenable beliefs about nature and history forbid us to believe that the same person who died on the cross now lives.

The point of these examples is not to single out Schleiermacher and Bultmann as exceptionally misguided interpreters of the New Testament's talk of Jesus' resurrection. On the contrary: within the epistemic and interpretive boundaries they broadly share, each offers an especially subtle and complex account of "Jesus is risen." The different interpretive difficulties in which each tends to get entangled when guided by his epistemic priorities illustrate instead the inherent problems of the project they undertake.

To be committed to the truth of a sentence is to be committed to the falsity of those sentences which, given the best interpretation we can provide, are inconsistent with it. The intensity of our commitment to different sentences does of course vary, and with that the readiness with which we are prepared to reject other sentences should they come into conflict with those to which we are committed. When sentences to which we are committed seem to come into conflict we can try to show that the conflict is apparent rather than real, or we can try to adjust the interpretation of some of the sentences to make them consistent with the others – thereby showing that we regard the adjusted sentences as epistemically subordinate to those whose interpretation remains fixed (and with that our more intense commitment to the truth of the sentences whose meaning we decline to adjust). But there are limits on the extent of the interpretive adjustments we can plausibly make. Those limits are reached when making a given adjustment in meaning would require us to attribute noticeably more falsity to sentences held true by speakers of the interpreted language than would result from simply holding false the sentences we are trying to adjust.

If these principles are roughly right, then our epistemic priorities will on the whole have to match our truth commitments. The modern theological dependence thesis, we can now observe, is basically an effort to arrange a divorce between the two: to hold at least some centrally Christian beliefs true in virtually all conceivable circumstances, while *not* being committed to rejecting virtually any conceivable belief which cannot be reconciled with those central Christian claims. For these truth commitments, the epistemic priorities lie elsewhere. In this effort to sunder the highest epistemic priorities from the deepest truth commitments something has to give, and the only thing left to give is plausible interpretation. This is not an all-or-nothing proposition, but admits of degree. The stronger our commitment to a given belief, the more likely we will interpret it badly if we fail to accord it an equivalent degree of epistemic primacy. If we are not willing to give up central Christian beliefs, and with them Christian identity, the only way to guarantee that we will interpret them plausibly is to treat them as epistemically primary without restriction. And correlatively: if we want to interpret central Christian beliefs plausibly, the only way to ensure that we will not have to give them up in the process is to treat them as epistemically primary across the board.

What to correlate?

Ascribing unrestricted epistemic primacy to the most central Christian beliefs might seem like a deliberately *anti-correlationist* position. But it would be misleading to put the objection to the dependence thesis here developed in this way. An anti-correlationist view would presumably be one which was concerned to deny something that correlationists want to affirm. But the foregoing considerations regarding how we may viably adjust the assignment of meaning, truth value, and epistemic status suggest that epistemic correlation in theology is not so much mistaken as empty. In order to locate the entities which standard accounts would have us correlate, we must already have excluded the possibility of the sort of epistemic correlation we are invited to undertake. Should the theological notion of epistemic correlation thus fail to state anything which could coherently be affirmed, there is no point in denying it; it needs not refutation, but elimination.[45]

The enterprise of epistemic correlation in theology seems to be that of distinguishing Christian belief from other regions of human discourse, and then comparing Christian talk with these other types of belief in order to see which beliefs in the various regions come out true. Correlationists mark off Christian belief from other areas of discourse in various ways, sometimes by distinguishing the presumed sources of beliefs (such as "revelation" and "reason," or as we saw with Schleiermacher in chapter 3, two different sorts of consciousness), at other times by adverting to what the beliefs are about (such as, in Bultmann's case, an objective world of spatio-temporal events and the world of human subjectivity).[46]

In order to identify beliefs as "religious," "historical," "scientific," or the like – in order to assign them their proper region – we have to know what the sentences mean which state the contents of the beliefs. If the relations between meaning, truth, and belief here outlined basically hold, we will on the whole not be able to figure out the meanings of sentences, and *a fortiori* the meanings of the words of which sentences are composed, except by assigning truth values to them which optimize

---

45. We are here concerned only with epistemic "correlation" aimed at judgments about the truth of Christian beliefs. This often goes together with an enterprise from which it is nonetheless distinct, namely a correlation which aims to establish the existential meaningfulness or relevance of Christian beliefs. See my *Christology in Conflict* for an argument against the latter sort of correlation, at least in its christological applications.
46. On "reason" and "revelation" as terms of epistemic correlation, see David Tracy's "Foreword" to Jean-Luc Marion, *God Without Being*, trans. Thomas A. Carlson (Chicago: University of Chicago Press, 1991). Tracy there rightly observes that non-correlational theologies are not for the most part those which unaccountably refuse to correlate terms like "reason" and "revelation," but which regard the very idea of epistemic correlation as "at best a category mistake" (p. x). The present remarks are an attempt to locate the mistake.

agreement about which sentences are true with speakers of the language in which the beliefs are stated. In order to assign beliefs to various regions, therefore, we must already on the whole have decided about their truth. And this leaves us nothing to correlate: no large regions of beliefs whose meaning we know, but whose truth value we need to find out, and might hope to discover by relating the regions to one another in some way. If we do not know the meanings of sentences believed, we have no bodies of belief to correlate, and if we have fixed sentence meanings we must have in large part already assigned truth values to sentences believed; there is no epistemic work left for correlation to do.

There will, of course, always be some leftovers the meaning of which we suppose we have fixed, but about the truth value of which we are unsure. When this happens we will not always have any clear way to decide whether to assign one meaning to a sentence and agree with our speakers in holding it true, or to assign a different meaning and hold it false. In the nature of the case this interpretive margin for error will have to be the exception rather than the rule. To the extent that we can settle such cases at all, they will presumably be decided by the most relevant beliefs whose truth value we know – which is to say, if we are thinking in terms of "regions" of belief, those to whose region the leftovers belong, rather those which make up some other area of discourse.

Appeals to epistemic correlation in modern theology have normally been made in defense of epistemic priorities suggested by the dependence thesis; the point has been to show that beliefs which belong to the Christian "region" are at least consistent with, and perhaps warranted by, the contents of other areas of belief. But the problem with such appeals has nothing specifically to do with the epistemic status of beliefs. The very idea of correlation turns out to be empty. It would make no more sense to try to correlate "reason" and "revelation" if revelation were epistemically primary, or if the correlation were "mutually critical," than it does when reason or *Wissenschaft* is epistemically primary. Insofar as the dependence thesis is at bottom the effort to divorce truth commitments from epistemic priorities in theology (or, one could say, to divorce central Christian beliefs from their properly primary epistemic function), one can be a dependence theorist without correlation, that is, without appealing to areas of belief that can be compared in the hope of favorable epistemic result. Yet it is not hard to see why the dependence thesis has so often taken an essentially correlationist form. Correlation holds out the promise that theologians can do justice both to the contents of Christian beliefs and to the epistemic priorities of modernity while keeping each in its place. Like the dependence thesis generally, correlation makes a promise which in the end it lacks the logical resources to keep.

Philosophical considerations thus support the conclusion we drew from an analysis of the content of the church's trinitarian identification of God: if central Christian beliefs are to be held true at all, they must have unrestricted epistemic primacy. A Christian view of things will be one which orders the whole open field of possible sentences or beliefs so as to achieve at least consistency with a christological and trinitarian center; in this way it will match its epistemic priorities to its truth commitments, and so hope to come up with a plausible interpretation of the whole field. These philosophical considerations also support the conclusion of our empirical analysis of Christian practice. Since we can only pick out central Christian beliefs in the first place by reference to their function across the whole field – this community's publicly observable commit-ment to retaining these beliefs in all possible circumstances, which dis-plays its conviction that they are epistemic trump – there can be no beliefs external to a Christian view of the world, nothing outside it with which it might conceivably be correlated. It is, of course, possible to order the whole field differently than the Christian community does, around dif-ferent epistemic priorities. But that is another matter, and the subject of the next chapter.

6

Epistemic priorities and alien claims

Fideism and epistemic priorities

The suggestion that the church's trinitarian identification of God enjoys unrestricted epistemic primacy may prompt a certain unease. To suppose that the Christian community is rationally justified – let alone correct – in rejecting as false any statement which is inconsistent with its own most central beliefs seems to have the whiff of fideism about it. Surely no one wants to be a fideist, so we need to see whether this opprobrious term fits the epistemic outlook so far proposed.

The charge of "fideism" labels the following contention. Far from answering the question of the church's right to hold its central beliefs, the argument so far has not yet succeeded in addressing it. To take the church's central beliefs as epistemic trump is to help oneself to a whole range of trinitarian and christological beliefs, simply assuming that these beliefs are true rather than producing any argument for them. But surely the question which most needs to be answered is why we should think these Christian convictions are true in the first place; the crucial question is what grounds, if any, there are for holding the central beliefs themselves true. By failing even to address, let alone answer, that question, we have taken a wholly fideistic position, the chief aim of which, so an objector might conclude, is to insulate Christian belief from criticism.

This objection exploits our deep conviction – surely correct and important, as far as it goes – that in order to hold a belief in an epistemically responsible way (to hold it rationally, rather than fideistically) we must be able to offer reasons for the belief. We do this in all sorts of ways, but in giving reasons we naturally appeal to beliefs which we and (we hope) our interlocutors already hold true. Reasons may in turn be requested and given for the beliefs to which we appeal, and so forth. Sometimes the charge of fideism seems simply to be that it is irrational to hold beliefs for which no reasons or "grounds" are given.

But surely this cannot be right. The giving of reasons has to come to an end.[1] Beliefs succeed in terminating justificatory arguments just in case we do not have to give reasons for them. Without a terminus to the regress of reasons we will lack a way to decide whether the reasons we have given are good ones, that is, whether they actually support the belief which prompted our search for reasons in the first place. This sort of decision has to rely, it appears, on a nexus of belief which can serve as a reason, but does not itself require the giving of reasons. Eventually the practice of justifying beliefs will have to appeal to beliefs which we and (again we hope) our interlocutors hold true, but for which no reasons are given – beliefs which, so far as we can tell, settle the matter with which we began. So holding beliefs rationally requires not only the ability to give reasons, but the ability to distinguish between those occasions when we need to give reasons, and those when we do not.

If we had to give a reason for everything, then *whatever* beliefs, Christian or otherwise, were invoked to justify other beliefs would be held irrationally, since beliefs terminate arguments when no reasons need to be offered for them. Since in that case it would be unreasonable to hold these beliefs, it would also be unreasonable to hold the beliefs which they are supposed to justify; reasonable beliefs presumably cannot be justified by unreasonable ones. So if it were fideistic to hold beliefs without giving reasons for them, then *all* of our beliefs would be irrational, both those which we hope to justify by giving reasons, and those which are supposed to do the justifying. Were this the case, Christian beliefs obviously could not be faulted by comparison with others for their lack of rationality. Understood in this way, the charge of fideism seems self-refuting.

To say that the Christian community's central beliefs are epistemically primary without restriction does not, of course, mean that these beliefs must terminate all justificatory arguments. Naturally they will conclude only a small portion of such arguments, namely those where the matter in dispute – what God is like, for example, or what human beings may

---

1. This way of putting the point is Wittgenstein's; see *On Certainty*, ed. G. E. M. Anscombe and G. H. von Wright (Oxford: Basil Blackwell, 1969), e.g., §§ 110, 192. But the thought goes back at least as far as Aristotle, e.g., *Posterior Analytics* I, 3 (72b, 5–24); *Metaphysics* IV, 4; 7 (1006a, 4–12; 1012a, 21–2).

hope for – is of a kind which makes appeal to these beliefs relevant to set-tling the dispute (cases, in other words, where the meaning of the dis-puted beliefs places them in logical space close to the narratives which identify Jesus and the triune God). Taking these beliefs as epistemically primary across the board does mean, however, that in general justifica-tory arguments cannot be accepted as yielding true statements when those arguments terminate in beliefs incompatible with the church's canonical narrative. If that narrative has epistemic primacy we cannot for the most part suppose, in other words, that we may regard statements as true whose supporting arguments depend on appeal to convictions incompatible with those narratives. Thus if the narratives which identify Jesus are epistemically primary, they are the final and decisive, though of course not the sole, criteria for deciding what count as good reasons for holding sentences true.[2]

So far, then, it seems epistemically permissible to hold central Christian beliefs true without giving reasons for them. Indeed if the church's central beliefs do have epistemic primacy, there will in the nature of the case be no way to show that these beliefs are true without appealing to these same beliefs as decisive tests of truth, no non-circular (and therefore epistemically trivial) way of offering reasons for them. That is part of what it means to say they are epistemically primary.

In response the charge of fideism might be more narrowly confined. It is not that all beliefs require reasons in order to be held rationally, but rather that these particular beliefs, the centrally Christian ones, need jus-tifying grounds, and cannot themselves suitably terminate justificatory arguments.

Were foundationalism tenable this version of the objection might have considerable force. In that case, beliefs would have to meet certain stringent requirements in order to terminate justificatory arguments in a rational way. Such beliefs would have to be self-evident, empirically evident, givens of immediate self-consciousness, or something of the kind. Indeed much of the appeal of foundationalism lay in the sense that without recourse to beliefs having certain marks which place them

---

2. The qualifications "in general" and "for the most part" are important here. In order to figure out whether a given claim is genuinely incompatible with central Christian beliefs it is necessary to establish strictly inferential connections between the claim in question and the negations of Christian beliefs. But many sorts of justificatory arguments yield their conclusions in less stringent ways, and in such cases a claim supported by reasons themselves genuinely opposed to the church's central beliefs might nonetheless be compatible with these beliefs.

beyond doubt for any rational person, there would be no adequate way to terminate justificatory arguments. This attraction has not been lost on theologians, who have tried to meet the requirements it imposes by packing their epistemic foundations with theological content, or showing that Christian beliefs were at least plausible, and perhaps more robustly warranted, by appeal to the supposed foundations.

As we have already seen, however, epistemic foundationalism seems untenable. Even if there are beliefs of the needed types (which is often disputed), they cannot plausibly be invoked for foundationalist purposes. Apart from foundationalist assumptions, it is not clear that central Christian convictions lack any marks (like empirical evidence or interior immediacy) which beliefs need to have in order to be epistemically primary, and so *a fortiori* to terminate justificatory arguments. Here too, the fideistic charge seems to require a distinction between rational and irrational ways of holding beliefs which turns out to be impossible to sustain.

Theologians have, however, often drawn a rather different lesson from the widely acknowledged demise of foundationalism. In order to avoid fideism in a post-foundationalist world, so the argument sometimes goes, we have to grant that all of our established beliefs, and with them all of our criteria of truth, are at hazard whenever we try to make decisions about what is true. The very idea that there could be permanently fixed epistemic priorities, let alone priorities which applied without restriction across the field of possible beliefs, is for this reason inherently fideistic – that is, irrational.

In this strong sense the further reformulated charge of fideism seems no more plausible than the earlier variants. It proposes a standard for rational (that is, non-fideistic) conversation which seems impossible to meet, in theology or anywhere else. It seems impossible that we could doubt all of our beliefs at once, or even be prepared to doubt them all. Perhaps the most familiar arguments against this possibility are those proposed by Wittgenstein: doubt is logically possible only against a background of beliefs held true, since doubt (or preparedness to doubt) requires reasons for doubting (or being prepared to), and giving reasons requires appeal to beliefs held true (that is, not doubted).[3] If foundationalism is untenable, and with it the necessity (and perhaps the possibility) of terminating justificatory arguments by appeal to putatively self-

---

3. See again Wittgenstein, *On Certainty*.

evident or self-justifying beliefs, then it becomes especially important to recognize that rational conversation and argument do not require, but rather preclude, holding all of our beliefs (including our criteria of truth) open to doubt at the same time.

Theologians sometimes compound the problem of inflated expectations about what may reasonably be doubted by basing the charge of fideism on a curious sort of self-loathing foundationalism. Such an outlook takes for granted the dualism of conceptual scheme and experienced content, and so is structurally foundationalist, but despairs of ever escaping the scheme so as to find the unblemished content – a kind of foundationalism which has given up on locating the foundations. On this view we will never be able to discover which conceptual scheme, if any, tells us the truth about the world and our experience of it, and for this reason we must regard all of our beliefs as up for grabs. But rather than trying to doubt all of our beliefs, the more plausible course would be, as chapter 4 argued, to jettison the dualism of scheme and content which tempts us to suppose that we could make sense of such doubt in the first place.[4]

So far it seems difficult to state the worry about "fideism" in a way which mounts a plausible objection to the unrestricted epistemic primacy of central Christian beliefs. Yet there is something to the worry, even if standard attempts to formulate it as an argument are unsuccessful. The collapse of foundationalism surely does not mean that we may believe whatever we like, nor does it mean that we may choose our epistemic priorities at will. Holding beliefs in an epistemically responsible way does not require that we be able to give reasons for every one of our beliefs. But our epistemic responsibilities do seem to require that we be open to changing any *one* of our beliefs if given sufficient reasons to do so. From the possibility of doubting any particular belief we cannot argue to the possibility of doubting all our beliefs, but the impossibility of doubting all our beliefs does not by itself entitle us to cling to any particular belief.

An account of the justification of beliefs, Christian or otherwise, therefore ought to include an explanation of the kinds of reasoning (as distinguished from the social or psychological motives) which might

---

4. For a theological example of the scheme–content distinction appropriated wholesale, see Gordon D. Kaufman, *In the Face of Mystery* (Cambridge, Mass.: Harvard University Press, 1993); on the putative need to play off language as a human contrivance against the ascription of truth to sentences, and so to regard the truth of our sentences as a question to which we can never hope to give an answer, see pp. 49, 347.

lead us to change our established beliefs, including our epistemic priorities. Explaining what might give us reason to change our epistemic priorities will very likely involve saying what gives us reason to keep them, so we could equally well say that we need an account of how we may justify our epistemic commitments – not simply our beliefs, but the priorities which guide our decisions about the truth of beliefs.

Since we have already offered an account of how the Christian community may justify its distinctive epistemic priorities, it may seem odd that this issue should now recur; the logic of the argument so far seems to suggest that this question has already received, for good or ill, the most complete answer we can give to it. Were that so, however, we would be left with a kind of standoff between the charge of fideism and the epistemic primacy of the Trinity. The objector to fideism has raised what seems like a reasonable question: why suppose that the beliefs which make up the church's identification of God are true in the first place? Though the objection has not succeeded in showing that the epistemic primacy of the Trinity is irrational, the objector still wants reasons for believing in the Trinity.

It might be replied that this demand is simply confused, and requires not to be met, but to be eliminated. The very idea of epistemic primacy is that for beliefs which have this property without restriction, there can be no further beliefs to which one might appeal in order to decide about their truth – that is, no beliefs of just that sort which the objector seems to think he needs in order to believe in the Trinity. But while right as far as it goes, this leaves us without a satisfying response to the objector worried about fideism. If we accept the objector's gambit we fall into the confusion of treating beliefs which (if held true) have to be epistemically primary as though they were epistemically subordinate; if we refuse the gambit we also decline to offer any reasons for the priorities by which we decide about truth which might have some epistemic purchase with those who do not already share them.

What we need is a way of giving reasons for beliefs without creating epistemic subordination and dependence. This would meet the anti-fideist's legitimate concern that we ought to be able to say something about the justification of our epistemic priorities themselves, without letting the objector's demand for reasons tempt us to lose track of those priorities. Identifying reasons of a kind which involves no epistemic dependence would permit a genuinely justificatory conversation about epistemic priorities between adherents of rival belief systems, individuated by different priorities. Armed with such reasons, the unrestricted epistemic primacy of central Christian beliefs would be entirely compatible with at least some of what has traditionally been called "apologetics."

Inclusion and assimilation

The success of the Christian community's belief system at coping with alien and novel beliefs – its *inclusive* and *assimilative power* – might count as a reason for having this community's epistemic priorities which nonetheless brings about no epistemic subordination of the beliefs for which reasons are given.[5]

By "alien" beliefs I mean those within the open field of possible belief which are not central to the belief system of the Christian community.[6] An alien belief is therefore one which a community may hold false without loss to its own identity. At any given time the church's belief system as a whole will likely contain countless alien beliefs. The capacity of the church's view of the world to permit the acceptance of alien beliefs when its holders meet with good reasons to hold them true is its *inclusive power*; possession of this capacity tends to justify, I will argue, epistemic priorities and belief systems which have it.

Alien beliefs may be regarded as occupying a position in the logical space of the Christian community's belief system ranging from medial to peripheral. For a claim to be alien is not necessarily for it to be rejected by the community; beliefs are "alien" only in not being central. Nor are alien beliefs those external to or outside of the church's belief system. If it makes sense to talk of beliefs "external to" a comprehensive belief system like that of the church, external beliefs will presumably be those which a

---

5. For a suggestion that a notion of "assimilative power" might have this sort of epistemic function, see George A. Lindbeck, *The Nature of Doctrine* (Philadelphia: Westminster, 1984), p. 131. For a critical analysis of Lindbeck's use of this notion, see my essay, "Absorbing the World: Christianity and the Universe of Truths," *Theology and Dialogue*, ed. Bruce D. Marshall (Notre Dame: University of Notre Dame Press, 1990), pp. 69–102. I now think this essay goes wrong in supposing that much sense is to be made of the notion that there are true beliefs "external" to a Christian view of the world, though I still think that its estimation of Lindbeck's views is basically correct.

6. The term is William Christian's, and I am applying it in his sense: "A claim that what is proposed in some assertion is true, or that some course of action is right, is an alien claim, with respect to some community, if and only if what is proposed in the claim is not an authentic doctrine of that community," where an "authentic doctrine" of a community is one which that community holds it is "bound to teach" – that is, what are here conceived as a community's "central" beliefs. The notion of "alien" claims is thus parasitic upon that of claims central to a communal belief system. *Doctrines of Religious Communities: A Philosophical Study* (New Haven: Yale University Press, 1987), pp. 145, 74.

community's epistemic priorities require it to reject, whereas there will be numerous alien beliefs the community will want to include. As the church's central, identity-constituting beliefs will tend to be distinctive to it rather than shared with other communities, so also the church's alien beliefs will tend to be those which it shares with other communities. The correlation, though, is not absolute; for example some convictions near the center of the church's belief system are also central for the Jewish people, and there might be beliefs which are distinctive to the church, but which are not central, and so are alien.[7]

Of particular interest for present purposes are beliefs which are not only alien for the church, but *novel*: claims which the Christian community and its members have encountered as live options for belief, but about whose epistemic status the community has on the whole not yet come to a decision. Novel claims are "live" options for belief when (a) they come with reasons attached which make the claims in some degree persuasive, and (b) they impinge closely enough on the Christian community's identity-forming belief and practice to make deciding about their truth worth the trouble for the community or its members.

For the Christian community to *assimilate* these novel beliefs is for the community to find a way of holding them true, a plausible interpretation of the novel claims which is at least consistent with the church's central beliefs. Assimilative and inclusive power obviously go together. Novel beliefs which have been assimilated are thereby included in the community's belief system, though inclusion need not involve any explicit or deliberate process of assimilation. When the epistemic status of the beliefs has been decided, whether by assimilation into the community's belief system or rejection from it, they are no longer novel.[8] By definition all novel beliefs start out as alien, and most will remain that way, but whether they do depends on how their epistemic status is settled. Novel beliefs may arise which the community eventually not only assimilates, but takes to be central; for many Christians, this is the case with, for example, the sinlessness and bodily assumption of Mary.

Since novel beliefs will for the most part already be held by people

---

7. For the case of Jews and Christians see the last section of this chapter. The converse case might be exemplified by beliefs bound up with the practice of devotion to a particular saint, which only highly socialized members of the Christian community are likely to have, but which the community does not regard as central to its belief system.

8. The line between novel beliefs or practices and those whose truth or rightness has been decided is not fixed; a belief or practice may seem decided for a long time, only to strike the community as novel once again (as, for example, the practice of ordaining only men to the church's pastoral ministry once seemed settled, but has now widely been reversed).

outside the community, the question about whether they can be assimilated is generally a question about whether the church can share a particular stretch of belief with at least some of those who are not its members. That is, at any rate, our chief concern here.

A community whose belief system displays an ongoing capacity to assimilate novel beliefs will naturally be one which shows itself capable of changing its established beliefs, and so of holding its beliefs in an epistemically responsible way. Pressure to change beliefs currently held very often comes from encounters with novel beliefs for which good reasons can be offered, though of course it can come in other ways as well (such as by continuing communal reflection on the meaning and implications of its own most central beliefs – it was chiefly in this way, for example, that the church rejected its own previous tolerance of slavery). Rejecting such novel beliefs does not, of course, require changing established communal convictions, but assimilating them often will. Assimilation often requires, that is, rejecting established beliefs inconsistent with the novel claims to be taken in.

In cases of this kind, the more closely novel claims impinge on the community's central beliefs, the more difficult they will be to assimilate. Should a community be able to accept novel claims only at the cost of rejecting beliefs which are epistemically primary for it, this would not exhibit the assimilative power of that community's belief system, but signal the end both of the belief system and the community whose identity depends on holding true the rejected beliefs. A communal belief system will thus have assimilative power to the extent that it can incorporate novel truth claims without making the community give up its own most central beliefs, and so abandon its identity-constituting epistemic priorities.

Encounters with novelty

The church's engagement with novel beliefs and belief systems has been ongoing since its earliest days. As the full corpus of Aristotle's writings made its way into the Latin West in the twelfth and thirteenth centuries, the Western church found itself confronted by a belief system whose explanatory power seemed to exceed that of any philosophical outlook which the church had previously confronted and assimilated. This compelling belief system appeared not only to be at odds with teachings long regarded as indispensable by the church (such as the immortality of the soul and the creation of the world in time), but to support the teachings of a rival religion – Islam – whose theologians were practiced at using it as an apologetic tool. In this encounter the strategy which prevailed in the church after long struggle was to assimilate Aristotle, by showing that his philosophy can be accepted in virtually all of its particulars without generating inconsistency with any central Christian beliefs, and indeed that Aristotle in some important respects strongly supports Christian claims.

Were such inconsistency to arise it would, all but a few were agreed, be too bad for Aristotle. But there seemed good reasons to accept Aristotle's physics, metaphysics, psychology, and cosmology over the available alternatives, even though this meant changing well-established (mostly Platonistic) habits of thought. In a series of highly technical debates (on issues like the creation of unformed matter and the number of intellectual souls) Christian thinkers in the medieval west became widely convinced that they could have it both ways: their commitment to Christian teaching did not require them to give up being Aristotelians (that is, to reject as false the results of a textually persuasive interpretation of Aristotle).[9] This close reading of Aristotle in the Christian community left neither the ancient philosophy nor the western church's view of the world unchanged, though the changes were of different kinds. The church's success at taking Aristotle in created a transformed and much expanded Aristotelianism, arguably superior to other assimilations of Aristotle, and it greatly altered the ways in which the Christian community and its members would explain and defend their most central beliefs, though not the beliefs themselves.

Sometimes, however, assimilation of novel beliefs does lead to communal reassessment of central convictions. The geological discoveries of the eighteenth century, and Darwin's development of an evolutionary biological theory in the nineteenth, made it seem incredible, despite what Christians had long tended to suppose, that the stories in Gen. 1–11 could be true – that the origin of the world and humanity could plausibly have taken place as they describe. One widespread (though by no means universal) Christian response to the community's encounter with this particular set of novel beliefs has been to propose a shift in the literary genre to which these stories are assigned. They are not to be taken as science or history, but as myths, sagas, or realistic (but in this case fictional) narratives. As such they can still be mined for beliefs about God,

---

9. For analysis of one example of this procedure – Aquinas's assimilation of Aristotle's account of matter to the creation narrative of Gen. 1 – see Marshall, "Absorbing the World," pp. 90–7.

the world, and humanity which remain abidingly central to the Christian community: that in every respect the world's existence depends upon God's creative will, that among all of God's creatures human beings are created in and for a distinctive and uniquely intimate relationship with God, and so forth.[10] But reading Gen. this way also means taking some beliefs long regarded as relatively central to a Christian understanding of the world as simply false: that Adam and Eve were the first humans, that the rest of humanity is biologically descended from them, and that the lost condition from which humanity is redeemed by the triune God can be traced in a quasi-causal way to this first pair.

Here the assimilation of alien and novel beliefs has meant a restructuring of the communal belief system relatively close to the center, since beliefs once seen as bound up with the most central ones are not merely relegated to the periphery, but discarded altogether. Perhaps in part for this reason the genre shift which funds the restructuring still meets with resistance in the Christian community. Those who support the shift argue, however, that it brings needed clarity, distinguishing those beliefs which are genuinely central and indispensable to communal identity from those which have simply been around for a long time. One form of this argument, suggested by Kierkegaard and exploited by theologians like Reinhold Niebuhr and Paul Tillich, maintains that the Christian doctrine of original sin makes much more sense if Adam and Eve are not regarded as the historical first parents of humanity than if they are; shorn of its cumbrous historical trappings, the doctrine becomes at once a genuinely central Christian teaching and a truth about human existence perspicuous to any honest and attentive analysis of self – indeed the indispensable means by which modern people can make sense of Christian teaching at all.[11]

Karl Barth gives the argument a quite different form, in which the

10. The suggestion that these texts have manifold meanings beyond their sense as descriptions of events in nature and history is, of course, an ancient Christian commonplace. And since finding sense in the texts does not depend on taking them as science or history, supposing that they propose true and important beliefs about God and humanity does not require supposing that those beliefs are of a scientific or historical sort – a point generally upheld by those ancient interpreters who also assume their scientific and historical veracity, and emphasized by those who, like Origen, entertain some doubts on this score.

11. See, e.g., Reinhold Niebuhr, *The Nature and Destiny of Man* (New York: Scribners, 1941), vol. I; Paul Tillich, *Systematic Theology* (Chicago: University of Chicago Press, 1951–63), vol. II. On the centrality of sin and its conceptual variants as an apologetic device in modern Protestant theology, see Hans Frei, *The Eclipse of Biblical Narrative* (New Haven: Yale University Press, 1974), pp. 124–30.

impossibility of appealing to Adam and Eve to justify any account of the human condition helps to bring out a cardinal point of which the tradition had (he supposes) at best only partial sight: that an adequate grasp of the human condition requires (rather than being required by) a grasp of Jesus' identity as the redeemer of humanity, by contrast with whom our own condition emerges as a "bizarre antitype" and so as sin.[12] In cognate fashion Karl Rahner argues that christological assimilation of an evolutionary view of the world highlights rather than diminishes the unsurpassability of Jesus Christ.[13] For both Barth and Rahner, decentralizing traditional claims about Adam and Eve as historical figures has the effect of emphasizing the centrality of the church's christological and trinitarian beliefs – that body of beliefs whose epistemic status must remain stable if the attempt to take in novel claims is to display the assimilative power of a belief system rather than to prove its undoing.

This sort of effort to include and assimilate alien and novel beliefs stems from the church's own most central commitments – from the narratives which identify Jesus. These narratives require that those who hold them true should not simply be prepared to cope with unfamiliar claims, but should actively seek out novel beliefs and try to find a place for them in a Christian vision of the world. As Paul puts it, Christians are called to "take every thought captive to obey Christ" (II Cor. 10:5). To hold true at all the narratives which identify Jesus and the Trinity calls for an always ongoing communal effort by Christians to interpret and assess whatever novel claims they encounter, and whatever they think they already know, by trying to find a place for them in the world created through and for Jesus Christ, and put at peace with God by the blood of his cross – the world of the triune God, who makes all things new by drawing them into the interior space of his own life through Jesus' passion and resurrection, where nothing has exactly the place we would otherwise have thought.[14] The imperative to take in alien beliefs is therefore not imposed on the Christian community from without, but goes with holding a Christian view of the world in the first place. It calls for an effort of interpretation

12. Barth argues this point extensively in the volumes which make up his doctrine of reconciliation; the quoted phrase is from *Kirchliche Dogmatik* IV/3 (Zurich: Evangelischer Verlag, 1932–67 [for the complete work]), p. 426 (ET, p. 369).

13. See his "Christology within an Evolutionary View of the World," *Theological Investigations* (New York: Seabury and Crossroads, 1961–), vol. 5, pp. 157–92.

14. This way of putting the matter is suggested by Hans Urs von Balthasar, *Herrlichkeit*, vol. I: *Schau der Gestalt* (Einsiedeln: Johannes Verlag, 1961), p. 594; see p. 127 (ET: *The Glory of the Lord*, vol. I: *Seeing the Form*, trans. Erasmo Leiva-Merikakis [San Francisco: Ignatius Press, 1982], pp. 615, 135).

and assessment which will be ongoing as long as there are novel beliefs to encounter, that is, until the end of time.[15]

But the church's primary *criteria* of truth will not furnish the primary *reasons* for holding most beliefs true. The Christian community and its members will naturally be able to decide the truth of relatively few proposals for belief by direct appeal to those beliefs which are epistemically primary for the church, since beliefs themselves inconsistent with one another will often alike be consistent with that narrative and its interpretation. Confronted with alien or novel beliefs, we will for the most part be unable to tell whether they conform to the Christian community's epistemic priorities except by a process of reasoning which strives to work out inferential connections, often of a complex and indirect sort, between the beliefs in question, the reasons we have for holding them, and those beliefs which are centrally Christian. Only by striving to include them, in other words, will the Christian community and its members be able to tell whether alien and novel beliefs cohere with their central convictions. And since all beliefs have to be consistent with the narratives which identify Jesus and the Trinity in order to be held true, the scope of the Christian community's assimilative effort has to match the scope of the community's epistemic priorities: both must be universal and unrestricted.[16]

The epistemic force of inclusive power

But why should success at including alien beliefs and assimilating novel ones count in favor of the Christian community's belief system? Conversely: why suppose that in order to be justified in holding their

15. It might be thought that this effort to assimilate the novel, to "take every thought captive", reflects an illicit "totalism" which theology ought to reject (on which see Emmanuel Levinas, *Totality and Infinity*, trans. Alphonso Lingis [Pittsburgh: Duquesne University Press, 1969]). If "totalism" is the view that all possible beliefs have in some sense already been assessed, so that there can be no genuinely novel beliefs and, on that account, no possibility that we will have to change our epistemic priorities, then the present argument is anti-totalistic: there will be novel beliefs until the eschaton, and they might lead us to change our minds at any point. If, by contrast, "totalism" is the view that there may be beliefs with unrestricted epistemic primacy, beliefs whose epistemic scope is the whole open field (perhaps to a large extent yet unexplored) of possible belief, then in this sense theology is totalistic, because Christian belief is itself totalistic; it is not even possible to say what counts as "Christian" belief except by reference to the entire open field of possible belief, across which some beliefs have a decisive epistemic role.

16. Under the limitations of actual practice the truth value of some beliefs will of course be left undecided, since they seem too remote from the community's chief concerns to make deciding about their truth worthwhile. At the same time any belief, no matter how remote it might seem, could become one whose truth value urgently required deciding.

own most central beliefs, Christians need to maximize *agreement* precisely with people who do not hold those beliefs? The notion of inclusive power calls for just such agreement; the greater the assimilative capacity of a belief system, the more extensively its holders will find themselves sharing beliefs proposed by people outside the community. But surely the gospel radically calls into question all of our beliefs, and in particular all of the epistemic priorities we humans are otherwise inclined – or tempted – to hold. This, it might seem, precludes extensive agreement in belief between the members of the Christian community and those who have other epistemic priorities, or at least rules out any epistemic need for such agreement. In that case failure of inclusive power would not count as a reason to suppose the Christian community's central beliefs were false, nor would successful inclusion of novel beliefs count as a reason to hold them true.

In order to see why inclusive and assimilative power count in the epistemic favor of a system of belief structured by the church's priorities, and also why assimilative failure counts against it, we need to reflect a bit further on the connections between meaning, truth, and belief. More exactly, we need to bear in mind the ties which bind the way we interpret a speaker's sentences, the truth value we assign to them, and the extent of our agreement with the speaker in the assignment of those truth values (the extent of our agreement, that is, with the speaker's beliefs). Is it even conceivable that we could have a set of epistemic priorities, and with that a belief system, which permitted (let alone required) us to disagree with other speakers most of the time?

Such a scenario could be conceived only if it were possible to interpret a speaker's utterances correctly on the whole, and still find the speaker for the most part mistaken, his utterances (and so the beliefs we attribute to him) generally false. A workable but non-circular theory of interpretation suggests, however, that this is not possible. If we are to interpret plausibly, we will have to find speakers for the most part correct in the truth values they assign to sentences, which is to say that we will for the most part have to agree with them. Radical interpretation has to presume, in other words, that all speakers have mostly the same set of beliefs. The more extensively we find ourselves disagreeing with others – holding false the sentences they hold true, and conversely – the more we will have to suspect that we have misunderstood them. Under the guidance of the principle of charity, we will have to reinterpret their words so as to agree with them on the whole, though not of course at every point.

With regard to the issue at hand, this implies that epistemic priorities which would permit us to find the utterances of others massively false are not simply undesirable, but impossible to sustain. If we have epistemic priorities which seem to be placing us in increasingly broad disagreement with other speakers, we will eventually have to take one of two possible paths. (1) We can reinterpret sentences which we hold false but others generally hold true, so as to find them more in agreement with our epistemic priorities, and so more generally true. Or (2) we can hold false the beliefs which require such broad disagreement with other speakers, that is, we can change our epistemic priorities. In one way or the other we will have to find ourselves in agreement, for the most part, with other speakers.

These options mutually limit one another, and so cannot simply be chosen at will. Just because plausible interpretation has to optimize agreement among speakers, epistemically troublesome sentences can be reinterpreted only to the extent that revised assignments of meaning tend to diminish, rather than increase, disagreement with those who hold them true. We cannot, for example, reinterpret the sentences which constitute evolutionary theory so as to bring them in line with Christian epistemic priorities, if our reinterpretation tends to increase rather than diminish our ascription of falsity to the sentences held true by other speakers (including, though not only, speakers who hold evolutionist beliefs). The result would be a less, rather than more, plausible interpretation of the troublesome sentences.

The economic alternative to bad interpretation, as we observed in the previous chapter, is to revise the assignment of truth values. What guides the assignment of truth values, as the current problem brings out, is the principle of charity, which optimizes agreement. If a particular set of epistemic priorities can only be sustained at the cost of massive disagreement with other speakers, and so at the cost of interpreting their utterances badly, the only plausible interpretive course is to hold false the beliefs which make up those epistemic priorities, and with that to revise the priorities themselves. In this way, the failure of our epistemic commitments to yield broad agreement with other speakers, and so with beliefs which for us are alien and novel, counts against those commitments; conversely, success at generating agreement – inclusive power – counts in their epistemic favor.

It may seem, however, that granting the inclusive power of Christian beliefs turns out not to support their unrestricted epistemic primacy, but instead to eliminate it. We have argued all along that for central Christian beliefs to be epistemically primary across the board means that all other beliefs have to agree (be consistent) with them in order to be regarded as true. But the argument just developed for the epistemic relevance of a belief system's inclusive power turns on the thought that for these Christian beliefs themselves to be held true, they have to agree on the whole with the rest of what everyone, including Christians, mostly believes. This seems an unhappy result, since we were looking for reasons for holding central Christian beliefs which do not create epistemic subordination.

This conflict, however, is apparent rather than real. The need to optimize agreement among speakers plays a different role in the admission of beliefs into our overall view of the world than does the requirement that any belief we hold must be consistent with our epistemic priorities. Conflict would arise only if we assigned the function of epistemic priority first to one set of beliefs, then to another and different set. In order to dispel the appearance of conflict, we therefore need to distinguish clearly the epistemic role played by "most of" our beliefs from the role of those which we take to be primary.

We can admit and retain in our belief system only those sentences which, in our ongoing effort to interpret the utterances of other human beings, allow us to share most of the beliefs we attribute to them. But the requirement that we optimize agreement is a coarse net; it will filter out countless possible beliefs, but will admit countless more, including many which are in conflict with one another. The need to optimize agreement gives us nothing to go on when it comes to resolving these conflicts – the ones which arise between interpreted sentences which have already passed the test of agreement with most of the beliefs we and other speakers have to share in order to make sense of one another. In order to have a largely coherent system of beliefs, we will regularly have to decide between contradictory claims alike compatible with most of the convictions we and others share. We will therefore have to fail of agreement with beliefs maintained by lots of other speakers, either because we have no opinion on the matter, or because by our own epistemic standards we find their beliefs false – as we will inevitably do in some cases, precisely in order to agree with them on the whole.[17] We can agree with others on a

---

17. See Davidson's comments on this point in "A Coherence Theory of Truth and Knowledge," *Truth and Interpretation: Perspectives on the Philosophy of Donald Davidson*, ed. E. LePore (Oxford: Blackwell, 1986), p. 318.

host of trivialities sufficient in breadth to establish that we are interpreting each other well ("Snow is white," "Grass is green"), and still disagree about what each of us takes to be most important ("On the third day Jesus rose" – or "did not rise" – "from the dead"; "God was" – or "was not" – "in Christ reconciling the world to himself"). When either of two conflicting beliefs would allow us to agree with most of what our interlocutors hold true, and so be good interpreters, we need epistemic priorities to resolve the conflict – to decide which of the beliefs, if either, to accept.[18]

The unrestricted epistemic primacy of central Christian beliefs thus seems quite compatible with the requirement that a plausible set of epistemic priorities exhibit inclusive power: no contradiction arises from saying both that an interpreted sentence can be held true only if it is consistent with the church's central beliefs, and that the same sentence can be held true only if it is consistent with most of the beliefs we attribute to others. Both are, in other words, necessary conditions for deciding about the truth of beliefs; neither is, by itself, sufficient.[19] Indeed the present objection (that we have unwittingly eliminated the epistemic primacy of central Christian beliefs) itself points up the need for concrete epistemic priorities – particular beliefs by adverting to which we make decisions about the truth of other beliefs. If agreement with "most" of our beliefs were sufficient as well as necessary for deciding what belongs in our belief system, then all of our beliefs would be epistemically subordinate to most of our beliefs. But this is absurd. If all of our beliefs were epistemically subordinate, there would be no beliefs left over for them to be subordinate to.

None of this presents any obstacle to the thought that the gospel itself is radically novel, given the ways we human beings are otherwise inclined to look at the world. The epistemic novelty of the church's central beliefs does not depend on the apparently hopeless suggestion that the gospel is opposed to most or all of the beliefs which the rest of humanity holds true, but only on the contrast between the gospel and the epistemic *priorities* human beings are otherwise inclined to have. The gospel does not call all or even most of our beliefs into question ("Snow is white," and so

18. In practice we do not, of course, first decide which beliefs to admit and then decide upon our epistemic priorities; rather in seeking to understand one another we inevitably test the priorities we already have against the limit of excessive disagreement.
19. There would, of course, be a contradiction if consistency with central Christian beliefs were supposed to be a sufficient condition for the truth of all other beliefs. But, as we have argued, it neither can nor need be that sort of condition.

forth), and it is not for this reason that the gospel overturns our settled epistemic priorities. The gospel does, however, conflict with some of the conventional beliefs which are closest to it in logical space, and in particular with the inferences we are inclined to draw from some of the obvious beliefs we all share (beliefs, for example, about what happens when we die, as observed in the previous chapter). Since we will readily use these conventional beliefs as standards by which to judge the truth of the novel claims of the gospel, believing the gospel requires a reversal of the epistemic priorities we would otherwise have, but it does not require that we reject most of the beliefs we would otherwise have.

Here the traditional theological distinction between nature and grace helps clarify matters – or, more precisely, the distinction between the *status integritatis* in which God created human beings (not to be confused with the entirely hypothetical state of "pure nature") and the *status corruptionis* in which human beings now live. Fallen human beings *want* to reject the triune God (even granted that, at another level, they implicitly desire God), and so inevitably fashion epistemic priorities inconsistent with the gospel by which God identifies and gives himself to us. So for fallen humans the novelty of the gospel requires a reversal of epistemic priorities – and with that holding false some beliefs we are otherwise deeply inclined to hold true – if we are going to believe the gospel at all. This means that in the nature of the case, believing the gospel requires a change of heart as well as a change of mind (a point to which we will return in the next chapter).

Were human beings still in their original created condition, without sin, the gospel – which is to say, the Spirit's disclosure to human beings of "the deep things of God" (see 1 Cor. 2:10) – would not meet the resistance of epistemic priorities already opposed to it; such resistance presupposes sin. But the novelty of the deep things of God would still be beyond the epistemic capacities of nature. The epistemic priorities we could otherwise have (say, those given by Quine's and Davidson's occasion sentences) would not be opposed to these novel beliefs, but would leave us with no basis for deciding about them one way or the other. In order to be justified in holding these beliefs true at all, we would have to take them as epistemically primary. So in either case, in the *status integritatis* as well as the *status corruptionis*, the novelty of the deep things of God requires the epistemic primacy of the beliefs by which we apprehend them.[20]

---

20. Thus, to recall a precedent, Aquinas's insistence (*Summa theologiae* II–II, 5, 1, c) that even Adam and Eve in paradise needed faith to know the Trinity; see the discussion in Marshall, "Faith and Reason Reconsidered," *The Thomist* 63/1 (1999), p. 14.

The limits of epistemic judgment

The usefulness (as distinguished from the logical force) of inclusive power as a test of epistemic priorities lies in its employment of shared beliefs in order to assess the epistemic rights of those which are not shared. Others need not agree with our epistemic priorities, but need only be sufficiently diligent, in order to discover whether those priorities tend to display inclusive power over time. It has long been observed that reasoned argument is possible only on the basis of convictions shared by all sides.[21] The present claim is that even when it comes to beliefs of unrestricted epistemic primacy, the convictions we share with those who do not hold these primary beliefs will always provide ways of testing the claims we take to be primary, a test whose force can be acknowledged regardless of one's epistemic priorities.

But the same feature which makes this a readily sharable test also limits its effectiveness. Failure of assimilative power rules out epistemic priorities, and with that the belief systems structured by those priorities. Lots of conflicting beliefs, however, can pass the test of agreement with "most of" what we and others alike hold true. This creates the possibility of conflicting epistemic priorities. Successful assimilation over time of alien and novel beliefs seems to be a feature of manifold actual belief systems which conflict with one another at crucial points, not least in their epistemic priorities; this includes a number of religions. The justificatory force of assimilative power is thus strictly negative; it can eliminate beliefs and epistemic priorities as false, but it cannot fix the truth value of those which remain – it cannot individuate a single true set of epistemic priorities, still less a single true belief system.

That we will always share enough beliefs with one another genuinely

---

21. So Thomas Aquinas, for example, argues that when it comes to first principles (e.g., in metaphysics or, above all, theology), one "enters into argument with a person who denies one's own principles if the adversary concedes at least something, but if he concedes nothing it is impossible to argue with him, although one can dismantle the reasons he gives" – that is, we can show that our first principles do not involve absurdity or contradiction with what we otherwise have good reason to believe (*Summa theologiae* I, 1, 8, c). Thomas thought of this as an idea which came to him from Aristotle, in particular from *Metaphysics* IV, 7–8 (1012a 18–b 10). Commenting on this passage, Thomas makes a suggestion strikingly similar to some of the Davidsonian considerations of which we have made use. Should we find another disagreeing with us in seemingly peculiar ways about what there is, we "can ask that he grant that the words mean something; without this the argument vanishes (*disputatio tollitur*)." In *Duodecim Libros Metaphysicorum Aristotelis Expositio*, ed. M.-R. Cathala and R. Spiazzi (Turin/Rome: Marietti, 1964), 4, 17 (no. 740). That is: if we do not mean the same thing by our words – if we are not talking about the same thing – then we do not disagree ("disputatio tollitur"); if we do mean the same thing by our words, then we will find, Thomas goes on to suggest, that we cannot hold utterly divergent beliefs.

to test one another's epistemic priorities does not, therefore, entail that we will always be able to settle conflicts of belief, and in particular conflicts about which beliefs ought to have epistemic primacy. "Settle," that is, in a fashion acceptable to all sides in an argument; we inevitably resolve some disputes by appeal to beliefs and epistemic priorities which are not shared with at least some of the people with whom we are talking, and so do not elicit their assent. There need be nothing irrational in such appeals to unshared beliefs. They merely point up the epistemic limits of what is shared, the room for rational disagreement which even massive agreement leaves open.

In the nature of the case, differences of epistemic priority (especially when the priorities structure comprehensive belief systems, like religions) are differences over what count as good reasons to hold or reject beliefs, particularly in disputed cases. The apostle Paul argues that belief in Jesus' resurrection makes a good, indeed decisive, reason for believing in the resurrection of those who have faith in Jesus, but he also acknowledges that his *modus ponens* may – to their detriment – be the Corinthians' *modus tollens*: their skepticism about the future resurrection might lead them to deny Jesus' resurrection as well (see I Cor. 15:16–17). Within the limits of plausibility established by inclusive power, adherents of conflicting beliefs and epistemic priorities will often differ not only about what is true, but about what confers or fails to confer epistemic right.

Commensurability

This last thought is sometimes expressed by saying that beliefs and epistemic priorities can turn out to be "incommensurable." If this term simply labels the sort of conflict between beliefs which cannot be resolved except by appeal to the disputed beliefs themselves, then the foregoing argument for the epistemic significance of assimilative power allows for "incommensurable" beliefs and epistemic priorities. But the term is often used to suggest two much stronger claims, both of which are ruled out if appeal to assimilative power has any epistemic force.

1. It is sometimes argued that beliefs and systems of belief (or "conceptual schemes") can be incommensurable in that the adherents of one communal belief system simply cannot understand the adherents of another communal belief system. It is not merely that the two communities hold different beliefs – one either rejects or suspends judgment on various beliefs proposed by the other – but that one community has no access, in whole or in part, to the contents of the other community's

beliefs; the conceptual resources available to the one have no equivalents for what is affirmed in the beliefs of the other. The assumption that (at least for humans) having beliefs depends on having a language connects the notion of incomprehensible beliefs to that of untranslatable languages: holding beliefs we cannot understand goes together with speaking a language we cannot interpret, one with no potential equivalents in our own linguistic stock.[22] Should this strong notion of incommensurability prove out, the power to include the beliefs of others, to count them right most of the time, will be of little use as a test for our own epistemic priorities. The very beliefs we will seek to assimilate, namely ones we do not already have, may well turn out to be convictions which, as non-adherents, we cannot understand, let alone decide whether to count right.

Everyone acknowledges that dramatic differences of both belief and meaning sometimes come to light. The question for our purposes is whether these support the claim that there can be incomprehensible cultural outlooks or untranslatable languages: beliefs we can understand only by holding them, communal convictions which we necessarily distort unless we adhere to them, or languages which permit their users to hold sentences true which we cannot interpret.

The arguments against this strong notion of incommensurable beliefs are now widely familiar. In order to say that the beliefs of another community belong to a worldview which is for us alien or foreign, we have to know what their beliefs are – we have to understand them. Beliefs we cannot comprehend are obviously beliefs we cannot classify as either foreign or domestic. Now it seems that we can only attribute beliefs to others, and discriminate among their beliefs in the fine-grained way we routinely do, if we understand what their words mean. Speakers of a language which we cannot interpret (or translate) using the resources of our own tongue will therefore likewise be creatures whose beliefs, to the extent that we cannot fix the meaning of the sentences they hold true, we

---

22. So for example John Milbank, following Alasdair MacIntyre, argues that "in certain cases, the signifying terms of one cultural outlook simply cannot be translated into the signifying terms of another, without betrayal and distortion," and infers from this that "for the insider" to a religious or other cultural tradition, "without belief, understanding can only be partial. So any claim to full understanding on the part of the outsider must negate the alien tradition's own self-understanding." *Theology and Social Theory: Beyond Secular Reason* (Oxford: Blackwell, 1990), pp. 340–1. For the background in MacIntyre, see especially *Whose Justice? Which Rationality?* (Notre Dame: University of Notre Dame Press, 1988), pp. 370–88. With Milbank's concern that theology avoid captivity to "secular reason" – that theology keep its epistemic priorities straight – I concur; the question at present is whether the notion of incommensurability helps make this point.

can judge neither incommensurable nor commensurable with our own. They will, indeed, be those to whom we have no apparent grounds for attributing beliefs in the first place. The idea that we might run across a communal worldview so foreign we could not understand it seems like an idea we do not really have. Given what we mean by a worldview (a big collection of mostly coherent beliefs, expressible in a language), our interpretive failure would eventually signal not that we had encountered a radically foreign worldview, but no worldview at all.

Advocates of radical incommensurability try to handle this problem by saying that we do not comprehend the beliefs of an alien community by translating their language into our own; rather we become "bilingual," we learn to speak their language like natives.[23] Moving the supposedly untranslatable language into the head of the interpreter does little, though, to make sense of the notion of radically incommensurable beliefs. Suppose that I, a speaker of L_1, acquire native fluency in L_2 (I need not, of course, *learn* L_2 primarily by translating it into L_1). If I, the speaker of L_1, cannot interpret L_2 in L_1, then I can no more tell whether or not the beliefs I have when I hold sentences in L_2 true are incommensurable with those which I have when I use L_1 than I could when L_2 was spoken by somebody else. Likewise I the speaker of L_1 will have no way to tell whether my interpretation of what I say as a speaker of L_2 betrays and distorts my L_2 utterances. In fact if I cannot translate these languages into one another, then when I speak L_2, I, the speaker of L_1, will not know what I am saying. The beliefs I have as a speaker of L_2 will consequently be incomprehensible to the speaker of L_1, that is, to me. This assumes, of course, that "I" refers to the same thing when I speak L_1 and L_2. If it does not, then we are back to the more familiar problem of alien speakers whom we do not understand; moving the two speakers into the same head has not helped make sense of the notion of radically incommensurable beliefs.

It therefore also proves difficult to get a fix on the claim, which often seems to drive appeals to radical incommensurability, that others might have convictions we could understand only by sharing them, or conversely that we (for example, we Christians) might have convictions which others must accept in order to understand them. As it turns out, either we need not share any particular belief of another in order to understand that belief, or sharing the belief will leave us as much in the

23. "Bilingual" is Milbank's phrase (*Theology and Social Theory*, p. 341); MacIntyre calls this, oddly, learning a "second first language" (*Whose Justice? Which Rationality?* pp. 364, 374).

dark about its content as we were in the first place. To reject the beliefs of others is by itself neither to distort their view of the world nor to lack comprehension of it, but simply to disagree with it. To differ in other ways from their beliefs (by suspending judgment on convictions they cherish, for example) is neither to betray nor to misunderstand their view of the world, but simply to hold a different one.

Of course we often enough fail to understand one another. Sometimes this happens because of differences in what we mean, sometimes because of differences in what we believe. We are practiced at coping with both kinds of difference, against the background of that massive sameness of meaning and belief assumed by the principle of charity, which funds plausible interpretation in the first place.[24]

Our concern here is with understanding the beliefs of others, with grasping the meaning of the sentences they hold true. "Understanding" is often used in a broader way, as when we try to "get a feel for" the situation and outlook of another. This affective and perhaps volitional sort of "understanding" surely *does* depend on sharing to some extent the beliefs of those we hope to "understand," assuming that emotions are belief dependent. If the foregoing argument is correct, then sharing the beliefs of others and so getting a feel for their situation depends on grasping the contents of their beliefs, which one need not share the beliefs to do; we can understand the beliefs of others well enough to know whether we also want to get a feel for their situation. Even this affective sense of understanding does not necessarily require conversion to the disputed beliefs of the other, since there is no one-to-one correlation of affections with beliefs, and we will in any case share most of the other's beliefs. There is also such a thing as willful misunderstanding and distortion of others, a deliberate refusal to grasp the sense of their utterances and beliefs. This we normally regard as a vice. It does not support the notion of incommensurable beliefs; if distortion were unavoidable then we would presumably not hold others morally accountable for engaging in it.

2. A less radical idea of incommensurability turns not on the notion of meaning, but of justification or warrant. It picks up the suggestion

---

24. Coping with difference successfully – understanding one another – does not require that there always be a clear way of deciding whether understanding is best served by taking differences as matters of meaning or of belief. As Davidson observes, "When others think differently from us, no general principle, or appeal to evidence, can force us to decide that the difference lies in our beliefs rather than in our concepts" ("On the Very Idea of a Conceptual Scheme," *Inquiries into Truth and Interpretation* [Oxford: Clarendon Press, 1985], p. 197).

that differences in epistemic priority entail differences in what count as good reasons for holding beliefs, and proposes that any belief system with reasonably clear epistemic priorities will always succeed by its own lights. Decisive criticism of such systems is therefore impossible; they will always turn out true by their own criteria of truth, and include the beliefs which conform to those criteria. As an epistemic test inclusive power is not just limited, but useless; all belief systems will pass it.

Just as the requirements of plausible interpretation limit the extent to which our beliefs can be supposed to differ from those of the speakers we are trying to understand, so the same requirements limit the degree to which we and they can differ on what count as good reasons for beliefs. Since we have to assume for the most part that our beliefs are the same as theirs, and good reasons are relations of evidence, support, agreement, and so forth, among beliefs, there is no chance that we can differ massively from them on what to count as good reasons, any more than we can differ massively on what to believe. Combine this with the earlier observation that even the most central beliefs will generate only a fraction of the primary (that is, most decisive) reasons for holding sentences true within a total belief system, and it becomes obvious that any belief system, no matter how comprehensive, will always be able to fail by its own standards.[25]

Conceiving such epistemic failure is not difficult. It threatens whenever beliefs which a community has good reason to hold, or which seem too obvious to deny, imply the negations of the community's most central convictions. Various strategies for meeting such threats present themselves. The community can try to assimilate the alien beliefs, arguing that they do not in fact imply the negations of its central beliefs (as with Aristotle for the Christian community in the thirteenth century). It can argue that the beliefs negated by the novel claims are not really central for it (as with evolution in the nineteenth century), though there are evident limits to pursuing *this* strategy; eventually the community will run out of beliefs to decentralize. It can mount a counterargument seeking to show that the reasons for rejecting the troublesome beliefs are better than the

---

25. A communal tradition, as MacIntyre argues, can undergo an "epistemological crisis," and may find that it has suffered "defeat in respect of truth" at the hands of an "alien tradition," when the latter provides the resources (which it lacked) for solving its epistemological crisis (*Whose Justice? Which Rationality?*, pp. 361, 365). MacIntyre's analysis of epistemological crises has bite, to be sure, only if his analysis of radical incommensurability is wrong – only if we can understand, without (or without yet) belonging to, traditions which might defeat us, including, presumably, those most different from our own.

reasons for accepting them (as Christians in the thirteenth century did not so much with Aristotle as with Muslim interpretations of Aristotle). Or the community can grant that the problem is insoluble, that it has no insight into the way in which novel claims which it has good reason to believe hang together with its most central convictions, though it is convinced that they must. This may involve a determination to keep working on the problem in the hope that greater light may come, but the difficulty may also be one whose solution we should not expect in advance of the eschaton. The decision to live with this sort of epistemic tension can be made only sparingly. Though armed truces can under some circumstances go on indefinitely, if the front on which one attempts to fight this delaying action becomes too broad, or the battle goes on too long, outright collapse becomes more imminent – less metaphorically, giving up central beliefs increasingly looks like the only plausible course.

Strong objections

This suggests that the strongest objections to Christian belief – those most telling to adherents of a Christian view of things – will not stem from arguments whose force depends heavily on acceptance of rival epistemic priorities. On the assumption that the Christian community's central beliefs cannot be its epistemic priorities, modern theology has often thought it necessary to revise the church's central beliefs precisely in order to accommodate alternative epistemic commitments. But such calls for revision rarely carry the force of necessity suggested by their advocates. *Ceteris paribus*, the more clearly the demand for revision relies on alternative epistemic commitments, the more easily the Christian community will be able to reject the demand – to take it as one of those places where we can count our interlocutors wrong in particular without endangering our agreement with them in general.

The strongest objections to Christian belief, as to any comprehensive belief system, will rather stem from matters on which everybody agrees – the more obvious the agreement, the better. A really forceful objection to the Christian community's belief system will be one where the community's central beliefs lead it to expect a particular state of affairs which manifestly fails to obtain. Take, for instance, the eucharistic disunity of the church. The New Testament seems to propose that the temporal missions of the Son and the Spirit from the Father have created a single human community, united chiefly by the eucharist (see 1 Cor. 10:16–17), in a way visible to all (see Jn. 17:21, 23). The bonds which are visibly to unite this temporal community are nothing less than those which eternally unite the Son with the Father and the Spirit in love (see Jn. 17:11, 21, 26). If the gospel (the narrative of the missions of the Son and the Spirit from the Father) is true, therefore, we should expect to find in the world a single community embracing all who celebrate the eucharist.

But we find no such community. Instead, obvious to Christians and non-Christians alike, multiple communities celebrate the eucharist while (in many cases) refusing to share it with the others. Multiple communities recognize one another as Christian communities, but lack the visible eucharistic bond which the missions of the Son and the Spirit were supposed to create in the world by giving the world a share in their own eternal bond of love. The existence of this community would not, of course, demonstrate the truth of the gospel, but its absence bespeaks the gospel's falsity. Though perhaps not the sort of objection which those who do not share the church's beliefs are likely to press, *here* we find a novel state of affairs which bears quite directly on the church's most central beliefs, and which the Christian community has had relatively little success in assimilating. Whether the church nonetheless has resources to cope conceptually and practically with the epistemic problem posed by its own divisions is therefore a particularly pressing question for Christian belief, a question not evaded but intensified by regarding the church's trinitarian identification of God as epistemically primary.[26]

Taking the Christian community's central beliefs as epistemically primary without restriction does not, then, prevent alien and novel claims from counting as good reasons against the church's central beliefs, calling for arguments in reply. Assimilative power is not useless as an epistemic test of this (or, *mutatis mutandis*, any other) community's belief system; success at assimilating novel beliefs will have to be earned, and does not come automatically once communal epistemic priorities are fixed. And this means that the unrestricted epistemic primacy of the beliefs which identify the Trinity is quite compatible with the now commonplace notion of rationality to which we alluded at the outset: the

26. On the argument of this paragraph see my essay, "The Disunity of the Church and the Credibility of the Gospel," *Theology Today* 50/1 (1993), pp. 78–89, but especially Ephraim Radner, *The End of the Church: A Pneumatology of Christian Division in the West* (Grand Rapids: Eerdmans, 1998). The end of the church as a coherent community will come, Radner provocatively argues, not from failure or inability to maintain its epistemic priorities, but as the divinely willed outcome of the divided church's willful failure to conform, in its life and practice, to what it claims its highest priorities to be.

view that being reasonable does not require (or even permit) us to doubt all of our beliefs at once, but does require that we be prepared to give up any particular belief, even the most central – and so be prepared to change our epistemic priorities.

Locating conditions under which there would be good reasons to give up the Christian community's most central beliefs, and thereby to abandon its epistemic priorities, is not especially difficult. Consider the following scenario.[27] A letter is discovered in an ancient Mediterranean, now Turkish, village, addressed to one Paul, formerly Saul, of Tarsus.

> I can hardly believe we got away with it. The place where we hid the body was so obvious, and it took so long before we could finally get rid of it, that I'm amazed no one discovered it. And that story we cooked up about seeing him alive after they crucified him – not just once, but for forty days! Admittedly a few Athenians thought this was pretty funny, but it's astonishing how many people have believed it. So let's press on to Rome and see how far we can carry this thing. Be careful, and write when you are able . . . As ever, Peter

That Jesus is not dead, though he once was, is utterly central to the Christian community's belief system. The New Testament also seems to link the very possibility of having the belief that Jesus is risen to hearing the testimony of others – ultimately, of a small group who did not hear about it from anyone else, but met the crucified one in his risen flesh, and were taught about the resurrection from the source.[28] So if we have good reason to believe that those upon whose testimony we depend in order to

---

27. Which I owe to a suggestion of Michael Root.

28. On this see Heinrich Schlier, "Kerygma und Sophia. – Zur neutestamentlichen Grundlegung des Dogmas," *Die Zeit der Kirche: Exegetische Aufsätze und Vorträge I*, 4th edn (Freiburg: Herder, 1966), especially pp. 215–17 (on I Cor. 15:1–11). Modern exegetical and theological discussions of Jesus' resurrection have, to be sure, often vehemently contested the idea that justified belief in the resurrection entails belief in the veracity of a handful of first-century Jews whom the New Testament presents as having seen the risen Jesus – have contested, in other words, the thought that anything depends on the truth of the claim that Schlier offers as an interpretation of Paul: "The resurrection of Jesus Christ occurred in front of witnesses, precisely in the sense that the risen one unmistakably appeared to them as such" (p. 215). It is perhaps not accidental that objection to this idea tends to go together with what we have argued are implausible interpretations of the New Testament resurrection texts, viz., those which try to avoid attributing "is risen" to the same referent to which they attribute "was dead," and so try to avoid seeing the resurrection as an event which happens to the dead Jesus. On such interpretations one will of course not expect anyone to have seen the crucified Jesus, risen, so believing in the resurrection does not depend on believing in the veracity of ancient witnesses who claim to have done so. If, by contrast, rising to life (however more precisely construed) is an event which happens to the dead Jesus, having the right to believe in the occurrence of this event would seem to depend on either seeing its unambiguous result – Jesus' risen flesh – or on hearing about that flesh from those who have.

believe in Jesus' resurrection were lying or deceived, we have good reason to think that what they said is false.

Of course the counterfactual scenario we have just imagined would be really forceful only if it could be developed much more elaborately than we have the space to do here. Naturally one Christian response to this fancied discovery would be to question the provenance of the letter, and to argue that it could not be attributed to its putative author. But suppose that scientific tests on the paper and ink ruled out a modern origin for the letter, that it fits with our best historical knowledge about Paul's journeys, and so forth. The Christian community would then find it increasingly difficult to deny the authenticity of the letter without rejecting wide stretches of seemingly obvious belief common to Christians and non-Christians alike; eventually the failure of assimilative power brought on by trying to maintain the belief that Jesus is not dead would call for dropping the belief altogether.

That we can state conditions under which Christians would be prepared to give up the belief that Jesus is risen does not, however, require that this belief be held tentatively, or that it be regarded as uncertain and therefore corrigible. What it rules out is taking certainty and incorrigibility as descriptive rather than normative concepts. Foundationalism took these to be descriptive notions. Confronted by the right kind of evidence, a functioning mind could not help having empirically evident or self-evident beliefs. Certainty and incorrigibility were made parasitic on these types of belief; eliminating the latter eliminates the former.

The Christian tradition, however, has generally taken the church's central beliefs to be certain and incorrigible, while explicitly denying that these beliefs are self-evident, empirically evident, or even very widely held. This position treats certainty and incorrigibility as normative concepts.[29] To hold the Christian community's central beliefs at all is, in virtue of their content, to regard them as giving the holder a share in

---

29. Thus Luther: "This is the reason why our theology is certain: because it tears us away from ourselves and puts us outside of ourselves, so that we may rely not on our own powers, conscience, sense, person, or works, but on that which is outside of ourselves – that is, on the promise and truth of God, which cannot lie" (*WA* 40/I, p. 589, 25–8). But equally Aquinas: "A human being is much more certain about what he hears from God, who cannot be deceived, than about what he sees by his own reason, because his reason can be deceived" (*Summa theologiae* II–II, 4, 8, ad 2). Therefore, "The believer's assent to what belongs to the faith is greater and more stable even than assent to the first principles of reason" (*In I Sent.* pro., 1, 3, iii, c). For a discussion see "Faith and Reason Reconsidered," especially pp. 15–16.

God's own creative knowledge – a veritable God's-eye view of the world.[30] We who hold these beliefs should therefore regard them as certain and incorrigible – incapable of turning out to be false – not because we have evidence which would compel anyone in our situation to hold the same belief, but because the triune God's creative knowledge, in which he graciously gives us a creaturely share by way of adherence to the church's epistemic priorities, cannot be deceived or corrected. To acknowledge conditions under which Christians would have to give up their own most central beliefs is not, therefore, to concede that these beliefs are uncertain and corrigible, but to express the confidence, rooted in the contents of these beliefs themselves, that these conditions will never be met.

A test case: religious diversity

The election of Israel
Christians are not, of course, likely to be alone in having this sort of confidence in the truth of their most central beliefs. Other communities, in particular other religious communities, will no doubt often have reasons, linked to the contents of their own most central and identity-forming beliefs, for supposing that these beliefs cannot turn out to be false. Encounters with the beliefs and practices of other religious communities pose special problems for a theological account of how to decide what is true.

One problem is epistemic. Encounters with other religious communities confront the church not simply with alien and novel beliefs, but with alternative epistemic priorities. Other religious communities will order the whole field of possible belief differently than the church does, around different convictions of unrestricted epistemic scope. How then

---

30. Some philosophers regard the notion of a "God's Eye point of view" as an essentially humorous one, useful for mocking the pretensions of epistemologies they reject (the quoted phrase is Putnam's, *Reason, Truth and History*, p. 49; see Richard Rorty, "Wittgenstein, Heidegger, and the Reification of Language," *Essays on Heidegger and Others*, p. 59). The humor is supposed to lie in the pretense that we can leap out of our conceptual schemes, our social practices, our skins, or whatever, in order to obtain a more surely veridical view of the world than these philosophers allow. But in order to obtain a God's-eye view of the world we need do nothing so dramatic; we need merely hold true the narratives which identify Jesus and organize the rest of our beliefs accordingly. The Holy Spirit's gift of wisdom thereby gives us "an exhaustive view from on high, which makes our perspective that of the Trinity" (M. M. Philipon, *Les dons du Saint-Esprit* [Paris: Desclée de Brouwer, 1964], p. 137). This is, to be sure, seeing "in a mirror dimly" (1 Cor. 13:12), but it is sight nonetheless; we will one day see better, but we are not on that account now blind.

can either community (though our present focus is of course on the Christian side of the encounter) genuinely learn from the other – assimilate the other's beliefs and change its own – without sharing the other's epistemic priorities, and thereby losing its own identity?

The encounter of conflicting religious truth claims also poses a moral problem. This sort of epistemic confrontation never takes place in a social and political vacuum, and rarely in a situation where power among the communities is more or less equally distributed. When one community wields vastly more power than another, it will face the temptation to mistake its political, economic, military, or even sheer numeric dominance for an epistemic triumph. Assuming epistemic victory naturally tends to foreclose the possibility of constructive dialogue between communities, since those who make this assumption will tend to suppose that they can have nothing to learn from the putatively defeated community, or, less harshly, that they have already assimilated whatever there is of value in the other community's view of the world. And while we need not, of course, abuse those from whom we suppose we have nothing to learn, this supposition does regularly serve as justification for abuse.

The historically dominant attitude of the church to the Jewish people is a particularly striking case of a larger religious community taking social and political power over a smaller one for epistemic triumph. We may usefully reflect, therefore, on whether the church can learn from the Jewish people about matters at the heart of its faith, without having to give up its own epistemic priorities – and without demanding that the Jewish people give up theirs, so that learning becomes the occasion for epistemic triumph. Should the epistemic outlook we have developed so far allow for an epistemically more constructive and morally less problematic relationship of the church with the Jewish people, the plausibility of the account would presumably be strengthened; should it not, there would be good reason to find the account unsatisfactory.[31]

For present purposes we will limit ourselves to brief consideration of a single topic, the election of Israel.[32] Jewish belief in Israel's election, to

31. It might be objected that the distinctive relation of the church to Israel, such that the church claims to worship the same God as the Jewish people, and takes Jewish scripture as the word of this God, makes the church's encounter with Israel a poor test case for the genuinely interreligious consequences of the epistemic proposal for which this book argues. At least as *worshipping* communities, however, the church and the Jewish people appear to regard each other as sharing no members in common. In that quite basic sense – at the point where their epistemic priorities are most clearly on display – it seems fair to call the relation between the church and the Jewish people an interreligious one.
32. For a fuller account of some of the issues discussed in this section, see my essays "The

summarize roughly, seems to include at least the following basic elements. (1) God freely chooses Israel – the descendants of Abraham, Isaac, and Jacob – from among the nations of the world for an enduring relationship with himself, one both uniquely intimate and intended for the ultimate good of all the nations. Israel responds to God's election, but does not originate it. (2) God gives the Torah to Israel; its obligations provide the chief content of this unique relationship, and their fulfillment is central to its aim. The gift of the Torah is thus inseparable from, but not identical with, Israel's election. (3) God's choice of Israel and his revelation of the Torah to her distinguish Israel from the nations.[33]

Belief in Israel's election is not only among the historically central doctrines of the Jewish community, but is clearly regarded by some Jewish thinkers as having unrestricted epistemic primacy. Michael Wyschogrod, for example, argues that the most basic feature of Jewish identity is neither a distinctive system of beliefs nor the observance of a distinctive legal code, however indispensable both are. Rather, "the foundation of Judaism is the family identity of the Jewish people as the descendants of Abraham, Isaac, and Jacob. Whatever else is added to this must be seen as growing out of and related to the basic identity of the Jewish people as the seed of Abraham elected by God through descent from Abraham."[34] Thus "the most important part of the whole [of Judaism] is the existence of the Jewish people as the earthly abode of Hashem," such that "everything else must be seen in this light. Only because it is true is everything else true."[35]

Remarks of this kind suggest that in Judaism, at least as construed by a Jewish thinker like Wyschogrod, belief in Israel's election is the primary criterion of truth.[36] When it comes to deciding about truth, God's unshakable electing love for Israel forms that conviction within the open

Jewish People and Christian Theology," *The Cambridge Companion to Christian Doctrine*, ed. Colin Gunton (Cambridge: Cambridge University Press, 1997), pp. 81–100, and "Truth Claims and the Possibility of Jewish-Christian Dialogue," *Modern Theology* 8/3 (1992), pp. 221–40.

33. This characterization is drawn in particular from David Novak, *The Election of Israel* (Cambridge: Cambridge University Press, 1995).

34. Michael Wyschogrod, *The Body of Faith: God and the People Israel*, 2nd edn (Northvale, New Jersey: Jason Aronson, 1996), p. 57.   35. *The Body of Faith*, pp. 223, 118.

36. Or at least one of the primary criteria. David Novak argues that Wyschogrod's account implicitly subordinates Torah to election, whereas the two ought to be regarded as equally basic to Jewish identity and to Judaism; see *The Election of Israel*, pp. 241–8. For our purposes this dispute is not decisive, since both locate election among Judaism's primary beliefs. In modern times some Jewish thinkers have, to be sure, argued that the Jewish people and the Jewish religion would be better off without the traditional doctrine of Israel's election; for a critical treatment of one such proposal from a Jewish perspective, see David Novak, "Mordecai Kaplan's Rejection of Election," *Modern Judaism* 15 (1995), pp. 1–19.

field of possible beliefs which the faithful Jew is most unwilling to give up or reinterpret, and correlatively that with which all other belief and practice must at least be consistent in order to be held true or regarded as right.

This way of understanding the epistemic structure of Judaism displays an obvious similarity to the account of Christianity's basic epistemic structure proposed here. In each case unlimited epistemic primacy is ascribed to a complex body of beliefs which identifies a particular – the Jewish people as the object of God's electing love and his dwelling place in the world; the resurrection and exaltation of the crucified Jesus of Nazareth as the self-identification of the triune God for the world.[37]

This structural affinity highlights, of course, a criteriological disagreement. If Wyschogrod and I are right about our respective communities, Jews and Christians both assign unrestricted epistemic primacy to descriptions of particulars. But we ascribe this decisive epistemic role to descriptions of *different* particulars. Once adequately picked out and described, these two particulars – Abraham's descendants as God's elect, Jesus crucified and risen – cannot be mistaken for one another; they are manifestly discernible (fail to have all the same properties) and therefore not identical. Since descriptions of two different particulars are epistemically primary for the two communities, the epistemic conflict between these communities seems irreducible: there is no chance that, so long as each survives, the two communities will agree on the decisive criteria by which to evaluate beliefs – including, of course, each other's beliefs.

Does this mean that the two communities are fated never to learn from, and perhaps never even to understand, one another? Or for present purposes, does ascribing unrestricted epistemic primacy to the narratives which identify Jesus foreclose the possibility that Christians could learn from Jews, even about matters at the heart of the Christian faith, and by the same token raise the specter of abuse directed at those from whom we cannot learn?

Conceiving religious diversity

Recent attempts, theological and otherwise, to cope conceptually with the plurality of religions have regularly tended to suppose that the answer to these questions must be yes. If different religious communities are genuinely to learn from one another, such that one comes to share

---

37. Wyschogrod is aware of this affinity, and takes Karl Barth as his model for a Christian theology which displays this sort of epistemic structure. See *The Body of Faith*, pp. 75–81.

beliefs important to another, they cannot finally decide about truth in disparate ways, still less by appeal to descriptions of different particulars. Rather they will already have to share not only many of the same beliefs, but at least implicitly the same epistemic priorities.

This point is sometimes put as a need to avoid religious "exclusivism." To ascribe unrestricted epistemic primacy to descriptions of a particular, and with that ultimate significance to the particular so described, is *eo ipso* exclusivistic. It requires those who make such an ascription to regard those who do not as either ignorant or mistaken about ultimate matters. Exclusivism is at once epistemically overcommitted and morally problematic; it embodies, so the argument goes, just the sort of attitude which leads people to suppose that others cannot teach them anything.

The suggestion that different religious communities in fact share the same epistemic priorities can be developed in a variety of ways.[38] It might be argued that underlying their apparent diversity of belief and practice, all religions finally have the same objective aim – "God," "reality," or "the transcendent," for example. Or it might be argued that all religious belief and practice expresses the same basic experience – of "love," for example, or, once again, "God," "reality," or "the transcendent." Some versions of each approach hierarchize the various religions according to the relative adequacy with which they lead toward the common aim or express the common experience. These tend to identify the aim or experience in relatively definite and, in the case of theological versions, predominantly Christian, terms. Other versions resist hierarchy and attempt to interpret all religions as equally adequate, although only partial, accounts of the common aim or expressions of the common experience. These tend to identify the common aim or experience in relatively vague terms, such as "reality," or "the transcendent." Epistemic primacy belongs, so these accounts variously imply, to those beliefs which locate the common aim or express the common experience. The assumption that this aim or experience is shared by all religions serves as warrant for the claim that they all at least implicitly have the beliefs which locate it, and indeed at least implicitly regard them as primary in decisions about truth.

Such strategies for coping with religious diversity need not rule out the possibility that the shared beliefs to which epistemic primacy belongs

---

38. For an argument in support of the typology briefly sketched in this paragraph, see J. A. DiNoia, O. P., *The Diversity of Religions: A Christian Perspective* (Washington: CUA Press, 1992). The approaches I here characterize as hierarchical DiNoia calls "inclusive," those which resist hierarchy he labels "pluralistic."

identify and describe a particular. But one can see why the proposals they make for the common religious aim or experience generally fail to include any identification and description of particulars. These proposals have to render plausible the suggestion that diverse communities not only share (at least implicitly) various relevant beliefs, but (at least implicitly) regard these shared beliefs as epistemically primary. Beliefs whose contents identify and describe particulars (God's elect people Israel; Jesus crucified and risen) are those which different religious communities are most evidently prone not to share, let alone jointly regard as epistemically primary. So a search for common criteria of truth will naturally tend to settle on beliefs whose content is abstract or indeterminate enough to make credible the claim that they are shared. The reference of the term which is supposed to locate the aim of the common quest or the content of the common experience will be correspondingly vague. Such expressions may be usable as singular terms (as is "the transcendent," or even "reality" or "mystery," which are singular in the way "water" or "blue" is singular), but they will almost surely not enable us to identify any particular (even singular terms whose reference is entirely clear may fail to support the identification of a particular, like "the first dog to be born at sea").[39]

These approaches rightly strive to account for the possibility that one religious community could come to share beliefs held by another. It is not clear, though, that they actually succeed.

In various ways these approaches reject the idea that descriptions of particulars can be epistemically primary in religious belief systems, and instead interpret these systems so that referring terms of a vague or general kind, with more or less rich descriptions attached, take on this epistemic role. We locate a community's epistemic priorities, however, by finding out which beliefs that community is least willing to give up or modify. Proposals about a community's epistemic priorities are thereby proposals about its identity. If descriptions of different particulars are epistemically primary for the Jewish and Christian communities, then interpretations of Judaism and Christianity which seek to dislodge these descriptions from their epistemic place are proposals for basic changes in the identity of the two communities. But this seems an odd way to think about a mutually instructive dialogue between the two communities. It would require Jews to stop being Jews, and Christians to stop being

---

39. To use P. F. Strawson's example of a "pure individuating description"; see *Individuals* (London: Methuen, 1959), p. 26.

Christians, in order for a dialogue to take place; a Jewish–Christian dialogue would not be the result. This seems not so much to account for the possibility of genuine dialogue between the two different traditions as (borrowing a metaphor from Donald Davidson) to arrange a shotgun wedding between them – one which, moreover, does not marry the original mates.

To this kind of objection it might, of course, be replied that descriptions of particulars are not in fact central to the belief systems of the Jewish and Christian communities (or of other historic religious traditions). The sort of interpretation which wants to centralize such descriptions, rather than that which aims to move them to the periphery, actually distorts the identity of the communities involved.

Even were such suggestions empirically plausible, they would not help with the matter at hand. Decentralizing descriptions of particulars in the belief systems of religious communities does not solve the problem of finding a morally tolerable approach to epistemic encounters between them. It defines the problem out of existence, and then declares it solved. By suggesting that religious communities which share no members nonetheless have, at least implicitly, the same primary criteria of truth, this approach in effect proposes that religious diversity is epistemically superficial: when it comes to criteria of truth, there is no warrant for the existence of separate communities (there may of course be warrants of other kinds). This thought fails to explain how we can learn from those with whom we have genuinely basic disagreements, religious or otherwise – in particular, disagreements about which beliefs are epistemically primary. The assumption, on the contrary, seems to be that we can only come to share the beliefs of those with whom we already agree on the most basic matters, those who are basically like us, at least when it comes to beliefs. Other communities with whom we assume agreement may, of course, fail to realize how little difference there is between us. They may actively resist the suggestion that they already share our beliefs – a hazard of assigning to them implicit beliefs, convictions they are unaware of having, and which they may see as inconsistent with their own explicit epistemic priorities.

Nor does epistemically decentralizing descriptions of particulars succeed in avoiding religious "exclusivism." Any belief system structured by epistemic priorities of unlimited scope is the same *size* as any other. Each includes the same totality of possible belief; worldviews differ not in being more or less inclusive, but in assigning truth values differently across the totality of possible belief which they already share. Religious belief systems which ascribe epistemic primacy to descriptions of a particular, like Judaism and Christianity, admit in principle no more or fewer beliefs, are no more inclusive or exclusive, than those which do not – however differently they assign truth values in individual cases. And to assign truth values differently than others is to regard others as mistaken. If this is exclusivism, outlooks which epistemically decentralize descriptions of particulars no more succeed in avoiding it than those with highly particularistic priorities. Error about matters of ultimate significance is still attributed to some, and not to others; we differ only as to whom.

We should perhaps ask, therefore, whether a religious community which grants unrestricted epistemic primacy to descriptions of a particular is in fact incapable of acquiring beliefs from another religious community. In the present case: is it possible after all for the church to learn from Jews to believe in the election of Israel?

Christological inclusion of Israel's election

The Christian community now widely, and in some cases officially, teaches the permanence of Israel's election.[40] Repudiating the claim that God has rejected or abandoned the Jews has evident moral implications; it counts as a strong reason (though of course not the only one) for opposing the church's historic hostility toward the Jewish people, and for changing Christian practice accordingly.

Through most of its history the Christian theological mainstream had, of course, affirmed God's election of Israel and his gift of the Torah to her, but had maintained that both the election and the gift were temporary. The church, so the historically dominant view goes, has superseded – taken the place of – Israel as God's elect, and sacramental worship has, roughly speaking, taken the place of the Torah in structuring the basic relationship between God and his chosen people. A genuinely postsupersessionist understanding of election in Christian theology is therefore one which affirms the permanence of Israel's election, and with that

---

40. Thus Vatican II: "According to the Apostle the Jews remain most dear to God on account of their fathers, since God does not repent of his gifts or his call [see Rom. 11:28–9]" (*Nostra Aetate*, § 4; see *Lumen Gentium*, § 16). Norman Tanner, S.J., ed., *Decrees of the Ecumenical Councils*, 2 vols. (London: Sheed and Ward, 1990), vol. II, pp. 970, 861. For a collection of Protestant statements see *The Theology of the Churches and the Jewish People* (Geneva: WCC Publications, 1988). For more on some of the issues discussed in the next several paragraphs, see "The Jewish People and Christian Theology."

the permanence of the divinely willed distinction between Jew and Gentile. The rallying point for this renewed understanding of Israel's election in Christian theology has been Rom. 9–11, where Paul's effort to come to grips with the relationship between Israel and the church culminates in a vigorous affirmation of God's unshakable love for and fidelity to Abraham's children (see Rom. 11:28–9). Indeed Paul seems to have a doctrine of Israel's election so strong that it might not be possible to conceive a stronger one. On his account it seems impossible that Jews can stray so far as to lose their election, since those Jews who have already done what Paul takes to be the worst thing they can do – reject the Messiah – are nonetheless "beloved for the sake of their forefathers" (Rom. 11:29).

However, just as there were many ways of being a supersessionist in Christian theology, so there are many ways of not being one. In order to get beyond supersessionism, some theologians argue that the Christian community has to rearrange its long-standing epistemic priorities. The church has to give up, in particular, the conviction of Jesus' universal primacy, and with that the epistemic priority of the Trinity. Perhaps the most obvious way to make this point is to argue that Israel's God has established two covenants or saving arrangements in the world, one for Jews (through election and Torah) and the other for Gentiles (through Jesus).

Though stemming from understandable motives, this adjustment of epistemic priorities looks like an unpromising strategy for post-supersessionist Christian theology. Any religious community will naturally resist the suggestion that it give up its most central, identity-forming convictions, and will likely endure even discomfiting associations of these convictions (in this case, supersessionism) if it sees rejection of its own most central beliefs – and with that infidelity to its God – as the only alternative. So a successful post-supersessionist theology will have to show that belief in Israel's permanent election is at least compatible with, and if possible more strongly implicated in, the unrestricted epistemic primacy of the narratives which identify Jesus, and thereby in the doctrines of the incarnation and the Trinity.

Here there is room for only two brief suggestions. Belief in the permanence of Israel's election, and so in the permanence of the distinction between Jew and Gentile, surely seems at least *compatible* with belief in the universal primacy of Jesus of Nazareth, and so with the epistemic primacy of the narratives which identify him. Nothing about the one belief manifestly contradicts the other, requiring us to choose between them, though a consideration of the complex entailments of each set of beliefs would be necessary in order to see if this appearance of consistency were borne out in the long run. Paul, at any rate, evidently thinks the two convictions are compatible, and so commits those who regard his writings as scripture to find ways of spelling out their compatibility.

In so doing, it ought to be possible to make a case for a tighter relationship between Jesus' unrestricted primacy and the election of Israel than mere compatibility. According to the traditional Christian doctrine of incarnation, for example, in the person of the Logos God makes his own the flesh of the particular Jew, Jesus of Nazareth. God's ownership of this Jewish flesh is permanent. In the end, when all flesh shall see the glory of the Lord, the vision of God will, so the traditional Christian teaching goes, be bound up ineluctably with the vision of this Jew seated at God's right hand. So in willing his own incarnation, it seems that God wills the permanence, indeed the eschatological permanence, of the distinction between Jews and Gentiles. But Jesus cannot be a Jew, or be identified as such (as he will be even in the eschaton), all by himself, in isolation from his people. He is a Jew, like any other, only in virtue of his descent from Abraham, and thus in virtue of his relationship to the Jewish people as a whole. And this suggests that in owning with unsurpassable intimacy the particular Jewish flesh of Jesus, God also owns the Jewish people as a whole, precisely in their distinction from us Gentiles; he cannot own the one without also owning the other. The two forms of ownership are not identical – the one involves nothing short of union, the other something like indwelling – but neither are they totally disparate. As both Jewish and Christian theologians have sometimes observed, the Christian doctrine of incarnation is an intensification, not a repudiation, of traditional Jewish teaching about the dwelling of the divine presence in the midst of Israel.[41]

In the end this Christian teaching clearly says more than the Jewish doctrine of Israel's election, and more than Jews can accept. But for present purposes the key point is that the Christian doctrine of God's incarnation does not say less than the Jewish belief in the eternal election of Abraham's children. That the Christian community could come to share this central Jewish belief, and thereby change its own historic teaching, may readily be understood in light of the foregoing account of the way communal belief systems may assimilate novel or alien claims.

41. For some penetrating observations on this point from the Jewish side, see Wyschogrod, The Body of Faith, pp. 211–15.

Since a community's primary criteria of truth will generate relatively few of the reasons the community and its members will have for holding beliefs, a viable communal belief system will be one which allows those who hold it to take in novel or alien claims when they have reason to do so, yet without giving up their own epistemic priorities. In the present case, however, the bond is much closer than this. Israel's permanent election seems not simply to be compatible with the Christian community's epistemic priorities, but actually to be required by them. The Christian rejection of supersessionism seems like a case of an initially alien claim – one central to another community but rejected by the church – which the Christian community finds it has good reason not only to assimilate, but to locate near the center of its own belief system.

God's faithfulness to his election of the Jewish people is not, of course, exactly a novel claim for Christians; belief in it goes deep enough into the community's system of beliefs to have not only textual, but scriptural fixity. A soon largely Gentile church more or less thought it could reject this belief without sacrificing plausible interpretation of its own scriptural text. The claim had to become novel again in order for the church to interpret its scriptures and order its belief system more coherently – in order for the church to have truth commitments on this matter which matched its epistemic priorities.

7

The epistemic role of the Spirit

180   Deciding about the truth of Christian beliefs so far seems to bring one of the trinitarian persons to the forefront – Jesus the Son – and to call for attention to the Father and the Spirit only as implicated in the distinctive epistemic work of Jesus Christ. Yet while the Son seems to have the leading role in a trinitarian response to the question of epistemic right, our christologically oriented answer to this question leaves another equally important matter largely untouched: how is it that we come to ascribe this epistemic role to the Son?

We recognize the ultimate epistemic right which belongs to Jesus Christ by organizing our total system of belief around the narratives which identify him, crucified and risen. If we ascribe this epistemic significance to Jesus, we shall be unwilling to hold true any belief which we recognize to be inconsistent with these narratives, and, conversely, unwilling to regard these narratives as false for the sake of holding true any other belief, should that belief conflict with them. Whence, though, comes this willingness to hold the narratives true in the face of whatever epistemic opposition the believer may encounter? How – without recourse to foundations or epistemic dependence – do we succeed in recognizing the epistemic ultimacy of Jesus the Son?

To this question the tradition has tended to respond by appealing to a distinctive epistemic role of the Holy Spirit: "No one can say 'Jesus is Lord,' except by the Holy Spirit" (1 Cor. 12:3). If the Gospel of John identifies "the truth" with Jesus Christ, the Word incarnate (14:6; cf. 1:14, 17), 1 John identifies "the truth" with the Holy Spirit, precisely in virtue of the Spirit's faithful witness to Jesus Christ: "the Spirit is the truth" (1 Jn. 5:6).[1]

---

1. Ignace de la Potterie makes much of this last passage, together with 1 Jn. 4:6, in *La Vérité dans Saint Jean*, 2 vols. (Rome: Biblical Institute Press, 1977); see especially pp. 286–328, and the summary, pp. 1012–14.

The Spirit's role as witness comes through with equal clarity in the Gospel's farewell discourses (cf. Jn. 15:26: "he will testify on my behalf," also 14:26; 16:13–14). In virtue of the Spirit's own unique location within the triune life of God, these passages suggest, he must be the one who empowers us to recognize the epistemic ultimacy of Jesus Christ – who teaches us how to order all of our beliefs around the narratives which identify the Father's crucified and risen Son. As Thomas Aquinas puts the point, "To make the truth manifest belongs uniquely to the Holy Spirit (*convenit proprietati Spiritus sancti*). For it belongs to love to disclose hidden things," and in God the love which opens up that which is hidden is the Holy Spirit himself: "the Holy Spirit is nothing other than love."[2]

The Son's distinctive epistemic role is therefore inseparable not only from that of the Father (see chapter 5), but also from that of the Spirit. That both the faith which assents to the church's central beliefs and the wisdom which judges all other beliefs accordingly depend on the continuing action of the Holy Spirit already indicates, as Christian theologians have long maintained, that there is no hope of generating what William James calls "coercive arguments" for the church's chief convictions (though the Christian community expects that it will be able, at least in the long run, to meet almost any argument which is brought against these beliefs, by showing that objections to them are not rationally coercive, either). The Spirit's epistemic work is thus to teach us how to believe – and to judge all things in accordance with – claims whose denial will always, at least in this life, be rationally plausible.

How does the Spirit do this? Acquiring a Christian view of the world calls for a persistent willingness to overturn the epistemic priorities (though not the totality of belief) we would otherwise be inclined to have. In at least this sense, ordering one's beliefs such that Jesus Christ has unrestricted epistemic primacy requires a change of heart and not simply a change of mind. The gospel of Jesus Christ, it seems, proclaims a truth which cannot be known unless it is also loved (see II Thess. 2:10). More than that: grasping the truth of the church's beliefs apparently requires a life which enacts a wide range of dispositions rooted in a Spirit-wrought love for God and neighbor. "Whoever says, 'I have come to know him,' but does not obey his commandments, is a liar, and in such a person the truth does not exist" (1 Jn. 2:4). The Spirit's induction of human beings into the Christian community's way of belief thus seems bound up with the creation of that purity of heart or holiness without

---

2. *In Ioannem* 14, 4 (no. 1916). The last thought is, of course, characteristically Augustinian.

which, as the New Testament has it, "no one will see the Lord" (Heb. 12:14; cf. Matt. 5:8).

Stirred by texts like these, Christian theologians have long sought to forge strong links between grasping the truth of the church's central beliefs and following from the heart a way of life these beliefs commend. "Anyone who does not love the truth," Gregory the Great observes in comment on I Jn. 2:4, "has not yet known it (*adhuc minime cognovit*) . . . I tell you that it is not by faith that you will come to know the light of truth [= Christ], but by love; not by mere conviction, but by action."[3]

The pragmatic thesis

This apparently deep-seated Christian claim that the triune God has to be loved in order for the truth about him to be known sometimes suggests a particular epistemic thesis. According to the "pragmatic thesis," successful practice on the part of the Christian community and its members helps to *justify* the community's central beliefs.

A "practice" in this sense is simply an action, as distinguished from an event (actions are intentional and purposive, while events just happen). Uttering and inscribing sentences obviously count as practices so defined, but there are countless others, many of which have a specifically moral bearing. "Successful" practice is the public presence of those actions enjoined by the community's beliefs about what is true and right. To this – to the communal and individual virtue of Christians – advocates of the pragmatic thesis make their epistemic appeal. Theological pragmatics does not always tie successful Christian practice specifically to the work of the Spirit, but to the extent that it does, the pragmatic thesis is one way of trying to account for the Spirit's distinctive epistemic role.

Though the pragmatic thesis is not unique to modernity, theologians have deployed multiple versions of it in order to meet distinctively modern epistemic challenges. A weak version will claim that the presence of practices in which those who hold Christian beliefs ought to engage is a necessary condition for holding Christian beliefs true. The absence of appropriate practices by holders of Christian beliefs undercuts the epistemic right to hold them and the epistemic responsibility of non-Christians to adopt them. A stronger version will take the presence of the relevant practices as positive evidence for holding Christian beliefs true;

3. *Homilia in Evangelia* 14, 3–4 (PL 76, 1129A–B).

it helps give Christians the right to hold their beliefs and helps create an epistemic responsibility for non-Christians to adopt them. A maximally strong version will regard the presence of relevant practices not simply as genuine evidence for Christian beliefs, but as sufficient reason for holding them true.

Within roughly the same theological milieu as Schleiermacher, Albrecht Ritschl develops a strong version of the pragmatic thesis, a practical justification of Christianity which he contrasts with the effort (doomed, as he sees it) to offer a speculative or metaphysical justification.[4] The impulse to "spiritual personality" – to an ethical mastery over nature and its limitations – Ritschl regards as a basic datum of human life. To anyone who grasps the character of his own interior life the Christian doctrine of God thereby becomes unavoidable, since only a creator who governs nature in such a way that human beings are destined for actual mastery of it can ensure, in the face of nature's obvious resistance to spirit, that the impulse to spiritual personality will finally be satisfied. So far Ritschl proceeds much as Schleiermacher does, but he regards the argument as incomplete. The interior spiritual impulse which founds the Christian doctrine of God will be epistemically reliable only if we have adequate grounds for supposing that it is actually destined for satisfaction – that spirit's desire for mastery over nature is not a "baseless fantasy."[5]

Here practice, Ritschl suggests, has to do the decisive epistemic work. Actual achievement of at least partial mastery over nature, by participation in the reconciled community and the practice of the Christian life, justifies the conviction that the impulse to this mastery is not baseless, and so that the Christian doctrine of God rests on an adequate foundation.[6] In this way the practical fruits which are supposed to spring from holding Christian beliefs are not only a necessary condition, but the ultimate evidence, for regarding those beliefs as true.

While justificatory appeals to practice in an earlier day tended to

4. "The scientific proof (*wissenschaftliche Beweis*) for the truth of Christianity may be sought only in the line of thought already singled out by Spener: 'whoever wills to fulfill the will of God will know that the proclamation of Christ is true' (Jn. 7:17)." *Die christliche Lehre von der Rechtfertigung und Versöhnung*, vol. III: *Die positive Entwickelung der Lehre*, 3rd edn (Bonn: Adolph Marcus, 1888), § 3, pp. 24–5.

5. "Eine falsche Einbildung." *Rechtfertigung und Versöhnung*, vol. III, § 29, p. 213.

6. "If," Ritschl argues (again with appeal to Jn. 7:17), "in the active fulfilling of the will of God one becomes convinced that Christ has really revealed God, then this includes the conviction that one has in that very way arrived at this insight: the practical end posited for human beings in Christianity is at the same time the final end for which God creates and governs the world." *Rechtfertigung und Versöhnung*, vol. III, § 29, p. 215.

regard properly Christian practices as closely bound up with the distinctive achievements of modern Western culture, and so took the development of the West as part of the practical evidence for the truth of
Christianity, theological pragmatics in the twentieth century has become
almost entirely counter-cultural. Ritschl's theology nicely exemplifies
the earlier outlook; for him the ethical kingdom of God, while by no
means identical with the social practices of Bismarck's Germany, can
grow only out of those practices, when believers carry out the social roles
which the practices define in a manner consistently shaped by the
Christian imperative of the universal love of neighbor. Liberation theologies clearly exemplify the more recent, counter-cultural, outlook –
although not all counter-cultural pragmatics in recent theology is liberationist (in the more specific sense of being oriented around the aims of a
particular group of oppressed people, with oppression defined in terms
of class, race, or gender).

The dominant social practices and institutions of the modern West are
for most liberation theologians incompatible with the Christian community's struggle to live for the sake of and in conformity with the coming
kingdom of God, and Christian acquiescence in these practices counts as
the most serious evidence against, not for, the truth of Christian beliefs.
Conversely, those practices which genuinely aim at the kingdom of God –
and as such are epistemically decisive with regard to Christian belief –
embody an effort to create social structures radically alternative to the
ones now in place. This outlook finds its most pointed epistemic application in the biblically resonant insistence of many liberation theologians
that "to know God is to do justice" – specifically, justice to the poor and
oppressed.[7]

In liberation theologies epistemic significance generally attaches to
the sheer persistent engagement of the Christian community in the right
sort of practices. At least under the present circumstances of massive
oppression what matters epistemically is that the community persevere
in that quest for justice which serves the coming kingdom of God, not
that its practices produce immediately noticeable results. *Participation* in
the community's practices thus tends to be decisive for the justification of
beliefs in liberationist versions of the pragmatic thesis. Unlike the earlier

7. See Gustavo Gutiérrez, *A Theology of Liberation*, trans. Sr. Caridad Inda and John Eagleson
(Maryknoll: Orbis, 1973), p. 195: "To know Yahweh, which in Biblical language is
equivalent to saying to love Yahweh, *is* to establish just relationships among men, it *is* to
recognize the rights of the poor. The God of Biblical revelation is known through
interhuman justice. When justice does not exist, God is not known; he is absent."

pragmatic outlook represented by Ritschl, liberationists generally do not suppose that outsiders will value the community's practices, and so take them as evidence for the truth of what the community believes. Liberation theologies often incline toward maximally strong versions of the pragmatic thesis about justification: at least for participants, the liberating practice of a Christian community is not only a necessary, but a sufficient standard by which to establish the truth of that community's beliefs about God and God's purposes in the world.[8]

The epistemic limits of virtue

Appeals to the epistemic support of practice are not limited to Christianity and Christian theology. Most religions include claims which could pass for versions of the pragmatic thesis about justification. Something like the pragmatic thesis also plays an important role in the justification of scientific beliefs. And the scientific thesis seems like a more refined version of a pragmatic assumption by which we make all sorts of everyday decisions about what is true. The quotidian root of the pragmatic thesis may be crudely put: true beliefs succeed, they get results, while false ones fail. We may thus decide between competing scientific claims or theories, and between more routine proposals in daily life, by seeing which get results and which do not. Pragmatically oriented theologians seem to make a similar claim: true beliefs get the result of virtuous conduct. Observing the rough parallel with science will help focus some objections to the pragmatic thesis.

Granted both the principle (true beliefs succeed) and the parallel, the epistemic bearing of appeals to Christian practice nonetheless proves elusive. Scientific theories, it is now commonplace to suppose, are underdetermined by the practical (more precisely, experimental) results which support them. Experiment regularly enables scientists to decide between alternative proposals and to build plausible theories, but does not – and this is the crucial point – guarantee that the proposal or theory thereby adopted *uniquely* accounts for the experimental evidence and meets the other desiderata of scientific theory (such as simplicity).[9] Other theories than the one actually adopted might conceivably meet the explanatory

---

8. This is not to say that liberation theologies always appeal to communal practice specifically as evidence which justifies beliefs; they embody the pragmatic thesis only to the extent that they do.

9. So, for example, Quine: "in general the simplest possible theory to a given purpose need not be unique" (*Word and Object* [Cambridge, Mass.: MIT Press, 1960], p. 22).

desiderata equally well; these alternative theories might be made up of beliefs which no one has held or will ever actually hold or even entertain, and they might include at least some beliefs inconsistent with parts of the adopted theory. That is: we might be faced with two sets of beliefs which cannot both be true, but between which no relevant consideration enables us to decide.

Acknowledging the underdetermination of explanatory theory by descriptions of practice does not require rejecting the assumption that true beliefs succeed. This assumption can be stated in standard conditional terms: if the belief that p is true, then the state of affairs s will obtain. Should we be in a position to know, for some values of p and s, (1) that p is true, and (2) that the conditional itself is true (that p cannot be true and s fail to obtain), then we can of course infer that s obtains, and know that we are correct. And if we are in a position to know (3) that $-s$ obtains, then (2) allows us to infer that p is false, and know that we are correct (this form of argument – *modus tollens* – is indeed highly useful in science, since, assuming the conditionals with which it works are true, it weeds out theory candidates effectively). What we cannot do is use s as a basis on which to claim that p is true. That is: even granted (2), and granted also knowledge (4) that s obtains, we cannot infer (1) that p is true. The principle that true beliefs get results may hold, but it does not license a strategy of argument which takes particular states of affairs as results from which the truth of explanatory beliefs may be inferred; this strategy falls afoul of the ancient logical stricture against affirming the consequent.

The parallel between Christian practice and scientific experiment is, to be sure, inexact. As the martyr's willingness to die for her faith in Christ most vividly shows, undertaking the life of obedience for which the gospel calls goes hand in hand with being convinced that the gospel is true, while scientists undertake experiments precisely in order to become convinced (or dissuaded) that an otherwise hypothetical set of beliefs is true. Failure of predicted results, moreover, tends to disconfirm the theory which underwrote the predictions, while Christians think they may and should believe the gospel precisely in the face of their own abject failures to live in a way congruent with it.

But the partial disanalogy apparently fails to bear on the relevant similarity of Christian beliefs to scientific hypotheses: the successful practice ·
of the Christian community and its members might be explained otherwise than by the truth of the beliefs held by those who engage in the prac-

tice. An objector to the pragmatic thesis might agree to a significant extent with the Christian community's description of a practice (might agree, for example, that St. Maximilian Kolbe acted with selfless love when he voluntarily took the place of a condemned prisoner at Auschwitz), and might agree that the practice is good and right, but might propose a different, indeed incompatible, account of why the practice goes on and succeeds (a non-theistic one, for example). Such an alternative account would acknowledge, of course, that for Christians themselves engaging in these practices is bound up with holding true a range of distinctively Christian beliefs – but an alternative account need not suppose that the beliefs *are* true in order to show how *holding* them true motivates or otherwise supports the practice. In that case the objector and the Christian community would in effect have alternative theories to account for the same practical data, and no amount of appeal to relevant practices by either side would seem capable of settling the matter, even when (indeed, precisely when) they largely agree on the description and value of those practices.

A defender of the pragmatic thesis might rejoin that this argument assumes an implausible level of agreement between Christians and non-Christians on the description and evaluation of Christian practices. Christians will describe St. Maximilian as a martyr, whose innocent death bears eloquent witness to the indwelling Holy Spirit's power to join believers to Christ himself, so that they may follow the way of their master even to the point of laying down their lives for their friends. Non-Christians will naturally be unwilling to accept this trinitarian and martyrological description of St. Maximilian's death. They will have their own descriptions of the action (perhaps regarding it as an expression of noble and lofty elements in the human spirit, though one motivated by some mistaken beliefs), and their own criteria of "successful" practice (perhaps regarding this as, on the contrary, a futile gesture of questionable moral worth). These descriptive and criteriological differences, so the rejoinder goes, obviate the objection that epistemic appeals to practice fail to discriminate adequately between competing accounts of the practice. St. Maximilian's death only makes sense within a distinctively Christian view of the world, and this is the only view which it supports.

Pressed too far, this rejoinder becomes self-eliminating. If descriptions of a practice differ extensively enough, they cease to be alternative descriptions of the same practice, and become descriptions of different practices. When that happens, the problem of underdetermination arises again in each case. Pressed within plausible limits, this approach heightens rather than diminishes the inextricability of practices and their description from the larger web of belief in terms of which practices are described. As the rejoinder rightly stresses, to say that St. Maximilian's death is described truly and most adequately as a martyrdom – an act by which one who receives and shares in the cruciform self-sacrificial love of the triune God for the world shows that very love to the world in his own way of dying – requires that one also hold true a complex body of beliefs about God as Trinity and about the nature and aims of God's action in the world. Thus deciding whether the description of practice is true goes hand in hand with deciding whether the larger web of belief to which it belongs is true. The description of practice is therefore not in a position to contribute decisively to the epistemic assessment of that larger system of belief.

The objection we have been pursuing observes, in effect, that even granted the truth of a conditional like "If (p) Jesus is risen, then (s) saints will die for the faith," there is no legitimate inference from (s) "Saints do in fact die for the faith" to (p) "Jesus is risen." This apparently rules out all but weak versions of the pragmatic thesis. A weak version simply holds that absent specific patterns of communal and individual action on the part of Christians, Christian beliefs must be regarded as false: should the conditional "If (p) Jesus is risen, then (s) saints will die for the faith" be true, the absence of saints dying for the faith $(-s)$ would imply that "Jesus is risen" is false $(-p)$. On this weak version of the thesis there will be practical criteria for deciding that Christian beliefs are false, but none for establishing that they are true – though whether even these purely negative criteria could be applied conclusively within the field of view open to finite human beings is another matter.[10]

Apart from this, it seems fair to observe that virtue is distributed in roughly equal measure among the world's religions. One need not resort to a highly generalized (and correspondingly attenuated) notion of "virtue" to grant this point. Different religions, as well as communal belief systems normally considered non-religious (like Leninism), may indeed have quite different and perhaps sharply conflicting standards and models for what counts as "successful" practice and so as virtue. And

---

10. Defenders of the pragmatic thesis rarely consider a further difficulty. On any version of the thesis, in order to be justified in holding true the community's central beliefs, one would have to be justified in believing conditionals of the form "If (p) Jesus is risen, then (s) saints will die for the faith." But how, according to the pragmatic thesis, would one justify *these* beliefs – the conditionals themselves, and not simply their antecedents? Surely *practice* will be of no help here.

these religions generally have long and rich communal histories, in which they can point to numerous examples of profound communal and individual success at leading lives congruent with the religion's distinctive overall pattern of belief. Even were a strong version of the pragmatic thesis plausible as an argument, the problem would not be finding practice which could support belief, but that so much practice would support so many different beliefs; practice seems unable to narrow the field very far when it comes to deciding which beliefs are true.

One can, to be sure, deny the rough parity of religious virtue, and at the same time avoid a tepidly generalized notion of virtue, by defining virtue such that only Christians have it. Indeed all religions will naturally do this to some extent. Given their own particular paradigms for successful practice, they will likely identify certain kinds of practical excellence which normally may be realized only within their own community by adherents of the religion.[11] But this in its own way vitiates the pragmatic thesis as an argument, since in order to regard a distinctive communal practice as genuinely virtuous (and not perhaps vicious), one would already have to subscribe to that community's belief system to a significant extent – that is, to the very beliefs for which the community's successful practice was supposed to count as evidence. One would thus have to regard oneself as already having the epistemic right to these communal beliefs, which would make any evidence supplied by successful practice at best redundant, and at worst circular.[12]

11. So, for example, Christians have classically regarded love as a virtue accessible in some degree to all human beings, but in its highest form – the fathomless self-giving of *caritas*, according to traditional interpretations of 1 Cor. 13:12 the greatest of all virtues – normally accessible only to Christians, since it requires the grace which ordinarily comes only through the distinctive communal practices of baptism and the eucharist.

12. While each religious community will rightly define virtue to some extent in its own way, this can – when joined to other kinds of assumptions – have consequences more menacing than logical circularity. So Ritschl, observing that "the Chinese and Hindus" have proven noticeably insusceptible to Christianity, suggests that they may not be entirely human. Should they fail in the long run to be convinced of Christianity by the merits of Christian practice, "the universality of Christianity should not thereby be doubted. Rather the extent of that humanity which is destined for the highest spiritual task would have to be fixed more narrowly than is often the case . . . Accordingly one would have to judge that peoples who show no prospect of becoming Christian are hindered therefrom by their abnormality – their distance from humanity" (*Rechtfertigung und Versöhnung*, vol. III, § 22, p. 131; see the discussion in Friedrich Mildenberger, *Geschichte der deutschen evangelischen Theologie im 19. und 20. Jahrhundert* [Stuttgart: Kohlhammer, 1981], pp. 131–2). One of the assumptions which leads Ritschl down this road, a supposition characteristic of much modern theological apologetics, is that Christian claims can be meaningful and intelligible only if they answer with supreme fitness a universal human need of which all people are at least implicitly aware (in Ritschl's version, a longing for ethical mastery over nature). This assumption is so important to Ritschl that when Christianity turns out to hold little attraction for the "Chinese and Hindus," he would rather regard them as subhuman than give it up.

For many advocates of the pragmatic thesis, the foregoing arguments fail to appreciate the basic point of the epistemic appeal to practice. They fatally assume a posture of analytic detachment in deciding about truth which the pragmatic thesis aims to overcome. That is: for theological pragmatists, observers of a practice are not on the same epistemic footing as participants in it. All the arguments marshaled so far against the pragmatic thesis seem to suppose that the mere presence or absence of the relevant practices, which anyone can observe, bears the epistemic weight. But that weight is borne, so the theological pragmatist (especially the strong pragmatist) might rejoin, only by participation in the practices.

Participationist versions of the pragmatic thesis might seem especially well suited to articulating the church's sense that its own Spirit-wrought practices have a decisive epistemic bearing. "Anyone who resolves to do" – and not simply to observe others doing – "the will of God will know whether [Jesus'] teaching is from God" (Jn. 7:17). It is difficult to see, though, how giving a participationist twist to the argument makes the pragmatic thesis any more plausible. If successful practice cannot count as evidence for the truth of Christian beliefs in the third person, how shall it do so in the first person? One can grant that people have a directness of access to their own practice, and perhaps thereby to its success, which is not available to observers – grant, in other words, that the agent, unlike the observer, need advert only to his own state of mind, and not to his overt actions, in order to know his good (or bad) intentions. One could even grant (though implausibly, if the interiority thesis is wrong) that people have access to features of their own practice which are simply inaccessible to others, depths which even the best informed observer could never plumb. This might be taken as a lode of evidence available only to the participant in a practice. But no amount or variety of evidence will validate the inference, by way of true conditionals with the form "If (p) Jesus is risen, then (s) saints will die for the faith," from successful practice to the truth of beliefs which call for or require that practice. Even the saint's surety about the success of his practice cannot warrant surety about the truth of his beliefs.

Even if it could, one wonders why the saint – especially he – would have any interest in treating his practice as evidence for the truth of his beliefs. Clearly the martyr's blood, however surely it must spring from that purity of heart without which no one will see God, does not count as evidence – the premise of a justificatory argument – for the *martyr*. He dies because he believes the gospel and loves the gospel's God, not in order to believe it. Conceivably a person might accept death rather than deny Christ not because of his surety that the gospel was true, but in order to find out whether it was true. Depending on its further motives, this might be assessed by the Christian community as misguided but pitiable (if it were seen to come from despair or desperation), or, more ominously, as that hubris which puts God to the proof, striving by heroic self-immolation to wrest from God an unambiguous epistemic triumph.[13] In any case, treating one's own practice this way will presumably not count as martyrdom, and the person who does so not as a saint – not, that is, as the sort of person who embodies with unique fitness the life for which the church's beliefs about what is true and right call.

So participationist versions of the pragmatic thesis end up in a paradox: the more excellently or successfully a person participates in the church's practices, the less need he has to treat those practices as evidence for the church's beliefs (or would have, were practice susceptible of being treated this way in the first place). Whatever epistemic bearing the saint's life has – and it surely, as the New Testament insists, has one – is for others, and not for the saint; however the saint comes by his conviction, it seems not to be by way of his own sainthood.

Practice and meaning

The crusader and St. Francis

How then should the epistemic significance of communal and individual Christian practice be conceived? The Spirit's epistemic work seems to be bound up with practices the Spirit creates, with human actions and dispositions that go together with having the beliefs which the Spirit brings us to hold. Yet what the practices have to do with holding the beliefs – how these practices "go together" epistemically with these beliefs – so far remains a bit mysterious. The pragmatic thesis suggested that the link was evidential. Save in its weakest (because purely negative and so epistemically indecisive) version, this looks implausible. The role practice plays in deciding which beliefs are true will, it seems, have to lie elsewhere than in *justifying* beliefs. What we need is a way of conceiving the epistemic bearing of the practices the Spirit creates without attempting to treat those practices as evidence for beliefs.

---

13. To paraphrase Donald MacKinnon, "Tillich, Frege, Kittel: Some Reflections on a Dark Theme," *Explorations in Theology 5: Donald MacKinnon* (London: SCM Press, 1979), p. 137.

Perhaps one important epistemic link of practice to belief lies not in the direction of evidence, but of meaning. Whether a sentence is true depends, at least in part, on what it means. The specific practical situation in which a sentence is uttered – what the speaker is doing when he utters the sentence in a particular context – plays a crucial role, in a non-question-begging theory of interpretation, in figuring out what it means. The *use* of words and sentences, as the point is often put, determines their meaning. If this is right, practice appears to have a crucial epistemic role by way of meaning: the Spirit-wrought practices of the Christian community enable Christians to mean by their utterances what they must mean in order, given the community's epistemic priorities, to be true.

We can sharpen the issue by borrowing a provocative example from George Lindbeck: the crusader who upon spotting, say, a fleeing Muslim cleric, gives chase at full gallop, and with a cry of "Christus est Dominus" cleaves the unfortunate fellow's skull with his mace.[14] What exactly is the crusader doing, linguistically and epistemically speaking?

If we suppose that the use of words in sentences fixes their meaning, where "use" embraces the non-linguistic practical and social setting of words and sentences as well as their purely linguistic context, then it may seem plausible (as Lindbeck suggests) to take the crusader's shout as a battle cry, and its purpose as authorization for the action of splitting open the skull of one whom the crusader regards as an infidel. If this context and purpose fix the meaning of what the crusader utters, then it surely seems implausible to suppose that when he says "Christus est Dominus," this sentence has the same meaning as it does when uttered by quite different people (St. Francis of Assisi, for example) in quite different contexts and for quite different purposes (such as to give a benediction, in the manner of II Cor. 13:13).[15] Assuming for the sake of simplicity that the crusader and St. Francis both mean the same thing by "Christus," such that this term is used by them as a name which singles out Jesus of Nazareth, their divergent practices seem to indicate that they mean quite different things by "est Dominus." What St. Francis means presumably includes a life wholly devoted to self-sacrificial redemptive service of a suffering world – the sort of life dimly mirrored in his own servant existence as a

---

14. See George A. Lindbeck, *The Nature of Doctrine* (Philadelphia: Westminster, 1984), p. 64. Lindbeck's case in point is not, unfortunately, so historically remote as we might wish. The *New York Times* on June 21, 1992 gave an eyewitness account of Serb soldiers who executed a Muslim cleric for refusing to make the sign of the cross (local edition, p. A8).
15. I am grateful to David Yeago for suggesting St. Francis as a fitting epistemic counterpoint to Lindbeck's crusader.

follower of Jesus of Nazareth – while the crusader apparently means by "est Dominus" a life of militant knighthood, devoted to conquest by violence.

If practice can fix the meaning of "Christus est Dominus" in roughly these divergent ways, then practice has a considerable epistemic bearing. People who believe that Christ is the Lord – that is, the redeemer through suffering service – will find "Christus est Dominus" as uttered by the crusader simply inconsistent with this belief, and so will hold what the crusader says to be false, without, of course, doubting that "Christus est Dominus" is true when uttered by others, like St. Francis. People like the crusader, who do not simply fail to believe that Christ is the Lord, but whose practice displays their belief that Christ is not *that* kind of Lord, will naturally be compelled to return the favor, and to hold what St. Francis says when he utters "Christus est Dominus" to be false.

To suggest that the truth or falsity of the sentence "Christus est Dominus" depends on the practices of the people who utter it may seem theologically disturbing. We may get the sense that somehow this puts Christ's lordship itself at hazard. Jesus Christ is and remains the Lord, Christians surely want to say, regardless of whether anyone recognizes this and lives accordingly – regardless of what any of us may or may not do. To say that whether "Christus est Dominus" is, as spoken, true depends on what the person who says it is doing at the time may seem to imply that it is the speaker's practice which makes this sentence true (or false). And it seems a short step from here to a "pragmatic definition of truth" for this sentence, of just the sort which even strong versions of the pragmatic thesis generally reject: a definition according to which for "Christus est Dominus" to be true just is for it to issue in a certain kind of life when spoken and believed (like that of St. Francis), and for it to be false just is for its affirmation to have other, less favorable sorts of practical consequences (as with the crusader). Better to suppose that "Christus est Dominus" means basically the same thing no matter who says it in no matter what circumstances, and that the crusader, in contrast to St. Francis, simply has some appallingly bad ideas about how people who hold this sentence true should act.

Formulated along these lines such theological suspicions are, however, ill-founded. The epistemic significance of practice so far proposed is not that what people do when they utter "Christus est Dominus" makes Christ the Lord (or worse, makes Christ not the Lord), but that what people do when they utter this sentence determines what the sentence itself means. It is therefore beside the point to emphasize that Christ's lordship fails to depend on the practices of those whose Lord he is, since the issue at hand is not whether Christ is the Lord, but whether the sentence "Christus est Dominus" is, as spoken, true. That surely depends on what it means. If as spoken "Christus est Dominus" means (or has a meaning which implies) "Christ is the suffering servant," then by the Christian community's epistemic standards it comes out true, but if it means "Christ is a knight errant," then by these same standards it comes out false, just because, so Christians believe, Christ is the Lord who conquers by accepting death and not by inflicting it.[16]

The bond of truth to meaning holds, it should be observed, regardless of how one conceives the way in which Christ's lordship constitutes the truth conditions for possible utterances – realist, coherentist, pragmatist, Tarskian, or whatever (on which more in the next chapter). However one thinks of what truth is for sentences and beliefs, whether a sentence is true depends on what it means. Thus the suggestion that the practices of speakers fix the meaning of the sentences they utter cannot be equated with, nor does it imply, a "pragmatic definition" of truth. If this suggestion is correct, it is quite compatible with the claim that the truth of sentences depends, as Davidson rather loosely formulates the point, on "how the world is arranged."[17] To indulge the theological suspicion that because the world is arranged in such a way that Christ is the Lord, no one can ever say "Christus est Dominus" and have it come out false, is therefore either to claim that this sentence is true regardless of what it means – which is absurd – or to claim that the practices of the people who speak it cannot make any important difference to what it means.

The autonomy of meaning

At just this point, however, the theological worry could be reconceived in a meaning-theoretical key. Despite the maxim that "meaning is use," there seems to be a crucial sense in which, if we are to succeed in interpret-

---

16. Even the most rigorous theological insistence that the truth of our talk about God depends entirely on what God is and does, and not on what we are and do, does not require denying that practice fixes meaning in an epistemically relevant way. So Karl Barth, for example, seems untroubled by the thought that if a Christian's "true witness is to be uttered as true by him," his whole self will have to be engaged, otherwise "it will, in spite of being entirely true, become a useless, indeed false witness with which he brings disgrace rather than honor to his Lord." *Kirchliche Dogmatik* IV/3 (Zurich: Evangelischer Verlag, 1932-67 [for the complete work]), p. 754 (ET, p. 658).

17. "The truth of an utterance depends on just two things: what the words as spoken mean, and how the world is arranged" ("A Coherence Theory of Truth and Knowledge," p. 309).

ing a speaker's utterances at all, what the speaker is doing when he utters a sentence cannot in fact make any difference to the meaning of the sentence he utters.

In order to get at the important way in which meaning does *not* depend on practice, it may be useful to recall the distinction, stemming from Frege, between three features any utterance may have: sense, force, and point. The sense of an utterance, we can say roughly for present purposes, is its meaning – what a useful theory of meaning or interpretation is supposed to tell us how to discover for sentences uttered in a given language. The force of an utterance is the act performed by speaking the sentence(s) uttered; linked to grammatical mood, the obvious cases are making an assertion, asking a question, and giving a command. The point of an utterance is the speaker's purpose in making it, the effect or result which the speaker intends his utterance to bring about: to inform, arouse, warn, inspire, amuse, and so forth.[18] The notion of "what a speaker is doing" (or of the "speech act" in which he is engaging) when he utters a sentence is manifestly ambiguous as between force and point. When it comes to the crusader, our chief concern is with point.

Perhaps the most obvious argument against the idea that the crusader's point fixes the meaning of the sentence he cries out is that it begs the question of how we can discover what the crusader's point is in the first place. The crusader's supposed point in uttering "Christus est Dominus" is to invoke the authority which licenses him to cleave infidel skulls; this purpose, so the argument goes, fixes the meaning of his utterance. Now we may surely grant that *some* grasp of a speaker's purposes is available to those who do not know how to interpret his utterances. An observer who does not know what "Christus est Dominus" means can nonetheless tell that the crusader intends to kill the person whose skull he is about to strike. But how can she tell, for example, that the crusader regards his victim as an infidel, or that his infidelity is the precise motive for the crusader's manifest intent to kill him? Even if she knows the victim is a Muslim cleric and that the crusader is a Christian, nothing about the crusader's overt action will, absent the capacity to interpret the language he speaks, enable her to assign precise beliefs and motives to him: to decide whether the crusader aims to kill the cleric because he believes him to be an infidel who must be eliminated for the greater glory

18. Sense, force, and point may correspond roughly to J. L. Austin's three types of "force": locutionary, illocutionary, and perlocutionary. See *How to Do Things with Words*, 2nd edn, ed. J. O. Urmson and Marina Sbisà (Oxford: Clarendon Press, 1975).

of God, a local resident whose land the crusader wants to acquire, a thief whom the crusader intends to punish for his crime, or the arbitrary victim of an afternoon blood sport played by crusaders. The same goes for the suggestion that the crusader cries "Christus est Dominus" in order to authorize his action. If the observer cannot tell what "Christus est Dominus" means, she will have no basis on which to impute to him the purpose of invoking an authority which is supposed to justify what he does to the cleric's skull.

To generalize: we can identify a speaker's purposes and intentions in even a modestly precise way only if we can figure out what the speaker believes. But accurately attributing beliefs to a speaker requires us to know what his words mean – not only the words which make up the utterance whose point we are trying to figure out, but enough of his language to get a fairly detailed picture of his beliefs, since a number of interwoven beliefs will no doubt be relevant to identifying the intention or point of his utterance (and in that sense the speech act in which he is engaged). Thus in a non-question-begging theory of meaning it is not so much the use of sentences – the extra-linguistic purposes for which they are uttered – which gives the interpreter their meaning, but the meaning which gives their use.[19]

The problem, indeed, goes further than this. Suppose, *per impossibile*, that an observer *could* discern the crusader's purpose in uttering "Christus est Dominus" without being able to interpret the utterance itself. How would this enable her to fix the meaning of the sentence he utters? Knowing, for example, that the crusader intends his utterance to authorize his action helps very little when it comes to figuring out what he is saying. There is no telling what the crusader might invoke as an authority for splitting skulls: the glory of God, the command of the emperor, the brotherhood of all true knights, the noonday sun, or whatever. Unless an observer knows what "Christus est Dominus" means, she has no way of knowing that it happens to be Christ's lordship which the crusader invokes to authorize what he intends to do. The converse is equally true. Just as utterances which mean quite different things might all be used for the same purpose, so the same sentence, uttered with the

19. Or more precisely, as Davidson puts the point, "interpreting an agent's intentions, his beliefs, and his words are parts of a single project, no part of which can be assumed to be complete before the rest is. If this is right, we cannot make the full panoply of intentions and beliefs the evidential base for a theory of radical interpretation" ("Radical Interpretation," *Inquiries into Truth and Interpretation* [Oxford: Clarendon Press, 1985], p. 127).

same meaning, might serve quite different purposes. "Christus est Dominus" might mean "Christ is the suffering servant" when used to bless a departing congregation, comfort a despairing sinner, instruct a class of novices, persuade a potential convert, and so forth.

The upshot of these considerations is that the meaning of sentences and the purposes for which they are uttered vary independently of one another. In the Fregean idiom with which we began, point does not suffice to yield knowledge of sense, nor sense knowledge of point, though we must grasp the sense of a speaker's sentences in order to know what his point is. What fixes the meaning of utterances therefore has to be something besides their use, if this means the extra-linguistic purposes for which utterances are made. Davidson calls this "the autonomy of meaning": an essential feature of language such that "the ulterior purpose of an utterance and its literal meaning are independent, in the sense that the latter cannot be derived from the former."[20] But the point is not a distinctively Davidsonian one. Dummett too argues that a plausible theory of interpretation has to account for meaning without violating its autonomy by making unfunded drafts on the beliefs, intentions, and purposes of the users of a language.[21]

Nor is there any gain to be made by objecting that the foregoing argument has to do with the way meaning is fixed for the interpreter of an utterance, rather than for its speaker. If linguistic meaning is to be public – if, that is, a speaker means just what an interpreter can correctly make out – then what fixes the meaning of sentences for the speaker has to be just the same as what fixes it for the interpreter. Since we all learn whatever language we know by listening to other people speak it and learning to interpret their utterances, were linguistic meaning not public in this way, it seems that none of us could become speakers of a language in the first place. Were meaning, moreover, not public – were utterances

---

20. "Communication and Convention," *Inquiries*, p. 274. See *ibid.*, pp. 113–14, 164–5.

21. Dummett especially criticizes "ordinary language philosophy" for promoting "a conscious disregard for the distinction between semantic and pragmatic aspects" of a sentence, the distinction, that is, of "what the sentence literally [says] from what, in particular circumstances, someone might seek to convey by uttering it" ("Can Analytical Philosophy be Systematic, and Ought it to Be?" *Truth and Other Enigmas* [Cambridge, Mass.: Harvard University Press, 1978], p. 445). The main target is Austin and his followers. Dummett regards Wittgenstein's notion of "use," while not productive of a genuinely informative account of meaning, as much more subtle and plausible than that of the "ordinary language" philosophers who appealed to him; unlike them, Wittgenstein "emphatically did not envisage a description of use as making free appeal to psychological and semantic concepts," but thought these descriptions of use had to provide whatever support there could be for invoking such notions (p. 446).

endowed with sense by something accessible to the speaker but not to the interpreter – it is hard to see how we could have any hope of interpreting speakers at all, any hope, that is, of understanding what they mean.[22] So even if the crusader could have a language whose sentences got their sense from his interior intentions and purposes, it would in the nature of the case be a language no one else could understand.

Meaning, total practice, and the Spirit

These considerations do not imply a repudiation of Wittgenstein's dictum that "the meaning of a word is its use in the language."[23] They do, of course, preclude one rather common way of construing this remark. But most recent theories of meaning argue that there is something fundamentally right about Wittgenstein's saying.[24] The problem, as with many of Wittgenstein's sayings, is to figure out the most plausible and productive way to take it – in this case, to figure out what sorts of use genuinely bear on meaning, and how they do so. In the present case we need to see how the practices of speakers as different as the crusader and St. Francis might fix the meaning of "Christus est Dominus" as uttered by each, without surreptitious or premature appeals to their intentions and purposes.

Let us suppose that our observer of the crusader's cry belongs to a community which first hears Latin on the lips of crusaders. This puts her and her community in a situation of radical interpretation, where they have to take the publicly observable behavior of crusaders, in particular the specific practical situations which prompt assent to and dissent from Latin sentences, as adequate evidence both for ascribing meanings to Latin words and ascribing propositional attitudes (especially beliefs, and with them purposes, desires, and so forth) to crusading speakers. What

---

22. This means that while the sense of any utterance is surely that which the speaker intends it to have, it does not have that sense *because* the speaker intends it to. If meaning is public, the notion that words get their meaning from an interior act (like intending) which speakers perform – what Dummett calls the "Humpty Dumpty" theory of meaning – has to be wrong, despite its intuitive appeal and long philosophical lineage. It has to be the case, rather, that "a word of a language does not bear the meaning that it does because a large number of people have chosen to confer that meaning upon it; they use it as having that meaning because that is the meaning it has in the language" (*Origins of Analytical Philosophy* [Cambridge, Mass.: Harvard University Press, 1993], p. 49).

23. *Philosophical Investigations*, I, no. 43, trans. G. E. M. Anscombe, 3rd edn (Oxford: Basil Blackwell, 1958). With characteristic caution, Wittgenstein proposes that this holds "for a *large* class of cases – though not for all – in which we use the word 'meaning.'"

24. Thus Davidson, though without direct reference to Wittgenstein: "I agree that we must find connections between how sentences are used and what they mean if we are to give a foundational account of language" ("Moods and Performances," *Inquiries*, p. 112).

would a radical interpreter who had heard Latin spoken only by crusaders make of "Christus est Dominus"?

Our resourceful interpreter begins by accumulating evidence which can fund plausible empirical hypotheses about the meaning of the crusaders' Latin sentences. The principle of charity (about the truth, on the whole, of crusader beliefs, not about the morality of their practices) plays an important role in ruling out implausible proposals. Striving to refine the hypotheses charity supports, the interpreter naturally attends with care to different situations which prompt assent to "Christus est Dominus," as also to other sentences using "Christus" and "Dominus" (let us suppose that she has fairly quickly figured out that "est" performs pretty much the same logical functions as "is" does in her own language).

She observes, for example, that the crusaders perform a ritual in which each kneels before one particular knight – the same one who leads them into battle – and says "Ego sum servus tuus, Domine mi." She is able to discern that this lead knight is not himself "Christus," since he too joins the others in calling out to Christus in various communal rituals of the crusaders. Initially puzzled by the fact that Christus seems nowhere to be present during this crusader ritual, her skill at interpreting Latin utterances eventually leads her to suppose that according to sentences the crusaders evidently hold true – for from her carefully chosen hiding place she has never seen them dissent from "Christus est Dominus" – Christus long ago waged battle with and triumphed over his enemies, now lives where God is, and commands the crusaders to do as he did.

Given the practical situations which elicit "Christus est Dominus" from the crusaders, and given further practices which prompt assent to sentences of the form "x est Dominus," the most plausible course for our interpreter might well be to take "Christus est Dominus" to mean that Christ is a kind of celestial knight errant, a murderous heavenly crusader who calls upon his followers to imitate him. Interpreting the sentence this way would of course go together with ascribing to the crusaders the belief that Christ is this sort of being, and might well also support the judgment that when uttered in connection with skull cleaving, this sentence is indeed being used as an authorization for the act.

To take the historical fancy one step further: suppose our interpreter, after having heard Latin spoken only by crusaders, chances to encounter Francis of Assisi – perhaps on the latter's journey to Egypt in 1219 with the crusaders of Gautier de Brienne. At first she supposes, reasonably enough, that Francis is another crusader. But he refuses to join the crusaders in battle, and appears to undertake no violent actions. Instead he assists the suffering – perhaps including some of the crusaders' own victims – at the same time saying to them "Christus est Dominus." He explains to all who will listen, including some crusaders returned from battle, that "Christus Dominus noster" does indeed triumph over his enemies, over those who oppose him. He does so, however, not by force of violence but by love, not by overpowering them but by suffering for them, offering himself "as a sacrifice and oblation on the altar of the cross," and in just *this* way "leaving us an example that we should follow in his footprints." Just because "Christus est Dominus," he continues, "let us love our neighbors as ourselves, and if there is anyone who does not wish to love them as himself, at least let him do no harm to them, but rather do good." As for "those who have received the power to judge others" – here he fixes his gaze on the crusaders in the group – they "should exercise judgment with mercy as they themselves desire to receive mercy from the *Dominus*."[25]

Confronted with this new evidence as to what can elicit assent to "Christus est Dominus" and what other Latin sentences can be found in its logical neighborhood, our interpreter might find that the most plausible course in dealing with Latin utterances overall is to assign different meanings to "Christus est Dominus" as spoken by the crusader and as spoken by Francis of Assisi – in particular, different meanings to the predicate "Dominus." If *everybody* who asserted "Christus est Dominus" were a crusader, then it would be quite appropriate to fix the sense of "Christus est Dominus" as "Christ is a crusading knight." But now it appears there are Latin speakers prompted to assent to "Christus est Dominus" in diametrically opposed circumstances, and by appeal to a body of sentences previously unsuspected as candidates to be uttered in support of assent to "Christus est Dominus." It seems quite unlikely that the contested sentence as uttered by *this* speaker should be taken to have the same meaning it does on the lips of the crusader; here it surely means something like "Christ is a suffering servant of all." Even though St. Francis and the crusader both hold "Christus est Dominus" true, attention to the practices which prompt assent to this sentence suggests that they mean different, indeed incompatible things by it, and so have not simply different, but opposed beliefs. Assuming, in other words, that a suffering servant is not someone who cleaves skulls, if what St. Francis

25. The quoted phrases are from the second version of St. Francis's "Letter to the Faithful," secs. 11, 13, 26–8, *Francis and Clare: The Complete Works*, trans. Regis J. Armstrong and Ignatius C. Brady (New York: Paulist Press, 1982), pp. 68–9.

believes about Christ's lordship is true, then what the crusader believes must be false, and conversely.[26]

To be sure, the available linguistic and practical evidence might best be accommodated in some other way. Depending on how the evidence fell out, interpretive economy might be better served by taking the crusader to mean pretty much what St. Francis means by "Christus est Dominus," and his deviance as moral rather than semantic. Christians are well familiar with this sort of situation, since they too know their own sinful failures to "follow in the footprints" of the Lord upon whom they call. Should a crusader return from battle and express to St. Francis regret for what he has done, and then engage in what the interpreter has learned to recognize as a public ritual of repentance and forgiveness pronounced in the name of "Christus Dominus," followed by retirement from crusading and entry into Francis's nonviolent band of followers, then the most plausible course for our interpreter might well be to suppose that even when cleaving a Muslim cleric's skull, the crusader did not mean or believe that Christ was a crusading knight.[27]

Nor are these the only available options. An interpreter might best save the available evidence by supposing that St. Francis and the crusader refer to different persons by "Christus," perhaps just because the sense and implications of "est Dominus" are so diverse in each case.[28] Or she

---

26. The foregoing scenario has been constructed in order make the salient points about meaning and belief as succinctly as possible, but a genuinely historical event could have served equally well. The sack of Constantinople by the armies of the Fourth Crusade in April 1204, with churches stripped bare, icons and sacred vessels plundered, and French prostitutes reveling on the patriarchal throne in Hagia Sophia, seems in effect to have convinced the Christian East that what the crusaders meant and believed when they said "Christus est Dominus" – and what a Latin-speaking church which tolerated such practices could mean by it – must be immeasurably far removed from what Greek-speaking Christians meant and believed when they said "Kyrios Christos." See the account of Steven Runciman in *The Eastern Schism* (Oxford: Clarendon Press, 1955), especially pp. 149–50.

27. The theological tradition has long had ways of observing the difference between semantic and moral failure. Thomas Aquinas, e.g., distinguishes between *infidelitas*, in which a person diverges from the Christian community's normative beliefs (even though he may assent to the same creedal sentences as the community; see *Summa theologiae* II–II, 5, 3, c; ad 2), and *fides informis*, in which a person holds the same beliefs as the rest of the Christian community, but has lost the love by which he cleaves to God in particular practical situations (e.g., a person who knows that adultery is forbidden by God, yet fails to act on this knowledge in a particular case; see II–II, 20, 2, c). On this see my essay, "Aquinas as Postliberal Theologian," *The Thomist* 53/3 (1989), pp. 377–9, 384–7.

28. The situation might, in other words, be that suggested by an example of Davidson's: "How clear are we that the ancients – some ancients – believed that the earth was flat? *This* earth? Well, this earth of ours is part of the solar system, a system partly identified by the fact that it is a gaggle of large, cool, solid bodies circling around a very large, hot star. If someone believes *none* of this about the earth, is it certain that it is the earth that he is thinking about?" ("Thought and Talk," *Inquiries*, p. 168).

might suppose that the crusader himself has contradictory beliefs about Christus, even though expressed by the same sentence; perhaps he means much the same thing as St. Francis when he assents to "Christus est Dominus" in public worship, but something quite different when he assents to it in public slaughter. Or the available evidence might not provide an interpreter any way to decide between alternative possibilities. Though it cannot be the norm, there must no doubt be a certain margin for error in the interpretation of a speaker's utterances – in particular, between assigning a meaning which finds speakers in agreement with one another (here, the crusader with St. Francis), or letting them disagree and assigning diverse meanings accordingly.

In the end, deciding what to make of the crusader's situated utterance requires finding the most plausible interpretation of Latin speakers on the whole. In this every practice of Latin speakers – the totality of the situations which elicit assent to and dissent from sentences in their language – is in play. In this sense attention to practice is indeed central to successful interpretation. But we cannot found our ascription of meanings, beliefs, and intentions to speakers only on those practices which seem to have a moral bearing, any more than we can weed out morally charged practices in the hope of showing that what a person's words mean floats free of the moral context in which he speaks. Such efforts are alike bootless because we can only discriminate between morally significant and insignificant practices, and between good and evil practices, *by* deciding what speakers mean. In the end – but not the beginning – we will sometimes no doubt decide that what people mean and believe remains fixed across morally significant and insignificant, as also good and evil, practices, and sometimes that what they mean and believe is profoundly determined by the moral context in which they speak and think.

This gives us a first take on the epistemic role of the Spirit. The Spirit creates a community – the church – structured by specific practices, and primarily these practices have to guide any effort to fix the meaning of this community's most central beliefs. Chief among this community's public practices is eucharistic worship, though there are many others. Grasping the meaning of the situated utterances which the eucharist elicits requires extended attention to the precise shape of that complex practice. Figuring out just what the community means when it says "Jesus is risen," to recall a basic case, depends on noticing that the eucharistic gathering continues to call upon him, even though it also solemnly remembers his death. Only by attention to such practices can we discern that when the community says "Jesus is risen," it means that he was once dead, but now lives. On grasping the meaning of situated utterances depends fixing the contents of the community's most central beliefs – those which identify Jesus Christ and, with him, the triune God. With a grip on belief can come discernment of the community's intentions, purposes, and so forth. It turns out that the Father and the Son most elementally identify themselves in the world by creating, through their Spirit's outpouring, a community of speakers on whose lips these sentences have the meanings they must in order to identify them. The Spirit teaches us how, by word and deed, to mean what we ought to believe.

The Spirit instructs the church – and thereby also the world – in the meaning of its own beliefs by his total mastery of the practical situations in which the community and its members (and indeed all human beings) speak. Since the Spirit creates and rules the total situation in which the relevant utterances are made, the meaning of those utterances depends primarily on the action of the Spirit himself, and only secondarily on that of the free human agents who make them. As the immediate agent of the unitary action of the Trinity in the world, the Spirit is the total cause of all that is not God: of, as the Nicene Creed says, "all things, visible and invisible." "All things" presumably includes the free acts of human beings as well as occurrences which have other sorts of causes; God, transcending the distinction between causes which produce their effects with necessity and those which produce them contingently, is free to create what exists in its totality, including the manner (necessary or contingent) in which each thing is.[29]

The community's own Spirit-wrought practices fix the meaning of its utterances "primarily," but not exclusively, since any practice in which speakers of a language may engage, whether or not members of this community, may have some bearing on fixing the meaning of any particular utterance in that language. But since in the nature of the case the sentences which express this community's most central beliefs are held true chiefly, and perhaps only, by the members of this community, it is mainly this community's own practices which fix the meaning of its utterances and the contents of its beliefs. Not only corporate practices, but those of individual members, can have this role. This holds particularly for the

---

29. There is no room here for a detailed defense of this claim, on which the Spirit's distinctive epistemic role in part depends. See Kathryn Tanner, *God and Creation in Christian Theology* (Oxford: Blackwell, 1988); for an analysis of Tanner's argument, see my review in *The Thomist* 55/2 (1991), pp. 321–6.

actions of those individuals – the saints – whose practical mastery of the complex connections among the community's central beliefs and of what it is right to say in ever-changing situations best embodies the community's grasp of the meaning of its own claims.

Love and belief

Attraction, habitability, and willingness to believe

How, though, does the Spirit create a willingness to judge all beliefs by their coherence with the church's central convictions? We get needed purchase on the epistemic role of the Spirit by tracking the links between practice and meaning. But this leaves unsettled the question of how we become persuaded to believe that the church's central beliefs are true, with the unrestricted epistemic primacy which the church attributes to them. It is of course quite possible for someone to mean by central Christian sentences just what the Christian community means by them, and to hold them false. We need, therefore, not simply an account of how the Spirit's action fixes the contents of central Christian beliefs, but an account of how the Spirit persuades people to hold these beliefs true.

As the problems faced by the pragmatic thesis show, a successful account of the Spirit's persuasion will have to avoid treating (descriptions of) the practices the Spirit creates as some form of evidence for the truth of Christian belief. There is no evidence for beliefs beyond the totality of belief to which any contested claims also belong, and the epistemic role of the Son already accounts for the distinctively Christian way of structuring this total field of belief. In the nature of the case the Spirit will not persuade by adding something to the totality of belief, by giving us reasons or evidence we do not already have, but by eliciting our assent to a way of structuring the whole.[30]

To fix the contents of the church's beliefs is to know what the world would be like if these beliefs were true. Willingness to hold these beliefs depends, presumably, on the attractiveness and the habitability of the world they describe – the world there must be if the beliefs are true. The community's beliefs will be attractive to hold if what they are about attracts: if, roughly put, the triune God who in love creates, redeems, and

---

30. Bonaventure suggests the notion of "persuasion" to characterize this aspect of the Spirit's epistemic role: "In faith, even though the intellect of the believer does not have a reason on account of which he ought to assent to the truth, it has the authority of the highest truth, who persuades his heart" (*In III Sent.* 23, 1, 1, ad 3; *Opera Selecta* III, p. 463a).

perfects all things is a being whom it would be desirable to be created, redeemed, and perfected in love by. But attractiveness alone is not enough for willingness; one might find a description of the world both plausible and attractive, but nonetheless regard it as imaginary. Willingness to believe thus seems to require an incentive beyond the attractiveness of what the beliefs are about.

The life of the Christian community constitutes the needed incentive, by displaying the habitability of the world which Christian beliefs describe. Communal success at holding these beliefs and living accordingly – the encounter with actual public willingness to suppose that the world described by these beliefs is not simply desirable but real – encourages and prompts its like.

This can happen in many ways. For example, people sometimes become especially attracted – or remain attracted, having been drawn from earliest memory – to the unmerited forgiveness which, so the church proclaims, the triune God bestows upon the undeserving in Jesus Christ. People may find themselves attracted, that is, to the triune God's will, which nothing can vanquish, to make right humanly irreparable wrongs. God's will to forgive, so the church supposes, reaches us in the most elemental way in public communal practices which are the Spirit's work – in baptism, confession and absolution, the preaching of the gospel, and the eucharist. One cannot coherently be attracted to this particular sort of forgiveness without also desiring to belong to this community and to believe its central claims (though of course a person might not realize this right away).

There are, of course, shades of desire or attraction here, and with that shades of belief. One might simply wish there were an omnipotently forgiving God, as one might wistfully desire to relive one's vanished youth. Such attraction does not require that one believe the truth of the church's central claims to be a serious possibility, any more than one believes time travel to be a serious possibility. One might positively desire the divine forgiveness of which the church speaks, but without actually partaking of the communal rites by which it is received. This does require taking the truth of the beliefs which identify the triune God, and specify the grounds for supposing that this God is unquenchably forgiving, as a serious possibility. It seems impossible genuinely to desire (and not just idly wish for) a good which one is committed to believing cannot be obtained.

One might, however, actively seek to receive the forgiveness which the triune God gives by accepting a share in the Christian community's life, and participating in those communal actions by which the triune God accomplishes his own forgiveness of sinners. This would seem to require not simply being open to the truth of the church's central claims, but actually believing them, since it seems impossible to seek forgiveness from a God whom one does not believe to be (that is, identifying descriptions of whom one does not hold true), or whom one does not believe acts forgivingly. One might, though, seek forgiveness without fully believing that the church's claims about this God are true, retaining some insecurity as to whether the forgiveness one is looking for has actually been received. One might, finally, trust in God's free and undeserved mercy in Christ, confident in the triune God's forgiveness in spite of one's sinful failings, and this would seem to require being fully convinced that the beliefs which identify and describe the forgiving God are true.

The Christian community's life displays the habitability as well as the attractiveness of a world in which God freely forgives sinners. In this community, people not only desire and seek forgiveness, but have utter confidence of receiving it, in spite of the wrongs which they themselves cannot make right. Members of this community display their trust in God's forgiveness not only by announcing their belief in it, but by forgiving those who have wronged them, even when this brings humiliation and suffering (not all do this, but some do it). As such they show that a world where the triune God freely forgives and commands us to do likewise is not only attractive, but viable. People actually succeed in living in this world; the sort of utter trust in God's forgiveness which enables people freely to forgive even those who hate them is, to be more precise, not simply possible but actual.

If, though, I want the forgiveness of this God to reach me such that I can know it and rely upon it, I have to hold true the church's central beliefs. At this point the manifest habitability, and not simply the attractiveness or desirability, of a world in which God freely forgives sinners plays a crucial role in eliciting belief that God forgives – belief that this is the way the world is.

It seems unlikely, though perhaps not impossible, that my desire alone, or even my active quest for forgiveness, could induce me to hold the beliefs without which I cannot trust or be confident in God's forgiveness. Since these beliefs cannot be regarded, epistemically, as either unavoidable or inadmissible, holding them requires a measure of willingness. But doing so simply because I desire what they promise perhaps demands too much of the will. That I want a good is surely an incentive to believe that it can be received, but seems by itself inadequate to sustain this belief, still less the belief that it actually has been received. When, however, I behold a community of people presently enjoying the good which I desire – confidence in God's free mercy – the burden on the will is reduced. The good already enjoyed by this community greatly increases the incentive to find my desire fulfilled by sharing in its life, and with that to hold the beliefs I must hold in order to enjoy the good which I seek.

The Spirit of course invites participation in the church's life in many other ways, and so has many other ways of eliciting assent to the beliefs which are necessary to enjoy the goods particular to that way of life. Perhaps more than anything else, so Christians hope and believe, the publicly visible love of this community's members for one another and for the world will invite all of humanity to share in that love, and so in the communal life constituted by it. Especially as it reaches to enemies and persecutors, this love displays itself as the Spirit's gift in its tendency to outrun the strength of those who, nonetheless, most clearly enjoy and enact it. But the features of Christian communal life which might elicit willing assent to the church's belief system are probably too numerous and diverse to systematize. Some basic patterns of attraction will no doubt be easy to observe, but the Spirit who lives in the church will endlessly fashion novel ways of inviting the world to share in its life.

Demand and love

Upon this community which offers love and forgiveness, however, demands are placed. The love which binds its members with one another and with Jesus Christ forever bears the form of the cross. Jesus Christ perfectly enacts his love for the Father and for us by accepting death and hell for our good. By creating and sustaining the church, the Spirit publicly invites the world into precisely this cruciform bond of love. The specific way of love in which the community and its individual members are called to follow, however feebly, Christ their head requires service, sacrifice, and suffering – if need be, unto death: "This is my commandment, that you love one another as I have loved you. No one has greater love than this, to lay down one's life for one's friends" (Jn. 15:12–13). Here especially, the cruciform holiness of the saints – perhaps above all of the martyrs, like St. Maximilian – displays the habitability of the demanding world which there must be if the church's central beliefs are true, the world into which the Spirit aims to draw us all.

If it requires this much, though, the world described by the church's central beliefs may not look especially attractive. The saints display the habitability of this world, but they do not on that account necessarily elicit willingness to inhabit it with them – that is, to share their beliefs. The very fact that they succeed in inhabiting this world may make it seem formidable, perhaps terrifying; this might be a world which one would be more comfortable to believe could not be inhabited. Resistance to adopting a way of belief which requires us to love God and neighbor even at the cost of our own life is, so Christians suppose, sin, which the saints, at least, recognize first of all in themselves. But it sharpens the epistemic problem. How does the Spirit persuade us to share in the church's life, and with that to hold its central beliefs, when the communal life the Spirit creates is more forbidding than attractive?

If we are to find the life of the Christian community attractive and habitable, in the end we will have to fall in love with the God who gives himself to the world in Jesus Christ. We will, that is, have to find ourselves drawn, beyond our capacity to resist, into the love the Father has for his crucified Son, a love which will let nothing be save through him and for him – a love, therefore, which will let nothing be save by raising him from the dead. We will equally have to find ourselves drawn into the love of this Son for his Father, a love which fully accepts even the Father's abandonment in order to secure for all things, but chiefly for those who have forsaken it, a share of the Father's love.

To fall in love with this God, to be drawn into the love of this Father and this Son for one another, seems an outcome which only their Spirit can bring about. Only the Spirit, and not we fallen human beings, can overcome our aversion to this love, born of our recognition that we cannot share it without unacceptable cost to our fallen selves. And even were we not averse to this love, it exceeds out strength; we can love this God only by sharing in his own love, and a share in God's love only God can give. To this end the Father and the Son send the Spirit into the world, and the Spirit consents to the mission they enjoin. At bottom, the Spirit gives to the world this highest possible gift – the eternal mutual love of the Father and the Son – simply by giving himself (see Rom. 5:5). All three conspire to share their love with the world, but it belongs to the Spirit, who perfectly expresses and rejoices in the love of the Father and the Son for one another, to make us participants in this love.[31]

The action whereby the Spirit induces us to love God by sharing in the mutual love of the Father and the Son is epistemically decisive: from it ultimately stems our willingness to hold true the narratives which identify Jesus and the triune God, and to order the rest of our beliefs accordingly.[32] We cannot love the triune God, let alone love him with his own love, unless we hold a complex collection of beliefs which together pick out and describe the actions in time by which this God identifies himself in the world, and thereby makes his life available to our desire. The Spirit elicits our assent to these central Christian beliefs precisely in order to share the love of the Father and the Son with us. We assent to them so that we may enjoy as a good the divine life which the Spirit holds out to us, despite all disinclination born of the demands that life places upon us. The Spirit persuades by inducing, we might say, a thirst which only a share in the life and love of God can slake. He works both the desire for this good and the actual enjoyment of it, and the road from origin to goal, from the first stirrings of the desire for God to their eschatological fulfillment, goes by way of holding the beliefs without which this good cannot be enjoyed.[33]

Here, as before, degrees of volition go together with shades of belief. In order to desire a taste of the peculiar cruciform love of the Father and the Son for one another, I need not actually believe that the crucified Jesus has been raised by the Father, but only have some understanding of this

31. See Balthasar, *Theologik III: Der Geist der Wahrheit* (Einsiedeln: Johannes Verlag, 1987): "The gift of the Son to the world opens up the space of love between the Father and the Son; it is, correlatively, for the Spirit to lead [us] into this open space of love, which is the truth" (p. 65). One can grant that it falls chiefly to the Spirit to induct the world into the mutual love of the Father and the Son regardless of how more precisely one conceives of the relation of the Spirit to the Father and the Son – regardless, in particular, of whether one supposes that there is a sense in which the bond of love between the Father and the Son just is the Spirit.

32. To focus on love here as the affective disposition toward God which is epistemically basic (as suggested, e.g., by 1 Cor. 13) is not to deny that the Spirit imparts a love which is linked to a broad panoply of epistemically relevant dispositions: trust, hope, joy, gratitude, and so forth. For present purposes the crucial point is that each bears in its own way, and together with others, on the willingness to hold true the church's central beliefs, but all will be joined in some way with love – with the desire for, and enjoyment of, the ultimate good which God has to give: himself.

33. At present we enjoy the good which the Spirit freely gives us, to be sure, in a way which anticipates immeasurably greater enjoyment yet to come. But in the nature of the case God can give us no greater good in the future than he has already given in the present, since there is no good greater than himself to give; what will be greater in the eschatological future is not the good we enjoy, but our enjoyment of it.

belief and what it entails (which is to say that I must be a competent interpreter of the sentences believers hold true).[34] In order actually to enjoy a share in this distinctive form of love, I will have to hold this belief and a host of others; since, presumably, the dead cannot love, I cannot rejoice in sharing Jesus' love for the Father unless I believe that he is risen, and so is in a position to return the Father's love.

In order to move from understanding the narratives which identify the Trinity to holding them true I must desire the good of which they speak enough to be willing to hold them true, where doing so requires accepting radical moral as well as epistemic demands. The intellect's assent to what God reveals, to put the point in traditional terms, can only happen "at the will's command" (*ex imperio voluntatis*). We believe the chief articles of Christian faith, and strive to order the rest of our action and belief accordingly, not because this course is rationally unavoidable, or because we have some way of ascertaining, without believing the articles, that they come to us from God, but because our will's grasp at the good, persuaded by the Spirit's grace, cannot help loving the God who depicts himself for us in them.[35]

Just how much desire is enough for willingness to assent is perhaps impossible to specify with more than rough precision.[36] It would seem,

---

34. There may also be an important sense in which all human beings desire God, regardless of their beliefs. Augustine's celebrated evocation of a universal human desire for the Trinity applies, so he and many others have thought, even to those who have never heard of, still less believed in, this God: "You have made us for yourself, and our heart is restless until it rests in you" (*Confessiones* I.i.1; *CCL*, vol. XXVII, p. 1, 6–7). This sort of desire for God differs from that currently under discussion, however, in being purely normative: attributing it to people does not involve ascribing to them any particular propositional attitudes (any beliefs and intentions which locate the object of the desire and orient a person toward it). A normatively ascribed desire only becomes capable of fulfillment when its object is in fact captured by a person's propositional attitudes; only thus can a person actually become aware that she has the desire, and direct her beliefs, intentions, and actions so as to realize the end which she seeks.

35. Reflection on the relation between desire, love, and faith has commonly argued that holding true the church's identification of God requires the will's *imperium*. So for Bonaventure "the intellect is not capable of assenting to divine truth on the basis of its own judgment, but requires the command of the will" (*In* III *Sent.* 23, 1, 2, c [*Opera Selecta* III, p. 466b]). Similarly Aquinas: "'To believe' is an act of the intellect, assenting to divine truth at the command of the will moved by God through grace" (II–II, 2, 9, c). And Luther, with "heart" doing duty for "will": "He is the sort of Spirit who confirms the truth in the heart and makes one certain of it" (*WA* 46, p. 53, 21–2). Like much of the western tradition's reflection on these matters, this thought owes much to Augustine. Thus, e.g., *De gratia Christi*, xiv.15: "When God teaches, it is not through the letter of the law, but by the grace of the Spirit. He teaches in such a way that what a person learns he not only grasps in thought, but also desires with the will, and accomplishes in action" (*PL* 44, 368).

36. Though the hope of exactitude on this score has drawn forth considerable theological labor. For the complexity of some of the modern debates over this topic, see Roger Aubert, *Le problème de l'acte de foi*, 3rd edn (Louvain: E. Warny, 1958).

though, that willingness to hold these beliefs requires that I treat the cruciform love which the divine Trinity bestows on the world not simply as a good, but as the highest good for the world and myself (I can probably do this without explicitly forming the belief that the Trinity is the highest good, just as a person can act honorably or speak grammatically without having formed any convictions about the principles of honor or grammar). Holding these beliefs requires not simply assent to them, but a reordering of all life and belief. *These* beliefs cannot be held true at all unless we are unwilling to give them up for the sake of any others. Willingness to sustain beliefs in this way would finally be senseless unless we took the good in which they give us a share as one which itself can be given up for the sake of no other – as, in other words, the highest possible good. Perhaps for this reason the gift of wisdom, by which the Spirit enables us to order and assess all of our beliefs in light of those which locate the triune God for us, goes hand in hand with that love for the Trinity which the indwelling Spirit sheds abroad in our hearts – the love which tastes, however faintly, the supreme goodness of the Father, and so by the Spirit's grace clings to the crucified and risen Jesus in spite of everything.[37]

Thus the Spirit's persuasion makes the church habitable for us. The Spirit draws us into that community structured by practices and beliefs which together give us a share in the forgiving and demanding love which is the life of the triune God. Seeing the Spirit's epistemic role in terms of his donation of a share in God's community-forming love may help us understand those scriptural texts which forge strong links between holding Christian beliefs and engaging in specific practices, and thus may seem to support the pragmatic thesis. "Whoever does not love" – which is to say, more specifically, "whoever does not obey his commandments" – "does not know God, for God is love" (1 Jn. 4:8; cf. 2:4). This need not be taken to suggest that the sinful failure of those who profess Christian beliefs is by itself incompatible with actually holding those beliefs. There is no one-to-one correlation of action with belief, and so no way to read off from any one act, either in our own case or that of

---

37. Aquinas observes that "a feeling for or intimacy with divine things (*compassio sive connaturalitas ad res divinas*)," such that its possessor has "right judgment concerning divine things" – the spiritual gift of wisdom whereby we judge all proposals for belief in a manner which mirrors the Father's own knowledge – "comes to be through love (*per caritatem*), which unites us to God" (II–II, 45, 2, c). For modern discussions of the *donum sapientiae* see M. M. Philipon, *Les dons du Saint-Esprit* (Paris: Desclée de Brouwer, 1964); Germain Leblond, *Fils de lumière* (Saint Léger-Vauban: Les Presses Monastiques, 1961).

others, an absence of Spirit-wrought love or desire for God, and with that of Christian belief. But the willingness actually to hold these sentences true has to come from the Spirit's donation of a share in the love which God is. And this donation cannot be without love toward companions who share it, and toward enemies who refuse it – cannot, in other words, be without obedience to the commandments of the God who is love. In just this sense, though not as pragmatic evidence for the truth of Christian beliefs, "anyone who resolves to do the will of God will know whether the teaching [of Christ] is from God" (Jn. 7:17).

Can we control what we believe?

The account so far given of the Spirit's distinctive epistemic role clearly assumes that human beings have some measure of control over their beliefs. This claim is, however, controversial. We cannot, it is often argued, simply decide to have this or that belief. I have spoken of "deciding what is true" in the sense of "being (or becoming) convinced that" a belief is true, especially in cases of conflict between candidates for belief. Being convinced that a belief is true presumably requires supposing that one has the right to hold the belief. The distinctive epistemic role we have ascribed to the Spirit, however, seems to rule out the possibility that supposing ourselves justified in holding central Christian beliefs could be enough to convince us of their truth. If the Spirit's epistemic role is chiefly to create the willingness to order the whole epistemic field around a particular set of beliefs, then it seems there must be a further sense in which we can "decide" to have a Christian view of the world, namely that we can in some fashion choose or opt for the beliefs which structure such a view as a whole. Is this a capacity which we can plausibly be supposed to have?

The short answer is that since the Holy Spirit actually gives us this capacity – and must do so if we are to have a Christian view of the world at all – then it must be possible for us to have it. We cannot, indeed, simply choose to hold true the narratives which identify the Trinity, and to order the rest of the epistemic field accordingly. Without the immediate action of the Spirit, we will lack the willingness to believe in this fashion. But if the omnipotent creator Spirit acts, then we will have willingness sufficient for assent to those beliefs which enable us to cling to Christ, and so even now to have a share, however partial and incomplete, in the life of the Trinity. The Spirit's action, it seems, is both necessary and sufficient for our actual willingness to believe in the Trinity, and so all the more for its possibility.

Different sorts of possibility, though, need to be distinguished. An event or action (in this case holding a particular collection of beliefs) might be possible in that it could take place under conditions which actually obtain ("real" possibility, this is sometimes called), or it might be possible simply in that the thought of it involves no contradiction (so-called "logical" possibility). Thus in order to be really possible an action must be logically possible, but not conversely.[38] If the Spirit's action fully accounts for our willingness to believe, then willingness to believe must be logically possible. It would be useful, though, to have some reasons to suppose that it is. With this in mind we can consider two objections to the notion that belief (or, more precisely, believing) can be voluntary.

It might be argued that we cannot simply choose or decide what to believe, because we have epistemic responsibilities and obligations – say, the Humean obligation to proportion all our beliefs to the evidence. Just choosing our beliefs as we will, without conformity to our epistemic obligations, would be irresponsible.

This is not, of course, an objection to the logical possibility that we can choose our beliefs. On the contrary, the objection seems to assume that we can choose our beliefs, otherwise we could have no genuine obligation to live up to epistemic responsibilities. To say that we "cannot" choose our beliefs is here to make a claim about moral rather than logical possibility.

In any case I have not argued that we can, in general, choose our beliefs at will. When it comes to the question of what beliefs we may have, the most basic limitations are imposed by the requirement of broad agreement with other speakers, and with that of plausibility in interpreting what they say. I cannot (really and perhaps logically, but not just morally) find myself in massive disagreement with other language users; I will be compelled to give up beliefs and epistemic priorities which point in this direction well before I can get to the point of generating such disagreement.

It seems unlikely that I could have either an obligation or a choice to agree on the whole with other speakers, since I most likely have to do so in

---

38. It may be hoped that these remarks are sufficiently modest to stand without entering into the debate about how to interpret the modal operators "necessary" and "possible," and the related arguments about what sense, if any, it makes to attribute necessity or possibility to objects, properties of objects, or states of affairs. For some now classic doubts on this last score, linked to puzzles about what to make of the modal operators, see Quine, *Word and Object*, pp. 195–200, 245–6; for an equally classic defense of modalities (interpreted in terms of possible worlds semantics) and their application *de re*, see Saul A. Kripke, *Naming and Necessity* (Cambridge, Mass.: Harvard University Press, 1980).

order to acquire a language at all, and acquiring a (first) language seems to be a matter of neither obligation nor of choice. Within this limit, however, there seems to be no barrier (certainly not a logical barrier) to affective and volitional factors playing a role in which beliefs and epistemic priorities we have, since these limits do not impose any particular belief or epistemic priority. Granted this, I still cannot "simply choose" what to believe, since the role played by desire and willingness in fixing belief presupposes a dense context of beliefs already in place. Room may no doubt also be found here for epistemic obligations. Some of these will be non-controversial (if you believe the premises of a valid argument, you are obligated to believe its conclusion). But it will naturally be difficult to disentangle in any thoroughgoing way the account we are inclined to give of human epistemic obligation from the beliefs and epistemic priorities we actually hold. Christians will be inclined to attribute to human beings an obligation to love God, and to see in the fulfillment of this obligation, as lately argued, a massive epistemic payoff. Others will of course see things differently, which returns us to the difficulty of settling disputes between rival belief systems and epistemic priorities without recourse to some of the beliefs which are in dispute.

Contrary to the line of thought which seeks to hold people to their epistemic obligations (however identified), it might be argued that we have no significant control over our beliefs. The naturalist tradition in epistemology (as exemplified by one important strand in Quine's philosophy) sometimes maintains that beliefs are responses, distinctive to organisms of the human kind, to environmental stimuli (or dispositions to respond to such stimuli).[39] In these responses willingness or choice play no important role, and since beliefs are thus not voluntary in any important sense, notions like obligation and responsibility have no epistemological work to do. On this sort of argument beliefs which depend on willingness to believe come close to being logically impossible; the very notion of belief more or less rules them out.

The foregoing account of the Spirit's epistemic role has focused mostly on the sort of situation where a person might explicitly choose to hold Christian beliefs, out of a desire to enjoy the good which they propose. The willingness to believe which the Spirit works need not, however, involve a deliberate choice (need not, in other words, involve adult conversion). Christians might, as many no doubt have, find that

---

39. This way of putting the anti-voluntarist claim is Isaac Levi's; see *The Fixation of Belief and Its Undoing: Changing Beliefs Through Enquiry* (Cambridge: Cambridge University Press, 1991), p. 71.

they had always been willing to hold these beliefs, and still were. But this by itself fails to meet the present objection, which seems to exclude any significant control over beliefs by those who have them, whether by deliberate choice or established disposition.

The objection does, however, fail to make sense of the fact that we do sometimes think we are entitled to hold people responsible for their beliefs, and to praise or blame them for beliefs they have (or fail to have). When one person makes a remark which, to her surprise, insults or hurts another, we sometimes think it entirely in order to tell the offending party that she should have known better – that she had both the ability and the responsibility to believe that her comment would offend. Were she simply a processor of epistemic inputs, who as such had no significant control over her beliefs, presumably we would not blame her for the ignorance which caused offense. If volition played no role in belief, it would never be right to say, as we sometimes suppose it is, "You should have known."

Of course we sometimes regard holding a particular belief as praiseworthy, just as we may regard holding a belief as blameworthy. We might praise a scientist who, having hit on a theoretical insight, holds to the beliefs at the heart of his theory over years of labor, struggles against opposition from his scientific colleagues, and eventually builds an overwhelming case for his theory. The credit we give the scientist is not only moral, of the sort we might give to any person who persevered in a good cause despite opposition, but distinctively epistemic: without his willingness to stick to the contested beliefs, even when he lacked strong evidence for their truth, the justifying evidence would never have come to light, and a contribution to knowledge would have been lost. This points up a second difficulty with attempts (naturalistic or otherwise) to exclude volition from belief. Did will and choice play no role in belief, it is hard to see how we could, by deliberate and sustained engagement in a course of inquiry, change our beliefs – enlarge (or reduce) the stock of beliefs we think we are justified in holding. We might, by detecting previously unsuspected inferential connections, become explicitly aware of beliefs we did not know we had. But absent some appeal to volition, it seems difficult to account for rationally (as opposed to simply causally) induced changes in our beliefs, of the sort we routinely take our practices of inquiry, everyday as well as professional, to yield.[40]

Something similar applies in the case of sticking to Christian beliefs,

---

40. For a sustained argument to this point, Peircean in spirit, see Levi, *The Fixation of Belief*, especially pp. 71–116.

which merits praise, so Christians have held from the earliest days, because it requires not only volition, but perseverance. Christians will inevitably encounter a kind of epistemic affliction, because they not only hold true, but insist on treating as epistemically primary across the board, beliefs which will be rationally contestable until the end of time.[41] The Christian's willingness to believe, like the scientist's, has a goal in which it can come to rest – to see God as he is (1 Jn. 3:2) – but not a goal whose attainment he can ordinarily expect to enjoy in this life. Not only do these beliefs lack, for those who hold them as much as for those who reject them, any characteristic which would make them epistemically or rationally unavoidable. (Perhaps, as we have earlier suggested, no particular belief has any such characteristic.) The affliction which goes with holding these beliefs may go beyond having to bear out their contestability; one may have to die in order to avoid giving them up. For the martyr's willingness to die for her faith in Christ, a perseverance no less arduous for being wholly the Spirit's gift, is rightly reserved the highest praise.

As it turns out, the Spirit's epistemic role is not to justify the beliefs Christians hold. Conferring the right to believe belongs rather to the crucified and risen Son. That we have the right to hold a particular set of beliefs does not, however, by itself account for our actually holding them; that we actually believe in Jesus crucified and risen depends wholly on the Spirit's gift of the willingness to do so. By enjoining these distinctive epistemic roles on the Son and the Spirit, the Father undertakes to give us a share in his own knowledge. If a share in the Father's creative and definitive knowledge is the end of the epistemic road, and the narratives which identify Jesus crucified and risen – not all alone, but as they are used to order the whole field of belief – are the road itself, then we traverse this road from beginning to end by partaking of the communally embodied love the Spirit imparts.

Thus the Trinity teaches us how to decide what is true. About what we thereby decide – about what truth is – we have so far assumed much, but said little. That lack needs to be made good.

---

41. On this see Barth's account of "The Christian in Affliction," especially the comments on 1 Cor. 1–2 (*Kirchliche Dogmatik* IV/3, pp. 724–6; ET, pp. 632–3).

8

The concept of truth

It may seem odd that we have come this far in a book devoted to a theological account of truth without making any attempt to say what truth is. The foregoing theological reflections on deciding what to believe may seem to accentuate the oddity, since we have from the outset made use of the concept of truth in the process of saying how we should make such decisions.

Leaving truth to the end, however, need not be taken to pose any special difficulties. The concepts of meaning, belief, and truth can only be grasped together, but obviously they cannot all be presented at once. Something has to come first, and leaving truth to the end has advantages. At least in some respects the concept of truth is about as clear a notion as we have; we have a better intuitive grasp of it than we do of the concepts of meaning, belief, and (*a fortiori*) epistemic decision. It was thus easier to presume upon that grasp in giving an account of the other notions than it would have been to proceed in the opposite direction.

Realism in search of a truth bearer

An ancient tradition holds that realism best captures the concept of truth. "Realism" comes in many different varieties, and involves more than simply a way of conceiving truth. But one hallmark of realism is the thought that truth is a relationship of correspondence between two quite different sorts of things: the mind, thoughts, propositions, or beliefs on the one hand, and reality, the world, or states of affairs on the other.

Christian theology has often thought about truth as a relationship of correspondence, and so along realist lines. Thomas Aquinas, for example, proposes that "the first relationship (*comparatio*) of being to the intellect is that being corresponds to the intellect; this correspondence is called the adequation of reality and the intellect, and in this the meaning (*ratio*) of 'true' is formally attained."[1] The *correspondentia* or *adaequatio* which defines truth can also be characterized as a *conformitas* or *aequalitas* of one thing (the intellect) with another (reality).[2]

Though such remarks may seem mere commonplaces, they conceal an ambiguity. Like the medieval scholastics generally, Aquinas tends to trade, without distinguishing explicitly, on what have since come to seem like two different views of what truth is. Modern philosophy has tried to sort out these two views and has widely come to regard one of them as implausible. The difference between them turns on what the bearer or vehicle of truth is.[3]

Sometimes Thomas (to continue with him as our example) thinks of the correspondence of mind to reality which defines truth as brought about by forms, when they come to exist in the intellect by passing through different media which link the intellect to the world. In this vein Thomas develops a complex metaphysics of knowledge, basically elaborating and refining that of Aristotle's *De Anima* and *Metaphysics*, which (to give a rough summary) traces the path of substantial and accidental forms from their original existence in individual objects, through their incorporeal existence (caused by the original objects) in sense organs and the imagination, to their existence as general concepts or *species* in the passive intellect, a mode of existence itself brought about by the abstractive power of the agent intellect.[4] When the intellect combines forms the way they are combined in reality – when it combines the *species* "grass" and "green," for example – then the intellect is true; it corresponds to reality. When it combines them otherwise – if it joins the *species* "grass" and "purple" – then the intellect is false; it fails to correspond to reality. Thomas's "conformitas" aptly characterizes the sort of correspondence of the mind to reality brought about by forms existing *in re* and then, by way of the senses, *in intellectu*. The forms give the intellect their own shape, the way a signet ring precisely shapes the wax in which it is imbedded; thus

1. *De Veritate* (= *De Ver.*) 1, 1, c. S. *Thomae Aquinatis Questiones Disputatae*, vol. I, ed. Raymund Spiazzi (8th edn, Turin: Marietti, 1949).
2. On *conformitas* see *De Ver.* 1, 1, c, and *Summa theologiae* I, 16, 2, c; on *aequalitas* see *De Ver.* 1, 3, c.
3. For the medievals, a "truth bearer" or "truth vehicle" is not simply whatever "true" is said of (the standard modern usage), but what brings truth – the relationship of correspondence – about.
4. For Thomas's detailed discussion, see *Summa theologiae* I, 84–6.

the mind (when it judges or combines rightly) corresponds to reality as fitly as the wax to the ring.[5]

At other times, however, Thomas thinks of truth as borne and brought about by sentences or utterances. So in his theology of the incarnation, for example, he poses a series of questions of the form, "Whether this is true...", followed by a sentence whose truth or falsity he aims to decide. Thus: "Whether this is true, 'God is a human being'?"[6] Several other formulations similarly serve the purpose of introducing sentences as truth bearers, such as "Whether it can be said (that)..." (*utrum possit dici* or *utrum sit dicendum*).[7] Whether a sentence is true depends (at least in part) on what it means, so Thomas attends to the precise interpretation of each sentence introduced by these second-order locutions, usually distinguishing senses in which it may be held true from senses in which it may not. He thus shows himself practiced in the devices of semantic ascent.[8] Like the scholastics generally, Thomas appreciates the gain in clarity about the shape of a problem and its possible solution (or dissolution) which may often be had by moving from talk about what there is to talk about talk of what there is, and in particular to talk about whether particular sentences are true under specified interpretations. Thomas's semantic ascent seems unbound, moreover, by his metaphysics of knowledge; he regularly treats sentences as truth bearers (that is, he fixes their sense and assigns a truth value to them) without ever referring to, still less depending on, his convictions about forms existing *in re* and *in intellectu*.

Of course, Thomas himself thinks that these two different ways of conceiving the bearer of "true" are not only compatible, but naturally fit for one another; they serve as complementary components in a unitary account of truth as the correspondence of mind to reality. In general, Thomas holds, the subject of an indicative sentence points to or signifies some object in the broadest sense (some *res*), while the predicate points to or signifies a form or forms. But linguistic subject and predicate can also signify the cognitive equivalent of the form (the *species* or *intentio intellecta*) and that of the object (its *phantasmatum*, if the object is a material

5. Thus *Summa theologiae* I, 16, 2, c: "The intellect, to the extent that it knows, is true insofar as it takes on the likeness (*similitudinem*) of the thing known, which is the form of the intellect insofar as it knows." For Aristotle's simile of the ring and the wax, see, e.g., *De Anima* II, 12 (424a 17–22).

6. *Summa theologiae* III, 16, 1, c; for a list of christological sentences completing "Utrum haec sit vera...", see the *prooemium* to III, 16.   7. See *Summa theologiae* I, 31, 2; 39, 2.

8. The phrase is Quine's; see his discussion in *Word and Object* (Cambridge, Mass.: MIT Press, 1960), pp. 270–6.

particular, otherwise another *species*). When in an act of judgment we assert or deny a predicate of a subject, the intellect inwardly combines or declines to combine the cognitive entities which the words signify; if forms and objects go together in the world the way the mind combines their cognitive equivalents, then the mind acquires that likeness or conformity to the world by which truth is defined.[9] Since they can be tied in this way to the cognitive apparatus which conforms the mind to the world, sentences as well as forms can be taken as vehicles, if secondary and dependent ones, of this conformity or correspondence.

This picture of truth and its vehicles has proven remarkably durable. Rationalist and empiricist philosophies overthrew both scholasticism's metaphysics of knowledge and the Aristotelian natural science which had backed it up, but continued to think of truth primarily as a correspondence or agreement of mind and reality. They also tended to treat both the non-linguistic contents of the mind (now "ideas," "sense impressions," and so forth) and their linguistic counterparts as means by which this relationship of mind to reality is brought about. Thus John Locke defines truth as "nothing but the joining or separating of Signs, as the Things signified by them, do agree or disagree one with another ... So that Truth properly belongs only to Propositions: whereof there are two sorts, viz. Mental and Verbal; as there are two sorts of Signs commonly made use of, viz. Ideas and Words."[10] Since ideas stand for things outside the mind while words stand for ideas in the mind, words are genuine but dependent truth bearers. Ideas are true just in case we join them, and the extra-mental things for which they stand "agree," or we separate them, and the things for which they stand "disagree"; whereas joined or separated words are true just in case the joined or separated ideas for which the words stand are themselves true. The "Truth of Words" thus depends on "mental Truth."[11]

Here the truth borne by mental contents, and *a fortiori* its verbal counterpart, has lost some of the lucidity it had in the world of Aristotelian forms. Whether a combination of ideas is true depends on whether extra-mental things agree with each other, but Locke makes rel-

9. Thus, "in every proposition [the intellect] either applies some form signified by the predicate to something signified by the subject, or removes the form from it" (*Summa theologiae* I, 16, 2, c). Words signify not only objects and forms, but the cognitive entities generated when the intellect strives to know the world of objects: "The intention itself [= the likeness conceived in the intellect of the thing understood] is called the interior word, which is signified by the exterior word" (*Summa contra Gentiles*, IV, 11 [no. 3466]).
10. John Locke, *An Essay Concerning Human Understanding*, IV, 5, § 2, ed. Peter H. Nidditch (Oxford: Clarendon Press, 1975), p. 574.   11. Locke, *Essay*, IV, 5, § 6 (p. 576).

atively little attempt to describe the relationship of mind to reality in which truth is held to consist (as distinguished from giving a causal account of the way in which it comes about). Where the Aristotelian tradition had thought in terms of an ontological, even quasi-physical isomorphism of mind and reality (the ring and the wax), Locke merely says that the mind (or a "Mental Proposition") is true when it joins ideas "as" the things for which they stand agree. He appears to take the notion of connecting signs "as" things are connected, along with the equally crucial notion of signs standing for things or ideas, to be clear enough to need no further explanation.

Modern theological conceptions of truth often follow this pattern. Friedrich Schleiermacher and Karl Barth both seem to take it as obvious that truth needs to be characterized in terms of correspondence. "That thought is knowledge," Schleiermacher proposes, "which is presented as corresponding to a being which is thought."[12] The relationship between thought and being which defines truth Schleiermacher variously labels "correspondence" (Entsprechung, Correspondiren) or "agreement" (Übereinstimmung); since thought and speech, while distinct, are inseparable, both may be conceived of as means by which this correspondence comes about.[13] Barth too proposes that in order to be true, human speech must "coincide and agree as precisely as possible, materially and in subject matter, with the one Word of God," that is, with Jesus Christ himself; like Schleiermacher, he has a handful of terms with which to label the relationship of speech to the world in which truth consists.[14] Indeed Barth seems to hold that the truth (or falsity) of *all* human speech consists in its agreement (or lack of agreement) with Jesus Christ, and not only the truth of that speech (for example, sentences in which the name "Jesus

---

12. Friedrich Schleiermacher, *Dialektik (1814/15). Einleitung zur Dialektik (1833)*, ed. Andreas Arndt (Hamburg: Felix Meiner Verlag, 1988), p. 16, § 87. In Schleiermacher's case the notion of a correspondence between thought and being is tied to lofty speculative ambitions: "Our [account of knowledge] rests on the fact that the agreement of thought and being ingredient in the idea of knowledge is derived from the primordial identity of the two in the absolute." *Dialektik (1811)*, ed. Andreas Arndt (Hamburg: Felix Meiner Verlag, 1986), p. 33; see pp. 17, 32.

13. Indeed "thought" may be defined as "the activity of the mind which is completed by speech," in such a way that "also inwardly every thought is already word." Friedrich Schleiermacher, *Dialektik* (Beilage 1822), ed. Ludwig Jonas, *Friedrich Schleiermacher's sämmtliche Werke*, division III, vol. IV, part ii (Berlin: G. Reimer, 1839), pp. 448–9; see the discussion in *Der christliche Glaube*, 2nd edn (ed. Martin Redeker, Berlin: de Gruyter, 1960), § 15, 1.

14. *Kirchliche Dogmatik* IV/3 (Zurich: Evangelischer Verlag, 1932-67 [for the complete work]), p. 123 (ET, p. 111). Barth here variously characterizes this relationship not only as "to coincide" (zusammentreffen) and "to agree" (übereinstimmen), but also as "to correspond" (entsprechen), "to confirm" (bestätigen), "to testify" (bezeugen), and "to mirror" (spiegeln).

Christ" appears) which is manifestly "about" him.[15] But unlike their medieval Aristotelian predecessors, Schleiermacher and Barth devote little attention to what the relationship of correspondence itself (as distinguished from the poles it aims to join) is supposed to look like.

The vigorous reintroduction of semantic ascent in philosophy after Frege has brought out at least two latent difficulties in this long-running effort to conceive of truth as a four-way affair uniting sentences, mental contents, the world, and human beings. Both affect the appeal to mental contents as truth bearers.

1. Everybody concedes the existence of sentences, knows how to use and interpret them, and ascribes truth values to interpreted sentences; everybody treats interpreted sentences as truth bearers. The existence and nature of the various types of non-linguistic mental entities to which philosophers and theologians have assigned truth-bearing capacity is rather less clear. Attempts to figure out what to make of "truth" and its cognates will naturally gain plausibility if they focus on giving an account of "true" when applied to sentences, and forgo appeals to truth bearers of the more obscure and dubious sort. Clarity about what truth is will profit from treating truth as at most a three-way affair, involving sentences, the world, and human beings. "The strategy of semantic ascent," as Quine observes, "is that it carries the discussion into a domain where both parties are better agreed on the objects (viz., words)."[16]

2. In reply to this difficulty it might be argued that while an account of truth ought to start on the agreed basis of interpreted sentences, it may be necessary for explanatory purposes to posit non-linguistic mental contents along the way.

This cannot, of course, be ruled out in advance, but it ought to be recognized as a counsel of despair. It will be difficult enough to say just what truth as ascribed to sentences has to do with the world, with objects and events, or with some other term whose existence everyone concedes. It seems unlikely that much will be gained by positing as truth bearers entities whose existence and nature is far less obvious than those whose relation we are trying to explain. Elusive mental entities there may of course be, but we will probably be better off, at least when it comes to explicating truth, not relying on them.

Sorting out plausible from implausible truth bearers may seem like an esoteric pursuit, but it deeply affects the more important question of how

15. We will return to this thought, suitably modified, in the next chapter.
16. *Word and Object*, p. 272.

to think about truth. So long as some version of the distinction between "mental" and "verbal" truth bearers was taken for granted, it made sense to think of truth as the correspondence of mind to reality, brought about by mental contents (especially when mind, contents, and reality were conceived in a basically Aristotelian way). But if mental entities can no longer fruitfully be regarded as truth vehicles, does it still make sense to think of truth as the correspondence of mind to reality? And if it turns out that the truth borne by interpreted sentences cannot be that of correspondence, how should we think about truth?

Different ways of rejecting realism

Anti-realism

One outcome of the modern philosophical debate about truth is in fact widespread rejection of the possibility that the truth of sentences or beliefs can successfully be characterized as any sort of correspondence. But the reasons for which "the correspondence theory of truth" gets abandoned vary considerably, as do the correlative suggestions for how to think about truth in the absence of correspondence.

One family of views rejects the notion of truth as correspondence because it makes truth radically non-epistemic (to use Hilary Putnam's phrase). Theories which rely on this notion suggest that a sentence is true when it has a certain relationship – correspondence – to an actual state of affairs. Whether the sentence enjoys this relationship depends on only two things: what the sentence means (or traditionally, what its mental equivalent is) and whether the relevant state of affairs obtains. Whether anyone has good reason to hold the sentence true, indeed whether anyone believes it at all, is irrelevant to its truth. The truth or falsity of sentences thus floats free of whether the sentences express justified beliefs, and in that sense truth is "non-epistemic." We can speak the truth without knowing it, and indeed without having any hope of finding out whether or not what we have said is true. To recall one of Michael Dummett's examples, on a correspondence theory of truth the statement "A city will some day be built here" is determinately either true or false, even though no speaker could ever be in a position to verify it.

Dummett has given the label "anti-realism" to those views which reject any account according to which truth turns out to be non-epistemic. Going anti-realist about truth has various motivations. In Dummett's own case, as we have observed, the chief incentive lies in the theory of meaning. But more often anti-realism stems from the desire to ensure that truth be accessible. Sentences and beliefs are the obvious bearers of truth, and if the truth they bear is conceived as a non-epistemic relationship of correspondence, so various pragmatic and coherentist versions of anti-realism tend to worry, it will be outside the reach of human beings.[17]

This motive sometimes seems to be bound up with a perceived conceptual problem. By being non-epistemic, so the worry goes, realist views of truth ask the impossible; in order to tell whether our beliefs are true, the realist would have us go out of our own skins (as William James puts it). Supposing we could make sense of the notion of sentences we hold true "corresponding" to a non-linguistic state of affairs, we would nonetheless be powerless to tell whether that relationship actually obtained, because we have no way to occupy a position from which to compare our beliefs with the world. Even if we thought we observed the belief that *p* corresponding to an actual state of affairs *P*, that observation could only become an item of knowledge for us, something we could tell is true, if we *believed* that *p* corresponds to *P*, and were justified in that belief. We are enmeshed in our beliefs in such a way that we can readily compare them with one another in search of justificatory relations, but cannot escape from them so as compare them with the world.

At other times the desire to get rid of realism and correspondence in the name of truth's accessibility gets tied to broader ambitions, such as an interest in fostering a "post-Philosophical future" in which beliefs are valued for the contribution they make to an ongoing and open-ended cultural conversation about what is good for us to believe, rather than for their correspondence (or lack of it) to reality.[18]

17. These differences among anti-realists suggest something of the complexity of "realism." For Dummett the chief mark of realism is not the correspondence theory, but bivalence (the claim that every meaningful sentence has a truth value), while other anti-realists are mainly concerned about realism's non-epistemic character. While these three features of realism tend to go together, they fall short of being mutually implicative. Thus Frege, who accepts bivalence and strongly regards truth as non-epistemic (and to that extent merits the label "realist"), rejects the correspondence theory. See Michael Dummett, *Frege: Philosophy of Language*, 2nd edn (Cambridge, Mass.: Harvard University Press, 1981), pp. 442–3.

18. Richard Rorty, "Introduction: Pragmatism and Philosophy," *Consequences of Pragmatism* (Minneapolis: University of Minnesota Press, 1980), p. xvii; see pp. xxxvii–xliv. Rorty has since dropped the pragmatist (as he calls it) notion of truth as "what-it-is-good-to-believe" (p. xxxvii), in favor, he sometimes claims, of a view like Davidson's; see "Pragmatism, Davidson and Truth," *Truth and Interpretation: Perspectives on the Philosophy of Donald Davidson* ed. E. LePore (Oxford: Blackwell, 1986), pp. 333–55. To the extent that Rorty settles on any particular notion of truth, however, it tends to be a "minimalist" or "deflationary" account (on which more below), which Davidson rejects.

Either way: since we can never succeed at being realists the sensible course is to give up trying, and content ourselves with the sort of truth which is within our reach. The truth we can grasp is that which consists in a relationship among our sentences or beliefs themselves, rather than in a relationship of sentences or beliefs to something else (like the world, reality, facts, or states of affairs). In order to be accessible, truth itself has to be epistemic: for a sentence to be true just is for people to be justified in believing it.

Of course people believe all kinds of things for all kinds of reasons, so anti-realism requires an account of precisely what sort of justification is sufficient to constitute truth, and of the kind of person (epistemically speaking) whose beliefs are likely to be justified in the relevant sense.[19] For some anti-realists, justified beliefs are those which fully rational persons, at the ideal end of inquiry, would accept, or regard themselves as warranted in asserting; the truth of a belief consists in its being among those which would meet this condition.[20] Other anti-realists impose less stringent conditions on their inquirers. Justified (and so true) beliefs are those which generally reasonable and self-critical people, or the participants in a generally rational (by its own standards, presumably) social or communal practice, would accept. Others propose that justification is relative to a conceptual scheme or paradigm, so true beliefs are those which come out justified according to this or that paradigm.

Anti-realism so conceived faces a number of problems. "Idealized warranted assertability" seems at least as remote and inaccessible a measure of truth as the "correspondence to reality" which, on account of inaccessibility, it was supposed to replace. Easing this problem by tying truth to current rather than ideal epistemic practices brings out the difference rather than the identity of truth and justification, since justification admits of degrees and can be lost, while truth, as anti-realists themselves generally concede, does neither: beliefs can be "sort of" justified, but since the sentences which express them are (if they have a truth

19. In Arthur Fine's formulation: anti-realism "portrays the truth of a statement P as amounting to the fact that a certain class of subjects would accept P under a certain set of circumstances." "And Not Antirealism Either," *The Shaky Game: Einstein, Realism, and the Quantum Theory* (2nd edn, Chicago: University of Chicago Press, 1996), p. 138. The sketch of alternative anti-realisms in this paragraph basically follows Fine's.

20. So, for example, Putnam: "Truth is an idealization of rational acceptability. We speak as if there were such things as epistemically ideal conditions, and we call a statement 'true' if it would be justified under such conditions." *Reason, Truth and History* (Cambridge: Cambridge University Press, 1981), p. 55. Peirce is usually assumed to lie in the background of such views.

value at all) either true or false, they cannot be "sort of" true; justified beliefs may become unjustified, and conversely, but their truth value does not change with their epistemic status.[21] If truth is relative (via its identity with justification) to a reasonable paradigm or communal practice, problems worse than losing it loom; since there are alternative paradigms and practices which have fair claim to reasonability, the same interpreted sentence or statement could end up being both true (in one paradigm) and false (in another, which accepted its negation). The anti-realist's notion of truth as what persons S would accept under epistemically ideal (or at least better) circumstances x may be viciously circular, and in that sense incoherent.[22]

Whether there might be convincing replies to these objections we need not decide. At least to the extent that they rely on the claim that realism makes truth inaccessible, epistemic views of truth fail to raise a relevant objection to realism in the first place. Correspondence theories never depended on the assumption that truth was accessible. On the contrary, their claim is precisely that reality makes sentences or statements determinately true or false even if we have no way of finding out whether they are true or false. One may think it a bad thing for truth to be inaccessible, and so define truth in epistemic terms. But even if anti-realists are right that the correspondence theory makes truth inaccessible, "the realist could simply reply," as Davidson has observed, "that his position is untouched; he always maintained that truth was independent of our beliefs or our ability to learn the truth."[23]

Realism and the correspondence theory of truth seem able to hold their own against the epistemic assumptions about truth usually offered as reasons for rejecting them. Nonetheless, there are good reasons to suppose that the notion of sentences or beliefs corresponding to reality is not so much false as empty, and so useless for saying what truth is. Consequently, to the extent that truth has to be borne by sentences, truth

---

21. If Dummett is right in his rejection of classical logic, then there will be some interpreted sentences which are neither true nor false, but there will still be none which are "sort of" true or "sort of" false.
22. As Fine suggests in "And Not Antirealism Either," pp. 141–2. The problem seems to go something like this. According to the anti-realist, we cannot recognize S's present acceptance of p as constituting the truth of p unless we can also say that S *would* accept p under x circumstances. But what S would make of p in case x is just what we need to find out, and have no hope of discovering unless we can take S's present acceptance of p as our point of departure. And we cannot do that (we cannot reach the point of saying that S would accept p in case x) unless we can recognize S's present acceptance of p as constituting the truth of p. Thus the circle.
23. "The Structure and Content of Truth," *The Journal of Philosophy* 87/6 (1990), p. 303.

cannot usefully be thought of as the correspondence of mind to reality. "The real objection to correspondence theories," as Davidson puts it, "is that there is nothing interesting or instructive to which true sentences might correspond."[24]

The slingshot argument

The train of thought which supports this contention has come to be known as the "slingshot argument," for its David-like ability to humble a certain kind of outsized claim, of which the definition of truth as correspondence is a good example. Stating the argument precisely requires putting it in formal terms, but its point is perhaps most easily grasped by starting with an example.

According to correspondence theories of truth, the sentence "Northfield is east of Lonsdale" corresponds to the fact that Northfield is east of Lonsdale, and in this the truth of the sentence consists. As it happens, Northfield is the town where St. Olaf College is located. Surely, therefore, "Northfield is east of Lonsdale" also corresponds to the fact that the town where St. Olaf College is located is east of Lonsdale. Northfield, it further happens, is the town which is such that St. Olaf College is located in it and Yellowknife is in the Northwest Territories. So "Northfield is east of Lonsdale" further corresponds to the fact that the town where St. Olaf College is located is east of Lonsdale and Yellowknife is in the Northwest Territories. We can, it appears, keep going for as long as we can keep stating facts, that is, indefinitely. If "Northfield is east of Lonsdale" corresponds to the fact that Northfield is east of Lonsdale, it seems to correspond equally well to the fact that Red Square is in Moscow.

To generalize the point: in expressions of the form "the sentence s corresponds to the fact that p," the values of s and p can be any true sentences. In other words, all true sentences correspond to all facts. If a sentence, moreover, corresponds to any fact, it corresponds to them all; by the same token, all true sentences correspond to the same thing – the totality of the real. Presumably advocates of the theory did not have *this* in mind when they said that truth was correspondence to "reality."

This line of thought may seem more than a little suspicious. It starts with a substitution which seems obvious and unproblematic (putting "the town where St. Olaf College is located" for "Northfield"), but ends with one which seems utterly counter-intuitive (putting "Red Square is in Moscow" for "Northfield is east of Lonsdale"). In order to allay the

24. *Ibid.*

suspicion, we need an argument to show that taking the first unproblematic step commits us to taking the last, seemingly counter-intuitive one.

The "slingshot argument" aims to fill this need.[25] It proceeds by the consistent application of two logical principles which in themselves are uncontroversial. One is that in expressions which permit the substitution of terms with the same extension (that is, terms which refer to the same thing) without changing the truth value of the expression, any term with the same extension can be substituted. For example, an expression which allows us to substitute "the town where St. Olaf College is located" for "Northfield" with no change in truth value is an expression which permits the substitution for the terms within it of any co-extensive terms. The sentential operator "s corresponds to the fact that p" is evidently such an expression, since, as we have seen, it allows us to substitute "the town where St. Olaf College is located" for "Northfield" in a sentence we put for the value of p. This operator creates what logicians call an "extensional context," that is, one where terms with the same extension may be substituted while preserving the truth value of the expression as a whole.[26]

The other logical principle in play here is that in expressions which allow the substitution *salva veritate* of sentences which are logically equivalent, any logically equivalent sentence may be substituted. Logical equivalence is a technical notion; sentences are logically equivalent which must always have the same truth value (the significance of this notion will become more apparent momentarily). In an extensional context, logically equivalent sentences, like co-extensive terms, may be substituted without changing the truth value of the expression in which the substitution occurs.

The goal of the slingshot argument is to establish the truth of the general point, suggested by our example, that in expressions of the form

25. The impetus for the argument goes back to Frege; Davidson gives a terse summary in "True to the Facts," *Inquiries into Truth and Interpretation* (Oxford: Clarendon Press, 1985), pp. 41–2; see also "The Structure and Content of Truth," pp. 303–4. For a fuller and more helpful presentation, see Simon Evnine, *Donald Davidson* (Stanford: University Press, 1991), pp. 136, 180–2. The version I give here is close to Evnine's.
26. The contrast here is with "intensional" contexts, those which do not permit the substitution of co-extensive terms *salva veritate*. Contexts involving belief are a standard example. In the expression "Ralph believes that Northfield is east of Lonsdale" we cannot substitute "the town where St. Olaf College is located" for "Northfield" while preserving the truth of the expression, since Ralph may be unaware that St. Olaf is in Northfield, or may believe that St. Olaf is in Faribault. The sentential operator "R believes that p," in other words, creates an intensional rather than an extensional context for the values of p.

"the sentence *s* corresponds to the fact that *p*," the values of *s* and *p* can be any true sentences. The argument goes as follows.

We have already seen that from

(1) "Northfield is east of Lonsdale" corresponds to the fact that Northfield is east of Lonsdale

we may safely infer

(2) "Northfield is east of Lonsdale" corresponds to the fact that the town where St. Olaf College is located is east of Lonsdale.

Permitting this inference establishes that "'Northfield is east of Lonsdale' corresponds to the fact that . . ." is the sort of expression which creates an extensional context for whatever completes the expression.

We next observe that

(3) $\hat{x}(x=x$ and Northfield is east of Lonsdale$)=\hat{x}(x=x)$

is logically equivalent to

(4) Northfield is east of Lonsdale.

Perhaps (3) seems a bit daunting, but what it states is not difficult to grasp. The symbol "$\hat{x}$" means "the set of objects *x* such that . . ." Statement (3) therefore asserts the identity of two sets with one another: on the right, the set of objects which are identical with themselves, and on the left the set of objects which are identical with themselves, and are such that Northfield is east of Lonsdale. Since everything is identical with itself, the set named on the right includes everything. What the set named on the left includes depends entirely on the truth value of "Northfield is east of Lonsdale." Should "Northfield is east of Lonsdale" be true, the set named on the left will include everything, since everything will be such that it is identical with itself and Northfield is east of Lonsdale. The sets named on the left and the right will both include everything, and (3) will be true. Should "Northfield is east of Lonsdale" be false, the set named on the left will include nothing, since nothing will be such that it is identical with itself and Northfield is east of Lonsdale. The set named on the left will include nothing, while the one on the right will include everything; (3) will be therefore be false. This means that (3) is true just in case (4) is true, and false just in case (4) is false; (3) and (4) are logically equivalent.

Applying the principle that in extensional contexts we may substitute logically equivalent sentences, we substitute (3) for "Northfield is east of Lonsdale" in the operand position of (1), and get

(5) "Northfield is east of Lonsdale" corresponds to the fact that $\hat{x}(x=x$ and Northfield is east of Lonsdale$)=\hat{x}(x=x)$.

In extensional contexts, however, we may also substitute co-extensive terms. This means that if we can find a term which has the same extension as "$\hat{x}(x=x$ and Northfield is east of Lonsdale)," we can substitute that term in (5). Because "Northfield is east of Lonsdale" is true, the extension of "$\hat{x}(x = x$ and Northfield is east of Lonsdale)" is everything; the set named by this term includes all things. As it happens "Red Square is in Moscow" is also true, so the extension of "$\hat{x}(x = x$ and Red Square is in Moscow)" is also everything; here too, the set which includes all things is named. Substituting these co-extensive terms, we get

(6) "Northfield is east of Lonsdale" corresponds to the fact that $\hat{x}(x=x$ and Red Square is in Moscow$) = \hat{x}(x=x)$.

Now we follow in reverse the reasoning which allowed us to substitute (3) for (4). We observe, in other words, that

(7) $\hat{x}(x=x$ and Red Square is in Moscow$) = \hat{x}(x=x)$

is logically equivalent to

(8) Red Square is in Moscow.

This puts us in a position to apply for a second time the principle that we may substitute logically equivalent sentences in extensional contexts. Thus we end up with

(9) "Northfield is east of Lonsdale" corresponds to the fact that Red Square is in Moscow.

By this series of steps the slingshot argument shows that the operator "the sentence s corresponds to the fact that p," since it creates an extensional context for the values of p, is truth-functional. However much the sentences put for s and p differ in meaning (like "Northfield is east of Lonsdale" and "Red Square is in Moscow"), we cannot bar them from being values of these variables as long as they are true. This makes "corresponds to the fact that . . ." useless for defining or characterizing truth, insofar as truth is borne by sentences and beliefs.

The expression "corresponds to the fact that . . ." is supposed to *explain* truth; correspondence theorists maintain that this operator tells us something about truth which we would not otherwise know. But as it turns out we understand truth better than we understand correspondence. That Red Square is in Moscow may be taken, according to the truth-functional logic of the correspondence operator, as the fact to which "Northfield is east of Lonsdale" corresponds, but we would never think of taking "'Northfield is east of Lonsdale' is true if and only if Red Square is in Moscow" as a satisfactory statement of the truth conditions for "Northfield is east of Lonsdale." This alerts us to the hopelessness of regarding "corresponds to the fact that . . ." as an informative substitute for "is true if and only if . . ." Rather than giving us an explanation of truth for sentences, "correspondence to reality" tells us nothing useful we do not already know, and know better, from whatever grasp of "true" we already have.

The slingshot argument does not, to be sure, meet with universal approval. For some, that this sort of argument allows us to infer from the apparently harmless (1) to the obviously unacceptable (9) shows not that the correspondence operator should be discarded, but that the argument should. John Searle suggests that the argument goes wrong at (5).[27] The fact that Northfield is east of Lonsdale is not the same fact as the fact that $\hat{x}(x=x$ and Northfield is east of Lonsdale$) = \hat{x}(x=x)$; facts about Northfield have nothing important to do with facts about the self-identity of all possible objects. This, Searle proposes, is just intuitively obvious to us. Given this intuition, we cannot substitute "$\hat{x}(x = x$ and Northfield is east of Lonsdale$) = \hat{x}(x=x)$" for "Northfield is east of Lonsdale" to get (5) from (1), and the slingshot argument breaks down.

At least two problems arise with this response. One is that the intuitions which block the unwanted inference from (1) to (5) equally well block the seemingly benign inference from (1) to (2). If the inference from (1) to (2) is allowed, then the sentential operator "s corresponds to the fact that . . ." creates an extensional context for the sentences operated upon, since it permits the substitution *salva veritate* of co-extensive terms in those sentences. Granted that, the substitutions which make the slingshot argument go are fully in bounds.

Searle tries to handle this problem, it seems, by saying that the substitution by which we infer (2) from (1) intuitively preserves "identity of fact" while that by which we infer (5) from (1) intuitively does not.[28] Identity of fact so construed (like the expression "the fact that . . .") is, however, an intensional rather than an extensional notion; claims about identity of fact do not permit substitution *salva veritate* of co-extensive terms.[29] That being the case, the only way to allow (2) but block (5) would be to say that the operator "s corresponds to the fact that . . ." is extensional in (2) but intensional in (5). Rather than explicating an intuition which is supposed to defeat the slingshot argument, this sort of recourse

---

27. John R. Searle, *The Construction of Social Reality* (New York: The Free Press, 1995), pp. 221–6.   28. *Ibid.*, p. 225.   29. As Searle insists; see *ibid.*, p. 226.

seems to stipulate intuitions at will, in the hope of granting the logical principles on which the argument is based without having to accept its conclusion. One may, indeed, take the disputed operator as genuinely intensional, but then we can no more get (2) from (1) than we can get (5) from it. With that we return to the result of the slingshot argument; all we are then permitted is "'Northfield is east of Lonsdale' corresponds to the fact that Northfield is east of Lonsdale," which tells us nothing we do not already know from "'Northfield is east of Lonsdale' is true if and only if Northfield is east of Lonsdale."

Supposing, though, that we allow an objector freely to treat "s corresponds to the fact that p" as either extensional or intensional, depending on whether substitutions in sentences put for p do or do not preserve "identity of fact." The difficulty remains of individuating facts or states of affairs, and of specifying when they are identical.

Perhaps the most obvious recourse is to say that there is a fact for every true statement.[30] As a strategy for explaining truth as borne by statements this has the disadvantage of assuming that we already understand the notion, since it requires us to invoke the concept of truth for a statement in order to pick out the fact which is supposed to make the statement true. Apart from that, it leads to undesirable results simply as a strategy for individuating facts. By this criterion

(10) Northfield is ten miles east of Lonsdale

would be a different fact from

(11) Northfield is sixteen kilometers east of Lonsdale,

since "Northfield is ten miles east of Lonsdale" and "Northfield is sixteen kilometers east of Lonsdale" are different statements, but alike true. This criterion clutters the world with too many facts – so many, indeed, that substitution which preserves identity of fact becomes impossible; every time we make a substitution we get a new statement, which states a new fact.

But if we cannot pick out facts by reference to true statements, how can we individuate them? Consider

(12) Lonsdale is ten miles west of Northfield.

Is this a different fact from (10), or the same fact? Since Northfield, Lonsdale, and the Minnesota real estate between them are the same in

---

30. This seems to be Searle's idea: "The only way to identify a fact is to make a true statement" (*ibid.*, p. 205; see pp. 210–12).

both cases, perhaps they are the same fact. But since west is a different direction from east, perhaps they are a different fact. It is not at all clear that we have any intuition about whether (10) and (12) are or are not identical facts, and to rely on intuition to tell us when facts are identical is in any case to concede that we have no clear, or even statable, criterion by which to do the job. As a rebuttal to the slingshot argument the need to preserve identity of fact was supposed to let us know which substitutions were licit and which were not, but it turns out that we have no clear idea when identity of fact is and is not preserved, and so no clear idea what is wrong with the slingshot argument.

More is the pity, in a way, since if Searle were right the theological job we have to do would likely be easier. As the next chapter will argue, a theological account of what truth is cannot get by without making something of the notion of correspondence, and it would probably be an aid toward this end if we could get correspondence into what truth is for sentences. But the obstacles in the way of this are formidable enough that we are well advised to look elsewhere for an account of truth as borne by sentences and beliefs. When it comes to truth, as to any other matter, theology should seek to bring under its own discipline the most plausible account currently available to it, not the account that makes its own job go more smoothly.

Truth without realism or anti-realism

What then should be made of the concept of truth, if anti-realism is unpersuasive and correspondence (and to that extent realism) is vacuous? An alternative to anti-realism, but without any appeal to correspondence, might go as follows.

Realists and anti-realists alike appear to assume that "truth" is an especially obscure and elusive notion, for which conceptual equivalents need to be found which we can more readily grasp. But Davidson in particular has suggested that this assumption has the matter backwards, as the problems had by both realists and anti-realists in coming up with an informative or plausible substitute for "true" in part attest. Far from being a daunting puzzle, truth is about as basic and obvious a concept as we have. The notion of truth is much more clear to us – we have a much firmer grip on it – than any concept we might use to analyze or explain it. "Why on earth should we expect to be able to reduce truth to something clearer or more fundamental? After all, the only concept Plato succeeded in defining was mud (dirt and water)."[31]

Taking truth as conceptually basic, and so insusceptible of an informative equivalent or intensional definition, does not mean that nothing can be said about it. We do have a statable grasp of the concept of truth, Davidson argues, for every sentence in our language. Supposing that language is English, our grasp of the concept "true" as applied to the sentence "Grass is green," for example, is expressed in our untroubled assent to the sentence "'Grass is green' is true if and only if grass is green." Our grasp of the concept of truth for any particular language is expressed in our untroubled readiness to assent to all such trivialities, that is, to all sentences of the form "*s* is true-in-*L* if and only if *p*." We get a T-sentence (as Davidson calls them) from this formula by replacing *s* with the description of a sentence (usually by quoting it) and *p* with the sentence itself (or a translation of the sentence, if the language of the T-sentence itself – the "metalanguage" – is different from the language of *s*), and by letting *L* denote the language to which the sentence described by *s* belongs (the "object language"). Sentences of this form are trivial in that their truth seems obvious and unworthy of dispute, but they are not on that account uninformative. Each of them shows us how "is true" works for a particular sentence of a given language (here, English), by giving the conditions under which it applies to that sentence.[32] Taken together, they show us how "is true" works for all the sentences of the language – that is, they define truth for that language.

The definition thus arrived at is purely extensional, and so perhaps not what we usually think of as a definition. It completely specifies, for a given language, the sentences to which "is true" applies and the conditions under which it does so, but does not tell us, in the ordinary (intensional) sense, what "is true" means – it provides no concepts equivalent to "true." Daunting technical problems arise over how to construct an adequate extensional definition of truth, and also over whether the procedure for

---

31. Donald Davidson, "Afterthoughts, 1987" (to "A Coherence Theory of Truth and Knowledge," published earlier in *Truth and Interpretation: Perspectives on the Philosophy of Donald Davidson*, ed. E. LePore [Oxford: Blackwell, 1986]), *Reading Rorty*, ed. Alan Malichowski (Oxford: Blackwell, 1990), p. 136. See "The Structure and Content of Truth," p. 314.

32. Tarski takes this way of specifying truth conditions for a sentence to be a refinement of Aristotle's definition of truth: "To say of what is that it is not, or of what is not that it is, is false, while to say of what is that it is, and of what is not that it is not, is true" (*Metaphysics* IV, 7, 1011b, 25–9; see VI, 4, 1027b, 17–29). See Alfred Tarski, "The Semantic Conception of Truth and the Foundations of Semantics," *Collected Papers*, vol. II, ed. Steven R. Givant and Ralph McKenzie (Basel: Birkhäuser, 1986), pp. 666–7.

defining truth extensionally can be applied to natural languages.[33] Our present concern is only to point up the plausibility of the suggestion that sentences which conform to Tarski's schema embody a grasp every language user has of the concept of truth, and provide a clear way of stating it.[34] If this suggestion is correct, then whatever else may be said in answer to the question "what is truth?" will need to have some intelligible tie to this shared grasp of truth and the sentences which express it.

By declining to offer a conceptual substitute for "is true" as applied to sentences, it might seem as though Davidson has committed himself to the view that T-sentences tell us everything there is to know about truth. This is, roughly put, the contention of "minimalist" or "deflationary" theories of truth. Views of this kind argue that truth, while not a dispensable concept, is at bottom a trivial one. Everything there is to be said about what it is for "Grass is green" to be true is stated by the sentence "'Grass is green' is true if and only if grass is green," and so on for all other sentences. Everything there is to be said about the concept of truth is thus, in the words of one deflationist, "expressed by uncontroversial instances of the equivalence schema

(E) It is true *that p* if and only if *p*."[35]

Correlatively, "the traditional attempt to discern the *essence* of truth – to analyse that special quality which all truths supposedly have in common – is just a pseudo-problem based on syntactic overgeneralization."[36]

At this point, however, Davidson admits to a certain unease. He agrees with the deflationists that T-sentences capture something quite basic about the concept of truth, and so are indispensable to any workable theory of truth. He further agrees that the concept of truth cannot be inflated in either realist or anti-realist fashion. Yet he forcefully rejects deflationism.[37]

---

33. Tarski devised a way to meet these technical problems, though he thought it worked only for formalized languages (those shorn of indexical elements like demonstratives and tenses). See Alfred Tarski, "The Concept of Truth in Formalized Languages,"*Logic, Semantics, Metamathematics*, trans. J. H. Woodger (Oxford: Clarendon Press, 1956), pp. 152–278; for the specification of conditions for an adequate (extensional) definition of truth ("Convention T"), see pp. 187–8. Tarski gives several relatively non-technical introductions to his own project; in addition to "The Semantic Conception of Truth," *Collected Papers*, vol. II, pp. 661–99, see "Truth and Proof," *Collected Papers*, vol. IV, pp. 399–423. Davidson argues that Tarski's procedure may be applied to natural languages in, *inter alia*, "Radical Interpretation," *Inquiries*, pp. 125–39.

34. As Davidson puts the point, "Convention T embodies our best intuition as to how the concept of truth is used." "On the Very Idea of a Conceptual Scheme," *Inquiries*, p. 195.

35. Paul Horwich, *Truth* (Oxford: Blackwell, 1990), p. 7; see p. 11.   36. *Ibid.*, p. 6.

37. See on this, and for what follows, "The Structure and Content of Truth," pp. 280–95; "Pursuit of the Concept of Truth," *On Quine: New Essays*, ed. Paolo Leonardi and Marco Santambrogio (Cambridge: Cambridge University Press, 1995), pp. 7–21; "The Folly of Trying to Define Truth," *The Journal of Philosophy* 93 (1996), pp. 263–78.

The reasons are in part technical, having to do with whether the deflationist position can be stated in a coherent way.[38] But the deeper reason stems from an ancient philosophical concern: Davidson thinks it essential to preserve the unity of truth, and thinks deflationism cannot help failing to do so. Tarski showed how to give an extensional definition of truth for particular languages – how, that is, to define the class of sentences to which the predicate "true-in-L" applies for certain values of L. As he himself was aware, however, he did not locate a general or unitary concept of truth, applicable to all languages; he did not, as Davidson often observes, show what his various definitions of a truth predicate for particular languages have in common.[39] If there is a single concept of truth applicable to different languages, there has to be more to this concept – and thus to the predicate "true-in-L" in each of the T-sentences which express our grasp of the concept – than any given T-sentence, or all of them taken together, captures. What, though, would "more" be in this case? Davidson evidently needs to steer a course, if one can be found, between defining truth and trivializing it. He needs to make some plausible generalizations about truth, some claims which articulate its unity, without pretending to find a conceptual substitute for it.

Davidson ventures generalizations of two different kinds. One has to do with the ties which bind truth to meaning and belief, connections which Davidson takes to be "partly constitutive of the concept of truth."[40]

A T-sentence tells us that the truth of the sentence described on its left branch depends only on (i) what that sentence means and (ii) whether the truth conditions uniquely specified on its right branch are met. T-sentences involving translation bring this out: our untroubled assent to "'Gras ist grün' is true if and only if grass is green" tells us that the truth of "Gras ist grün" depends on (i) whether it means "Grass is green" and (ii) whether grass is green. Truth as captured by T-sentences is thus not at all an epistemic notion; whether the sentence named on the left is true depends on what it means and on whether its truth conditions are met, but not on whether anyone is justified, or regards herself as justified, in

---

38. See "The Folly of Trying to Define Truth," pp. 272–4.

39. "Unless we are prepared to say there is no single concept of truth (even as applied to sentences), but only a number of different concepts for which we use the same word, we have to conclude that there is more to the concept of truth – something absolutely basic, in fact – which Tarski's definitions do not touch." "The Structure and Content of Truth," p. 288.

40. Ibid., p. 281; see p. 295. We met with some of these connections from a different angle when we discussed Davidson's theory of interpretation in chapter 4.

holding it true. To that extent traditional correspondence theories are right, though this is only half the story.

Truth has constitutive connections not only with meaning, but with belief. Whether a sentence is true depends only on what it means and whether its truth conditions are met. Interpreting sentences correctly, however, requires knowing whether their speakers believe them to be true, and what truth conditions they assign to the sentences to which they assent. At least in the most accessible cases, figuring this out in a non-circular fashion depends on taking the circumstances which prompt assent to a sentence as constituting the truth conditions for that sentence (such that falling snow, for example, causes Erich to utter "Es schneit").[41] Locating with sufficient precision the truth conditions for a particular sentence, and weeding out aspects of the situation in which the sentence is uttered which do not actually prompt assent to it, can be accomplished only as part of a plausible theory of interpretation for a language as a whole, and not sentence by sentence. Assigning truth conditions requires, in other words, consistent application of the principle of charity. What speakers mean by their sentences has to be, on the whole, what makes the sentences to which they assent – which is to say their beliefs – come out true. "What saves truth from being 'radically non-epistemic,'" Davidson argues, "is not that truth is epistemic but that belief, through its ties with meaning, is intrinsically veridical."[42]

As we noted a while back, the claim that belief is on the whole veridical meets with the obvious objection that beliefs are sometimes false, and so might be false most of the time: plausible interpretation requires that speaker and interpreter largely agree about what to believe, but it does not require that their beliefs largely be true.[43]

In reply, Davidson observes that having the concept of belief requires a grasp on the notion of objective truth, since the concept is basically that of a sentence which is held true, but might not actually be true. The concept of belief thus enshrines the objection's distinction between agreement (shared belief) and truth (which shared beliefs might lack). In order to have this concept at all, we have to know how to use it, and we use it precisely in interpersonal communication and interpretation. Having the concept of belief enables us to sort out from among a speaker's utterances

---

41. As Davidson puts the point, "what ultimately ties language to the world is that the conditions that typically cause us to hold sentences true *constitute* the truth conditions, and hence the meanings, of our sentences." "The Folly of Trying to Define Truth," p. 275.
42. "Afterthoughts, 1987," p. 136.   43. See chapter 4, note 35.

those where he is in error – where he takes the concept of objective truth to apply (as specified by Tarski-style truth conditions), while we judge that it does not. In order to interpret speakers at all we must (as the objection grants) avoid attributing to them massive error. But since the interpreter has no choice but to read his own standards of truth into the utterances of the speaker, we can avoid the ascription of massive error only by supposing that most of the speaker's beliefs are not only held true, they are true: as objective a concept of truth as we have has to apply to them. And conversely: since the interpreter's own standards of truth enable her to locate the truth conditions (in the first place the causes) of a speaker's utterances, and so to grasp what the speaker means, if the interpreter's own beliefs are not mostly true, she will obviously not be able to locate truth conditions for utterances in a generally correct way, and so will have no way correctly to figure out what speakers mean.[44]

Should this be right then truth, while not an epistemic notion, is also not inaccessibly divorced from belief (and so from justification) in the way it seemed to be in correspondence theories, which led anti-realists to go epistemic in their accounts of truth. If successful, Davidson's proposal is thus a genuine alternative to both realism and anti-realism.

On his account the concept of truth turns out to be pivotal in both our ascription of meanings to sentences and of beliefs (and with them thoughts, attitudes, desires, and the like) to speakers. The ties of truth to meaning and belief help display the unity of truth, and so tell us more about truth than Tarski's schema by itself. On account of these ties we can relate Tarski's extensional definitions of truth to language as actually used by humans to talk about a shared public world. What unifies truth is the role that it plays in enabling us to *interpret* other speakers, no matter what language they speak. A concept which can play this role must be the same for the speaker and the interpreter, and must therefore be a single concept for whatever languages they speak.

A second sort of generalization, about which Davidson is much more tentative, has to do with what to make of the right branch of a T-sentence

---

44. On this see especially "Thought and Talk," *Inquiries*, pp. 168–70, and "A Coherence Theory of Truth and Knowledge," pp. 314–19. Davidson's argument that our beliefs have to be mostly veridical is evidently not an epistemological claim to have "jumped out of his own skin," or to have assessed beliefs one by one. Instead epistemology is here "seen in the mirror of meaning" ("Thought and Talk," p. 169): in order for the sentences we and others hold true to *mean* what they do, we and they have to be generally correct about what we hold true, and so our beliefs have to be generally true.

– with whether it is possible to generalize in an informative rather than misleading way about truth conditions.

We have no trouble generalizing about what the left branch of a T-sentence does; it describes a sentence. But what, in general, does the right branch do? To say that it uniquely specifies truth conditions for the sentence on the left is no doubt correct, and this is enough to be quite informative, in the context of a radical and holistic approach to interpretation, about the meaning of speakers' sentences and the content of their beliefs. But it may not seem to tell us much about truth itself, and so may tempt us to try for more informative generalizations.

Davidson sometimes appears to give in to this temptation. "What Convention T, and the trite sentences it declares true … reveal is that the truth of an utterance depends on just two things: what the words as spoken mean, and how the world is arranged."[45] This suggests that the right branch of a T-sentence in general isolates truth conditions by describing, or being about, an "arrangement of the world," a state of affairs in virtue of which the sentence described on the left is (or would be) true. This suggests the further thought that the truth of the sentence described on the left depends only on (i) what that sentence means and (ii) whether the arrangement of the world or the state of affairs described on the right actually obtains.

It may seem as though we have quickly learned more about truth in general than T-sentences explicitly tell us, encouraged by the structure of T-sentences themselves. But on Davidson's own grounds, appearances here are largely illusory. Tempting though it may be, we cannot take formulations like

(13) p describes (or: is about) the state of affairs that …

or

(14) p describes (or: is about) the arrangement of the world such that …

to tell us more about what it is for s to be true than we already know from

(T) s is true if and only if p.

More precisely, these generalizations about the values of p fail to tell us anything about the truth conditions specified by p, and so about the meaning of "is true" in (T), that is not told by (T) itself. The problem is that (13) and (14) look to be fodder for the slingshot argument; like "p corresponds to the fact that …", they look ready to be taken as truth-functional

45. "A Coherence Theory of Truth and Knowledge," p. 309.

sentential operators, in which case they will not tell us more about truth than (T), but less.[46] We can block this result by insisting that the sentence upon which (13) and (14) operate be the same as the sentence put for p, but this only makes it plain that (13) or (14) do not elucidate (T), but are elucidated by it. Whatever understanding we have of

(13') "Gras ist grün" describes the state of affairs that grass is green

depends on the understanding we have of

(T$_1$) "Gras ist grün" is true if and only if grass is green.

Our grasp of (13') depends, that is, on our ability, when puzzled, to take truth as explaining description, and not conversely.

Apparently a generalization like Davidson's "the truth of an utterance … depends on the way the world is arranged" does not really tell us more about truth than we can gather from Tarski's definitions, since we have to rely on T-sentences to understand the generalization. This does not rule out such generalizations, but encourages us to be conscious of their explanatory shortcomings.

Much the same goes for the notions of what "makes" a sentence true or what a sentence is true "in virtue of." Truth theorists sometimes seem allergic to these expressions (especially when the theorists have deflationist tendencies); Davidson himself seems capable of rejecting and accepting them in pretty much the same breath.[47] The point of such apparent insouciance seems to be that generalized notions like "true in virtue of" and "made true by" are harmless enough, as long as we realize that what grasp we have of them depends on the grasp we already have of the connection of the left branch of a T-sentence to the right. Notions of this kind may, indeed, serve an important use: to remind us, in a general way, that language is tied to the world. The problem with such notions lies in our readiness to ignore their explanatory limitations, not in the thought that language is tied to the world. It is truth that ties language to the world, in the fashion displayed by each T-sentence. The difficulty we

---

46. This suggests that an account of truth like that recently offered by Alston, while more austere than Searle's, is unsatisfying for much the same reason. In order to give content to the concept of truth, Alston relies on notions involving truth-functional operators, like "what the maker of a statement is saying to be the case" and "what the maker of [a] statement is attributing to what the statement is about." See William P. Alston, *A Realist Conception of Truth* (Ithaca: Cornell University Press, 1996), pp. 23, 26.

47. "Nothing, however, no *thing*, makes sentences and theories true: not experience, not surface irritations, not the world, can make our sentences or theories true." Yet: "In giving up the dualism of scheme and world, we do not give up the world, but re-establish unmediated touch with the familiar objects whose antics make our sentences and opinions true or false." "On the Very Idea of a Conceptual Scheme," pp. 194, 198.

have in finding notions which allow us to generalize effectively about this tie need not suggest that the tie is puzzling or mysterious, still less that it is absent. Our conceptual frustration attests rather to the utterly basic way in which the concept of truth captures this tie.

Let us suppose, then, that a view like Davidson's, which accepts realism's fall but not anti-realism's rise, is the most plausible outcome currently available of the long philosophical debate about what truth is. What should Christian theology, committed to an explication of the claim that Jesus Christ is "the truth," make of this result?

9

Trinity, truth, and belief

Truth under theological discipline

Truth borne by a person

In a theological account of truth, as Donald MacKinnon suggests, any understanding we may acquire of that notion without reference to Christian beliefs will no doubt be "radically disciplined and changed," although – we hope – "not annihilated."[1] The New Testament seems to regard "is the truth" as a genuine predicate both of Jesus Christ (see Jn. 14:6) and of the Holy Spirit (see 1 Jn. 5:6). The discipline to which theology subjects any philosophical proposal about truth is thus obvious, and radical: if Jesus Christ is the truth, then truth is borne, not only or chiefly by sentences and beliefs, but by a person. More than that: if the New Testament is right, then in the end truth *is* a person. The same applies, though differently, to the person of the Spirit.

Should the Tarski–Davidson notion of truth outlined in the previous chapter prove incompatible with the claim that truth is each of these persons, and so intractable to theological discipline, it faces annihilation (to use MacKinnon's term). At first glance, though, it might seem that a Tarski–Davidson account of truth states the truth conditions, and so displays the workings of "is true," for statements which express central Christian beliefs as well as it does for any other statements. Surely Christians want to say, for example, that the following sentence is true:

(1) "Jesus is risen" is true if and only if Jesus is risen.

---

1. "The Problem of the 'System of Projection' Appropriate to Christian Theological Statements," *Explorations in Theology 5: Donald MacKinnon* (London: SCM Press, 1979), p. 81.

Jesus is risen, so Christians proclaim; therefore "Jesus is risen" is true. The person who holds "Jesus is risen" true therefore has a true belief, and the person who holds it false has a false belief. This not only looks theologically acceptable, but appears to capture in a more informative and less misleading way at least part of what traditional theological appeals to truth as correspondence were driving at, especially where the traditional view stressed sentences rather than mental contents as truth bearers. So far, it seems, so plain. Theological discipline appears to leave a Tarski–Davidson account of truth pretty much intact – indeed untouched.

We do not, however, learn anything from (1) about how a person is the bearer of truth. The person Jesus figures in the truth conditions specified by the right branch of (1), such that if and only if he is risen, "Jesus is risen" is true, but this does not make Jesus himself "true," still less "the truth," with respect to the sentence "Jesus is risen." Or, if you like, it makes the person Jesus a truth bearer for "Jesus is risen" in exactly the same sense as grass is a truth bearer for "Grass is green." If having this location on the right branch of a T-sentence makes Jesus "the truth," it equally well makes grass "the truth" – not, presumably, what John's Gospel means when it predicates "is the truth" of the person Jesus.

This may prompt the thought that when Davidson and the Gospel of John speak of "truth," they are simply talking about two different things. Truth as borne by sentences and beliefs has nothing in particular to do with "the truth" as borne, according to the New Testament, by the person Jesus. Supposing otherwise, so it might be argued, is to read passages like Jn. 14:6 in a needlessly literalistic way. We do not suppose that we need a theological biology because Jesus there says "I am the life," or a theological geography because he says "I am the way." Why do we need a theological aletheology – an account of truth for sentences and beliefs – because Jesus says "I am the truth"?

Standard exegetical approaches do not suggest that a passage like Jn. 14:6 may be taken as utterly metaphorical, so that "I am the truth" amounts to something like "I am the most important thing there is." To be sure, even when exegetes draw freely on philosophical ideas to interpret the concept of truth in John, they tend to connect it at best loosely to truth as applied to sentences and beliefs.[2] But a link between the two uses

2. As, for example, in Heinrich Schlier's broadly Heideggerian "Meditationen über den Johanneischen Begriff der Wahrheit," *Besinnung auf Das Neue Testament. Exegetische Aufsätze und Vorträge II* (Freiburg: Herder, 1964), pp. 270–8.

of "truth" is nonetheless implicit in the common view of recent exegesis that in Jn. 14:6 (as also in 1:17), Jesus is "the truth" in that he is the unique "revelation" of the Father, the one who alone adequately makes the Father known.[3] Jesus is able to bring about knowledge of the Father by others on account of his own unique relation to the Father: as the Father's Word become our flesh, this human being is the one who "expresses the total being of the Father."[4]

For human beings, however, having knowledge requires having true beliefs. To have a belief is to have the disposition to hold sentences true which express the contents of the belief. The knowledge of the Father which Jesus brings about – and this is the crucial point for present purposes – is thus impossible for us save by having beliefs and holding sentences true. The text of John seems to confirm this. Jesus' unique relation with the Father is what enables him to make the Father known, but he imparts the knowledge in words: "I declare what I have seen in the Father's presence" (8:38) and thus, in a different context, "The words that I have spoken to you are Spirit and life" (6:63; cf. 18:37: "Everyone who is of the truth listens to my voice").

The following conditionals therefore seem exegetically sound:

(2) If Jesus Christ is the truth, then he imparts knowledge of the Father to us

and

(3) If Jesus Christ imparts knowledge of the Father to us, then we have some true beliefs (and we hold true some true sentences).

Taken together, these two conditionals imply

(4) If Jesus Christ is the truth, then we have some true beliefs (and we hold true some true sentences).

Exegetically, therefore, "truth" as applied to sentences and beliefs is logically necessary for the "truth" which the person Jesus Christ is. However

---

3. Cf. Ignace de la Potterie, *La vérité dans Saint Jean*, 2 vols. (Rome: Biblical Institute Press, 1977): "The truth of Christ is the unveiling of his Sonship, in his life of love and obedience to the Father. This *revelation of Christ*, this *truth*, has to reach its culmination on the cross" (p. 1011), also Raymond E. Brown, *The Gospel According to John*, 2 vols. (Garden City, NY: Doubleday, 1966), vol. II, p. 630. The connection between the truth which Jesus is and the knowledge he brings about was not missed by classical exegesis of John, though generally without reliance on the notion of revelation. "Truth belongs to [Christ] on account of who he is, namely the Word . . . And because no one can know the truth unless he clings to it, it is necessary that everyone who desires to know the truth cling to this Word" (Thomas Aquinas, *In Ioannem* 14, 2, no. 1869). This sort of remark suggests that our grasp of truth (both the concept and its application to each sentence) depends universally, and not just in some cases, on Jesus' being the truth; we will return to this point.

4. To recall Aquinas, *In Ioannem* 1, 1, no. 29.

we connect more precisely these two applications of "truth," it seems clear that the Gospel of John and Davidson are not simply talking about different things when they use the term.

We confront, therefore, the following problem. A Tarski–Davidson approach cannot by itself be adequate for a theological account of what truth is, because it gives us no clue about how to connect truth to a person as its bearer. At the same time, the concept of truth as applied to sentences and beliefs cannot be utterly disparate from the concept of truth which applies to the person Jesus. Assuming that a Tarski–Davidson approach gives us the best available account of truth for sentences, theological discipline will have to go beyond merely showing that this approach is compatible with central Christian claims. We need an explanation as to why the content of the concept of truth as characterized by Tarski and Davidson should be regarded as incomplete, and how it may be expanded theologically without losing an intelligible tie to the characterization Tarski and Davidson give.

Truth as an act of the Trinity

Did this characterization of truth capture adequately the way "is true" works for "Jesus is risen," then the truth (or falsity) of "Jesus is risen" would be, as it were, automatic. Tarski's schema for T-sentences, after all, states not simply necessary ("only if...") but sufficient ("if...") truth conditions for the sentence described on its left branch. Should a sentence conforming to this schema express a grasp of the concept of truth adequate to "Jesus is risen," then anyone's utterance, "Jesus is risen," will be true depending only on what she means by the words and whether Jesus turns out to be risen (and not dead), just as her utterance, "Grass is green," will be true if she interprets it in the usual way and grass is green (and not orange). Since the truth of beliefs depends on the truth of the sentences which express them, if Jesus is risen anyone who holds "Jesus is risen" true will have a true belief, brought about by the attitude he has toward that sentence. The truth of the belief, like that of the interpreted sentence which states the contents of the belief, will be automatic.

Why should the truth of the belief that Jesus is risen not be automatic in this sense? Here we need to bear in mind two points.

1. Having true beliefs is a necessary condition for having knowledge of Jesus, and so of having any relation to Jesus which depends upon having knowledge of him. Knowing the risen Jesus requires having the belief that Jesus is risen, and it requires that the belief be true. If (as we

have argued in chapter 2) having the belief that Jesus is risen is requisite
for identifying him, then knowing Jesus *at all* requires having the true
belief that he is risen. To have knowledge of Jesus is to have a certain relation to him, but many other relations to Jesus depend on having knowledge of him, and in that sense have a cognitive component: loving,
worshipping, following, and so forth. (Relations to Jesus which require
no cognitive component, like sharing descent from Abraham, can presumably obtain for someone who lacks the belief that Jesus is risen, or any
other belief about him.) To be sure, one can apparently worship a figure
who does not exist (though whether one can love the inexistent is
perhaps less clear), and to that extent worship requires only that one have
certain beliefs, not that the beliefs be true. For the worshipper's intention
to succeed, however – for his attitude to relate him to a really existent
term – he not only has to hold the relevant beliefs; the beliefs also have to
be true. Having (successful) love or reverence for Jesus does not, of course,
consist wholly in having true beliefs about him, but such relations apparently cannot do without true beliefs sufficient to identify him.

2. Any relations which created reality has to Jesus depend as a whole
on Jesus himself. This comes out perhaps most clearly in the way the New
Testament characterizes Jesus' resurrection. The Father raises Jesus by
his own free and sovereign action, which is to bestow his Spirit upon the
slain Jesus. This gift to the crucified Jesus fully enacts the Spirit's mission,
begun at Jesus' baptism, to abide in and on the Son. The Spirit gives the
dead Jesus the divine freedom to rise from the dead, by including Jesus
once again in an ordered but mutual bond of being, knowledge, and love
with the Father. Jesus rises, therefore, in the utterly sovereign, self-deter-
mining freedom of God.[5] The action of the risen Jesus thus takes place in
the full spontaneity of the being and all the acts of the triune God. The
risen Jesus is not passive or inert, and therefore not at the disposal of
human beings, or of anything created – except, of course, insofar as he
freely gives himself to them. Jesus' being at their disposal, one could say,
is not itself at their disposal, but only at his own. Upon his own action,
therefore, depends any relation to him which creatures may come to
have.[6]

5. For a reading of the resurrection narratives along these lines, see Hans Urs von
Balthasar, *Mysterium Paschale*, trans. Aiden Nichols (Grand Rapids: Eerdmans, 1993), pp.
203–15; on the pneumatological aspect in particular, see pp. 210–12.
6. At this point the logic of genuinely transcendent and therefore non-competing agency
(as articulated, e.g., by Tanner in *God and Creation*) seems indispensable to making sense of
the narratives which identify Jesus. If the human being Jesus is God, he cannot simply be

Taken together, these observations suggest why the truth of the belief that Jesus is risen cannot be automatic. The content of the belief itself seems to preclude the possibility that the relations of the rest of humanity to the risen Jesus could be brought about save by Jesus' own action. Any element necessary for such relations to obtain must, it seems, depend in some way upon Jesus' action. Cognitively dependent relations of other human beings to the risen Jesus, relations like knowing and (successful) loving, require having the true belief that he is risen. Therefore the *truth* of this belief must itself be brought about by an action which belongs to Jesus.

The resurrection narratives indicate this in a striking way: even though they see him and talk to him, the two disciples on the Emmaus road and Mary Magdalene at the empty tomb cannot recognize Jesus, and so have the belief that he is risen, until his own deliberate action – his eucharistic blessing in the one case (Lk. 24:30), his personal address in the other (Jn. 20:16) – enables them to do so.[7] Their true belief that he is risen depends on his self-presentation to them, his utter self-giving. This goes *a fortiori* for those who have not seen the risen Jesus, and whose belief must come by way of the worship and witness of the Christian community. The point is not that believers are passive. They hold "Jesus is risen" true, and this is obviously their own attitude and, in some circumstances, their explicit act. The point is rather that this attitude and act seem not, even in conjunction with the state of affairs that Jesus is risen, sufficient to yield a true belief. A Tarski–Davidson approach cannot, therefore,

at the disposal of creatures, but his divine agency cannot be defined simply as the negation of creaturely disposability, lest he fail to be a genuine human being. The divine agency of the human being Jesus must rather include his unlimited freedom to put himself at the disposal of creatures. Karl Barth puts the point with characteristic expansiveness: "God in Christ . . . is no doubt absolute, infinite, high, active, untouchable, and transcendent. But he is in all this the one who loves in freedom, who is free in his love and thus not his own prisoner. He is all this instead as the Lord, and thus in such a way that he embraces the oppositions designated by these concepts, while he is at the same time superior to them. He is all this as the creator, who has made the world as that reality different from him, but willed and affirmed by him, and thus as his own – as the world which belongs to him. In relation to it he can be God and act as God both in an absolute and in a relative, in an infinite and in a finite, in a high and in a lowly, in an active and in a passive, in a transcendent and in an immanent, and finally: both in a divine and in a human way" (*Kirchliche Dogmatik* IV/1 [Zurich: Evangelischer Verlag, 1932–67 – for the complete work], p. 204; ET, pp. 186–7).

7. This point about the resurrection narratives has long been noticed. See, for example, Gregory the Great (*Homilia in Evangelia* 25, 5; *PL* 76, 1192C–D): " 'Jesus says to her: Mary' [see Jn. 20:16]. After he had called her by the common word for her gender, and had not been recognized, he calls her by name. It is as if he said openly: 'Recognize him, by whom you are recognized . . . I do not know you in a general way, along with everyone else, but in a special way.' And so Mary, because she is called by name, recognizes the one who is speaking."

offer an adequate characterization of what it is for the belief that Jesus is risen to be true.

This may seem to go a step too far. That someone has the true belief that Jesus is risen, it might be argued, may depend on Jesus' own action, but that the belief is true does not: it depends only on whether the sentence "Jesus is risen" is true. A belief, in other words, has two components: an interpreted sentence which expresses its contents, and a holding true of that sentence. The argument so far shows only that the holding true, not the truth of the sentence, depends on something more about Jesus than that he is risen. Crediting Jesus, or indeed any person of the Trinity, with bringing about the attitude of believing does not, it seems, add anything to the truth conditions for the sentence as captured by the Tarski–Davidson schema. *Having* the belief that Jesus is risen is not automatic, but the *truth* of the belief still is, assuming that the biconditional truth conditions for the sentence which states its content are met.

Just because the distinction between these two components is basic to the notion of belief, though, the truth of the belief that Jesus is risen has to depend on the deliberate act of the risen Jesus. If the risen Jesus is not at all at the disposal of creatures, then creatures will have whatever they need in order to acquire a certain relation to him only because he wills that they have it. Cognitively dependent relations like knowing and loving require not only that we have the attitude of holding suitable sentences true, but that the sentences be true. So the truth of "Jesus is risen," and not only the attitude which holds it true, must depend on Jesus' own will and action. It cannot, by contrast, depend only on his being risen. That Jesus is risen does not seem subject to being taken as an "arrangement of the world," on hand to make our sentences (automatically) true in Tarski's biconditional fashion when we get their meanings right.[8]

Were it otherwise, then we could know the risen Jesus regardless of whether he wanted us to – he would be cognitively at our disposal. Presumably it is possible to generate the attitude of belief toward "Jesus is risen" (or some other sentence with the same meaning) on our own,

---

8. Barth insists on this point in his own way, though it is not unique to him. "The fact [of the existence of Jesus Christ] which God has posited is not a mute but an eloquent fact, a fact which speaks for itself, which bears witness to and explains itself; it has and uses the power to proclaim itself adequately in its truth, and thereby to communicate and share itself in its reality" (*Kirchliche Dogmatik* IV/3, p. 253; ET, p. 221). God – here precisely the crucified Jesus – "does not deliver himself captive to human thought and speech . . . God himself alone can make [human thought and speech] true" (p. 473; ET, p. 410).

though this attitude best comes to us, so Christians suppose, as a gift from Jesus himself. If the truth of "Jesus is risen" (suitably interpreted) depended only on Jesus' being risen, then anyone who held this sentence true would have a true belief, even when the holding true was her own doing rather than his. She would thereby know the risen Jesus, it seems, against (or at least without) his will, and might (other things being equal) have further cognitively dependent relations to him as well. That the risen Jesus is not at our cognitive disposal cannot, it seems, be guaranteed simply by regarding him as the primary cause of the attitude of belief.[9]

In any case credit for bringing about the attitude of belief towards the rightly interpreted sentence "Jesus is risen" belongs, among the divine persons, chiefly to the Spirit, not to the Son. Our having the true belief that he is risen cannot be the work of the risen Jesus alone; all three persons of the Trinity consort to bring this result about. It is the Spirit who acts immediately upon human beings to elicit the belief that Jesus is risen, who directly leads the world "into all the truth" (see Jn. 16:13). Jesus himself is, of course, the truth into which the Spirit's action leads the world. Were responsibility for creating the *attitude* of believing sufficient to characterize Jesus' own action in bringing about the true belief that he is risen, there would be no distinction between Jesus' role in the one divine action of bringing about this true belief and the role of the Spirit in that action.

Perhaps when it comes to creating true beliefs about him, the Son's distinctive role is simply to send the Spirit, who does the actual work of bringing about the attitude of belief. Jesus does send the Spirit for this purpose. But limiting Jesus' work in the creation of true beliefs about him to the job he sends the Spirit to do would miss the distinctive relation to each of the three persons which any divine action creates, in virtue of the particular role each person has in the action. In bringing about true beliefs, as in carrying out any divine action, Jesus brings about in us a direct and immediate relation to him, and not only to the other persons of the Trinity. John 16:12–15 indicates this: the Holy Spirit is to lead us into all truth, in the first place by bringing about the attitude of believing true

9. The tradition has often distinguished sharply between the cognitive situation of a person who holds sentences of scripture and creed true by God's grace, and that of a person who does so "by his own will." Aquinas, for example, argues that those who assert "Deus est" (and presumably also "Iesus Christus resurrexit a mortuis") "by a certain opinion rooted in their own will" rather than by the grace of God (he takes heretics for the chief instance of the class) lack a true belief that God exists (*Summa theologiae* II–II, 5, 3, c; cf. 10, 3, c; for the argument see "Faith and Reason Reconsidered," *The Thomist* 63/1 [1999] pp. 8–13).

sentences about Jesus, like "Jesus is risen." Jesus cannot be the truth into whom the Spirit leads us in that he too brings about the same attitude. Otherwise there would be no distinction between the Spirit's leading and what the Spirit leads us into; instead of leading us into the truth (by way of leading us to have true beliefs), the Holy Spirit would, redundantly, lead us into leading us into the truth.[10] Jesus must be "the truth" with respect to a sentence like "Jesus is risen" in some other way than that he elicits the attitude of assent to it which yields a true belief.

For cognate trinitarian reasons – and not simply because it would put him involuntarily at the disposal of creatures – Jesus' role in creating the true belief that he is risen cannot consist in his being risen (that is, in having a property such that Tarski-style truth conditions for "Jesus is risen" are met). In the action of bringing about the true belief that he is risen, Jesus' role needs to be distinguished from that of the Father as well as from that of the Spirit. The Father's role is to raise Jesus from the dead, to bring it about that Jesus is risen.[11] The Father's own part in the action is, as it were, to see to it that Tarski-type truth conditions for "Jesus is risen" are met. *Jesus* cannot be responsible for this, since the Father acts to raise a person who has gone to the dead, and the dead do not themselves act.[12] Did Tarski's conditions adequately capture what it is for "Jesus is risen" to be true, then Jesus himself would have no place in the divine action of bringing about the true belief that he is risen. The Father's act would bring it about that the relevant biconditional truth conditions were met, and the Spirit's act would see to it that people actually held "Jesus is risen" true; the Son would have nothing to do.

If Jesus is to have a role of his own in this action, the truth of our belief that he is risen requires not only that the Father act on him, but also that he act on us. Since the Spirit brings about the will to believe, Jesus has to act on

---

10. Jesus also has to do something other than send the Spirit in order clearly to distinguish his role in the action of leading us into the truth from the Father's, since the Father also sends the Spirit. See Jn. 14:16–17, 26 (where the Father gives and sends the Holy Spirit) over against Jn. 15:26 and 16:7 (where Jesus promises to send the Spirit). As the tradition has noted, though, Luke/Acts suggests that the action of sending the Spirit is itself not undertaken in exactly the same way by the Father and the Son; having received the Spirit in fulfillment of the Father's promise, the risen and exalted Jesus "pours out" the Spirit on all flesh (Acts 2:33; see Acts 1:4; Lk. 24:49).

11. In the action of raising Jesus – which is, of course, not the same as the action which yields the true belief that Jesus is risen – the Spirit too has a distinctive role; the Father raises Jesus by persevering in his baptismal donation of the life-giving Spirit to Jesus even in Jesus' "going to the dead" (to borrow Balthasar's phrase).

12. Belief in Jesus' resurrection brings particular clarity to the different way in which each of the divine persons undertakes the act of creating true beliefs, since at least in this case the specific action of the person the belief is about apparently *cannot* consist in causing the state of affairs or "arrangement of the world" in virtue of which the belief is true.

us in a different way. He must, it seems, make himself accessible to the person who (at the Spirit's bidding) believes that he is risen; he must act upon the mind as the Spirit acts upon the will. For someone who assents to "Jesus is risen" to have a true belief, Jesus must not only be risen, he must bring it about that the sentence they hold true, is true. When the Father has done his work on the dead Jesus, and the Spirit has done his work on us, whether our belief that Jesus is risen is true depends on Jesus himself, on his free self-presentation, his spontaneous creative willingness that the belief that he is risen be true. In at least this specific sense he is "the truth."

That the truth of "Jesus is risen" depends on Jesus' own spontaneity does not make its truth serendipitous or occasional. This sentence and the belief expressed by assenting to it are true without any such qualification if Jesus freely gives himself to make them true without such qualification, which he does. Theologians have regularly held that at least some people who hold creedal sentences like "Jesus is risen" true nonetheless lack a true belief, but even on quite traditional grounds we may grant that Jesus' gracious self-presentation reaches them, and grants them too a true belief.[13] The tradition has usually supposed, after all (following Jas. 2:19), that even demons have a true belief in Jesus' resurrection, though they hate what they find themselves compelled to believe. This suggests *a fortiori* that people who hold "Jesus is risen" true apart from the grace of God, or who do so even though they have spurned Spirit-wrought love, may also have a true belief.[14] The conditional "If Jesus did not act to make it so, then 'Jesus is risen' would not be true" does not assert that Jesus fails to act, any more than "If humans had not sinned, God would have become incarnate" asserts that human beings have not sinned (to recall another, widely discussed, counterfactual scenario). Our argument does not, therefore, fall afoul of the traditional thought that even the demons can have the true belief that Jesus is risen. On the contrary, that they have this true belief simply suggests the generosity of God: though the demons wish it otherwise, the gracious act by which Jesus makes the belief that he is risen true extends even to them.

Divine action and appropriation

The foregoing argument against taking the truth of "Jesus is risen" as automatic presumes that Jesus' action must be different from those of the

---

13. Cf. note 9 above. There might, of course, be other reasons why their belief was not true, e.g., that what they meant by "Jesus is risen" did not make for a true belief.
14. See Thomas Aquinas, *In Gal.* 5, 2 (no. 287): "What demons believe displeases them, and the baseness of will in a human being who refuses to believe is not so great as that in a demon who hates what he believes."

Father and the Spirit. His presentation and gift of himself to the world as the risen one belongs to a single act by which the Trinity brings about the true belief that he is risen. In this unitary act each of the persons has, however, his own distinctive role: the Father gives Jesus the freedom to rise in their common Spirit, so that the risen Jesus' free self-presentation to the world, grasped through the gift of that Spirit, is itself sustained by the Father's absolute initiative.

This may seem incoherent. If three agents engage in actions which are alike in the relevant ways, we may say that they do the same thing – that their actions are qualitatively identical. Should Peter, James, and John all make sandals, we may say that they do the same work, meaning that they perform the same *kind* of action. We do not mean by this, however, that they perform the *very* same action – that their actions are numerically identical. In this sense we normally count actions and agents together: one agent for each action, and conversely. Peter's sandal making is one action, James's another, and so forth. If the Father, the Son, and the Holy Spirit engage in a single action, therefore, it seems natural to count them as a single agent. But this is hard to square with the way the narrative which identifies the three depicts the interaction between them. The Father sends the Son, and the Son obeys the Father (by accepting the Father's mission); if these two were the same agent, the Father would send himself, the Son would obey himself, and so forth. Taking the three as the same agent threatens, moreover, to eradicate any distinction between them at all.[15] If the numerical unity of their action eliminates Father, Son, and Spirit as distinct agents, it eliminates *a fortiori* the differences between their actions proposed in the foregoing account of the way they bring about true beliefs, differences which apparently rule out qualitative (to say nothing of numerical) identity.

15. In the following way. If the divine action is numerically one, then when we assert (e.g.) "The Father creates," we can equally well substitute *salva veritate* "the Son," "the Spirit," "the Trinity," or "God" for "the Father." This is just what we want theologically, since it allows us to say both that Father, Son, and Spirit all create, and that they are one God and one creator. But it also means that the intersubstitutable terms should all refer to the same thing (assuming that the substituted position is, in Quine's phrase, "purely referential" – roughly, that these assertions do not take place in indirect discourse, statements of propositional attitude, or some other context which obscures reference). And this implies that the Father, the Son, and the Spirit are the same thing, viz., are numerically identical with one another. One could of course argue that while Father, Son, and Spirit are one agent, they are distinct in some other way. Assuming, though, that only individuals act (in traditional terms, only *hypostases* or *supposita*, so that "actus sunt suppositorum"; cf. Aquinas, *Summa theologiae* I, 29, 1, c; 39, 5, ad 1), if Father, Son, and Spirit were one agent, they wold have to be one individual (one *hypostasis* or *suppositum*), which presumably they are not. The main difficulty posed by the numerical unity of divine action therefore lies not, as is often supposed, in explaining how it allows us to *know* that the divine persons are distinct from one another, but how it allows there to be any distinct persons to know.

This might induce us simply to drop the thought that the three divine persons can undertake numerically the same action. Bringing about the true belief that Jesus is risen should be taken not as a single action, but as a class name for three different actions, one for each divine agent. This gives us the desired difference of Jesus' action from those of the Father and the Spirit, frees us from having to take the Father's raising of Jesus and Jesus' self-presentation to the world (or the Father's sending and Jesus' obedience, and so on) as somehow belonging to the same action, and leaves us with three numerically distinct agents.

Yet from an early point reflection on the works of the triune God has tended to insist that every action shared by the Father, the Son, and the Spirit has to be numerically, and not simply qualitatively, the same for all three. On the numerical unity of the divine action has seemed to depend the possibility of taking the three as one God who acts in the world, rather than three gods who do similar things. Did Father, Son, and Spirit not undertake numerically the same action, they could no more be one God than Peter, James, and John, plying generically the same trade, could be one tradesman.[16] The coherence of the Christian identification of the one God as the Trinity seems to require that Father, Son, and Spirit, while numerically distinct agents, share the very same action.[17]

16. Gregory of Nyssa is among the first to argue this point explicitly. "The Holy Trinity undertakes no action which is divided according to the number of hypostases, but there takes place one motion . . ." *Ad Ablabium: Quod non sint tres dii, Gregorii Nysseni Opera*, vol. III, part 1: *Opera Dogmatica Minora*, ed. Frideric Mueller (Leiden: Brill, 1958), p. 48, 20–4. "No activity is separated with regard to the hypostases, as though it were brought to completion by each of them individually or separately, apart from their shared oversight" (p. 50, 17–20). Consequently, "we cannot count as three gods those who surely enact their divine power and activity of overseeing us and the whole creation in complete agreement and inseparable mutuality" (p. 49, 4–7). Augustine argues, similarly, that Father, Son, and Spirit have to be distinct agents, since (e.g.) only the Son was born of the Virgin Mary and rose from the dead, only the Spirit descended in the form of a dove upon the baptized Jesus, and only the Father spoke from heaven, "You are my Son." In each case the action (or passion) belongs to one, "and not to all three" (*nec eandem trinitatem*), "yet just as the Father, the Son, and the Holy Spirit are inseparable, so they also act (*operentur*) inseparably." *De Trinitate* I, 4, 7 (CCL 50, pp. 35–6).
17. Concern to avoid tritheism sometimes leads to the suggestion that Father, Son, and Spirit not only undertake a single action, but are a single agent. Karl Rahner, for example, apparently rules out taking them as three agents ("three different centers of action"), and thus as three "subjectivities" capable of saying "you" to one another ("Der dreifaltige Gott als transzendenter Urgrund der Heilsgeschichte," *Mysterium Salutis*, vol. II: *Die Heilsgeschichte vor Christus*, ed. Johannes Feiner and Magnus Löhrer [Einsiedeln: Benziger Verlag, 1967], pp. 343, 366, note 29. ET: *The Trinity*, trans. Joseph Donceel, 2nd edn [New York: Crossroads, 1997], pp. 43, 76). In part for these reasons he shares Karl Barth's hesitation about thinking of the three as "persons," and proposes an alternative ("distinct ways of subsistence") similar to Barth's (see pp. 385–93 [ET, pp. 103–15] and Barth, *Kirchliche Dogmatik* I/1, pp. 370, 374–83 [ET, pp. 350–1, 355–63]). Some of the obstacles to taking the three as a single agent – at least when this is played off against the thought that each is himself an agent – have already been pointed out.
    The issue might, however, be parsed so that the triune God came out as a single agent,

We need, then, a way to count agents without counting actions. "Appropriation" is the traditional technical device for accomplishing this. The term is medieval; as Aquinas defines it, "to appropriate" is "to draw that which is shared" by all three persons "toward that which is unique" to each (*commune trahere ad proprium*).[18] So defined, "appropriation" labels two different though related thoughts.[19]

1. Every attribute and action common to the three persons belongs primarily to one of them. The primacy here in question is that of likeness (*similitudo*, as the medievals put it) rather than of causality or existential dependence, where the Father always comes first (the Son and the Spirit, since they come forth from the Father, depend for their being and all their attributes on him; correlatively, he can receive no attribute from them). The content of each attribute and action shared by the three persons will naturally have a special fitness with features unique (or "proper") to one of the persons. In virtue of this likeness that person "draws" or appropriates the common attribute or action to himself. Noticing the way each action of the divine persons displays this likeness of what they share to what (as unique or proper) they do not, we in turn ascribe or "appropriate" each attribute and action chiefly to one of the persons.[20] In this sense "truth" has often been taken as a shared attribute appropriated to the Son; to this thought we will return in the next section.

2. Every attribute and action common to the three persons belongs to each of them in a different way. The difference stems from the characteristics, unique to each, by which the persons are distinct from one another. Just as the *propria* of one person establish an especially intimate likeness of a shared attribute or action to that person, so each person possesses each attribute or action in a unique way. This idea precedes the use of the term "appropriation" to label it. Athanasius already notes that Father, Son, and

while each person remained an agent in his own right. This would relocate the problem we are trying to solve, and perhaps make it more daunting: we would need to look not only for a way of counting agents without counting actions, but also for a way of counting individuals who act without necessarily counting agents. Some terms do need to be predicated in the singular both of the three persons taken one by one and of the three taken together; the most basic case is "God": the Father is God, the Son is God, and the Holy Spirit is God, yet they are not three gods, but one God (see Augustine, *De Trinitate* v, 8, 9; for a later semantic analysis see Aquinas, *Summa theologiae* I, 39, 3). Whether "is an agent" conforms to the semantic pattern of "is God," and so whether Father, Son, and Spirit are in a sense one agent as well as three performers of a single action, we can leave undecided for present purposes.   18. *De Veritate* 7, 3, c.

19. On this see also Bruce D. Marshall, "Action and Person: Do Palamas and Aquinas Agree about the Spirit?" *St. Vladimir's Theological Quarterly* 39/4 (1995), pp. 394–401.

20. As Aquinas puts the point, "each divine action is better suited to be appropriated to one of the persons than to another, insofar as the attribute which is appropriated to that person is more clearly manifested by the action." *In* III *Sent.* 4, 1, 1, i, c (no. 18).

Spirit undertake each shared action in an irreversible sequence, and thereby in a certain fixed relation to one another: "In effect, the Father does everything through the Word, in the Spirit, and it is in this way that the unity of the Trinity is preserved."[21] The unique place of each person in this sequence is sufficient, so Nyssa and others suggest, to establish that each person undertakes the shared action in a different way.[22]

The Western middle ages develop fuller accounts of the *propria* of each person, and with that strive to specify how each possesses in a unique way what is common to all. Aquinas's account of divine "adoption" furnishes a clear example. For God to adopt Adam's fallen offspring as his own children (cf. Rom. 8:15–17, 23, 29; Gal. 4:5) is a single act undertaken by all three persons, but each in his own way. The Father is the source of this act. He not only initiates it, but has the prerogative to share with those who are not his natural offspring the goods he imparts to the one who is, so that we become his adopted children ("to adopt" thus belongs primarily to the Father). As the Father's natural offspring by eternal generation, the Son is the pattern or exemplar of our adoption; in his infinite possession of the Father's goods – the divine nature itself – the divine act of adoption gives us a share. And the Spirit joins us to the Son; he "imprints" upon us the pattern constituted by the Son, and so completes the divine act which adopts us.[23]

21. *Epistulae ad Serapionem* I, 28 (PG 26, 596A).

22. "There takes place one motion and distribution of the good will which passes from the Father, through the Son, to the Spirit" (*Ad Ablabium*, p. 48, 22–49, 1). God's power to oversee creation (viz., God's providence) "is one in Father, Son, and Holy Spirit . . . it starts out from the Father as its source, it is enacted by the Son, and its grace is completed in the power of the Holy Spirit" (p. 50, 13–17).

23. See *Summa theologiae* III, 23, 2 ad 3: "Adoption, while it is common to the whole Trinity, nonetheless is appropriated to the Father as source (*auctori*), to the Son as exemplar, and to the Holy Spirit as the one who impresses upon us the likeness of this exemplar."

   Recent discussions of appropriation sometimes take the point of the notion to be the opposite of that stipulated by this sort of remark, apparently assuming that to appropriate a shared attribute or action denies, rather than asserts, that it is possessed or undertaken by each of the three divine persons in a unique way. Rahner, for example, habitually speaks of "merely" appropriated relationships of the divine persons to creatures, contrasting these unfavorably with "proper" or "not-appropriated" relationships (see "Der dreifaltige Gott," pp. 329, 336–7, 366–7; ET, pp. 23, 34–5, 76–7). He seems to regard appropriation as a symptom, and perhaps a cause, of the eclipse of the Trinity as a vital mystery of salvation (see pp. 322–3; ET, pp. 14–15); at best it admits of a harmless construal which keeps it from getting in the way of what Rahner apparently fails to notice is its traditional *point*: that "the activity which is common to all three persons . . . is (like the divine essence) possessed by each of the three persons in the way unique to him" (p. 367; ET, p. 77). Though doubts about "merely appropriated" relationships were on the scene before Rahner's treatise, one is a bit puzzled to find him concerned about this; if each of the divine persons fails to be an agent in his own right, how can his action set up a relationship to creatures in any sense different from that of the other two persons? In any case, Thomas's own rejection of "mere" appropriations is unmistakable: "The likeness of the appropriated attribute to that which is unique to the person [to whom it is appropriated] establishes the fitness of the appropriation ontologically (*facit convenientiam appropriationis ex parte rei*); it would obtain even if we did not exist." *In* 1 *Sent.* 31, 1, 2, c.

So understood, appropriating a divine action differently to each of the three persons apparently gives us a way of counting agents without counting actions. With regard to the case at hand: in the sentence

(5) God brings about the true belief that Jesus is risen

we can substitute "the Father," "the Son Jesus," and "the Holy Spirit" *salva veritate* for "God." This displays the numerical unity of the divine action, and with that the unity of God. At the same time we can give descriptions of the action which specify the unique role of each person in it:

(6) The Father brings about the true belief that Jesus is risen by raising Jesus

(7) The Holy Spirit brings about the true belief that Jesus is risen by enabling people to hold this belief true

(8) The Son Jesus brings about the true belief that he himself is risen by freely presenting himself such that when this belief is held true, it is true.

In these sentences we *cannot* substitute *salva veritate* "the Father," "the Son" and "the Holy Spirit" for one another. Failure of intersubstitution in these cases guarantees that the referents of these terms are not identical, despite their intersubstitutability in (5), and so displays that Father, Son, and Spirit are agents numerically distinct from one another.

Ascribing to Jesus his own unique role in the divine action of bringing about the true belief that he is risen is thus compatible with the unity of the triune God, and conversely. Jesus' action is different from that of the Father and the Holy Spirit not numerically, but in the manner in which he carries out the very same act.

This perhaps begins to give a sense of what it might mean to say that truth is, and is borne by, a person. Theological discipline modifies – though it does not, I think, annihilate – the Tarski–Davidson account of truth in two ways.

1. Jesus is the ultimate bearer of the truth of "Jesus is risen," and of the belief expressed by this sentence. At least in this life, human beings can have the true belief that Jesus is risen only by holding this sentence (or one which translates it) true. The sentence therefore remains a genuine truth bearer for us, without any need to invoke mental contents. But it is a secondary and dependent, rather than a primary, truth bearer. It bears truth only because the person Jesus does, and causes it to do so.

2. Jesus' own unique role in the action of the triune God which presents him risen to the world is necessary in order for "Jesus is risen" and

its cognates to be true. Reference to this action thus seems necessary in order to capture the way "is true" works for "Jesus is risen." It is probably not most useful to interpret the modification which the Christian doctrine of God brings to a Tarski–Davidson account of truth as an addition of further truth *conditions* beyond those specified by Tarski's schema.[24] This would require eliminating the biconditional in T-sentences, which would doubtless have unfortunate repercussions elsewhere – not least in the theory of meaning and interpretation, since speaker and interpreter alike have to be able to grasp when truth conditions for a speaker's utterance are met, which requires the capacity to locate sufficient, and not simply necessary, conditions. A further, more theologically pertinent reason is that the truth conditions for a sentence are unique to it (and to sentences which translate it), and apply to it regardless of whether it is true or false; the biconditional brings both of these features out. Jesus' truth-bestowing action, by contrast, is not similarly unique to any particular batch of intertranslatable sentences, but applies – with one important type of exception, as we shall argue in the next section – to all true sentences; it obtains, however, only for true sentences and not for false ones.

To be sure, a puzzle here arises which there may be no conceptually satisfactory way to solve. By taking the role of Jesus himself in bringing about the true belief that he is risen as part of the concept of truth for this belief, rather than as a condition of its truth, we avoid one problem, but create another, equally serious. It seems incoherent to grant that a Tarski-style biconditional gives the truth conditions for this belief, and then to insist that an action of the risen Jesus is necessary in order for the belief to be true. How can necessary and sufficient truth conditions for a belief be met, and the belief still not be true – at least not yet?

The specter of incoherence here can, I think, be put down, but at a cost. Tarski's and Davidson's T-sentences can be taken as giving the sufficient *created* conditions for the belief that Jesus is risen to be true. But the truth of the belief also requires a divine action: not simply, we have argued, the action of creating the arrangement of the world which would make the belief true, but also an action, admittedly somewhat elusive, of the risen Jesus, which we have characterized as his self-presentation. A specific divine action is thus requisite for the truth of the belief. Since this action is uncreated, however, it fails to compete with

---

24. I mistakenly thought otherwise in " 'We Shall Bear the Image of the Man of Heaven': Theology and the Concept of Truth," *Modern Theology* 11 (1995), pp. 108–9.

the created truth conditions for the belief.[25] Because it is of course the divine persons themselves (chiefly the Father) who create these conditions, this comes to saying that the components of the triune act of bringing it about that we have the true belief that Jesus is risen fail to compete with one another.

We have thought clarity best served by taking Jesus' truth-bestowing act as part of the content of the concept of truth, rather than as a further truth condition (lest Tarski-style conditions be taken as insufficient), but one could equally well parse the matter by saying that the action of the risen Jesus is the specifically uncreated (or divine) truth condition for the belief, in contrast with the created conditions isolated by Tarski. In either case, the appearance of contradiction – of saying that sufficient truth conditions are insufficient – is removed, because we cannot group divine and created conditions together under a single notion of "condition," and so cannot suppose that "sufficient conditions" means the same thing in each case. The cost is obscurity. We cannot conceive of uncreated truth conditions except by qualifying and negating elements in our concept of created conditions, which avoids the suggestion of competition but denies us a clear concept of the truth-bestowing role of divine action. As a result we have no clear way now to explain how two elements which we take to be necessary to the concept of truth, at least for one belief – Tarski-style conditions and the action of the risen Jesus – fit together in a single concept, even though we are committed to thinking that they have to do so. The best we can do is block the suggestion that they are positively incompatible. This is what theological discipline regularly does to philosophical notions. It exacts a price in obscurity which one perhaps has to have distinctively Christian epistemic priorities to think worth paying.

There cannot, at any rate, be any objection on Davidsonian grounds that there is more to what truth is for sentences than their truth conditions as specified by Tarski, since Davidson often insists on this with regard to the bearing of truth on meaning and belief. Only a strict minimalist about truth could raise an objection on this score – which suggests that minimalism about truth would have to be theologically unsatisfying, even if it were philosophically preferable.

25. There is a parallel here with the relation between genuinely sovereign divine agency and free human action (see note 6 above and chapter 7, note 29), and also with the conceptual limitations imposed by the need to characterize that relation as non-competing. This is not surprising, since the case at hand – where we find reason to assert both a divine act of making true and a human act of locating truth conditions – is itself an instance of the relation between divine and human agency.

The trinitarian shape of the concept of truth

So far we have indicated how an action of the Trinity, undertaken differently by each of the persons, belongs to the concept of truth for one belief. If we had to take beliefs one by one this would not be much of an advance, but it ought to be possible to take "Jesus is risen," and the belief expressed by holding that sentence true, as a pattern for the way the action of the Trinity shapes the concept of truth for sentences and beliefs generally.

We are looking, after all, for a single concept of truth applicable to all true sentences and beliefs. Suppose the action of the Trinity bore in a different way, or not at all, on the concept of truth for each belief – differently, say, on what truth is for "The Holy Spirit is poured out on all flesh" or for "Grass is green" than for "Jesus is risen." In that case we would have a different concept of truth for each sentence and belief, rather than the unitary concept we are looking for. We would, in effect, be back to the minimalist view, where each sentence, since it has truth conditions unique to it, has its own concept of truth. Philosophers from Plato to Davidson have argued against breaking up the concept this way, and in any case it seems ruled out theologically. If Jesus Christ and the Holy Spirit are, each in his own way, "the truth," then it seems as though the action of each has to bear on what truth is for all sentences and beliefs (otherwise each would be at best "a truth"), and that it has to do so in basically the same way for all sentences and beliefs (otherwise each would be a plurality of truths, for a plurality of sentences).

It will, however, be useful to distinguish, in accordance with their contents, between two sorts of beliefs: those about the Trinity and those about creatures. Roughly put, we will treat separately sentences (like "The Holy Spirit is poured out on all flesh") whose Tarski-style truth conditions include terms referring to the persons of the Trinity, their attributes and actions, and sentences (like "Grass is green") whose truth conditions lack such terms, but may include terms referring to anything else.

Beliefs about the Trinity

Not only in the raising of Jesus, but in their totality, the being and acts of the triune God are not at the disposal of anything created. What applies to relations to the persons of the Trinity which depend on holding "Jesus is risen" true applies, therefore, to relations which depend on any belief about the divine persons. Since the relations themselves depend on the action of the Trinity, the truth of those beliefs which the relations require must do so as well.

Together with the need for a unitary concept of truth for all sentences and beliefs, this apparently licenses us to take the belief that Jesus is risen as the pattern for any true belief about the Trinity: a unitary action of the divine persons, undertaken differently by each, belongs to the concept of truth for any such belief and the sentences which express it. With regard to the belief that the Holy Spirit is poured out on all flesh, for example, the Father sees to it that the truth conditions for sentences expressing this belief are met – sees to it, in other words, that the Holy Spirit is poured out on all flesh. The Spirit himself sees to it that people hold these sentences true, that they form the conviction that he has been outpoured. And the risen Jesus sees to it that the belief which people thus hold true, is true.

The roles of the persons in the action by which they see to it that we have true beliefs should not, however, be confused with their roles in the actions the beliefs are about. As the Greek fathers suggested early on, the Father initiates every divine action. When it comes to our having true beliefs concerning the Trinity, the Father's initiative brings it about that "the world is arranged" such that sentences expressing those beliefs are true, but this does not mean that the Father is always either the primary or the immediate divine agent by which that "arrangement of the world" comes to be. Depending on the action – especially the actions of the divine persons in relation to one another, which are our present concern – any of the persons might be the primary agent (the one with whose *propria* the action has the greatest likeness) or the immediate agent (the one whose role terminates the action). So the Father is the primary agent of Jesus' resurrection, and the Spirit apparently the immediate agent; the same goes for our adoptive share in Christ's natural relation to the Father. The Father sometimes seems to be both the primary and immediate agent of the outpouring of the Spirit, though sometimes he seems to have entrusted the latter, and perhaps the former, role to the risen Jesus.[26] By contrast the Spirit seems to be both the primary and immediate agent of the conception of Jesus as the incarnate Word in Mary's womb.[27]

Our having true *beliefs* about these various divine actions appears to depend upon the immediate agency of the Spirit, since the Spirit leads us

26. See note 10 above.
27. See Aquinas's account of the appropriations pertinent to this action in *Summa theologiae* III, 32, 1, c; ad 1.

to hold true the appropriate sentences about these actions, namely those whose truth conditions the Father, by ensuring that the actions get done, guarantees are met. It seems right, however, to take the risen Jesus as the primary agent of the divine action by which we come to have true beliefs regarding the Trinity, the one to whom this action is chiefly "appropriated." None of the divine persons is at the disposal of creatures. It belongs to the risen Jesus, however, to display the specifically cognitive indisposability of the triune God in the most unambiguous way. He retains (as the appearance narratives suggest) his indisposability even in the face of his apparent spatio-temporal availability, and at the same time grants cognitive access to the Trinity by that self-bestowal which makes beliefs we have about the divine persons true. In this sense it belongs chiefly to the risen Jesus to manifest the Trinity to the world – not only by making it possible for us to identify the Father and the Spirit along with him (as we discussed in chapter 2), but by bringing it about that the beliefs which constitute the identification of the triune God are true.

What exactly does the risen Jesus manifest? We have been concerned so far only with the actions of the Trinity in time, but basic Christian practices suggest that the creative, redeeming, and consummating work of the Trinity gives us access to the divine persons themselves, and not only to the work they do. We have already indicated how the liturgy, especially in the creed and the eucharistic prayer, ascribes to the divine persons not only features which enable us to identify them, but features which seem genuinely constitutive of their identities, of who they are. To recall the creedal cases: the Father eternally "begets" the Son, the Son is eternally "begotten" by the Father, and the Spirit "proceeds" from both (in the case of our sample liturgy).[28] Chiefly by way of the risen Jesus' self-bestowal, the Trinity apparently grants us true beliefs sufficient to acquaint us with the persons themselves, and not just with their temporal actions.

It may be tempting to suppose that knowing the persons of the Trinity just is knowing their actions toward us – that to grasp their personal identities just is to have true beliefs about their actions. But this is implausible. As we have observed in chapter 2, Christian liturgy and scripture characterize the whole life of Jesus as a gift of the Father to the world, and the outpouring of the creator Spirit on all flesh likewise as a gift of the Father and his risen Son. That these are gifts implies that the acts which give them – the sendings of the Son and of the Spirit – are free.

28. See chapter 2, pp. 27–8, 40.

If they are free, then they are contingent: the acts themselves do not have to take place, and likewise any event which depends on those acts. The whole redemptive and consummating work of the Trinity depends on the incarnation of the Son and the outpouring of the Spirit, and so is contingent as a whole. Creation too, it is often argued, depends on the Trinity's resolve that the Son be incarnate and the Spirit be outpoured, but in any case liturgy and scripture give adequate witness to creation's contingency. The totality of the temporal works of the Trinity – or more precisely, of all divine acts whose description includes reference to actual creatures – are therefore contingent.

The *identity* of a person *x*, to recall our earlier formulation, is made up of whatever must be true of some person in order for him to be *x* – in order, we might roughly say, for a person to be himself, and not someone or something else. If the sending of the Son and the Spirit, or more broadly any divine work of creation, redemption, or consummation, belongs to the identity of any of the divine persons, then those persons cannot fail to engage in that action and still be themselves. In that case there would be two possibilities. (1) The missions or other temporal actions would not be contingent, and so would not be free and would not be gifts. Just because they are Father, Son, and Spirit, the divine persons could not help undertaking these actions; they would have to create, redeem, and consummate the world lest they cease to be themselves and become some other persons. (2) The personal identities of Father, Son, and Spirit would be as contingent as the temporal acts they undertake. Some divine persons with other identities would become Father, Son, and Spirit by creating, redeeming, and consummating the world. These seem like equally unacceptable outcomes. They alike fall afoul of the liturgical and scriptural conviction that on Easter and Pentecost Father, Son, and Spirit give themselves to us in their personal uniqueness, even though they – these same persons – did not have to make us at all, let alone give themselves to us without reserve.

The point is not that free acts (or more likely patterns of free acts) can never be identity-constituting for persons. At least when it comes to created persons, it is plausible (if controversial) to say that who a person is – her very identity – depends upon her actions and reactions in particular settings. The personal identities of created agents may, in other words, plausibly be regarded as contingent. But whatever may be the case with created persons, it seems impossible that the identities of the divine persons could be contingent. Christian liturgy and scripture variously embody the belief that the Father, the Son, and the Spirit who freely allow us to become acquainted with them in time also freely create the total situation in which they graciously give themselves to us. That this creative act is free implies that these same agents might not have made this – or any – world at all. Each would be the person he is, the person with whom we are allowed to become acquainted in time, even if there were no creatures – nothing besides these three divine persons. So whatever features of the divine persons constitute the identity of each, the possession of these features by each cannot be contingent on any act which involves creatures.[29] In traditional terms: the Father would beget, the Son would be begotten, and the Holy Spirit would proceed just as they do even if there were no creatures, and in these relations of origin the identities of the three consist (there is not, to be sure, universal agreement that precisely these three features do the job of constituting personal identity in God).[30] We may be able to take the creative, redeeming, and consummating actions of the Trinity as a basis for grasping the identities of the divine persons, but we cannot take our grasp of their identities to consist in the knowledge of these actions.

Recent discussions of how to link up the divine persons with their actions toward us tend to insist on the principle that the "economic Trinity" and the "immanent Trinity" are identical.[31] The term "economic Trinity" apparently refers to three divine persons who undertake the actual "economy" of salvation which scripture narrates; they create, redeem, and consummate the world. The referent of "immanent Trinity"

29. The same result could be obtained simply by taking non-contingency as a basic feature of divine (as opposed to created) being; the task would then be to find a way of distinguishing divine being from divine acts, since the latter *are* contingent.

30. The tradition has tended to distinguish between those features which are common (though differently appropriated) to the persons, those features which are unique to each (their *propria*), and that sub-class of *propria* which are genuinely person-constituting for each (see, e.g., Aquinas's summary in *Summa theologiae* I, 32, 3, c). Identity-constituting features have to be *propria* in the traditional sense, but not all *propria* can be identity-constituting, since they include features (like the Son's being incarnate and the Spirit's being poured out on all flesh) which, as the results of contingent acts, cannot belong to the identities of the persons who possess them. Any *proprium* can, by contrast, be a feature by which we pick out or identify its possessor. Whether there is anything to be made of the distinction between *propria* which are identity-constituting and those which are person-constituting we can leave aside for present purposes.

31. Here too Rahner has been especially influential; see "Der dreifaltige Gott," especially pp. 327–9, 382–4 (ET, pp. 21–4, 99–103), also "Bemerkungen zum dogmatischen Traktat 'de Trinitate'," *Schriften zur Theologie* (Einsiedeln: Benziger Verlag, 1954–84), vol. IV, pp. 115ff. (ET, pp. 87ff.). Whether or not they take it from Rahner, however, most extended treatments of the Trinity in the last generation or so have accepted the principle he articulates, if often with qualifications. Basically the same thought, if not the formulation, predates Rahner. Barth, for example, is emphatic about it; see *Kirchliche Dogmatik* I/1, pp. 352, 503 (ET, pp. 333, 479).

is more elusive. In Rahner's formulation, the term refers to three divine persons who are "in God, setting aside his free self-communication."[32] Presumably no divine persons actually exist apart or "aside" from the economy of salvation; the point seems rather to be that the "immanent Trinity" consists of three persons considered "aside from" any reference they may have to actual creatures – three divine persons as they would be even if there were no economy of salvation. The principle that these two trinities are identical is thus the claim that the persons in one Trinity are the same as the persons in the other.

Much is often thought to hang on this principle, from whether belief in the Trinity has any relevance for Christian life and experience to whether it is possible for us to know the persons of the Trinity at all. Depending on how one takes it, though, the principle seems either trivial or absurd. It might be taken to assert that the three persons who make up the "economic" Trinity are the same *persons* as the three who make up the "immanent" Trinity, and conversely. Surely this is right, but it fails to make a claim which anyone ever thought to deny. No one has maintained that there are six divine persons, three who act in the "economy" and, with personal identities different from any of the economic agents, three others who do not. Taken this way, the principle simply seems like an awkward way of making a point upon which trinitarian theology has pretty much uniformly insisted since the Nicene settlement: the identities of the three divine persons who freely give themselves to us in creation, redemption, and consummation are the same as they would be even if the three had not decided to create and give themselves to us. If this is its sense, the principle turns out to eliminate the possibility that any features the persons of the Trinity have because they undertake the economy of salvation (such as the Son's being human, or the Spirit's being poured out) can belong to their *identities*; this would contradict the claim that the persons who act in the economy are the same three as they would be "aside" from it.

The tone in which the principle is often put forth indicates, however, that it is not intended to be taken as trivial. Asserting the identity of the economic and the immanent Trinity is supposed to correct a profound error which has long crippled trinitarian theology (at least in its "Western" versions), perhaps as far back as Augustine. This suggests that the principle be taken differently. Not only do the same persons make up

32. "Der dreifaltige Gott," p. 383 (ET, p. 101).

both the economic [...] teristics are the same in [...] Trinity, but their *features* or charac- immanently as well as economically. Being incarnate belongs to the Son belongs to the Spirit immanently, being poured out on all flesh Taken this way, the principle asserts [...] economically, and so forth. same features because they enact the economy [...] vine persons have the have had if there had been no economy of salvation [...] on as they would features in. If this is its sense, the principle is not just false to have these tradictory.[33]

The persons of the Trinity, it seems, bring it about that we have true beliefs sufficient to grasp their identities, and not only their actions toward us. At the same time, we apparently cannot reduce the contents of true beliefs about the identities of the divine persons to the contents of true beliefs about their actions.

Correspondence

Under theological discipline the concept of truth has to include the action, ascribed chiefly to the risen Jesus, by which the triune God enables us to have true beliefs about him. Reflection on the *outcome* the Trinity apparently intends by this truth-bestowing act indicates a second basic way in which the notion of what truth is – precisely for sentences and beliefs – needs theological expansion.

33. That the "economic" features of the persons also somehow belong to them "immanently" is sometimes thought necessary in order to avoid the thought that the Son's cross and the Spirit's outpouring fail to convey to us what God is really like. It might seem, for example, that Barth's doctrine of election requires this doubtful trinitarian claim. Barth insists that God's decision to be the particular human being Jesus, and therewith to live in covenant love with human beings, is an act by which God has primally determined himself, so that this determination now belongs to him as much as everything which he is in and for himself" (*Kirchliche Dogmatik* II/2, p. 6 [ET, p. 7]); this decision therefore precedes and controls God's resolve to create a world and rescue it from sin. That this primal decision is contingent (and Barth, at least, seems to think it is: "it is however, that it is not identity-constituting for Father, Son, or Spirit, and so cannot be an "immanent" feature of any of them. This is not to say, however, that the decision, once made, is somehow less true of God than "everything which he is in and for himself," nor that it might be revoked or superseded, nor that its enactment fails to give access to the non-contingent identities of the three persons who undertake it. Even less does the standard medieval view (see chapter 5, note 8) that the acts which result in the possession by the divine persons of "economic" features are eternal, while the features themselves are temporal, require the claim that "economic" features are also "immanent." This view is compatible both with the contingency of the possession of "economic" features by the three persons and with various ways of thinking about the sequence of divine decisions (e.g., with the view that God's decision to be incarnate is in fact contingent upon human sin).

sustains by his Spirit the self-pr... ...the crucified Jesus to the
world for the life of the w... ...s creation radically. The New
Testament describes the ...esus' rising on the world, and on
human beings in part; ...gs affected by his resurrection: we will be his
risen Jesus and h... ...erms of a distinctive relation between the
icons. Even as we shall bear the ...orne the image (εἰκόνα) of fallen Adam, "the man
of dust," s...(see 1 Cor. 15:49). image of the man of heaven, the risen
Jesus C... ...to be (note Paul's use of καθὼς here) a kind of participation which
see... ...cludes existential dependence. Those who bear the image of the risen
Jesus are shaped by this person himself in their total reality, as they once
were shaped by the person Adam; they are "conformed (συμμόρφους)" to
the risen Christ (Rom. 8:29; cf. Phil. 3:21).

This conforming of human beings to the crucified and risen Christ is a
unitary action of the whole Trinity, and indeed seems to realize the most
interior and primal purposes of the triune God. The Father has eternally
and effectively willed – predestined – our conformity to his Son (cf. Rom.
8:29; Eph. 1:5), who, by accepting incarnation and the death from which
the Father raises him, constitutes that original form of which we are the
intended images. The Spirit is the agent who, poured out from the Father
by the risen Son and dwelling in us, immediately joins us to Christ and
makes us his icons (see Rom. 8:9–11, 14). The New Testament of course
talks about the outcome of Jesus' resurrection in many other ways, but
the notion of "bearing the image of the man of heaven" seems to express
both the final aim and the original intention not only of the resurrection,
but of the totality of divine acts involving creatures. While for now we are
icons of the risen Christ in fragmentary and partial ways, in the end the
Spirit will enable us to see him as he is, and so be as much like God as it is
possible for creatures to be (see 1 Jn. 3:2). With the perfection of this work
of the Spirit will coincide the liberation of all creation; no further divine
aim for creation will remain to be realized (see Rom. 8:22–3). The notion
that we will be Jesus' icons thus seems as basic as any description of the
outcome of his raising.

Though conformity to the risen Jesus in heart, mind, and will preserves the distinction between the particular person Jesus and those
persons who are conformed to him, it nonetheless involves a sharing by
others in his own affections, thoughts, and desires. Being a bearer of
Christ's image is therefore a cognitively dependent relation. Having
affections, thoughts, and desires which succeed in making us like

another person requires having a range of true beliefs – in this case not only the belief that Jesus is risen, but countless others about the way his action and passion embody the purposes of the triune God, about what counts as virtuous action and affection, about how we should treat our neighbors, and so forth. To be sure, the belief-dependence of this relation may not be permanent. At the last, when we have become Christ's icons in a fully unsurpassable way, our cognitively dependent likeness to him may be able to do without true beliefs and the sentences which express them ("we shall see him as he is").[34] At least in this life, though, being Christ's icon apparently depends on having some true beliefs. Their truth, like that of any belief which a particular relation to the persons of the Trinity may require, depends on the action by which these persons together bring it about that we have true beliefs.

The act by which we come to have true beliefs concerning the divine persons is therefore apparently not an end in itself, but serves the Trinity's purpose of making us bearers of Christ's image. This is the intended term or goal of the act, and as such a feature or component of the act itself. Given the unrestricted freedom shared by the divine agents, this outcome cannot fail to be present where the act occurs. And since the act itself belongs to what truth is for this belief, so does its term. That believers bear the image of the risen Christ itself belongs to the concept of truth for whatever beliefs this relation requires, and similarly for the sentences which express those beliefs.

But bearing the image of another is obviously a relation of correspondence. Between those who bear Christ's image and him whose image they bear obtains a complex likeness or similarity (indeed a participatory likeness), that is, a correspondence. While "mysterious" in the standard theological sense – its richness is ever greater than our fullest apprehension of it – the relation to the risen Jesus by which we become his icons is not, in contrast to the notion that the truth of a sentence consists in its correspondence to reality, "mysterious" in the pejorative philosophical sense: conceptually empty or hopelessly puzzling. It is a relation among persons, in which one person joins numerous others to himself by faith, hope, and love, and in that way makes them like himself in mind, heart, and will. It is thus a relation of subject to term in which the subject can, in an unpuzzling sense, be like – correspond to – the term.

34. As Luther, for example, suggests: "In the future life believing will cease . . . When faith ceases the brilliant light (claritas) of glory will follow, in which we will see God just as he is" (WA 40/I, 428, 29 – 429, 13).

This correspondence belongs to the concept of truth for at least some sentences and beliefs (we will see momentarily whether it may be extended to all true sentences and beliefs). It is not that the sentences or beliefs correspond to anything. But when assented to as the term of the threefold truth-conferring action of the Trinity, they are an indispensable means by which a definite relation of correspondence comes about, and this is part of what it is for them to be true. In the correspondence of person to person by which the Trinity makes us Christ's icons one may hear an echo of the ancient idea that truth is the correspondence of mind to reality, though here it is the whole self, and not just the intellect, which shares in the relevant conformity. In this sense the created persons affected by the truth-bestowing action of the Trinity may themselves be seen as truth bearers. As whole selves, they can become "true" when the action by which the triune God enables them to have the relevant true beliefs brings about their conformity to the risen Christ.[35]

This need not, I think, fall afoul of our earlier scruples about correspondence. On Davidson's account T-sentences give us the basis of an adequate grip on what it is for each sentence (on the left) to be true; "correspondence" adds nothing to the understanding of "is true" we already have for sentences. In effect the foregoing argument reverses, on trinitarian grounds, this sequence of inference, at least for some sentences. An account of "is true" for these sentences has to include a distinctive way in which persons are "true," namely by sharing in a philosophically unmysterious relationship of correspondence to one person in particular. Truth for these sentences must consist at least in part in their having a share in constituting this relationship; therefore T-

---

35. On this see Anselm's *De Veritate*, which also links in an ordered way different aspects of the concept of truth with different bearers. The *rectitudo* of each bearer unifies the elements which make up the concept of truth. A truth bearer has *rectitudo* when it "does what it ought" (*De Ver.* 2, p. 179, 2). Divine purpose determines what each truth bearer ought to do (see *De Ver.* 3, p. 180, 12–13, 15). Each ought to do something different, but there are relations of dependence among truth bearers, and with that among aspects of the concept of truth. Thus the truth of utterances (*enuntiationes*) depends, in a fashion not far removed from Tarski's ("to signify that what is, is," *De Ver.* 2, p. 178, 22–3), on what Anselm calls "the truth of the essence of things," which in turn depends on the *summa veritas* ("There is truth in the essence of all things which are, because they are in essence what they are in the highest truth," *De Ver.* 7, p. 185, 18–19), as does the truth ascribed to all other bearers (see *De Ver.* 10, p. 190, 1–12). The *summa veritas* is Jesus Christ himself (*De Ver.* 4, p. 180, 21–2: "veritas ipsa"; see *Monologion* 46, p. 62, 22–6), and not only the divine nature (see *Monologion* 18, p. 33, 22–3). References are to F. S. Schmitt, ed., *S. Anselmi Opera Omnia*, vol. I. For a theologically provocative analysis of Anselm's treatise, see Michel Corbin, "L'événement de Vérité," *L'inouï de Dieu* (Paris: Desclée de Brouwer, 1980), pp. 59–107.

sentences cannot by themselves give an adequate grip on what it is for these sentences to be true. But at no point have we suggested that by understanding truth for sentences as some sort of correspondence, we understand how persons can correspond to (bear the image of) the risen Christ; rather the reverse. Thus while there are good theological reasons for thinking precisely of truth as involving a certain kind of correspondence, in abstraction from Christian belief there may be no need – and perhaps no coherent way – to do this.

The Spirit creates, moreover, a twofold conformity or correspondence: not only of us to Christ, but also of us, in and with Christ, to the Father. As we have already observed in another connection, Jesus Christ crucified and risen (not only the eternal Logos, but precisely that Logos become our flesh) is himself "the icon of the unseen God" (Col. 1:15; cf. 1:20). He is the "exact imprint" or representation (Heb. 1:3: χαρακτήρ) of the Father, other than the Father yet completely expressive of the Father's total reality, and as such perfectly conformed to him. Consequently we cannot be bearers of Christ's image without sharing in his own correspondence to the Father, and so bearing, like him if imperfectly, the imprint of the Father himself.[36]

Since Jesus is presumably the Father's fully adequate image because of the unique way in which he comes forth from the Father – as the Father's only "Son," who as such fully possesses the Father's divinity – the New Testament also expresses the correspondence to the Father which we gain through Jesus by speaking of us as the Father's adopted children. Conformed to the Son by the indwelling Spirit's love, we share Jesus' own sonship, his own complete likeness to the Father; we become by adoption what he is by nature (cf. Rom. 8:15–17, 29; Gal. 4:4–7). In this way the Spirit gives us a share – as much as we creatures can take – in God's own life. By acquiring (in Thomas's phrase) a "participated likeness" of features unique to Jesus Christ (as the Father's only-begotten Son and perfect image), we not only share in those characteristics which the three have in common (see II Pet. 1:4), but take up a particular place in the non-contingent pattern of their personal relations to one another. We share, that is, in the very features which at once distinguish the Son

---

36. This was noticed early on. Thus Ignatius of Antioch: "In love, the faithful bear the imprint (χαρακτήρα) of God the Father through Jesus Christ" (Magnesians 5:2). Ignace d'Antioche et Polycarpe de Smyrne, *Lettres* (*Sources Chrétiennes* 10), ed. P. Th. Camelot (4th edn, Paris: Cerf, 1969), p. 82.

from, and unite him to, the Father and the Spirit, and so constitute his identity.[37]

Conformity to the Father, and not only to Jesus Christ himself, apparently belongs to what truth is, at least for beliefs concerning the Trinity. Granting to creatures a participated likeness in the incarnate Son's correspondence to the Father seems to be the final goal of the act by which the Trinity brings it about that we have true beliefs. There the matter ends: as the unoriginate origin of all things, the Father can have an image, but he is himself in no way the image of any other. He can be corresponded to – above all by his incarnate Son Jesus, in a conformity of one person to another than which a greater cannot be conceived – but he himself corresponds to nothing.

The correspondence to the Father at which the triune God aims by granting us true beliefs about himself is available to us only as a participated likeness of the incarnate Word's own perfect conformity to the Father. Insofar as correspondence is an element in what truth is for our sentences and beliefs, it therefore seems that the most basic form of correspondence belongs not to us, but to Jesus himself. Our conformity to him and (in him) to the Father both depend upon his own perfect likeness to

37. To show that being the Father's Son (non-contingently the recipient and full possessor of his nature) and thereby his image are genuinely constitutive of Jesus' identity as rendered in the Gospels would require an extended argument for which there is not room here. The argument would proceed by linking the uniquely divine actions Jesus performs, the mission from the Father in virtue of which he performs them, and the identity-constituting relation of origin to the Father which this mission assumes. It would have to address the conceptual problems posed by (1) the need to show that the Spirit, even though he is the full possessor of the Father's nature, is neither Son nor image, and by (2) the seemingly paradoxical result that being the Father's Son and image is identity-constituting for Jesus, but being Jesus is contingent, and therefore not identity-constituting, for the Son.

For present purposes we may simply observe that Jesus' capacity to impart to us the Father's likeness depends upon his own fully adequate possession of it, and his possession of it depends upon the relation of origin by which he receives the Father's entire divinity. That the Son terminates this relation of origin cannot, in classic accounts of "adoptive sonship," be a feature which he has contingently, and so is identity- (indeed person-) constituting for him. As we have briefly outlined, for Aquinas the Father freely grants us a "participated likeness" (*participata similitudo*) in Christ's own "natural" relation to himself (*Summa theologiae* III, 23, 4, c), assimilating us to "the eternal Word precisely in his unity with the Father," that is, to the non-contingent and identity-constituting *filiatio* of the incarnate Son (III, 23, 3, c). One may find this thought in perhaps unexpected places, as when Karl Barth describes *unio cum Christo* as the goal of God's call to Christian faith and discipleship. "Granted all their difference from one another," the bond of the Christian with Christ "is accomplished and consists in a complete self-giving (*Hingabe*) from both sides," from which issues "a single whole, one reality, an internally differentiated and animated, but pure, solid, unity." Therefore "when [Christians] are in Christ, they have and receive an immediate share precisely in that which, because in the first place and above all *God* is in him . . . is shown and given to them by God" (Barth's emphasis). *Kirchliche Dogmatik* IV/3, pp. 621, 627 (ET, pp. 540, 546).

the Father. So if our sentences and beliefs cannot be true without yielding our own correspondence to the Father, then their truth depends upon Jesus being the Father's Son and (as such) his perfect image. The truth which Jesus brings about with respect to us depends, in other words, on Jesus' unique relation to the Father, and not only on his leading role in the truth-bestowing action of the Trinity toward us. As the incarnate Word or image Jesus Christ is, as the medievals liked to say, the *veritas Patris*, "the truth of the Father."[38] To the extent that shared actions belong (and so are ascribed or "appropriated") differently to each of the divine persons on account of characteristics unique to each, the Son's perfect correspondence to the Father seems to be the basis for taking the divine act of granting us true beliefs as belonging chiefly, though of course not solely, to the Son.

If correspondence to the Father is itself identity-constituting and non-contingent for the Son, then "truth" belongs, in a sense, to God's own identity, in the form of the Word's perfect correspondence to the Father whose total reality he expresses. The Son would then correspond to the Father – would be "the truth of the Father" – even if he were not incarnate, and there were no world for him to be incarnate in. His identity-constituting relation to the Father would thus be basic to the truth of all possible true beliefs, even if there were no actual beliefs to be true. We have elsewhere suggested that the Son is the Father's way of uttering or expressing the whole Trinity, and not only himself.[39] The Son can have this role because of his distinctive place, as Word and image, in the pattern of personal relations constitutive of the identities of the divine persons – because, in other words, of his perfect correspondence to the Father. In that the Son cannot fail to be the Father's Word and image, there cannot fail to be an utterance (in an extended sense, to be sure) whose truth depends on the Son's perfect correspondence to the Father: the Father's utterance of the whole Trinity to himself, the Spirit, and also the Son. On account of the Son's correspondence to the Father, there would in a sense be truth, even if there were no world, no sentences, and no beliefs.

---

38. See Anselm, *Monologion* 46 (Schmitt, vol. I, p. 62, 22–6): "The Son may most suitably be called the truth of the Father, not only in the sense that his truth is the same as the Father's ... but also in the sense that we find in him not some imperfect imitation, but the complete truth of the Father's substance, since he is nothing other than what the Father is." The phrase shows up early in Lombard's *Sententiae* (Book I, Dist. 3); see the comment by Bonaventure, *In I Sent.* 3, 1, Dubium 4 (*Opera Selecta*, vol. I, pp. 57b–58a); see also Aquinas, *In I Cor.* 2, 2 (no. 100).   **39.** See Chapter 5, note 24.

Beliefs about creatures

If Jesus Christ is "*the* truth," then we should expect the truth-bestowing action of the triune God to unify all true beliefs, and not simply those about the Trinity. We are looking for a single, theologically adequate concept of truth for all true beliefs. It may seem as though the argument so far inevitably limits a trinitarian account of what truth is to sentences about the divine persons, their attributes, and their actions. Our point of entry for the thought that there is more to the concept of truth than Tarski and Davidson suppose was the observation that the persons of the Trinity are not at our disposal. That Jesus is risen – that this crucified Jew lives, presently available to the world – is wholly at the disposal of the Trinity; the truth of the belief that he is risen cannot therefore be automatic. That grass is green is, by contrast, not at all at the disposal of grass. This might lead one to suppose that the truth conditions Tarski provides adequately capture what it is for "Grass is green" to be true, and that the truth of the belief that grass is green may safely be taken for automatic.

Of course our account of truth has already implicated countless sentences which contain no terms referring to the triune God or his actions, since the cognitively dependent relation to the Trinity which we acquire by "bearing the image of the man of heaven" demands myriad beliefs about ourselves, the sort of life we ought to lead, the future of the world, and so forth. It seems unlikely, though, that the truth-bestowing action of the Trinity extends to sentences like "Grass is green" by making anyone who holds this sentence true an eschatological bearer of the risen Christ's image. In that case anyone who had a true belief would be a bearer of Christ's image, regardless of what the belief was. A cognitively dependent relation requires, however, some beliefs specifically about who or what the believer is related to. When it comes to beliefs about creatures, we need to account for the truth-bestowing role of the Trinity in some other way.

Everything corresponds to the Father in some fashion, however distant and remote. He is the unoriginate source of all things, and even the humblest creature is like him in some respect. In contrast with the perfect likeness of himself whom the Father eternally generates, those things the Father freely creates by way of the Son resemble him (whether individually or collectively) in more or less partial and incomplete ways. Part of this contrast between the perfect likeness of the Son to the Father and the limited likeness of creatures is that creatures resemble the Father only by resembling his image, who is as such the *exemplar* of all creation. The Father creates by giving all things a greater or lesser share not only in the Son's likeness to him, but also in the love which they have for one another through their Spirit. In all creatures there lies at least a trace, a *vestigium*, of the Trinity, such that they both resemble and desire the Father. Not only human beings, but all creatures, are ordered toward a share in the risen Christ's correspondence to the Father, if not precisely to being personal bearers of his image. The Spirit is conforming everything to the crucified and risen Christ, in and for whom all things were made and in whom all things hold together (see Col. 1:16–17); he is giving everything a more or less intimate share, depending on the kind of thing it is to be, in Christ's perfect likeness to the Father.

This suggests, however, that all truth conditions – the truth conditions for all sentences and beliefs – are wholly at the disposal of the Trinity. That Jesus' self-presentation is completely at the disposal of the Trinity may seem relatively obvious, because there the presented is also a presenter, and shares fully in the act of presentation. The "arrangement of the world" that grass is green does not display its presenter, or that there is an act of presentation in the first place, quite so clearly. Yet that grass is green is as much presented to the world by the triune God as that Jesus is risen. The Father as much sees to it that the truth conditions for "Grass is green" are met as that those for "Jesus is risen" are met. As Jesus Christ presents the truth conditions for the belief that he is risen to the world, in order that this belief may actually be true, so also he presents to the world all the truth conditions which the triune God wants to see met, and in this way brings about the truth of every true belief. And as the Spirit creates the conviction that "Jesus is risen" is true, so the Spirit may also be credited with creating the conviction that grass is green; any holding true of a true sentence, he brings about.

Moreover, "Grass is green" will be true not just if and only if grass is green, but also if green grass (more precisely: *that* grass is green) is a created trace, however remote, of the unoriginate Father. It will be like the Father, however, only if it can count as a vestige of the crucified and risen Son, in whom, as the *exemplar* of creation, all things hold together. The same goes for every sentence whose truth conditions the triune God contingently wills to meet, and for the beliefs expressed by these sentences.[40] For a sentence about creatures to be true, the "arrangement of

40. Problems arise, to be sure, with regard to sentences (e.g., in mathematics or logic) whose truth is not evidently contingent. Whether the truth conditions for such sentences can plausibly be regarded as in some way at God's disposal depends on a number of considerations (such as whether the analytic/synthetic distinction holds up) which we lack the space to pursue here.

the world" which would make it true, as specified by Tarski-style truth conditions, has to be at least a vestige of the Son's correspondence to the Father. In this way "the firstborn from the dead" (Col. 1:18) is *the* truth – the *veritas Patris* not just for some, but for all sentences whose truth conditions he wills, together with the Father and the Spirit, to present to the world.

This trinitarian account of truth conditions cannot, however, be applied to all sentences in quite the same way. Some sentences, like "Florensky was murdered in the Gulag," are obviously true, but the "arrangement of the world" which makes them true is not in any way an image or vestige of the Trinity.[41] Because there is evil in the world traceable to the doings of created free agents, there will be some actual states of affairs which correspond to nothing in God, arrangements of the world for which there is nothing in God of which they are the likeness, even remotely. The truth conditions for sentences about persons who suffer or do voluntary evil, events which are the outcome of voluntarily evil acts, and so forth, will remain at the *disposal* of the Trinity, granted genuine divine sovereignty over evil (an assumption which, to be sure, creates significant conceptual problems). But any evil state of affairs is not one which God actually wills to be. Sentences for which such states of affairs constitute truth conditions are not, therefore, sentences whose truth conditions the triune God wills to meet, nor are they sentences whose truth conditions the risen Jesus presents to the world. In these cases, while the sentences are true, there is no divine truth-bestowing act.

For this reason there will be some sentences for which a Tarski–Davidson account of truth is indeed adequate, and needs – indeed admits of – no trinitarian extension. "Florensky was murdered in the Gulag" is true if and only if Florensky was murdered in the Gulag; there is nothing further – in particular, nothing about God – to be said about the way "is true" works for this sentence (though there is much more to be said because the sentence is true). Though informative generalization is a bit difficult here (recall our reservations at the end of chapter 8 regarding the notion of what sentences are "about" or "describe"), we can perhaps state that a Tarski–Davidson account of "is true" will be adequate for those sentences, but only those, whose Tarski-style truth conditions one can say are, or are the result of, voluntary evil. That Florensky

41. On the fate of the great Russian theologian and scientist, see Sieglinde and Fritz Mierau, eds., *An den Wasserscheiden des Denkens: Ein Pawel Florenski Lesebuch* (Berlin: Kontext Verlag, 1991), p. 258.

was murdered in the Gulag locates the truth conditions for "Florensky was murdered in the Gulag," and that Florensky was murdered in the Gulag is, one can surely say, evil. It is precisely not the triune God who sees to it that the truth conditions for sentences which follow this pattern are met. With regard to these sentences, a trinitarian account of what truth is does not want to say anything more than the Tarski–Davidson approach already does.[42] This does not, I think, signal a weakness in the account; rather it signals that there are some sentences to which we should not expect the account to apply in full.

Trinity, justified belief, and truth

Our final task is to spell out the connection between truth and belief. We have developed a theological account of how to decide which beliefs are true, and we have just outlined a theological account of what truth is. It remains to make their coherent relation explicit – to say what holds together truth, justified belief, and the willingness to believe, or, if you like, keeps them from coming apart in the first place.

One way to see the issue clearly is to recall the ancient problem of skepticism. The skeptic worries that his beliefs, or those of human beings generally, might be largely or wholly false. The skeptic's problem has not to do with the justification of beliefs, or even with willingness to believe, but with the link of belief to truth. He worries that precisely those beliefs he is justified in holding and willing to hold might turn out to be false, and sees no good grounds for supposing that in deciding what to believe, we have thereby decided what is *true*.

Foundationalism is of course designed to overcome skepticism, by giving access to beliefs which cannot turn out to be false, and which can be recognized as such. Previous reflection has suggested that skepticism, especially when it comes to beliefs about a mind-independent

---

42. The history behind this thought is long, and cannot be analyzed here. By way of example, Aquinas argues that "things" (states of affairs, let us say) can be "false" when there is no original in the triune God to which, in some manner, they conform. This happens when free agents "withdraw themselves from the ordering of things in the divine intellect; in this consists the evil of guilt" (*Summa theologiae* I, 17, 1, c. See 18, 4, ad 4: "Evil things are in God's knowledge . . . but not in the sense that they are created by God or conserved by him, nor in the sense that they have a likeness [*rationem*] in God; rather they are known by God through the likenesses of good things"; on the latter see 14, 10). But of course the fact that there is nothing in God to which this withdrawal – this "falsity" – corresponds does not make sentences describing the agents who engage in it false (see I, 16, 2; 17, 3). For an analysis of Thomas's texts, see Bernard Lonergan, *Grace and Freedom* (London: Darton, Longman and Todd, 1971), pp. 111–15.

spatio-temporal world, actually depends on foundationalism in order to create the conceptual space in which it can arise in the first place. Should foundationalism be necessary for skepticism, then cutting the foundationalist ground out from under the skeptic (in the Davidsonian fashion outlined in chapter 4, for example) renders senseless his worry that his beliefs might be largely or wholly false; it deprives him of an idiom he needs to state his worry in the first place. But surely this leaves the job at best half done. Once we have gotten rid of the foundationalist idiom, the question still remains as to *how* even the most determined skeptic cannot help getting it right most of the time, how it is that his beliefs have to turn out true for the most part.

It is sometimes argued that we need not and perhaps cannot answer this question, and may safely content ourselves with showing that the skeptic's worry is baseless. Absent some positive account of what links belief and truth, however, even the most convincing narrative of foundationalism's collapse will perhaps only prompt the suspicion that skepticism has other plausible sources.

In particular, it may seem that skepticism depends on realism about truth, and that realism can create the conceptual space for skepticism even in the absence of a foundationalist epistemology. Realism ordinarily includes a correspondence theory of truth, but even where it does not, the realist is apparently committed to the bivalence thesis – the view that every meaningful sentence is determinately either true or false. Bivalence in turn seems to require that truth cannot be an epistemic notion: if bivalence holds, then a meaningful sentence is determinately either true or false regardless of whether we have any way of finding out what its truth value is, and regardless of whether we have any good reasons for holding it true or false.

We have avoided the label "realist" for views which reject the correspondence theory, even when they also deny that truth is epistemic (including those of Frege, Davidson, and Fine). Accepting even this much of realism, though, may seem to permit belief to become parted from truth. To say that truth is not epistemic is to say that with regard to any particular belief, truth, so to speak, outruns justification. On a view where truth is not epistemic and justification is not foundationalist (including the one developed here), the truth conditions for a belief (as located by the right branch of a T-sentence) fail to be identical with what gives us the right to hold the belief (namely some other beliefs that we hold). And this inherently leaves open the possibility that even a belief which we have very good reasons to hold true might in fact be false. So, the skeptic wants to know, what keeps this from happening all the time? What, in other words, keeps truth from being inaccessible, not just in particular cases, but on the whole? At this point we may, of course, be tempted to block truth's inaccessibility by suggesting that truth is epistemic after all. But if, as we have argued, this suggestion makes the cure seem worse than the disease, we need an account of truth's accessibility which does not force truth to go epistemic.

One such account is Davidson's. He proposes that we treat meaning as the tie which, on the whole, binds belief to truth. Meaning, as it were, makes truth accessible to belief, by requiring that belief be "intrinsically veridical."[43] Davidson's suggestion has given rise to controversy. Even if his argument holds its own against standard criticisms, however, it will be of little use to us here. Since we have found theological grounds for supposing that Davidson's notion of truth is incomplete, we cannot help ourselves to it when the time comes to connect truth with justified belief. Though the argument of this chapter still allows us to agree with Davidson that the sentences people hold true can only mean what they do if their truth conditions are generally met, truth under theological discipline cannot on the whole be made accessible to belief by way of meaning. With the exceptions (having to do with evil) which we have recently discussed, the truth of beliefs cannot be automatic – it cannot consist only in the truth *conditions* of the beliefs (or the sentences which express them) being met. For the most part the truth of beliefs requires the truth-bestowing act of the triune God, and in particular the free presentation of their truth conditions by the risen Christ. Davidson's aim is to show that our beliefs are mostly true when we take them to be. We need a reason for saying this – for supposing that justified beliefs are generally veridical – which squares with the theologically disciplined notion of truth at which we have arrived.

The chief standard for justified beliefs, we have argued, is that they at least be consistent with the narratives which identify Jesus and the triune God. These epistemically primary beliefs cannot, of course, serve as reasons for holding most beliefs, since reasons need to be in the logical neighborhood of the beliefs they support. To say that beliefs are generally true when we take them to be – when we regard them as justified – is therefore to say that beliefs which are at least consistent with

43. See chapter 8, p. 237.

the identification of Jesus and the triune God, and which we otherwise have reason to hold true (which largely fit with the rest of our beliefs), for the most part actually are true.

According to our theologically disciplined notion of truth, beliefs justified according to these standards will generally be true just in case the triune God – and especially, in his distinctive way, the risen Christ – undertakes his truth-bestowing act (1) with regard to belief in the narratives which identify him, (2) with regard to no belief inconsistent with these narratives, and (3) with regard to beliefs which there is otherwise good reason to hold. Truth will be *accessible* to belief if we can *count* on the triune God to do just this – if, when it comes to our own beliefs, his truth-bestowing act is not for the most part inaccessible to us. Presumably God bestows truth on no false beliefs, since true beliefs are all and only those to which he has granted truth.[44] But we need not always be able to tell which beliefs God makes true; it suffices that we can tell for the most part, and especially with regard to those beliefs which are epistemically primary. There need be no guarantee that a justified belief is true (there hardly could be, since in some cases people are justified in holding incompatible beliefs), only that justified beliefs are true on the whole.

Which beliefs get their truth conditions met is chiefly up to the Father, with the Spirit as his immediate agent. The Christian community's epistemic priorities cannot be the right ones, and nor can they rightly be taken as unrestricted, unless the Father sees to it that such beliefs as hold true the narratives identifying Jesus (and with him the whole Trinity) unfailingly get their truth conditions met, and any beliefs incompatible with this narrative identification never get their truth conditions met. The Father can be counted on to distribute truth conditions in just this way because, as we have observed, the narratively identified Jesus is his own image become our flesh, the one who perfectly expresses the Father's own reality. Around him the Father orders all things, and so determines which beliefs will have their truth conditions fulfilled. The Father cannot, indeed, fail to order all things around his own uniquely adequate

---

44. Beliefs pertaining to evil are again in part an exception, since there is no divine truth-bestowing act in their case (though if the beliefs are true, actually holding them depends on the Spirit; see below). But since no belief can be justified which fails to hang together with most of the rest of what we believe, beliefs pertaining to evil cannot themselves be true unless most of the rest of what we believe, which does not pertain to evil, is also true. In this way the truth of beliefs pertaining to evil depends upon the triune God's truth-bestowing act, even though they do not themselves receive it.

icon. The Father's icon might not have been incarnate, but in any case that image (as Logos) fully expresses the Father's knowledge of himself, the whole Trinity, and all things as the Father actually wills them to be, and he orders them according to this definitive knowledge. Just because he has Jesus Christ for his incarnate icon, the Father can be counted on to do his part in seeing to it that the beliefs which the Christian community takes to be primary in the order of justification are actually true, and that any belief which fails of consistency with them is false.

But the Son also needs to do his part. Truth will be accessible to belief only if the risen Jesus bestows truth on all the beliefs, and only the beliefs, whose truth conditions the Father sees to it get met. In particular, the beliefs which are epistemically primary for the Christian community cannot be true, nor can their epistemic primacy be unrestricted, unless the risen Jesus spontaneously but unfailingly presents truth conditions to the world as the Father has distributed them. This means presenting to the world, and so making accessible to belief, the very truth conditions for the narratives which identify him and the Trinity which the Father himself provides, and presenting truth conditions for no beliefs inconsistent with these narratives – no beliefs which the Father has declined to see get their truth conditions met.

The Son can be counted on to do this just because he has the Father as the one to whom he perfectly corresponds. As the incarnate Son, Jesus perfectly corresponds to the Father because the Father fully expresses himself in the person of the Son; expression and correspondence are here what the scholastics call *relationes oppositae*, relations where being the subject of one necessarily goes together with being the term of the other. Though other than the Father, the incarnate Son fully possesses everything the Father can give to another without ceasing to be himself. To him belongs, in the creedal formulation, the Father's own οὐσία or essence, everything (numerically, not just generically) which makes the Father God. As full possessor of the Father's own will and knowledge, but in the mode of recipient, not of giver, the Son cannot fail to order truth-bestowal the way the Father orders truth conditions. Taken together, the actions of the Father and the Son ensure that the beliefs which make up the Christian community's epistemic priorities are true, and any belief inconsistent with these priorities is false.

The actions of the Father and the Son settle which sentences and beliefs are true, and secure the basic connection between truth and justified belief by ensuring that the church's epistemic priorities are correct. By itself, however, this does not guarantee that most of the beliefs we take to be true actually are true. The Christian community's primary beliefs do not for the most part enable us to tell which sentences to hold true, since countless competing truth claims are alike consistent with these beliefs. Granting the truth and unrestricted epistemic application of the church's central beliefs on trinitarian grounds still leaves open the question why we should take most of the rest of what we believe to be true.

Here the action of the Spirit is decisive. The Spirit, as we have observed, brings about the conviction that the church's central beliefs are true, and teaches the community's members to order the rest of their beliefs accordingly. But all true beliefs are the Spirit's work: the Spirit sees to the holding true of any sentences whose truth conditions are met by the Father and presented to the world by the Son. The Spirit can be counted on to do this because he is, in the Johannine idiom, "the Spirit of truth," the one who will lead first Jesus' own followers, but through their communal life the world, to grasp not just some truths, but "all the truth" (Jn. 16:13). As the Spirit of the Father and the Son, he is sent by both to convince the church and the world of those beliefs the Father and the Son have, each in their own way, secured: "he will take what is mine and declare it to you" (Jn. 16:15). Just as Jesus Christ himself possesses all that belongs to the Father – the Father's own divinity – so also the Spirit possesses all that belongs to the incarnate Son. He is thereby uniquely in a position to declare, and will declare only, those beliefs which the Father and the Son have seen to it are true.[45]

This does not yet solve the problem at hand, since knowing that the Spirit brings us to hold all our true beliefs, and only our true beliefs, does not enable us to tell which beliefs the Spirit brings us to hold. There is probably no way to tell this on a case-by-case basis, especially when we are

---

45. Dispute arises concerning the inner-trinitarian background of the Spirit's work, or more precisely concerning which identity-constituting features enable the Spirit to accomplish his mission in the world – especially those features which bear on his relation to the Son. Jn. 16:13–15 has often been taken to imply, with particular stringency, the *Filioque*. Taken this way it provides especially strong background for the Spirit's role in uniting truth and justified belief, but of course this inference is much contested. Similar results might be obtained by conceiving the relevant background in terms of the Spirit's eternal coming forth from the Father to rest upon the Son (temporally manifested especially in Jesus' baptism) or in terms of the Spirit's place as personal bond of love between Father and Son (which it might be possible to work out without assuming the *Filioque*).

at some distance in logical space from the Christian community's central convictions, and surely not on any large scale. But there is no need for one. Part of the Spirit's business in leading us "into all the truth" is to make sure that we never stray too far from the truth – that for the most part our beliefs are true.

Ultimately, we recall, the triune God grants us true beliefs in order to give us a share in his own life. Countless beliefs about creatures are tied up with beliefs about the triune God and his purposes in the world, and there is probably no clear or effective way to draw a line between those which are and those which are not. The Spirit cannot, it therefore seems, lead us into the life of God without seeing to it that we hold mostly true beliefs, not only about God, but about everything else. Since we hold beliefs at all only insofar as they fit with the rest of what we suppose to be true, this is to say that the Spirit guarantees that our beliefs are generally – though of course not always – true when we take them to be. An account of truth, meaning, and belief like Davidson's might – now that the coincidence of true beliefs with those whose truth conditions are met has been christologically secured – be taken to describe the mechanism by which the Spirit accomplishes this. So at least we have argued here, but in the end we have trinitarian reasons for supposing that truth and justified belief will generally cohere, regardless of the created means by which one supposes that this takes place.

Evidently the coherence of truth, justified belief, and willingness to believe finally depends upon the unity of the triune God. Were the Son and the Spirit not united to the Father by full possession of the Father's own essence, received from him – the creedal *homoousion* – we would lack adequate grounds not only for upholding the Christian community's central convictions, but for supposing that the beliefs we take to be true, generally are true. There is, to be sure, more to it than this. The divine persons are united with one another, and live in one another, in more than one way – by will and not just by essence, in love as well as in being. In more than one way each can thereby count on the other, and we can count on them all, to do his part in the act by which together they bring it about that we have true beliefs, which we can recognize as such.

In what ways Father, Son, and Spirit may coherently be thought of as one God is a large topic, and one for another day. For now we may simply observe that when our beliefs are true – as they usually are – we are led by the Spirit's grace, though perhaps without yet knowing it, to retrace the pattern of relationships by which he and the Son are eternally united to the Father in being and love. When we get our epistemic priorities straight, we become acquainted with the divine persons in the intimacy of their relations to one another as well as to ourselves. More than that: we begin to take part in the love which is eternally the being and the life of the triune God.

Index